The Limits
of State Autonomy

Sponsored by the Foreign Policy Analysis Section
of the International Studies Association

The Limits
of State Autonomy

Societal Groups and
Foreign Policy Formulation

EDITED BY

David Skidmore
and Valerie M. Hudson

Westview Press

BOULDER • SAN FRANCISCO • OXFORD

This Westview softcover edition is printed on acid-free paper and bound in library-quality, coated covers that carry the highest rating of the National Association of State Textbook Administrators, in consultation with the Association of American Publishers and the Book Manufacturers' Institute.

Chapter 2 first appeared as "Internationale Umwelt, gesellschaftliches Umfeld und außenpolitischer Prozeß in liberaldemokratischen Industrienationen," *PVS-SH* 21(1990). Reprinted by permission.

Published in 1993 in the United States of America by Westview Press, Inc., 5500 Central Avenue, Boulder, Colorado 80301-2877, and in the United Kingdom by Westview Press, 36 Lonsdale Road, Summertown, Oxford OX2 7EW

A CIP catalog record for this book is available from the Library of Congress.
ISBN 0-8133-8449-4

Printed and bound in the United States of America

The paper used in this publication meets the requirements
of the American National Standard for Permanence of Paper
for Printed Library Materials Z39.48-1984.

10   9   8   7   6   5   4   3   2   1

Contents

Preface

The Limits of State Autonomy is the first product of an occasional series of edited volumes planned and sponsored by the Foreign Policy Analysis Section of the International Studies Association. The editors first became acquainted while simultaneously serving as section officers. In comparing notes on our respective scholarly endeavors, the two of us came to realize that while our academic training grew out of disparate research traditions,[1] we shared an interest in the domestic sources of foreign policy behavior. More specifically, aspects of our separate research agendas attempted to explore, in quite different ways, the role of societal groups in the foreign policy-making process. Our mutual agreement that this represented an important but largely untapped field of inquiry led to the present volume. Our distinct areas of specialization have allowed us to evaluate and incorporate a range of perspectives and approaches, while our interest in a common set of problems has, we hope, helped us to mold a focused and coherent collection of essays.

We received a large number of high quality manuscripts and proposals in response to our initial call for papers in the summer of 1990. The difficult job of selecting a manageable number of essays for inclusion was guided by our interest in showcasing diverse theoretical and empirical approaches while assuring that the volume as a whole addressed the role of societal groups in varying national contexts. Given the paucity of existing research, we also sought conceptually innovative works that might stimulate new interest and research on the role of societal groups in foreign policy formulation. Each of the papers finally selected went through a rigorous process of review and revision. We believe that the resulting volume will be of interest to a wide range of scholars in the fields of foreign policy analysis, international relations, and comparative politics.

---

1. Hudson's work has revolved around comparative foreign policy, political psychology, artificial intelligence, and formal modeling, while Skidmore's interests lie in the areas of American foreign policy, international political economy, and case study methods.

A large number of people played roles in helping to bring this project to fruition. We would like to thank Chadwick Alger, Jon Deal, Robert Denemark, William Dixon, Amy Eisenberg, Deborah Garner, Joseph Hagan, Ann Jackson, Jennifer Knerr, Thomas Lairson, Jack Levy, Janice Love, Martin Sampson, and Linda Wilson. The David M. Kennedy Center for International and Area Studies at Brigham Young University provided valuable financial support for this project.

David Skidmore
Valerie M. Hudson

1

Establishing the Limits of State Autonomy

CONTENDING APPROACHES TO THE STUDY OF STATE-SOCIETY RELATIONS AND FOREIGN POLICY-MAKING

David Skidmore and Valerie M. Hudson

This volume explores the influence of societal groups on foreign policy formulation in a variety of national contexts. The notion that politically organized groups might play an important role in swaying foreign policy choices is intuitively appealing. Yet work in the field of foreign policy analysis has barely tapped the rich insights potentially available through this line of inquiry. *The Limits of State Autonomy* is a step toward filling this gap in the scholarly literature.

Our introduction places this research agenda, and the essays which follow, into a larger theoretical context. We first examine the rationale for constructing an independent theory of foreign policy behavior. We argue that theories of international relations pitched at the systemic level of analysis may complement but cannot substitute for models which specify the domestic determinants of state behavior. Previous efforts to build domestic-centered theories of foreign policy behavior have, however, suffered from inattention to the significant causal role of societal groups. This omission may stem partly from the empirical and methodological difficulties of tracing group influence: a set of obstacles the essays in this volume attempt to overcome in diverse ways.

The heart of the chapter is a comparison of several distinct theoretical approaches to the study of state-society relations and foreign policy formulation. We employ the labels of statist, societal, and transnational to distinguish among these approaches, which rest on differing assumptions about the motives and interests of state decision-makers, the structure of society, and the relationships between state and society. Conclusions about the role and significance of societal groups in the process of foreign policy formulation vary greatly depending upon which model is embraced. The final section of our introduction surveys the contributions which comprise the volume and classifies each in terms of the models of state-society relations previously elaborated.

SYSTEMS, ACTORS, AND FOREIGN POLICY ANALYSIS

Recent years have witnessed renewed scholarly interest in the domestic sources of foreign policy behavior (Putnam, 1988; Ikenberry et al., 1989; Kegley, 1987; Barnett, 1990; Levy, 1988; Barnett and Levy, 1991; Risse-Kappen, 1991). A short list of contemporary phenomena suggests why this should be so. The growth of economic interdependence, along with rising literacy and the communications revolution, has blurred distinctions between domestic and foreign policy and heightened the domestic political salience of social, cultural and economic relations among states. Recent events in Eastern Europe and the (recently deceased) Soviet Union have once again demonstrated that changes in governing coalitions and regime structures can have dramatic consequences for international alignments. The spread of democracy, not only in Eastern Europe but also in Latin America and other parts of the Third World, seems likely to increase the domestic accountability of foreign policy elites in many countries. These few examples of the linkages between domestic politics and foreign policy could easily be multiplied.

Simply recognizing the need for investigation into the impact of domestic variables on foreign policy behavior is, however, inadequate for such a project to succeed. Empirical research is most profitable if embedded in a coherent theoretical model. In the field of international relations, such models are most easily found at the level of the international system. Balance of power, deterrence, and hegemonic stability theories predict systemic outcomes based upon various conceptions of international structure. Typically, systemic theories rest upon simplifying assumptions about the attributes of states. Realist models, in particular, treat states as rational, unitary actors. The purpose of doing so is to assume away or hold constant the effects of variation at the national level. This enables the theorist to deduce predictions based solely on variation at the systemic level (Keohane, 1986).

Unfortunately, the popularity of systemic theories of international politics has partially stymied or displaced efforts to develop independent theories of foreign policy behavior. Before proceeding to a discussion of the main themes of this volume, therefore, it is necessary to explain why the assumptions underlying systemic approaches are inadequate to support a theory of foreign policy behavior and why the latter must necessarily incorporate domestic variables.

Kenneth Waltz (1979) has argued that we must clearly distinguish between theories which aim at predicting systemic outcomes from those which predict actor behavior. For the former, in Waltz's view, it is defensible to assume similar attributes and motives across states, even while acknowledging that such an assumption departs from reality. In the same way, Waltz points out, simple microeconomic theories of the market are possible precisely because they abstract away from variation at the level of the firm. Conversely, however, market theories, being systemic, do not subsume or replace theories of the firm, although they may tell us something about the constraints which face similarly placed firms. To understand the behavior of particular firms, one must break with the assumptions of market level theories, including those of rationality and profit maximization, in order to examine the effects of organization, corporate culture, and other actor level attributes on firm behavior. This is particularly true where markets are structured oligopolistically, the situation which best mirrors great power competition in the international system. Oligopolistic firms are potentially capable of influencing their environment by colluding with or responding strategically to their rivals. Since market level constraints are looser (and potentially manipulable) under these circumstances, they provide less certain predictions regarding firm behavior.

Similarly, theories of the international system are inadequate to predict the foreign policies of particular states. Yet we often find scholars attempting to do just this (e.g., Lake, 1988). Actor behavior is inferred from systemic constraints, with the usual assumptions of state unity and rationality forming an explicit or implicit backdrop for the analysis.

There are three fundamental difficulties with this approach. First, systemic level forces are rarely fully determinate of state behavior. Systemic constraints allow for a bounded range of behavior. The scope of this range, in turn, varies substantially. More powerful states, for instance, typically have greater freedom to maneuver than less powerful states. Second, even where systemic constraints select certain ends or goals, multiple distinct and equally viable routes to these ends may be available. The choice among means, under these circumstances, will not be determined by the system itself. Third, if it is true that the international system rewards some types of behavior under given conditions, and punishes others, this is equally true on the domestic side. Foreign policy decision-makers are not simply agents of the national interest but political animals who must worry about their survival in office and the viability of their overall set of political goals, domestic and foreign. There exists little reason to expect that the pattern of domestic and international rewards and punishments for various sorts of foreign policy choices will naturally coincide. Where they do not, foreign policy officials may be compelled to choose between domestic rewards at international cost or international rewards at domestic cost. Systemic theory cannot predict which choice will be made except, perhaps, in the rare circumstance where the wrong foreign policy choice threatens the survival of the state itself.

For these reasons, systemic theory is incapable of explaining more than broad directions in foreign policy behavior. Systemic theory may account for circumstances where states with widely varying national attributes behave alike under similar external constraints. Such models are inadequate, however, where states situated similarly in the international system respond differently to common stimuli or where the same state alters its behavior significantly despite little change in its external circumstances.

A theory of foreign policy is needed to explain the substantial variation left unaccounted for by systemic theories. It must therefore be a theory about how differences in domestic factors alter foreign policy behavior across states or over time in a single state. To accomplish these tasks, such a model must answer two basic questions: Which domestic variables are likely to prove significant? How are such factors related to one another and to the behavior we want to explain?

THE DOMESTIC DETERMINANTS OF FOREIGN POLICY BEHAVIOR

Case studies and historical accounts have highlighted a bewildering variety of domestic influences on foreign policy behavior. An actor level theory of foreign policy must, however, distinguish the significant factors from the insignificant and those which apply to many nations from those which pertain only to one or a few. A good theory must also, of course, generate empirically testable hypotheses. Over the last two decades, there have been several attempts to design a research program which identifies significant domestic variables while also, in some cases, integrating these with systemic constraints. Not surprisingly, the earliest such efforts, during the seventies, began by negating one or another of the actor-level assumptions (i.e., state unity and rationality) posited by systemic theory.

The bureaucratic politics paradigm (Allison, 1971; Art, 1973; Halperin, 1974; Destler, Krasner, 1972; C.F. Hermann, 1978) questioned the assumption of state unity while the political psychology literature (Singer and Hudson, 1992; M.G. Hermann, 1984; Jervis, 1977; Steinbrunner, 1974; De Rivera, 1966; Janis, 1982) rejected the assumption of state rationality. On their own, however, neither of these two approaches proved adequate to provide a general theory of foreign policy behavior. Each largely confines itself to the state and state decision-makers even while breaking with the assumptions of unity and rationality. In neither case is the possible influence of society or non-state actors on foreign policy-making given more than passing attention. In this respect, these approaches accept the traditional realist distinction between the political processes governing the making of domestic and foreign policies. According to this view, while the determinants of domestic policy lie in the political system at large, including the influence of public opinion, political parties, and interest groups, foreign policy is a product of the state itself, relatively insulated from society.

This orientation is not universally shared within the foreign policy literature, but the notable exceptions still fall short of providing a theory of foreign policy formulation which fully incorporates state-society relations. There exists, for instance, a large literature on the foreign policy beliefs and opinions of the U.S. public (Wittkopf, 1990; Holsti and Rosenau, 1989; Chittick et al., 1992; Baugh and Southwell, 1992). Implicit in these discussions of foreign policy opinion is the underlying assumption that what the public thinks makes some difference to those who actually make foreign policy. This linkage is, however, seldom demonstrated in practice, nor is it incorporated into an explicit model of the policy-making process. An expansive literature (Katzenstein, 1978; Krasner, 1978; Mastanduno, et al., 1989) has also arisen on the relationship between state structure and foreign policy behavior. In some versions, these models treat the state's strength or weakness in relation to society as an independent variable. This is a first, though tentative, step toward incorporating societal variables. Yet, in most instances, analysts in this tradition limit themselves to the observation that weak states, in contrast with strong ones, are vulnerable to societal pressures which affect policy without specifying theoretically the source, nature, or content of the pressures that societal forces bring to bear.

What is missing in these approaches is attention to the domestic politics of foreign policy, i.e., consideration of the ways in which politically organized societal groups seek to influence policy and how state decision-makers either cooperate with, resist, or compromise with such groups. This sort of exercise is, of course, the meat and potatoes of those in the political science profession who study the making of domestic policy in the U.S. and elsewhere. Yet attention to the role of societal groups is strangely absent in most, though not all, of the scholarly literature on foreign policy behavior. (Some notable and recent exceptions from the foreign policy analysis literature include Hagan, 1987; Putnam, 1988; Hermann, Hermann, and Hagan, 1987; Levy and Vakili, 1989).

Taken as a whole, the studies in this volume suggest the need to treat societal group influence as an important variable in explaining foreign policy outputs. We seek to build upon the scattered but useful and suggestive work which has already been done and point toward new directions for research in this area. Although the essays which follow all focus on state-society relations in the making of foreign policy, they represent a diverse range of theoretical and methodological approaches. In our view, it remains far too early in the evolution of research in this area to close ranks around one approach.

ANALYZING STATE-SOCIETY RELATIONS AND FOREIGN POLICY BEHAVIOR: THE TASKS AHEAD

Research into the influence of societal groups on foreign policy formulation must confront a number of important challenges. A way must be found, for instance, to disentangle the influence of societal groups from other causal factors. Demonstrating a direct link between group activity and policy response is problematic. This issue raises substantive as well as methodological problems. To know which sorts of domestic pressures count, one must know something not only about the society and the political process generally, but also about the goals, motives and priorities of state leaders themselves. We must ask not only if societal groups have influence, but also when and under what conditions they are most likely to exercise it effectively. It is also crucial to know something about the groups themselves, as well as the nature of the issues they contest. What prompts societal groups to mobilize around foreign policy issues? Are some types of issues more likely to engender political activity than others? How does the arena of decision (e.g., executive vs. legislative) affect the likelihood of group influence? Are coalitions among foreign policy interest groups stable or do they shift easily across issues and over time? Do groups have the capacity to sway public opinion and enlist its weight in their cause? Can we generalize across countries or subsets of countries about the sort of societal group pressures that foreign policy officials experience or about the effects of differences in political structure on interest group dynamics?

These are important and interesting questions even if they do not yield ready answers. In order to generate hypotheses about these matters, one must begin with a theoretical model which posits the structure and nature of state-society relations as they relate to foreign policy-making. These models may then be compared and tested against one another, based upon the hypotheses they suggest, for any given country or used to differentiate among countries according to which model they best approximate.

Below we suggest three alternative models, along with variations of the first two. Each model or variant presents an ideal type, embodying different assumptions about the structure of state-society relations and how they relate to the making of foreign policy. Each corresponds in a general way to some body of thought or literature, though they are presented as logical constructs that do not precisely mirror any particular piece of work. Alternatively, the approaches may be seen as describing *types* of state-society relations that may exist in the world at any given time. One approach may be more descriptive of one nation, while a different approach may be more descriptive of another.

The statist model corresponds closely to Realist theory. Statists assume that state decision-makers formulate foreign policy largely autonomously of societal influences. Since differences emerge over how complete this autonomy is, we examine both strong and weak versions of the argument.

The Strong Version of Statism

The strong version of statism assumes full state autonomy of societal constraint on foreign policy issues. Statists posit that foreign policy-making is guided by the national interest. The national interest is itself defined variously in either objective or subjective terms. Most commonly, the national interest is derived objectively by the researcher from a state's position in the international system. The principal determinant of position is relative power, though factors such as geography and level of dependence on others are sometimes considered as well. The national interest is determined by the constraints and opportunities presented by the international system. External realities select certain behaviors. Whether consciously or not, state leaders tend to conform to systemic pressures over time.

The national interest can also be defined subjectively, as arising from fundamental attributes of a nation's political culture. The international goals and priorities of particular states generally correspond with the values most highly prized by the broader culture out of which decision-makers emerge and in which they are immersed (Krasner, 1978; Hartz, 1955; Packenham, 1973).

In either case, the national interest tends to remain relatively stable over time unless fundamental shifts occur either in international structure or political culture. Despite tactical shifts in the means of policy, strategic ends remain constant.

The strong version of statism assumes relative societal unity and a correspondence of interests and values between society and the state on foreign policy issues. Where an objective national interest is assumed, this occurs because security is indivisible. External interests, as determined by the international system, apply to the nation as a whole, not only to parts of it. The fundamental goal of any society—survival—is shared equally by all. Thus the nature of foreign policy, in contrast to domestic policy, promotes societal unity as well as deference toward the state. Much the same result is expected where the national interest is viewed as emerging from the nation's political culture. Once again, shared cultural values promote unity. In either case, a unified and deferential society frees decision-makers to pursue the national interest autonomously of domestic constraints.

One other variant of this approach must be mentioned. The possibility of societal opposition to particular foreign policy initiatives can be reconciled with the assumption of full state freedom and autonomy if one also assumes that the state is particularly strong vis à vis society. If, in other words, the structure of the political system so insulates decision-makers that they can safely ignore political opposition without fear of losing power or influence, then foreign policy can be conducted free of domestic constraints despite the existence of opposition. Thus the "strong" statist approach might be descriptive of some nations in the international system, but not of others.

If the strong version of statism holds, under some combination of the assumptions outlined above, then there exists no justification or need for examining the role of societal groups in foreign policy formulation. Depending upon how one defines the national interest, it is sufficient to study the ways in which international constraints or national political culture shape policy responses.

The Weak Version of Statism

The weak version of statism persists in claiming that central decision-makers are guided by the national interest, whether defined objectively or subjectively, in formulating their own policy preferences. It concedes, however, that foreign policy issues evoke particularistic as well as general interests within society. Foreign policy choices produce both winners and losers among different sectors of society, thus provoking coalitions which may either support or oppose existing policies. In the same vein, the values of the broad political culture may not be universally shared, thus giving rise to ideological opposition. Fissures may develop, therefore, within society as well as between particular societal groups and the state. The result will be political mobilization as different groups seek to influence government decision-making.

None of this affects state preferences, which continue to be shaped by the national interest. But societal opposition may affect a state's ability to realize or implement those preferences. If the state is strong and well insulated, as mentioned previously, then societal opposition can be ignored, at least until it reaches very high levels. If the state is weak, however, then state leaders may be constrained from fully carrying out their preferences. The necessity of preserving their future power and authority may compel state leaders to compromise with societal opponents. These circumstances are most likely to arise in democratic settings, although state weakness can be found in non-democratic systems as well.

Since state preferences remain stable in this variant of the statist model, policy should depart from the norm, i.e., the national interest, only occasionally when societal opposition reaches critical levels. Over the long run, foreign policy should reflect stable ends. We should, however, expect the process, and sometimes the end results, to reflect the efforts of policymakers to cope with opposition in a setting of decentralized power. Thus, the conduct of foreign policy will be characterized by lags, side payments, anomalies, and deception. State leaders may also attempt, often successfully, to influence the preferences of societal groups by manipulating the policy agenda, setting the terms of debate or shifting material incentives. While the study of societal groups is required to account for residual variation in both process and content, it is not central to the understanding of foreign policy outcomes overall.

SOCIETAL APPROACHES

What the weak version of statism views as exceptional, societal models treat as normal or characteristic. Societal groups are assumed to play a central and continuing role in foreign policy formulation. Once again, there exist two versions of the societal model, distinguished according to their assumptions about the structure of society and the motives of central decision-makers.

The Pluralist Model

A societal-centered model of foreign policy formulation necessarily adopts different assumptions about the motives and priorities of central decision-makers than statist models. The pluralist version of a societal approach posits that political leaders care most about maintaining a high level of domestic political support. Thus, foreign policy choices are judged first and foremost according to their effect on the central decision-maker's political standing at home. The rationale for this assumption is that domestic support is a prerequisite both for maintaining office and for maximizing influence and effectiveness across the full array of issues leaders must address. This approach preserves the assumption of rationality found in statist theories, but it substitutes different ends to account for policy choices—i.e., domestic for international goals.

The assumption that internal incentives outweigh external ones does not suggest that international considerations play no role in policy choice. Many foreign policy issues, especially those of a routine nature, attract little interest on the part of either the public or the major power bases in society. In such cases, international constraints and incentives will outweigh domestic ones since there is little at stake in the latter realm. In other cases, domestic and international incentives will point in the same direction. This is rendered more likely by the fact that "success" abroad can serve to mute opposition at home to a given policy, thus providing policy-makers with a domestic rationale for giving attention to the external viability of their policy choices.

Nevertheless, a societal approach assumes that many foreign policy choices, like those concerning domestic policy, evoke societal division and political mobilization. This occurs either because the material interests of various groups are affected differently—producing both winners and losers—or because foreign policy choices provoke ideological conflict over values and purposes.

In either case, any given policy choice on many important international issues will stimulate a range of support and opposition. Depending upon the balance of power among these forces, domestic incentives may conflict with international incentives. Where this is so, a societal model expects foreign policy choices to be driven by the former.

The pluralist version of the societal approach assumes that foreign policy interest groups are large in number, that cross-cutting cleavages exist among them, that coalitions shift easily across issues and over time, and that power is dispersed rather than concentrated. On issues where domestic salience is high, political leaders select policies which attract the support of dominant coalitions. Since coalitions change over time and across issues, policy consistency and coherence are rare. The pluralist model applies most readily to political systems featuring weak, poorly insulated states and competitive political processes.

Social Blocs

A societal model appears quite different from that described above if one alters assumptions about the structures of power and conflict within society. The label "social bloc analysis" is meant to encompass a variety of alternatives to pluralism, including elite, Marxist, corporatist and sectoral

Table 1.1 Comparing Theoretical Approaches: Independent Variables[a]

Principal Axes of Conflict in Society

		Horizontal	Vertical
Number of Organized Societal Blocs	One	Elite Theory	Corporatism
	Few	Marxism	Sectoral Bloc Analysis
	Many	(Empty)	Pluralism

a. We are indebted to James Nolt for his input into the design of this table.

bloc theories. Despite the considerable differences among them, these approaches each assume that power is concentrated in the hands of relatively few social blocs, cleavages among them are reinforcing rather than cross-cutting and coalitions are stable and enduring across issues and over time. Where a political system is dominated by only one or a few stable centers of power, it is unlikely that any political leader can rise to the top without affiliating with a particular power base. Thus, the policy preferences of top officials should reliably and consistently reflect the interests and ideological inclinations of the bloc with which they are associated. Political leaders therefore serve a stable constituency with well articulated interests rather than a series of fleeting coalitions which shift rapidly over time and across issues, as pluralists would have it.

While sharing these basic assumptions, the four models reviewed below differ along two important dimensions. Elite and corporatist theories view the politics of foreign policy formulation as dominated by a single bloc which, while composed of differing elements, functions in a coordinated and coherent manner. Marxist and sectoral approaches suggest that more than one organized bloc contends for power and control over policy. These models also differ according to whether they depict the principal cleavages within society as falling along horizontal or vertical lines. Horizontal cleavages divide segments of society which stand in a relationship of dominance and subordination to one another. Vertical cleavages distinguish among relatively equal social actors. Elite and Marxist theories assume societies divided by horizontal cleavages while corporatist and sectoral approaches depict vertical cleavages.

Elite theory focuses on the network of social ties and overlapping interests which organize institutional power holders. Elites, conceived of as a single relatively unified bloc, are distinguished from the mass of unorganized citizenry. A horizontal line divides the powerful from the powerless (Mills, 1956; Kolko, 1969).

In corporatist models, the allocation of political power is regularized through a functional division of labor among highly organized social groups. Each group is recognized by the state and incorporated into the policy-making process through peak associations. While corporatist polities are characterized by vertical cleavages, which distinguish a number of relatively equal social actors from one another, the structure of interest intermediation provides for stable and predictable policy trade-offs among varying social interests. This allows the ensemble of corporatist groups organized around the state to act as a single, though not undifferentiated, bloc (Schmitter, 1974).

Marxist theories identify class as the principal cleavage within capitalist societies. Since both capital and labor are organized, there exist two distinct and politically significant social blocs. However, the functional dominance of capital over labor leads to an asymmetry of power between the two. The outcome is class struggle. State policies generally reflect the interests of capital, but labor may, at times, mobilize the power to extract concessions (Lenin, 1975).

Sectoral blocs are organized around various factions of business, each possessing distinct interests and policy preferences. Typically, several highly organized business clusters compete for influence (e.g., nationalist versus internationalist). While the balance of power among rival sectoral blocs may vary, the cleavages between them are vertical. No functional or a priori relationship of dominance and subordination structures their interaction.[1]

Pluralist models can also be accommodated within this classification scheme. Many, rather than one or a few, politically organized groups compete for influence. Since there exists no pre-established hierarchy, the cleavages among them are vertical. Table 1.1 summarizes the above comparisons.

There are points of convergence and divergence among the models described thus far along two important dimensions of foreign policy formulation. These dimensions may be thought of as dependent variables. Statist and societal approaches lead to differing expectations regarding the substantive content of the interests which drive foreign policy. Statist approaches assume that national interests, whether derived from systemic

---

1. For examples of sectoral analysis, each of which distinguish between national and international blocs, see Ferguson, 1984; Frieden, 1988; and Nolt, 1992.

or domestic cultural sources, provide the primary criteria by which policy choices are judged. Societal approaches assume that foreign policy is the product of particularistic societal interests, while differing over which set of interests predominate. Along this dimension, then, there is considerable variation between statist and societal approaches, as well as among different versions of the latter.

A second significant dimension of foreign policy formulation concerns the degree to which the state is capable of acting in a unified, coherent and strategic manner, apart from which interests animate policy. While their predictions regarding policy content vary, the strong version of statism converges with the elite and corporatist models in expecting a high degree of coordination and consistency in state policy. The weak version of statism and the Marxist model each predict a somewhat less consistent but still ultimately coherent pattern of policy-making. State officials, whether motivated by the national interest or capitalist class interests, may be forced to compromise with societal opponents but will seek, in the long term, to guide policy back toward a strategic vision. Sectoral models suggest that policy consistency and coherence will vary with the balance of power among competing social blocs. Strategic action is most likely where one bloc achieves hegemony. Finally, pluralist approaches lead to expectations of policy inconsistency as rapidly shifting coalitions contribute to incoherent state behavior over time and across issues.

Table 1.2 Comparing Theoretical Approaches: Dependent Variables

Policy Coherence

Character of Interests		High	Medium	Low
	National Interests	Strong Statism	Weak Statism	(empty)
				Pluralism
	Particularistic Interests	Elite	Marxism	
		Corporatism	Sectoral Bloc[a]	

a. This categorization requires qualification: sectoral bloc theories suggest that policy coherence may assume a high value if one bloc achieves hegemonic status.

The Transnational Approach

A societal based model of foreign policy formulation traces the influence of nationally based societal groups and movements on the foreign policy behavior of their own governments. In their common emphasis on non-state actors, societal and transnational models share much in common. Where the transnational model differs is in its attention to the independent linkages among societal groups based in different countries. Thus, government to government interactions are mirrored by transnational societal interactions (Alger, 1984; Nye and Keohane, 1971).

In its broadest formulation, the transnational model points to the emergence of a nascent global society. Made possible by improved transportation and communications, the growth of economic interdependence, the increasing salience of global problems and the spread of information and values through a globally organized mass media network, the global society envelopes and thus constrains states and their behavior. Societal interdependence creates "new facts" internationally, forcing decision-makers to abandon the assumption of national autonomy when calculating interests and formulating policy (Morse, 1970; Burton, 1972).

The existence of transnational economic and cultural linkages among societal groups has important political consequences. Yet the political salience of transnationalism is often more direct and immediate. The transnational model assumes that societal groups with similar interests and objectives will form political coalitions which span across national boundaries. Such groups therefore serve to strengthen one another by sharing ideas, coordinating demands and strategies, pooling resources, and even devising working divisions of labor. The objectives of such transnational social movements may vary. They include bringing about the transformation of particular regimes (South Africa movement), overcoming existing structures of international conflict (the American and West European peace movements), placing new issues on the global agenda (the environmental movement), or shifting global norms, values and standards (the human rights movement). Transnational coalition building is not limited to mass based dissident groups. Elite groups with close ties to existing government or parties may also organize on a transnational basis (e.g., the Trilateral Commission).

While the bulk of political activity engaged in by such groups takes place within national settings, directed at influencing the foreign policies of one's own government, the linkages across political boundaries provide a given transnational coalition with influence beyond the sum of its national parts. Aside from formal linkages, the informal interdependence among similar groups located in different nations may lead to demonstration effects. The success of groups in one country may embolden those in other countries to mobilize while providing lessons which increase the effectiveness of later efforts (e.g., the contagion of revolution in Eastern Europe).

Governments each facing transnationally linked societal coalitions may be forced, by the experience of similar pressures, to respond by coordinating their own behavior (e.g, NATO nations' reaction to the peace movement of the early 1980s). They may collectively resist, co-opt or acquiesce to the demands placed upon them from below. In any case, the coordinated responses of many states when they each face simultaneous pressures from a transnationally organized movement are likely to differ from the adjustments one might expect any given state to undertake were it alone to experience the same demands in isolation. Alternatively, the transnational character of the movements may result in the state actor having to cope not only with the movement, but with a variety of other state actors as well. Inter-state relations may be affected by the policies the state actor pursues toward the transnational movement. In other words, the rules of the game states play when each must cope with oppositions emerging from within segmented and largely autonomous national political settings differ from those which obtain when societal resistance is organized and coordinated transnationally.

STUDYING SOCIETAL GROUP INFLUENCE ON FOREIGN POLICY FORMULATION: THEORY AND EVIDENCE

The preceding section introduced three approaches to the study of state-society relations and foreign policy formulation: statist, societal, and transnational. This volume's organization corresponds to these categories. With the exception of the strong version of statism, essays representative of each of these three models and their variants have been included. We have omitted works reflecting the strong statist perspective by design. This choice stems partly from the fact that examples of such approaches are already abundant in the existing literature. More importantly, however, the theoretical assumptions underlying strong statist models explicitly relegate the influence of societal groups on foreign policy formulation to a peripheral or non-existent concern. Such premises lie beyond the parameters of the research agenda this volume is intended to explore.

Our first contribution, by Thomas Risse-Kappen and Harald Müller, offers an overview of the debate concerning whether the primary determinants of foreign policy lie externally (in the international system) or internally (in the domestic sphere). Their wide ranging survey helps to place the narrower concerns of this volume—namely, the role of societal groups in foreign policy formulation—in a broader context. The authors review the evolution of the internal-external debate before addressing the literature relating to three specific areas of contention: (1) Are security issues less subject to domestic influences than international economic issues? (2) Which domestic variables most directly affect foreign policy-making: those relating to state structure or those having to do with political coalition-building? (3) Do democracies behave more peacefully toward contending states than other sorts of regimes?

Risse-Kappen and Müller suggest that an exclusive focus on either international or domestic variables is unwarranted. Instead, they argue that the most fruitful work in the field of foreign policy analysis has centered around hybrid models which incorporate both internal and external factors. In terms of the models reviewed earlier, these conclusions suggest a skeptical attitude toward either the strong statist perspective or any of the societal centered approaches. Risse-Kappen and Müller lean toward the weak version of statism which, like their own argument, views the state as a Janis-faced creature, concerned with both internal and external order. While external considerations are perhaps primary in the making of foreign policy, domestic factors may also work to alter the trajectory of a state's international behavior.

The chapter by Valerie M. Hudson, Susan M. Sims, and John C. Thomas, is a bold attempt to overcome the methodological obstacles to estimating the effect of domestic opposition group activity on foreign policy behavior in any given instance. To move beyond more vague assertions of the general vulnerability of a regime to such influence, as well as the confines of historical single case analysis, the authors posit a theoretical framework that is cross-nationally applicable and situation specific. Designed to be supplemented by the more detailed knowledge of a country expert, Hudson, Sims, and Thomas hypothesize that the crucial explanatory questions to be resolved is, "what tactic(s) will the national regime choose to cope with current opposition activity?" Determination of specific policy moves by the regime is contingent upon (a) the policy agenda of the regime, (b) the strengths and weaknesses of the regime, and (c) the characteristics of the opposition groups (size, cohesiveness, ideological salience, political proximity level of activity, and so forth).

Knowledge of the tactics that will likely be used by the regime then allows the researcher to project probable resultant effects on the state's foreign policy behavior. A variety of effects may be seen: no effects, tangential effects, and direct effects. As the authors are able to relate their projections to values of specific foreign policy attributes, their model is thus empirically testable through cross-national aggregate analysis, as well as through more detailed process-tracing techniques. To facilitate the testability of the model, the authors provide in-depth guidelines and complete operationalizations for all variables and propositions used. In some senses, the methodological breakthrough of combining more formal and more traditional approaches may be the nut that needs to be cracked in order for the larger research agenda to be realized.

Because of their emphasis on state response, and their assumption that the state will resist efforts by opposition groups to modify policy content or process, we would place the Hudson, Sims, Thomas model under the weak statist approach. The state, though it may not possess autonomy from societal groups, will consistently strive to maintain as much autonomy as it possibly can.

Richard Friman's examination of the British opium trade during the late nineteenth and early twentieth centuries also supports this assumption of the weak version of statism. British officials sought to extend the life of the opium trade against both international pressures exerted by the U.S. and domestic opposition mounted by anti-opium reform groups in Britain. Rather than comply with either set of demands, British leaders used deception to stave off, for a time, each set of pressures. British concessions to both international and domestic constraints were in fact less than met the eye.

Friman's argument suggests the need to distinguish between appearance and substance when evaluating foreign policy adjustment. While unwanted foreign and domestic pressures forced state officials to significantly alter the form and rhetoric of policy, actual behavior and outcomes shifted far less quickly or markedly. A strategy of deception does not provide the state with absolute autonomy. Deception can be politically costly if exposed and therefore serves mainly as a delaying tactic. Nevertheless, the use of "creative" diplomacy can render the relationship between domestic or international constraints and policy response far less simple or direct than many analyses commonly suppose.

Tamar Hermann's piece examines the rise and evolution of the Israeli peace movement. This case presents a significant challenge to the strong version of statism. The strong statist model, in one of its variations, contends that external threats promote societal unity and deference to the state. A second version of statism stresses the unifying effects of a shared national political culture. Few countries have faced more serious international threats to their security than Israel. Moreover, Israeli Jews have been united around a shared cultural heritage as well as a common commitment to Zionism.

Consistent with the expectations of statism, these conditions discouraged domestic challenges to the autonomy and power of the Israeli state in the realms of foreign and security policy during the first several decades of Israel's existence. Yet substantial societal discord over Israeli foreign policy began to emerge in the late seventies. The creation of the Peace Now movement was the most prominent of these challenges to the pre-existing consensus. Its expanding support grew out of changing domestic and international circumstances during the late seventies and early eighties.

Although the direct impact of Peace Now and similar groups on government foreign policy has remained limited, public debate over such issues has been much freer and dissent has been tolerated more readily over the past decade than in previous periods. The scope of public discourse on and political participation in foreign policy issues has expanded considerably. Thus, while the Israeli political system once served as a fair reflection of strong statist assumptions, it now more closely resembles the weak version of statism, demonstrating the possibility that the structure of state-society relations can shift over time in particular countries.

Douglas Van Belle's highly original contribution constructs a rational choice theory of foreign policy decision-making, albeit one based upon unique assumptions about leader preferences. In contrast with most rational choice theorists, Van Belle discards the notion that foreign policy decision-makers adopt the national interest as their central criterion of policy choice. Instead, he offers a cluster of related hypotheses built around the assumption that leaders judge policy options based upon calculations about how various choices will affect the leader's level of domestic support among relevant power bases. This allows Van Belle to account for foreign policy behaviors that appear anomalous from a national interest perspective (e.g., why foreign policy decision-making is reactive, dealing with problems only once they reach crisis proportions, why policies which stand little chance of international success, such as economic sanctions, are sometimes chosen or why leaders may prefer to cope with policy failure by diverting attention from the issue rather than search for better options).

Van Belle's argument proceeds from a pluralist conception of state-society relations. In its present version, the scope of the model is explicitly limited to democratic settings. Van Belle assumes a multiplicity of power bases arrayed along a normal curve ranging from strong supporters to strong opponents of the present leadership. Leaders direct their calculations toward the middle of this spectrum, where support can most easily be won or lost, while attempting to assemble winning coalitions around discrete policy choices. By implication, the composition of these coalitions may shift substantially across issues and over time.

Elizabeth Rogers' piece examines the conflict between ethnic and business interest groups as each sought to influence U.S. policy toward South Africa in the mid-eighties. Rogers' argument best fits the pluralist version of the societal model. She shows that black interest groups successfully pressured the Congress to adopt stringent economic sanctions toward the apartheid government in South Africa. This both demonstrates the sensitivity of the government to societal pressures on an important foreign policy issue while also undermining the assumption, found in many elitist models, of an omnipotent business class. Though well endowed with resources, business interests were divided and relatively few firms viewed the South African issue as a high political priority. Black groups were relatively poor in resources and possessed little experience in lobbying on foreign policy issues, yet they managed to maintain a united front and proved highly motivated. Rogers supports the notion that foreign policy issues often distribute costs and benefits unevenly through the society, thus prompting political conflict and mobilization. The composition of the coalitions which develop, as well as the balance of power among them, will, however, vary from issue to issue.

David Skidmore's contribution examines the struggle between two contending interest group blocs during the debate over ratification of the SALT II treaty. His analysis suggests that security issues can indeed prompt societal division and political mobilization. The elite consensus which characterized much of the Cold War era gave way during the early seventies, leading to competitive mobilization between liberal and conservative factions through the remainder of the decade as each sought control over U.S. foreign policy. The Carter years, in particular, brought repeated clashes between the President and his liberal supporters on the one hand and a coalition of conservative forces on the other. The climactic debate over SALT II revealed the superior strength and organization of conservative groups over their liberal counterparts. Faced with an unfavorable interest group environment, Carter was repeatedly forced to compromise along a range of foreign and security issues in an uphill battle to salvage SALT II's passage by the Senate.

Skidmore's analysis of the SALT II debate, as well as the foreign policy conflicts which led up to it, provides qualified support for the social bloc version of the societal model. While large numbers of groups took part in the SALT II debate, a handful of organizations on either side provided the bulk of political resources available to each coalition. The most influential groups were dominated by prominent representatives from government and business circles. On the conservative side, in particular, the core groups were characterized by overlapping memberships as well as close communication and coordination. Despite divisions within the liberal camp, cleavages among the principal foreign policy interest groups were reinforcing rather than cross-cutting during the seventies. The essential lineup of contending groups remained relatively stable across issues and over time. As suggested by the bulk of his appointments and policies, Carter was clearly affiliated with the liberal faction at the outset of his Administration, although the asymmetry of power in favor of conservative forces prompted a significant retreat on Carter's part over time.

Ellen Dorsey's contribution examines the recent proliferation of transnational social movements (TSMs). She argues that these movements herald an emerging global consciousness; one which has arisen in response to the failure of the modern state to provide its citizens with physical, social or economic security. TSMs therefore represent a significant challenge to state based patterns of political authority. Acting both within and external to established institutional channels, TSMs exert their influence on foreign policy and international relations along three major routes. First, nationally based groups attempt to alter state behavior directly by challenging particular policies as well as shifting the policy agenda. Second, TSMs engage in citizen's diplomacy, bypassing states to create significant linkages among groups based in different societies. Third, TSMs attempt to compensate for or subvert state policies considered destructive of human dignity or security. TSMs thus bring pressure to bear upon existing state structures from both above (the international system) and below (domestic systems).

David Meyer's argument that grassroots activism in both the Eastern and Western camps played a key role in bringing the Cold War to a close draws heavily upon the transnational social movement model. Meyer suggests that a transnational peace movement, spanning the U.S. and its NATO allies, helped to moderate and constrain the hawkish Western policies and rhetoric of the early eighties. In particular, he credits the mobilization of popular support for the peace movement as a key reason why the Reagan Administration felt constrained to re-embrace arms control in the mid-eighties. A more moderate Western stance provided Mihkail Gorbachev with the political space and opportunity needed to pursue an end to the Cold War.

Meyer also argues that the Western peace movement contributed to the conceptual development of Gorbachev's "new thinking" about foreign affairs and provided significant support for reformist groups attempting to carve out a "civil society" in Eastern Europe. Thus, grassroots movements in the U.S., Western Europe and Eastern Europe benefited from transnational ties among themselves and influenced the policies and agendas of the major powers.

CONCLUSION

The central purpose of this volume is to draw attention to the significance of societal group influence on foreign policy formulation, a relatively neglected topic within the field of foreign policy analysis. Our aim is to suggest the range of possible approaches to this task, as well as the rich potential of such research, rather than to endorse a specific model or paradigm. Indeed, the essays which follow embody varying assumptions about the nature of state-society relations. They also differ in other essential respects, such as the relative weight given to deductive and inductive logic in deriving generalizations. Nevertheless, all share a common concern with the question of how societal actors impinge upon the foreign policy process. At this stage in the evolution of research and knowledge on this subject, we think it appropriate to leave open certain crucial questions such as, for instance, whether the various approaches outlined earlier in this essay are necessarily competing or whether they may each prove applicable under different conditions and contexts.

This introductory essay has sought to provide a common theoretical vocabulary by which the diverse perspectives represented here can be compared and assessed. We have attempted to throw into sharp relief the differing assumptions underlying the disparate conceptual and empirical endeavors represented in this volume and the field at large. Clarity about basic premises and where they diverge is the first step toward fruitful dialogue and disciplinary progress.

Perhaps the most glaring omission from this collection is the absence of truly comparative and cross-national empirical research. Collectively, the essays which follow explore the processes of foreign policy decision-making in various national contexts. The more conceptual pieces (e.g., Risse-Kappen and Müller, Hudson, Sims and Thomas, Van Belle, and Dorsey) suggest strategies and hypotheses for comparative analysis. Yet none of our contributors extend their empirical investigations beyond a single country case. In part, this shortcoming reflects the difficulty faced by any given scholar in acquiring sufficient expertise to conduct cross-national research with confidence.

However, there are other, more basic reasons for this absence. Scholars pursuing this research agenda are doing nothing less than re-creating the field of foreign policy analysis. They are doing so by pushing up against three of the field's most long-standing, obstinate barriers to theoretical and empirical progression: (1) causality, (2) integration, and (3) testability.

As mentioned previously in this essay, theorists of domestic effects on foreign policy behavior are faced with a plethora of potential explanatory variables. Separating the disparate strands of causality can be an almost overwhelming task. Did the behavior reflect the influence of societal group activity or not? How can one say? Can one sort out the necessary and the sufficient causes for a particular behavior or types of behavior? One is almost reduced to envy of the systems theorists who cheerfully "black box" this "Pandora's box" of internal factors affecting state behavior.

If the strands of causality *can* be disentangled, the theoretical task has only just begun. Now the strands must be woven together to form a coherent and integrated explanation of foreign policy behavior. That is, a theory of foreign policy behavior must specify when societal groups will be impor-tant, and when other variables, such as leader personality of systemic constraints will be more important. Moreover, as no social explanation is unicausal, it must specify how societal group influence *interacts* will these other variables to produce outcome in specific cases. A meta-theory linking the theories in this volume to those at other levels of analysis must be posited.

Unless this can be done, testability is compromised. After all, if a theory of societal group effects is to be linked to outcomes in discrete situations, then the scope conditions of that theory must be carefully elaborated. Further complicating testability—at least in the cross-national, quasi-aggregate sense—is the clear implication of the chapters in this volume: that a large amount of rich, detailed qualitative data is indispensable to making the argument that societal groups in fact influence foreign policy behavior. Scholars pursuing this research agenda are engaged in "concrete theorizing" (Lane, 1990), which does not proceed by abstraction to heights of idealized simplification, but burrows in the trenches of detail that heretofore only country experts have braved. Methodologies affording use of such qualitative detail, while still retaining the social scientific desiderata of testability, generalizability, and rigor must be developed for empirical progression to keep pace with theoretical progression. (See Hudson, 1991).

Though the challenges to be met are stiff, the very existence of this volume speaks to the willingness of some to face them. We hope that the many promising ideas contained herein will inspire others.

PART ONE

Weak Statist Approaches

2

From the Outside In and from the Inside Out

INTERNATIONAL RELATIONS, DOMESTIC POLITICS,
AND FOREIGN POLICY

Harald Müller and Thomas Risse-Kappen

I s international politics explicable on the systemic level of the international environment and does, therefore, the foreign-policy of states primarily result from and react to external constraints and opportunities? Or does the study of world politics have to start on the unit-level of individual states and, thus, is foreign policy to be explained by the internal organization of a political system and its domestic processes? Scholars have struggled with these questions since world politics has existed as a subject of research. The following essay tries to make sense out of an ever-growing body of literature.

For the purposes of this paper, "domestic" refers to the constellation of political interests in a society, the aggregation of such demands, the debates on issue-areas, and the transformation of these processes into foreign policy outputs. We concentrate on state-society relations, domestic political structures, and coalition-building processes while largely disregarding decision-making analysis in the narrow sense (Hermann et al., 1987; Maoz, 1990), in particular bureaucratic politics (Allison, 1971; Halperin, 1974) and the individual or group-psychological dimension (Janis, 1982; Jervis, 1977; Jervis et al., 1985; Lebow, 1981).

Three major areas of controversy can be identified in the "external-internal" debate: (1) What determines international politics, the nature of the global system or the domestic environment of the actors? Our survey of the history of the debate attempts to show that to pose the question in an "either-or" form is to misconceive the problem. Instead, we see a growing consensus among scholars that a complex model of international politics has to integrate the three levels of analysis: society, political system, and international environment. (2) If it can be taken for granted that domestic factors do play a role, how do we conceptualize them? State-centered analyses focus on the institutional structure of political systems, while others emphasize the coalition-building processes among elites, interest groups, and societal actors. Again, we see an emerging consensus towards mixed approaches. However, related to that is the question of whether those domestic factors are issue-area specific, namely, whether there is a difference in the domestic environment of foreign economic policies as compared to security studies. (3) A third and final controversy concerns the relationship between domestic political structures and the content of foreign policy and goes to the heart of the liberal theory of foreign policy. The two main issues at stake here are (a) whether the foreign policy-making processes of liberal democracies resemble the pluralist model at all, and (b) whether there is any connection between democratization and foreign policy outcomes. Are democracies more peaceful? Do they pursue cooperative and free-trade-oriented foreign economic policies? Our review of the empirical literature leads us to conclude that a modified version of the liberal theory is indeed able to cope with the observable reality.

Throughout our review, we try to bring in findings of the European literature which is often ignored among American scholars. We conclude with suggestions for further research.

The "External-Internal" Debate and the State of the Art

The History of the Controversy

American scholars need sometimes to be reminded that the *realist* paradigm, which treats international politics as the result of power struggles between rationally acting states, was not invented by them. Some trace it back to Thucydides and ancient Greece. As an articulated position, however, it can probably be dated back to the German historian Leopold von Ranke and his followers who established the concept of the "primacy of foreign policy" back in the nineteenth century. Ranke's famous quote points to a basic ambiguity of his approach between description and prescription: "The position of a state in the world depends on the degree of independence it has attained. It is obliged, therefore, to organize all its internal resources for the purpose of self-preservation. This is the supreme law of the state" (von Ranke, 1936/1973, 117–18). The "primacy of foreign policy" was therefore often used by von Ranke's followers to justify authoritarian rule domestically and to promote an expansionist foreign policy of the German Reich disguised as a "policy of global power balance" (critical reviews in Czempiel, 1963; Dehio, 1961).

However, there also existed a purely analytical version of the concept. In 1906, historian Otto Hintze described the close relationship between political and military constitutions as a result of the external pressures to which states are exposed. Since the sixteenth century, the European great power rivalry necessitated an endless chain of efforts to restore and maintain the balance of power between them and, as a consequence, produced absolutist constitutions as well as the standing armies on the Continent. Britain, on the other hand, could exclusively concentrate on naval power because of her insular situation; since she didn't have to maintain a standing army, there was no need for an authoritarian state (Hintze, 1906).

Hintze's theory was an early attempt to develop a perspective which later became known as "the second image reversed" (Gourevitch, 1978). While Hintze referred to the international security environment as determining state structures, historians such as Alexander Gerschenkron (1962) and Barrington Moore (1966) tried to show in the 1960s that the pressures of the international economy had a crucial impact on the domestic political structures of "early industrializers" such as Britain and the U.S. as compared to the "late industrializers" Japan and Germany. The realist paradigm as developed by von Ranke became the subject of controversy very early on. After World War I critical historians became alarmed that von Ranke's followers, at the turn of the century, had supported Tirpitz's naval arms buildup and a German foreign policy hostile to Britain. In the 1920s, for example, Eckart Kehr (1928/1977) argued the "primacy of domestic politics." He explained the anti-British and anti-Russian policies of the German Reich prior to World War I as the foreign policy consequence of a domestic coalition-building between the East-elbian junkers and the bourgeoisie against strengthened social democratic forces. Unlike the Marxist theory of imperialism (Hilferding, 1910/1968; Lenin, 1917/1960) which analyzed international expansionism and colonialism as primarily driven by the needs of capitalist accumulation, Kehr pointed to the "politics of merging" (*Sammlungspolitik*), the alliance of *pre*capitalist farmers with industry oriented towards modernization. Thus, Kehr's "primacy of domestic politics" established the primacy of politics and not simply of the (capitalist) economy.

Social historians such as Michael Gordon (1974) and Hans Ulrich Wehler (1969) came back to Kehr's approach in the 1960s. Wehler, for example, elaborated the concept of social imperialism. He argued that the aggressive foreign policy of the German Reich was caused by the problems of economic growth which Germany faced during the post-1873 world economic crisis, on the one hand, and by the attempt of the ruling elites, on the other, to divert internal conflicts with industrial workers into the external environment. In the meantime, *realism* had won the day among American international relations scholars. German emigrants such as Hans J. Morgenthau (1948) developed von Ranke's earlier efforts into a sophisticated analytical approach. However, the 1960s saw the first challenge to the concept in the U.S. Coinciding with the political upheaval of the decade, "revisionists" explained U.S. policy during the Cold War as resulting from the expansionist needs of American capitalism after World War II and/or from the necessity to secure the domestic power position of the ruling elites (Kolko, 1968; Williams, 1962).

Revisionism had its impact on West European thinking, too. Drawing heavily on the critical theory of the "Frankfurt school" (Theodor W. Adorno, Max Horkheimer, Jürgen Habermas et al.) and combining it with insights gained from critical U.S. scholars, peace researchers such as Johan Galtung (1975–80) and Dieter Senghaas (1968, 1972) began to challenge realist assumptions. They criticized the prevailing model of arms races as action-reaction processes and pointed to domestic processes (*Eigendynamik*) to explain the East-West arms buildup. According to their view, armament dynamics were determined by growth imperatives of the arms industry or—in a more sophisticated analysis—by a mutually reinforcing spiral of technological, industrial, power preserving, and psychological factors.

This critical theory of foreign policy distanced itself from the realist "rational actor" model and emphasized counter-intentional and irrational political processes and consequences. At about the same time, scholars in the U.S. arguing from the liberal tradition challenged the realist assumption of the state as a unitary actor and pointed to the mechanisms of *bureaucratic politics* (Allison, 1971; Halperin, 1974). Moreover, the notion of a state-centered international system came under attack. Earlier attempts by Karl W. Deutsch (1966) and James N. Rosenau (1966) were reformulated into the concepts of "transnational politics" and "interdependence" according to which societal actors increasingly complement and substitute for the foreign policy of states and transnational ties penetrate the "hard shell" of national sovereignty (Kaiser, 1969; Keohane and Nye, 1971, 1977; Mansbach et al., 1976). Had this hypothesis been substantiated, the controversy between "external" vs. "internal" determinants of foreign policy would have become irrelevant, since the state as an international actor would have withered away. However, most analysts concluded that this line of argument went too far, that foreign relations between states still counted, and that state sovereignty consolidated itself besides and often above transnational relations (Bühl, 1978; Link, 1978; Lissner, 1977). In other words, the question has to be reformulated toward the analysis of the *conditions* under which transnational relations affect state behavior and inter-state relations.

Transnational economic relations also became the focus of a critical theory of international relations developed by scholars from the Southern hemisphere. "Dependency theory" (Cardoso, 1973; Frank, 1969) analyzed the economic relationship between the industrialized countries and the Third and Fourth World. Underdevelopment was claimed to result from the integration of Third/Fourth World countries into the capitalist world economy, the exploitation of the peripheries in the South by the metropolis of the North, and the ensuing political and societal penetration of Southern systems. Thus, while peace research thought to have understood the East-West arms race as primarily domestically driven, "dependency theory" argued against modernization theory that underdevelopment was predominantly caused externally.

Agreement in Sight: Toward Complex Models of International Politics

Studies of "transnational politics" led to the conclusion that the "external vs. internal" controversy would not just wither away because of the occurrence of transnational interdependencies and that the capitalist penetration of the world economy could even produce new forms of "external determinants" of domestic politics. At the same time, empirical studies on armament dynamics undertaken by European peace researchers concluded that the "domestic politics" explanation of the East-West arms buildup had oversimplified the processes at work. These analyses pointed to an interaction between international and domestic factors (Krell, 1976; Müller, 1985; see also Evangelista, 1988; Russett, 1983). Empirical tests of the "dependency theory" brought similar results. The "center-periphery" concept turned out to be too simplistic to account for the complexity of relations between the First and the Third/Fourth World and for the process of differentiation among the countries of the South. Development prospects depend upon a match between structural capacities of the state and society, the dominant development strategy of the country, and the opportunities and constraints provided by the international system (Menzel, 1985, 1986; Menzeland Senghaas, 1986; Senghaas, 1982). In sum, to simply contrast international system explanations with domestic politics concepts, has proven to be inadequate for our understanding of the processes at work (see also Moravscik, 1990).

Foreign policy behavior always seems to be "externally driven" to the extent that it usually reacts to information generated in the international environment which reaches the political system in part directly, in part indirectly via societal demands, which in turn have to process information from the international environment. Changes in the world economy, for example, force states to adapt independently of their strength and their political importance. Such adaptations not only entail the short-term provision of additional resources; the international economic environment more often than not forces decision-makers to redefine their political priorities against their own ideological preferences. Helen Milner (1988) has argued that the increased economic interdependence after World War II contributed to prevent protectionism in the 1970s and 1980s. Even states with strong national economies are not always able to use them solely according to domestic preferences.

Similar tendencies occur in the security area. External threats and alliance relations are important factors in this regard. Expensive social policies or fiscal conservatism to balance the budget frequently give way to increased defense expenditures, when forced by external threats. The perceived Soviet threat and pressure by West European governments, for example, led to the U.S. decision to build a Western alliance after World War II and to finally put an end to isolationism. In the late 1960s, detente between the superpowers exerted adaptive pressures on West Germany which culminated in the *ostpolitik* of the social-liberal government (Haftendorn, 1985). Western policies crucially affected coalition-building processes in the Soviet leadership (Snyder, 1989).

External factors not only influence individual political decisions, but also domestic structures themselves. The Soviet revocation of the Brezhnev doctrine, for example, which put an end to its penetration of the Eastern European Communist regimes, was the decisive catalyst for the democratic revolutions in those countries. Peter Katzenstein showed in his study on "Small States in World Markets" (1985) how domestic decision-making structures changed profoundly toward corporativism under the specific international conditions of the 1930s (for similar processes see Rogowski, 1989; Senghaas, 1982). Empirical studies of a similar analytical strength are still rare in security studies. However, Ernst-Otto Czempiel's (1979, 1989a) analysis of the origins of the U.S. security apparatus led to conclusions similar to Katzenstein's work. The U.S. "military-industrial complex" was formed when the American society was confronted with its superpower role in a bipolar conflict. When the arms buildup was institutionalized in social and political structures, the apparatus developed a self-interest in its own preservation and in the increase of its political influence to allocate security-relevant resources.

The study of international regimes adds to the analysis of how international processes influence national policies (Krasner, 1983; Kohler-Koch, 1989; Young, 1989). International regimes are only able to survive and fulfill their functions if the participants develop stable and reliable patterns of expectations of each other's behavior. This is not possible if political decisions are oriented ad hoc to the regime norms. Rather, these norms have to become embedded into the national decision-making rules. Regime efficiency can therefore be determined by its ability to alter national decision-making norms in the respective issue-area. The U.S. government, for example, used its obligations in the international trade regime to resist radical protectionist demands from domestic interest groups (Nau, 1989). In the security area, the non-proliferation regime had a discernible impact on changes in national legislation regarding nuclear export regulations (Müller, 1989b, 1991).

To conclude, changes in the allocation of resources, redefinition of priorities and finally the degree of domestic support are often the result of external pressures—both in economic and security policies. But a "primacy of the international environment" does not follow from these findings. In most cases, states have choices which then must be explained in terms of domestic politics and the goals of the different actors. The degree and the precise mode of adaptation to outside pressures depend on the domestic and social structure of the respective country. External factors rarely influence the political priorities of a state directly without being modified by the internal structures and coalition-building processes. Domestic political instabilities and the state of the national economy crucially affect decisions to join international alliances (Barnett and Levy, 1991; Most and Siverson, 1987), crisis behavior (Lebow, 1981), and decisions to go to war (Levy, 1988; Russett, 1990: chap. 2). As the "revisionist school" pointed out, U.S. cold war policies and its entry into NATO were determined by domestic factors to a considerable degree. In the case of the Federal Republic, conservative groups were strong enough to delay its adaptation to detente until 1969. In the early 1980s, on the other hand, the strong domestic consensus in favor of *ostpolitik* prevented West Germany from conforming to U.S. confrontational policies vis-à-vis the Soviet Union (Risse-Kappen, 1988a).

In sum, the debate on the primacy of the international system versus domestic politics does not adequately address and describe the problem. A complex model of international politics has to be conceptualized which integrates the three levels of analysis: society, political system, and international environment. Rather than adding up international and domestic factors to explain the foreign policy of states, the model should focus on the interaction of the three levels (Moravscik, 1990). Such a framework should be able to incorporate both externally and internally driven behavior as extreme cases without foreclosing the analytical angle in one direction. Several authors who developed such models over the last twenty years came to surprisingly similar conclusions:

Wolfram Hanrieder's (1967) "compatibility-consensus" concept views foreign policy as a balance between domestic consensus and compatibility with the restrictions of the international system.

In the late 1970s, Peter Gourevitch (1978) and Peter Katzenstein (1976, 1978b) debated over how to conceptualize the domestic environment of foreign economic policies of advanced industrialized states.

James N. Rosenau (1981) applied systems theory and the concept of adaptation to foreign policy analysis. His model linked adaptive behavior to specific combinations of internal and external demands to which a state is exposed.

Ernst-Otto Czempiel (1981, 1989b) conceptualized international politics as an "asymmetric broken grid of interactions," i.e., interaction patterns of various density and intensity between the political systems, their social systems, and the international environment.

Charles and Margret Hermann's (1987, 1989) work in comparative foreign policy focussing on "decision units" equally emphasizes the interaction of international and domestic factors.

Robert Putnam's (1988) "two-level game" model of international negotiations linked international goal attainment to the domestic restrictions to which state actors are exposed, and vice versa. His concept resembles Hanrieder's and Rosenau's earlier attempts.

Michael Mastanduno, David A. Lake, and G. John Ikenberry (1989) developed a "realist theory of state action" which tries to predict foreign policy as a function of both the state's international power position and its domestic structure.

These converging concepts portray states as the most important, though not the exclusive, international actors which however, are neither in complete control of their international nor their domestic environments. They are constantly exposed to internal, external and, more often than not, conflicting demands (also Skocpol, 1985). Political systems try to balance these demands by selecting options and by extracting the necessary resources for their actions. From this perspective, the alternative "primacies" do not emerge as mutually exclusive and generalizable hypotheses, but as the two poles of a continuum of possible combinations of external and internal factors influencing state actions.

FROM THE INSIDE OUT: DOMESTIC IMPACTS ON FOREIGN POLICY

We have tried to show that there is an emerging consensus in the international relations literature on the need to develop complex models to integrate domestic and international factors to explain the foreign policies of states. However, while most scholars have a clear idea of what counts in the international environment, they are far less precise as to what they mean by "domestic politics" as an explanatory variable. "Domestic politics" is often used as a catch-all notion covering almost everything from psychological predispositions of top decision-makers and bureaucratic politics within a government to party politics, business interests, public opinion, and interest groups. However, if international relations scholars want to specify more clearly the internal environment of state actions, they can learn a lot from their colleagues in comparative politics. The most fruitful controversies in the study of the domestic environment of international politics center around concepts stemming from comparative politics.

Unfortunately, the domestic politics dimension of national security policy has not been analyzed in the same depth and through systematic comparison as has been the case in the study of foreign economic policies (Nye and Lynn-Jones 1988, 24–25). The issue has received considerable attention in quantitative analyses, but the results remain to some extent inconclusive because of serious methodological problems in identifying the direction of causation or the interdependence among variables (Levy 1989, 267–76). On the other hand, a large number of single-case studies exist, many of them unknown to English-reading scholars (for example, Czempiel, 1979; Everts, 1983, 1985; Krell, 1976; Kubbig, 1988; Müller, 1985). Where the domestic dimension has been included in studies using the method of focussed comparison, the results point to the significance of these factors (for example, Barnett and Levy, 1991; Evangelista, 1988; Jervis et al., 1985; Lebow 1981, 169–91; Levy, 1988, 1989). We see two major debates in the literature regarding the conceptualization of domestic influences on foreign policy: (1) To what extent are variances in the responses of different countries to the same international pressures to be explained by domestic political structures or by coalition-building processes within political systems and societies? (2) Does the degree of domestic influences on the foreign policy of nations vary according to specific issue-areas? In particular, is there a difference between the domestic fabric of foreign economic as compared to security policies?

Institutions and/or Coalitions: Domestic Structures and Foreign Policy

Domestic structure approaches deal with the nature of the political institutions (the "state"), with basic features of the society, and with the institutional and organizational arrangements linking state and society and channeling societal demands into the political system (the "policy networks") Domestic structures determine the selectivity of political systems with regard to societal demands. Social movement research talks about "political opportunity structures" (Kitschelt, 1986). States differ markedly with regard to the governments' autonomy within the political systems and their societal environments. Following a proposal by Peter

Katzenstein (1976), Stephen Krasner (1978a, b) argued that state "strength" and "weakness" in relationship to the society are central to explain foreign policy (also Mastanduno et al., 1989; Ikenberry, 1988). "Weak" states are dominated by society; foreign policy decision-makers are restricted in their actions by public opinion, interest groups, parliament, and bureaucracies oriented towards domestic politics. As a result, policy-makers are unable to exploit the full scope of their margin of maneuver in the international environment. Foreign policy decision-makers in "strong" states, on the other hand, are relatively independent of societal demands and pressures. It is easier for them to extract resources from society in order to pursue foreign policy goals.

France seems to be the ideal candidate of a "strong state" among the Western democracies with its centralized political system and the extraordinary power, in particular in foreign and defense affairs, granted to the president by the constitution of the Fifth Republic. The U.S., on the other hand, is usually considered a typical "weak state" because of its federalist structure, the system of checks and balances between Congress and administration, and the extensive network of interest group representation. The Federal Republic of Germany assumes a middle position insofar as its federalist structure, the proportionate rule, and the permanency of election campaigns with national repercussions in the Länder require almost constant consensus-building in coalition governments; as a result, the German domestic structure comes close to the democratic corporatist model (Katzenstein, 1989).

The Japanese political system seems holds an intermediate position, too. On the one hand, it is highly centralized with a strong state bureaucracy and the stability of the Japanese government is illustrated by the ability of the Liberal Democratic Party to hold the government constantly over the last forty years (Johnson, 1982; Pempel, 1982). On the other hand, Japan may as well be regarded as another corporatist system insofar as consensus-oriented decision-making is deeply rooted in its political culture (Bobrow, 1989; Calder, 1988; Ishida, 1983).

The Japanese and the German cases show analytical problems of the "strong vs. weak state" dichotomy. First, the distinction is biased toward the institutionalized political structure and ignores the effects of political culture, ideology, and history. Second, "weak states" like the U.S. are sometimes able to pursue highly efficient policies, while "strong" ones might become victim of their own power (Ikenberry, 1986a, b; International Organization, 1988).

Most important, however, institutionalist approaches have been challenged as "apolitical," as unable to explain specific policy outcomes. Rather than emphasizing state structures, Peter Gourevitch suggested that one should analyze the *coalition-building processes* within the society and the political system in order to understand policies: "Majorities have to be built, coalitions constructed, terms of trade among alliance partners worked out, legitimating arguments developed..." (Gourevitch 1978, 904). Thus, coalition-building approaches focus on the "policy networks," i.e., the mechanisms and processes of interest representation linking the political systems to their societal environments, such as political parties and interest groups. This concept emphasizes the ability of political actors to build consensus among the relevant elite groups in support of their policies (Hagan, 1987; Milner, 1988; Rogowski, 1989).

To simply set off the coalition argument against the institutionalist approach seems to be inappropriate, though. First, domestic structures may be well suited to explain the ability of states to reach and implement decisions but do not determine the specific content or the directions of policies. For example, the frequent shifts in U.S. arms control policy from Carter to Reagan, and from Reagan's first to his second term, did not result from changed structures, but from changes in domestic coalitions. Second, however, simple coalition arguments cannot account for stability in policies when coalitions change. The continuity of West German detente and arms control policies since the early 1970s despite changes in the global East-West environment and in the governing coalition can only be accounted for when the specific German domestic structure geared toward consensus-building is taken into account. Third, coalition-building takes place in the framework of political institutions. The structures of society, of the political system, and of the policy networks between them determine the size and the strength of policy coalitions needed to create the support basis for specific policies (Evans et al., 1985). In the French case, for example, the combination of a highly centralized state with a strong and bipolarized party system does not require the President to take opposition demands into account under normal circumstances (except 1986–88). The absence of both factors in the U.S., on the other hand, raises the demands on coalition-building. Finally, domestic structures account for general features of foreign policies pursued by different countries, the degree of stability as well as the level of activity and commitment (Hagan, 1987).

As a result, a "mixed" approach taking into account both institutional structures and coalition-building processes seems to be adequate. In their later works, Peter Gourevitch and Peter Katzenstein who previously had argued about the respective merits of institutionalist versus coalition-based concepts, both moved towards combined approaches (Gourevitch, 1986; Katzenstein, 1978b, 1985). Katzenstein, for example, has suggested a differentiation between (a) the structure of the political system and the degree of its centralization, (b) the nature of society, i.e., the level of societal fragmentation and polarization, and (c) the "policy network," i.e., the linkage structure between the political system and society and the degree to which it is state-controlled, society-dominated, or corporatist. A mixed approach combining institutional settings and coalition-building processes, while less parsimonious than the purely institutionalist concept, seems to be better suited to account for structural differences in the decision-making processes as well as for variations in policy outcomes between different countries.

Economy and Security: The Impact of Issue-Areas

Domestic structure and coalition-building approaches have proven useful and are well established in the study of international political economy (Cohen, 1990; Gourevitch, 1986; Katzenstein, 1978a, 1984, 1985, 1989; Milner, 1988; Müller, 1989a; Rogowski, 1989). However, they are far less common in security studies. Here, von Ranke's "primacy of foreign policy" still looms. Stephen Krasner (1978b: 70), for example, has argued that, when it comes to issues of national survival, all states are "strong:" "A state that is weak in relation to its own society can act effectively in the strategic arena because its preferences are not likely to diverge from those of individual societal groups." As a result, domestic processes would be issue area specific. Some have even argued that the differences between domestic structures are less significant than those between issue-areas (Zimmerman, 1973; for an excellent review see Evangelista, 1989).

However, there is increasing empirical evidence from both American and European scholars suggesting that domestic structures do count in security policy. After all, peace researchers started their attack on the realist paradigm in the 1960s by using domestic structure arguments to explain the East-West arms competition. Among the most prominent concepts was the proposition that the "Military-Industrial Complex" (MIC) dominated the security policy network in the U.S. and other Western countries (Ilchman and Bain, 1973; Melman, 1970). Amalgamating neo-marxist political economy and C. Wright Mills's (1956) "power elite" concept, the MIC was defined as a social and political subsystem which integrated the armament industry, the military-oriented science community, the defense-related parts of the political system, and the military bureaucracies. They would combine their power to increase the chances that their particular interests prevail in the political system. The MIC concept assumed that these interest groups not only tried to increase their share in the allocation of economic resources, but also to secure stable preconditions for such a distributional pattern. Thus, it would favor an aggressive foreign policy and a military doctrine which guarantees the constant increase of defense expenditures.

Empirical research on the U.S. MIC, which is by far the largest among all Western political systems, did not confirm the hypotheses of the theory. Peace researchers systematically tested this and other domestic structure approaches (Gleditsch and Njølstad, 1989; Krell, 1976; Medick, 1976; Müller, 1985; Rosen, 1973; Schlotter, 1975). They concluded that, first, the political, military, and economic elites of the U.S. are more heterogeneous than the concept assumed (also Russett and Hanson, 1975). If at all, the MIC would have to be conceptualized as a loose coalition of actors and groups with different interests and goals. Second, defense policy formation in the U.S. seems to be less dominated by the economic interests of the armament industry than by ideological factors, threat perceptions, and strategic orientations. Third, the armament industry, too, is subject to business cycles. The MIC does not have unlimited access to budget resources, and, once its demands reach certain, though not clearly discernible, boundaries, it meets with strong and often successful opposition by counterveiling powers (Czerwick and Müller, 1976; Krell, 1981).

This does not mean, however, that an interest group-oriented concept is irrelevant for the analysis of foreign policy decision-making. The focus of the MIC concept on the amalgamation of economic, military, and political interests has been successful in explaining single weapons development and procurement decisions (Adams, 1984; Hampson, 1989). Moreover, it cannot be denied that public interest groups such as the "Committee on the Present Danger" influenced U.S. policies during the late 1970s/early 1980s by shaping both public and elite preferences (Sanders, 1983). Political-ideological interests produced a reallocation of resources towards defense in this case, with considerable distributional consequences. But even economically oriented interest groups do not necessarily work in only one direction, as illustrated by the Committee on the East (*Ostausschuß*) of the West German Federation of Industry which had a clear and positive impact on Bonn's detente policy since the mid-1960s (Kreile, 1978; Wörmann, 1982). In this case, economic interests promoted a cooperative foreign policy.

While the MIC concept has been disconfirmed in its more rigid version, it could nevertheless be shown that the analysis of domestic politics is relevant in security studies, too. In his seminal analysis of arms innovation processes, Matthew Evangelista (1988) made a good case for the domestic structure argument. He compared the technological innovation in the arms buildup of the U.S. with the Soviet Union and concluded that the variation in process resulted from the different social and political structures. Arms innovations are usually initiated in the U.S. "from below," by "technological entrepreneurs" who try to form coalitions in the defense bureaucracy, Congress, and the administration which ultimately lead to development and production decisions. In the Soviet Union, on the other hand, the process is much more "top down", i.e., demands to develop new arms technologies stem from decisions high up in the military and political hierarchy. Thus, the study basically confirms the "weak vs. strong state" distinction for the security area. Another study compared the impact of public opinion and public interest groups on security policy in several liberal democracies and found that—*ceteris paribus*—differences in domestic structures account for variances in public influence (Risse-Kappen, 1991a).

The available evidence seems to suggest that differences in domestic structures are more important than the peculiarities of issue-areas to account for variations in foreign policy choices across cases and countries. Whether in national defense or foreign economic issues, the U.S. policy network is considerably more society-dominated than the French. The West German structure resembles the corporatist model in both issue-areas. This does not mean that issue-specific factors are irrelevant. For example, other things being equal, states seem to be generally more autonomous vis-à-vis their societies concerning national security issues than regarding foreign economic policies (*International Organization*, 1988). However, it is far from clear whether these differences have to do with intrinsic qualities of security as compared to economic issues or whether they are simply due to the fact that security issues tend to be less politicized than economic problems. Once the public gets involved in security affairs and the issue salience raises, the political processes do not look much different from those in any other issue-area (Kubbig, 1988; Meyer, 1990; Risse-Kappen, 1988a).

POLITICAL STRUCTURES AND THE CONTENT OF FOREIGN POLICIES: HOW WELL-BEHAVED ARE LIBERAL DEMOCRACIES?

A third debate regarding the relationship between domestic politics and foreign policy concerns democratic theory. How democratic are the foreign policies of the highly industrialized liberal democracies? The question has in fact two parts. First, it has to be asked whether the foreign policy-making process of countries claiming to be democratic resembles the pluralist model. Second, if the first question can be answered positively, do pluralist democracies behave differently in international politics, as liberal theory would predict? Are democracies more peaceful and do they pursue more cooperatively oriented foreign economic policies than authoritarian regimes?

Democracy and Foreign Policy: The Re-discovery of the Public

Realism and revisionism—for all their disagreements—converge in the assessment that the public and democratic participation do not have a role to play in the conduct of foreign policy. Those arguing the "primacy of foreign policy" supported the notion that foreign policy should be the realm of the executive and its conduct should be unhampered from domestic pressures. The critical theory of foreign policy, on the other hand, claimed that in capitalist democracies—and even more so in nondemocratic systems—ruling elites essentially control the foreign policy consensus-building process (Chomsky and Herman, 1988; Ginsberg, 1986). Others argued that foreign affairs were far away from the daily life of ordinary citizens whose knowledge of these issues were almost negligible. Public opinion on foreign and security issues was claimed to be instable and volatile (Rosenau, 1961).

Three factors seem to determine the degree of public influence on the foreign policy of liberal democracies: (1) the structure of the political system and its openness to societal influences (see above); (2) the salience of the issue in the domestic debate; and (3) the degree of consensus and cleavages among elites and public opinion (cf. Everts and Faber, 1990; Russett, 1990).

A domestic structure conducive to public influence on foreign policy is only one pre-condition for societal actors to have an impact. There also has to be an articulated and informed public opinion. Indeed, empirical studies show for all Western democracies that basic foreign policy attitudes remain remarkably stable over time (Bobrow, 1989; Eichenberg, 1989; Flynn and Rattinger, 1985; Graham, 1989; Russett, 1990; Schweigler, 1985; Wittkopf, 1990). The image of a volatile public blindly following the agitated debates in the media and among politicians is questionable. A long-term study of the U.S. public showed that attitude changes more often than not coincided with changes in the international environment or in the available information. The public seems to be more "rational" than is often assumed (Shapiro and Page, 1988). Moreover, public opinion is only uninformed as far as technical details are concerned. People seem to acquire the functional knowledge necessary to make sense of information and to form an opinion on issues they are interested in (Graham, 1988). Public opinion cannot be called "irrational" simply because it judges certain issues according to different criteria than do the elites.

Finally, the assertion must be modified that the public in general is completely uninterested in foreign affairs. Americans, for example, pay much greater attention to these issues than is usually assumed. During election campaigns, majorities in the public knew the different policy choices to be debated and were able to pinpoint the candidates' positions (Aldrich et al., 1989). In Western Europe (except France), the salience of foreign and security issues has markedly increased in the public debate over the last fifteen years (Sabin, 1986; Everts, 1988; Szabo, 1988).

To determine the degree of domestic consensus on foreign policy in liberal democracies, general public opinion and elite shave to be distinguished. As far as elite opinion is concerned, data for the United States and

Western Europe suggest a high degree of consensus relating to basic foreign policy principles and goals (Holsti and Rosenau, 1986, 1988; Eberwein and Siegmann, 1985; Schössler and Weede, 1978). However, this unanimity only exists on a high level of abstraction. The U.S. elite, for example, while overwhelmingly supportive of "internationalism," has been deeply divided since the Vietnam war on whether the U.S. should pursue rather militant or cooperative policies in the world (Holsti and Rosenau, 1988; Mandelbaum and Schneider, 1985; Wittkopf, 1987). There is also a high correlation between elite attitudes on foreign policy and on domestic issues. "Hard-liners" are overwhelmingly conservative regarding social issues; domestic "liberals" more often than not support "accomodationist" foreign policies.

While, to our knowledge, no data of comparable sophistication exist for Western Europe and Japan, the available evidence suggests that there are similar divisions among the political elites in most Western democracies—with the remarkable exception of France (Coker, 1987; Everts, 1983, 1985; Howorth and Chilton, 1984). In sum, the available evidence on elite opinion on foreign policy in liberal democracies runs counter to the proposition of a ruling power elite with shared interests, attitudes, and goals.

The same holds true for mass public opinion. While consensus prevails on the level of fundamental foreign policy orientations, the public in most Western democracies is divided on specific issues. Military means, in particular nuclear weapons, are controversial. One could even call this a "stable dissent" (Bobrow, 1989; Eichenberg, 1989; Graham, 1989; Flynn and Rattinger, 1985; Russett, 1990). While the same political and social cleavages exist in the public as well as among the elites, mass and elite attitudes are not always in sync and changes in public and elite attitudes do not always occur simultaneously (Wittkopf, 1987; Ziegler, 1987).

To conclude, elites as well as masses are more pluralistic than previously assumed; controversies on foreign policy goals and issues are more common than consensus. This does not yet answer our question on the impact of the public on foreign policy decisions. The lack of consensus within the elites only provides a "window of opportunity" which might be filled in by the public.

There is new evidence that the public impact on foreign policy in liberal democracies is greater than is usually assumed (Risse-Kappen, 1991a). In the U.S. case, a long-term study of the relationship between changes in public opinion and policy shifts showed that the change occurred in the same direction in two thirds of the cases; public opinion usually changed before the policy shift took place. This finding relates to domestic as well as foreign policy issues (Page and Shapiro, 1983; Russett, 1990). Specific examples of public influence on U.S. policies include the cases of the Vietnam war and of the Reagan Administration's reappraisal of arms control in 1984 as a response to anti-nuclear protests in the U.S. and in

Western Europe (Joseph, forthcoming; Kubbig, 1988; Meyer, 1990; Small, 1988).

As for West Germany, the public impact on foreign policy increased since the 1970s. Public opinion primarily affected the elite cleavages. The stable public consensus on detente emerging in the 1970s, for example, caused a shift in the Christian Democratic Party's (CDU) stance towards *ostpolitik* which in turn brought about a new elite consensus. In the early 1980s, peace movements interacting with segments of the public caused a breakdown in the elite consensus on defense policy with regard to nuclear weapons. The Kohl government's resistance against the modernization of short-range nuclear weapons in the spring of 1989 was another example of public influence on West German security policy (Risse-Kappen, 1988a, 1991b).

While there is not sufficient empirical evidence to finally decide between a "top down" (elites manipulating the public) and a "bottom up" model, a modified version of the second hypothesis which points to interactive processes between segments of the public and parts of the elites seems to gain plausibility. Elites do not simply decide among themselves in liberal democracies; their ability to manipulate public opinion, while not deniable, is clearly limited. As in the cases of SALT II in the U.S. and the Euromissile crisis in many Western European countries, public opinion becomes a resource which competing elite factions try to mobilize for their purposes. Public opinion defines broader or more limited boundaries on the range of options available to the political system, depending on the degree and the specificity of the public consensus. Issue salience and domestic structure seem to determine the variances in the public impact on foreign policy in various democratic countries. The more important the issue in the domestic debate and the more fragmented the political process, the more influence the public has ceteris paribus on foreign policy decisions. Policy-makers are rarely able to govern against public majorities without losing general support for their policies. While public opinion has to compete with the demands of organized interest groups, its impact increases, the greater the consensus and the more specific the demands. On the other hand, public influence on foreign policy seems to be rather limited, if there is either a stable elite consensus—as in the French case—or if the structure of the political system favors stable majorities and allows decision-makers to act independently of societal demands—as in Margret Thatcher's Great Britain. But these cases seem to be the exception rather than the rule.

Security: Are Democracies More Peaceful?

If a certain degree of societal participation in the foreign policy-making process of liberal democracies can be taken for granted, what is the resulting impact on the content of these policies? The liberal theory of foreign policy in the tradition of Kant and Spencer asserted that pluralist democracy and liberal economic order would result in a peaceful foreign policy, at least toward other democracies. According to Ernst-Otto Czempiel (1981, 1986), liberal societies demand economic welfare and security from external threats; these demands are persistent over time. While territorial security as the pre-condition of welfare enjoys logical precedence, historical evolution strengthens societal demands for welfare as compared to security. In this sense, welfare evolves into a pre-condition of security. In a low-threat environment, the prioritization of welfare favors a risk-shy and defensive foreign policy. Only if their national security seems to be fundamentally threatened, do democratic societies support strengthening military organizations, increasing defense expenditures, more aggressive foreign policies, and, ultimately, the use of military force. Once the perceived need for security is fulfilled, welfare demands regain societal priority.

Czempiel argues that the low inclination of democracies to use force is based on an analogy of internal and external processes of value distribution: The low degree of violence which democracies enjoy in their domestic allocation of values, should intrinsically correspond to their foreign policy behavior. However, this analogy is neither theoretically imperative nor historically uncontroversial. Thucydides already showed that the Athenian Republic whose citizens enjoyed a relatively high degree of participation, nevertheless conducted an extraordinary expansionist foreign policy. Polybius concluded the same for the Roman Republic. Macchiavelli and Montesquieu even maintained that republics tend to be particularly war-prone, precisely because of the high degree of citizens' participation and the resulting legitimacy of state actions (Doyle, 1983, 1986; Forde, 1986; Gilpin, 1981: 101–3).

The liberal theory of foreign policy has to be based on the assumptions of a theory of individual action. It can only claim plausibility if the political subjects are motivated toward a peaceful foreign policy. Two such motivations seem to exist:

Cost-benefit calculations: welfare interests of citizens and their organizations are endangered by the potential risks of an aggressive foreign policy and by the costs of war.

Normative value-orientations: Individuals may regard the peaceful means of conflict resolution which democracies use internally, as morally superior to aggressive behavior and, therefore, demand that they be applied to international politics.

The empirical basis of these assumptions is questionable:

Quantitative research on the causes of war has shown that, since 1815, democracies did not behave more peacefully than authoritarian states and dictatorships. They participate in interstate wars about as frequently as nondemocracies and often initiate wars, in particular imperialist interventions (Gantzel, 1987; Maoz and Abdolali, 1989; Maoz and Russett, 1991).

The United States did not behave differently than the Soviet Union regarding the use of military threats during the Cold War (Blechman and Kaplan, 1978; Kaplan, 1981).

Threat policy and military interventionism are correlated with election years in the United States and in Israel. As far as the U.S. is concerned, this is particularly the case if election years coincide with economic recessions (Russett, 1990: chap. 2; Stoll, 1984; Tetlock, 1985).

At the same time, however, evidence does exist to support a modified liberal theory of foreign policy:

Since the end of the Napoleonic wars in 1815 democracies have not fought wars against each other. Even if wealth, contiguity, and alliance membership are controlled for, the correlation between stable democratic political structures and the non-use of force against fellow democracies still holds (Chan, 1984; *Journal of Conflict Resolution*, 1991; Maoz and Abdolali, 1989; Maoz and Russett, 1991; Russett 1990, chap. 5).

Since the 1970s democracies participated significantly less in wars than before. Individual democracies are gradually less inclined to use force over time (Gantzel, 1987; Rummel, 1983).

Democracies build stronger, denser, and less coercive structures of cooperation among themselves than other systems. Fragmentized, but stable political systems tend to conduct less aggressive foreign policies than statist or internally unstable systems (Geller, 1988; Rittberger, 1987).

Constant support for arms control cooperation and opposition to military interventions by Western public opinion forced even conservative governments in Western Europe and the U.S. to adopt more centrist and more cooperative foreign policies, except under extraordinary circumstances such as the Gulf war (Czempiel, 1989a; Kubbig, 1988; Müller, 1989a; Risse-Kappen, 1988a).

When societal demands for security clash with welfare interests, the latter are likely to prevail, except for high threat environments (Blank, 1978; Kelleher, 1987; Kreile, 1978; Rode and Jacobsen, 1985).

Historical research suggests that the resource dilemma is not new. States have persistently overstretched their domestic resources to pursue external goals which often resulted in vicious circles whereby further expansion in order to gain booty was necessary to pay debt resulting from earlier military endeavors (Kaiser, 1990). As Barnett and Levy (1991) have indicated, alliance choices are made frequently to evade the dilemma between foreign ambitions or security needs, on the one hand, and the risks entailed by domestic resource mobilization, on the other. However, late 20th century democratic welfare states are different from their predecessors and from less-developed or non-democratic countries in terms of their far greater exposure to societal demands for state services because of universal suffrage, pluralistic media, freedom of self-organization, and access to comparatively independent judicial systems. As a result, it has become more difficult for governments to extract societal resources for foreign policy adventures. Increasing defense budgets or going to major (costly) wars can only be legitimized when credible and significant threats are perceived by elites and the public alike. Thus, welfare objectives do not always dominate security goals, but they pose higher constraints on governments in democratic welfare states than in other political and economic systems.

The liberal theory of foreign policy has to be modified to integrate apparently contradictory evidence and to sufficiently account for the existing trends. Three conditions might lead democratic states to adopt aggressive and war-prone foreign policies:

Highly organized interests may be able to exploit an unequal distribution of participation in democracies and succeed in getting state help for private "marauding expeditions" in which the costs are shifted onto the less organized and fragmentized majority. However, these costs have to be relatively modest and must be broadly distributed in order not to induce the majority to effectively organize their interests.

The majority may succeed in offloading the costs of warfare onto a minority. Professional armies, for example, provide the opportunity to impose the existential risks of warfare on a group of specialists.

The overall costs of aggressive policies may be low. Imperialist interventions of the past often profited from an asymmetry in weapons technologies and in the organization of warfare. As a result, they assured victory and territorial, strategic, or economic gains in a short time period at low cost.

Public support for warfare in democracies is usually high at the beginning of wars and interventions. This "rally 'round the flag" effect (Mueller, 1973) can be interpreted as a psychological reaction. The conviction that something which causes fear and anxiety, is inevitable and morally justified, relieves the citizens from an awesome moral and decision dilemma. It is significant, however, that public support for warfare in democracies decreases the longer the fighting continues and the stronger the human and economic effects are felt domestically, except for undoubtedly defensive wars in high threat situations (Rosecrance 1986, chap. 6; Russett 1990, chap. 2).

The level of participation and the costs of war seem to be two crucial and interconnected factors. The level of participation is not simply determined by the domestic regime, but also by the respective intensity of competing interests. As a result, if the costs of aggressive policies increase significantly, the majority—or the concerned minority—will intensify the efforts to influence policy. This implies that the utility of the use of force will be diminished for the profiting minority (or majority).

But the institutional effects of democratic systems will only take roots over time. As long as major social mobilization processes are under way in the course of nation-building, governments may be anxious to channel the energies of mobilized or anomic masses against external threats (Levy, 1989). At the same time, the utility calculations concerning the use of force may differ considerably in younger democracies which often have not reached the welfare level of more stable democratic systems. On the other hand, the diversionary use of military threats is not completely absent in stable democracies, as the comparatively higher frequency of the use of force during election years suggests (Ostrom and Job, 1986; Russett, 1989).

However, these effects are mitigated by other processes in stable democracies. As argued above, societal participation in the foreign policy-making process seems to have increased. At the same time, the risks and costs of aggressive policies have multiplied, too. First, the existence of nuclear weapons adds to the dangers of escalation in even limited confrontations. Second, the proliferation of advanced weapons systems increases rapidly. While this doesn't offset the advantages of the superpowers, they are at least diminished. Thus, the human and economic costs of war increase dramatically, while the prospects for quick victories decrease—except in cases of extreme asymmetries like Grenada or Panama. Third, the higher degree of social mobilization broadens the basis for resistance in the country attacked as well as at the attacker's home front (Rosecrance 1986, chap. 6).

In sum, opposition against aggressive policies amplifies to the degree to which their costs are felt. It is not just that the policies themselves are costly. The opportunity costs of using military power rise together with the welfare demands of the citizens. If they no longer see the link between expansionist policies and national security, a consensus will emerge to reduce the costs of such policies (Gilpin 1981, 163–68). This interpretation of the liberal theory of foreign policy leads to the expectation that the peacefulness of democracies increases as a result of broader societal participation and rising costs of aggressive policies. It is also more consistent with the existing data than a static and dichotomous version of the theory.

The second line of reasoning in liberal theory assumes a normative orientation of individuals towards peace. If at all, this orientation only affects the relations between democracies. Here, the analogy between the peaceful resolution of conflicts in domestic affairs and in foreign policy seems to work. On the other hand, the democratic norm is less effective concerning the relations between democracies and authoritarian systems. Even democratic systems have developed normative justifications for aggressive behavior, from "manifest destiny" and "white man's burden" to the interventionist version of "making the world safe for democracy." However, attitudes opposing interventionism and favoring cooperative security relations with non-democratic systems have increased in Western democracies (Russett 1990, chap. 5). These attitudes are influencing politics and have been incorporated in international law primarily as a result of pressures by democratic systems.

Welfare: Cooperative Foreign Economic Policies?

Rising welfare demands are politically effective in democracies. Their fulfillment, however, increasingly depends on the international economy. This trend does not affect all states in the same way, though; unequal growth exists between regions of the world, states, and between economic sectors. The greater the socio-economic standard and the more comprehensive the level of participation in a given state, the more effective are established organizations in defending their assets and the less they are prepared to show flexibility (Knorr, 1977; Olsen, 1982). If there is a high degree of societal participation, policy-makers are, therefore, tempted to do everything to maintain a given pattern of distribution (Putnam and Bayne, 1984; Aggarwal et al., 1987).

Governments prefer strategies which externalize the problems of adaptation to those which lead to internal restructuring, forcing society to absorb costs and, thus, threatening to undermine the political support basis of governments (Ikenberry, 1986a, b). They can refuse foreign economic adjustment by bringing to bear economic or political strength; the United States used this strategy in its energy policy during the 1970s (Müller, 1989a). "Reaganomics" worked similarly in that it attracted capital from all over the world, but, at the same time, mobilized domestic support to prevent trading partners from behaving "unfairly" (Rode, 1988). Governments can also pretend cooperative behavior while in fact driving a hard bargain and minimizing their concessions. Examples are Western policies with regard to the United Nations Conference on Trade and Development (UNCTAD), the negotiations to restructure the Third World's debt, and the conference on the International Law of the Sea.

Compared with the premises of the liberal theory of foreign policy, the outcome is, thus, paradoxical (Gilpin 1987, 60–3). On the one hand, welfare interests in liberal democracies seem to pressure governments to conduct peaceful security policies. On the other hand, the same interests favor non-cooperative behavior in foreign economic policies. This does not necessarily include the use of force, but it does create conditions in the international environment which are prone to violence (Gilpin 1987, 389–95; Ikenberry, 1986a, b).

However, this outcome does not apply to all political systems. As Peter Katzenstein (1978b) has argued, liberal-pluralistic systems such as the U.S. prefer cooperative and free-trade foreign economic policies, but tend to limited protectionism if crises affect their economies or individual sectors. State-centered systems like France and Japan pursue mercantilistic strategies and use anticipatory policies to capture markets without paying much attention to the effects on their trading partners. Corporatist systems like West Germany and Italy show a comparatively "benign" record; defensive and sectoral protectionism is rather exceptional. The consensus-building effects of democratic corporativism tend to stabilize a liberal foreign economic policy. In a more recent analysis, Katzenstein (1984, 1985) has confirmed this proposition with regard to other European countries. Under conditions of interdependence, developments in the international economy inevitably affect national economies. Neocorporatist consensus-building might represent a domestic structure which leads to the necessary adjustments without jeopardizing internal stability (Höll, 1983; Weiss, 1989).

CONCLUSION

Our journey through the growing body of literature on the interaction between domestic politics, foreign policy, and international relations leads us to the following conclusions. First, the time of simple dichotomies and "either-or" explanations like the original "external vs. internal factors" debate is definitely over. We have tried to show in the first part of this essay that a growing consensus among scholars embraces models integrating the unit-level and the systemic level of analysis. Research is needed to submit these complex models to empirical tests. However, most of the existing empirical research doesn't really integrate the two levels and, thus, fells victim to the old dichotomy by choosing the international environment or domestic politics as the main frame of reference. As a result, complexity is reduced for the price of decreasing explanatory power.

Second, we perceive a lack of communications among scholars on at least two dimensions. To begin with, we have tried to show that considerable progress has been made in understanding the domestic environment of the international political economy. Domestic structure and coalition analyses have proven useful to submit the domestic politics conundrum to more parsimonious explanations. However, fruitful exchanges between theoretical approaches in international political economy and in security studies are rare. In security studies, ad hoc explanations for domestic politics phenomena still prevail, except for well-established cognitive psychological approaches. In particular, there is a lack of comparative studies on the domestic politics of national security which could build on the efforts by—mostly West European—peace research during the 1970s (exceptions: Barnett, 1990; Barnett and Levy, 1991; Evangelista, 1988; Lebow, 1981; Levy, 1988, 1989; Snyder, 1991). This also points to the other lack of communication which persists between American and European—not to mention Japanese—scholars. American authors rarely take notice of the works of their European colleagues (not to speak of Japanese)—and vice versa. Again, this is particularly true for security studies; a greater degree of transnational communication in the field of international studies would probably have relieved Americans from their intellectual obsession with realism earlier on.

Finally, we suggest that domestic structure and coalition analysis should be complemented by research on the "soft" side of domestic politics, i.e., the role of ideology, belief systems, and cultural phenomena. The revolutions in Eastern Europe, for example, would probably not have been possible without the transnationally shared values of human rights and democracy by the relevant actors. If anything, the collapse of the communist regimes and the subsequent end of the bipolar international order should have alerted the scholarly community to reconsider their theoretical preconceptions and to take the interaction of "hardware" such as power and "software" such as ideology in producing far reaching domestic and international change more seriously.

3

The Domestic Political Context
of Foreign Policy-Making

EXPLICATING A THEORETICAL CONSTRUCT

Valerie M. Hudson, Susan M. Sims, and John C. Thomas

T he study of the effects of domestic politics on international politics is enjoying a long awaited heyday. Probably traceable to Putnam's felicitous and influential metaphor of the "two-level game" (1988, 1989), it has of this writing been the subject of numerous articles (see Bueno de Mesquita and Zulman, 1990) and even an entire issue of the *Journal of Conflict Resolution* (Summer 1991). This sudden awakening no doubt bemuses authors who labored "in the wilderness" over this issue decades ago. For example, in 1966, Rosenau states,

> To recognize that foreign policy is shaped by internal and external factors is not to comprehend how the two intermix or to indicate the conditions under which one predominates over the other. And in these respects, progress has been very slow indeed. Rare is the article or book which goes beyond description of an internal factor and locates it in the ever changing interplay of variables—both external and internal—which combine to produce foreign policies. Even rarer is the work that contains explicit "if-then" hypotheses in which the "if" is a particular form of the internal factor and the "then" is a particular type of foreign policy.

And it was in 1973 that Dahl published his edited volume, *Regimes and Oppositions*, in which he examines types of opposition likely to form in response to different types of regimes, and the conflict resolution techniques likely to be used by the regimes in response to that opposition.

What seemed to happen in the late 1980s (as reflected in, for example, Lamborn and Mumme, 1989; Maoz, 1990; Mastanduno, Lake, and Ikenberry, 1989; Hagan, 1987, 1988, 1989; Hermann, 1987; Hudson, 1988; Levy and Vakili, 1989) was a growing realization that the key intellectual puzzle of International Relations would now be to explain the massive changes in the world system that culminated in the destruction of the Berlin Wall. Systems-level theories appeared inadequate to explain such sudden and system-wide change. As every chapter in this edited volume argues, such explanation requires a critical look "inside the black box" of the nation-state, with an acknowledgment that the nation-state must reckon with sometimes formidable powers within its borders that limit its autonomy in the policy-making arena.

It has been interesting to note the coincidence of this shift with a parallel shift methodological orientation in International Relations. As Lane (1990) notes, there is emerging a new "brand" of political theory—concrete theory. Whereas "abstract theory mounts from reality to ever higher (and emptier) concepts" (927), concrete theory places its emphasis on "political elites, on strategic decision-making processes, freed from narrow notions of economic rationality, and on a concern with the environment and institution within which choice occurs" (927). Very naturally, almost all work on the domestic context of foreign policy making falls in to the category of concrete theory. The subject matter itself, we would argue, demands such an approach. Psychological, sociological, anthropological, historical, cultural, political variables all play a role in understanding the context of decision. Welding a massive amount of qualitative data with a systematic, but not mathematically notable decision calculus is a recipe for the development of techniques to realize concrete theory. International Relations has taken the lead in the social sciences, in our opinion, in the development of such techniques, of which computational modeling is the vanguard. (see Sylvan and Chan, 1984; Hudson, 1991)

Computational modeling (or "Artificial Intelligence-type modeling") is a flexible tool for understanding human decision-making. Eschewing the oversimplification of reasoning by the rational-choice school for theoretical reasons (see Purkitt, 1991), the crucial question for the researcher becomes, how is a problem situation defined by a set of decision-makers? How will the problem solving process affect the decision outcome? A large amount of data—virtually always qualitative in nature—must then be organized and interrelated. A wide variety of specific tools—from Levenstein distances (Schrodt, 1991) to natural language processing (Mallery, 1991)—are used to accomplish this task.

THEORETICAL FOUNDATIONS

Basic Needs Theory

The general model developed here is rooted in two broad theories about human nature and the nature of politics. The first of these is the human needs theory of behavioral motivation, most closely identified with the work of Abraham Maslow (1943). Recognizing that political behavior is one aspect of human behavior, scholars suggest that the same basic needs driving human behavior drive political behavior as well. Representing this school of thought, James Chowning Davies explains:

> Humans, who do all the things that life forms from one-celled animals to primates do, also engage in complex information-gathering and decision-making activity. People usually engage in this activity in the process of fulfilling needs that range from survival itself to satisfying the love drive and gaining recognition. When the environment is supportive, people also do things that fulfill their unique, individual, idiosyncratic pattern of genetic endowment (1986, 49).

Although qualitatively different at the levels of the individual and that of the regime,[1] behavior at both levels is goal-directed and also determined by the prioritization of needs. Furthermore, needs can be posited as legitimately for institutions comprised of humans as they can for humans themselves. The work of Harold Lasswell (1976) is an example of how such theories of behavior motivation rooted in the field of psychology can be profitably applied to an understanding of complex political institutions. With reference to these needs, Davies continues, "The basic needs, which are genetic to every human being, include (1) substantive needs and (2) instrumental needs" (49).

The substantive needs include the need for physical security, for social interaction and communication, for legitimation and validation by others, and for the realization of goals derived from one's ideology or other closely held beliefs. Individuals actively seek fulfillment of these life-giving and life-enhancing needs. The fulfillment of instrumental needs allows for continued fulfillment of the substantive needs. Indeed, as fulfillment of the

---

1. Although the concept of regime is rather broadly conceived, we equate regime with the ultimate decision unit as used by Hermann (1987) and Hermann, Hermann and Hagan (1987): "a set of authorities with the ability to commit the resources of the society and, with respect to a particular problem, with the authority to make a decision that cannot be readily reversed."

substantive needs connotes achievement of a certain abstract state of being (e.g., "I feel secure"), the social science researcher must look to the more tangible manifestation of that state in order to assess to what extent such fulfillment has occurred. We argue that the tangible manifestation of the fulfillment of substantive needs can be found in the degree to which the subject has secured fulfillment of instrumental needs related to that substantive need (e.g. "I feel secure because I have a burglar alarm system"), though we recognize the imperfection in such an operationalization. The three broad categories of instrumental needs are the need for security, for knowledge, and for power.

Lasswell (1976) provided one interesting interpretation of these ideas in the context of regime activity. He suggested that for a regime to reassert or retain socio-political control, it must be able to wield eight specific tools that will assist in "a sequence of planning and striving" (117). He identifies these tools as power, enlightenment, wealth, well-being, skill, affection, respect, and rectitude (117). Whereas Lasswell makes no distinction between levels of needs and the components of regime tools, we offer a three-tiered view of need fulfillment. The fulfillment of substantive needs rests upon the fulfillment of instrumental needs, which in turn rests upon control over those elements that make up the instrument in question. These elements are the metal from which the regime's instruments or tools are created. The more and the more varied elements the regime obtains, the broader its options for pursuing the fulfillment of its needs. Indeed, control over one element may facilitate the regime's efforts to control other elements. Thus, the elements that fulfill an instrumental need can be mobilized by the regime to fashion policy tools in its quest to fulfill other needs. Furthermore, a listing of all those elements (e.g., stable military, cooperative bureaucracy, public support, and so forth) that would satisfy the regime's instrumental needs with a corresponding judgment as to the control the regime has over each would constitute a barometer of regime strength. In other words, the more elements the regime controls, the more instrumental needs are fulfilled, and the stronger the regime is.

Exchange Theory

While knowing these roots of political motivation is necessary, it is still insufficient to explain the political *process* involved in gaining control over the elements that would fulfill particular instrumental needs. For that task, we turn to insights from the second theory upon which this model is built—the exchange theory of politics (and its nexus with role theory). David Easton's formulation (1953), consistent with exchange theory, defines politics as the authoritative allocation of values in a society. These values are the direct analogue of the above-mentioned elements that provide for the fulfillment of instrumental needs. Because of this, value is attached to these elements within the society, and they will be sought after by the various societal participants. (See also Lasswell, 1976; Blau, 1967; and Lipson, 1954).

In one conceptualization of exchange theory (Walker, 1983, 1985, 1987), politics is viewed as the process whereby these valued elements are distributed among participants in society. The foundation of all governmental behavior is the establishment of the terms of this allocation, that is, setting the "value" or the "exchange rate" or "terms of trade" for these elements. (Hereafter we will abbreviate "valued elements" as "values".) Over time, a set of shared expectations regarding the terms of exchange arises. At this point (the nexus with role theory), these expectations may solidify into diverse roles that participants fill within the society, which roles largely determine their behavior. As the terms of exchange and the role expectations persist over an extended time, they may in fact become formalized into institutions (Walker, 1987).

These processes describe the political system under conditions of relative societal consensus. The most interesting episodes in politics, however, arise when consensus breaks down, resulting in political conflict. This process has two basic sources: ambiguity in the terms of trade that develops over time, and erosion of the shared expectations among participants in the value allocation process. It is during these times of political conflict that the government's primary task is to reassert control over the value allocation process.

Since political and societal consensus is rare, most governments find themselves in a perpetual state of political conflict. Indeed, as with shared expectations, conflict itself may become institutionalized, as in the case of some bitterly divided coalition governments. Our notion of political conflict should not be construed as necessarily connoting violence and hostility. The essence of politics is managing the competition between the opposing agendas of the regime and other societal participants. If a regime seeks to maintain control over its ability to authoritatively allocate the values in a society and to set policy (terms of exchange), then any force seeking to modify the control process or policy content will be viewed by the regime as political opposition.

How, then, will the regime choose to reassert control over the political process vis à vis its opposition and adapt to a changing political environment? The primary instrument is governmental policy, both domestic and foreign (Rosenau, 1981). In the language of exchange theory, "in order to pursue or maintain domestic policy goals, a state may also act to establish, maintain or disrupt a shared set of expectations or the allocation of values among other states" (Walker, 1987: 282). In fact, important foreign policy decisions are often linked to the regime's attempts to maintain or regain control over the domestic political exchange process. While this is not to say that a domestic political struggle is always the direct catalyst for such decisions, it may figure prominently in the regime's choice of foreign policy initiatives. As we view governmental policy as the selective use of available strategies by the regime, how and why certain strategies or tactics are selected (i.e., how certain policy moves are chosen) will be intimately tied to the threat posed to the regime's pursuit of its agenda of needs, which necessitates control over the exchange process.[2]

Figure 3.1 summarizes how the theoretical elements of the preceding discussion of the two theories underlying the model are interrelated. In sum, every human activity can be seen as an attempt to fulfill certain essential needs, both substantive and instrumental. That which fulfills these needs is valued in any society, and the terms of exchange for these values are established by the governmental political process that authoritatively allocates those values. Political institutions consequently form and create shared role expectations among exchange participants. Political conflict occurs when this created exchange deteriorates or role expectations change. As a result, the regime seeks to protect its control over values by attempting to reassert control over the exchange process through the

Figure 3.1: The Relationship of Human Needs Theory and Exchange Theory in the Explanatory Construct

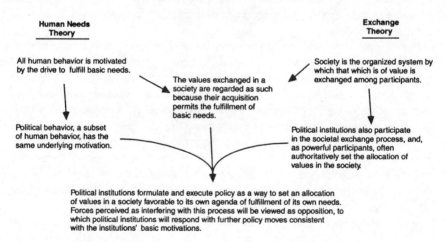

<hr />

2. We do not pretend to explain or even view the totality of domestic politics. Rather, we focus on the interaction between regime and opposition at levels or in situations where that interaction intensifies to the point of challenging the regime's control over one or more of the values associated with instrumental needs.

use of domestic and foreign policy, which itself draws upon those values the regime already controls. Without such adaptation, the government would face radical transformation and a new system of exchange would arise.[3]

ELEMENTS OF THE EXPLANATORY MODEL

The Rationale

With the model's theoretical basis established, it is possible to enumerate the elements of the explanatory model, which attempts to synthesize cross-national and country-specific approaches to understanding regime behavior. The former without the latter lacks the detail and richness necessary to apply findings to discrete circumstances, while the latter alone is theoretically adrift and cannot contribute to the cumulation of knowledge in this area. Merging country experts' knowledge with the generalized, systematic treatment offered by a cross-national explanatory framework is a challenging task. Those familiar with a cross-national approach may find this methodological hybrid untidy and imprecise—while those accustomed to traditional, more descriptive modes of inquiry may think it overly regimented and systematized. Yet we have found that only such a hybrid allows for application of a relatively powerful theory to real-time situations in all their complexity and uncertainty.

The model is designed to help explain how foreign policy behavior is affected by domestic politics. The explanatory journey is not direct but involves a two-step inference process. In our estimation, the foreign policy behavior of the regime will, under certain circumstances, depend on the regime's response to domestic opposition activity at a given time. Therefore, regime response to opposition serves as the pivotal dependent variable for this study, while foreign policy behavior effects of the response are the ultimate dependent variable. Figure 3.2 graphically represents this two-step process. The choice of regime response, in turn, depends on two clusters of variables. The first determines the status of the regime's agenda of needs; the second relates to the capabilities of domestic opposition groups to disrupt the pursuit of this agenda.

---

3. We exclude from the purview of our model an analysis of such extreme circumstances, restricting the scope of our efforts to regimes that are able to mount adaptational policies.

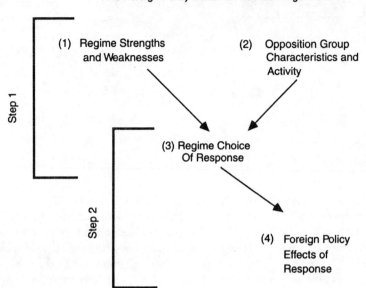

Figure 3.2: The Relationship Between Domestic Political Conflict
And Foreign Policy Behavior. See also Figure 3.5.

Our analysis of these variables produces four types of information: which opposition group will likely be the primary opponent and likely subject of regime concern; which regime responses to that group are possible and impossible under given circumstances; which possible responses are more likely and which are less likely; and what the foreign policy effects of the more likely responses will be. The first three are derived from step one of Figure 3.2; the last corresponds to step two. Because all four items can be checked in some manner for congruence with reality, empirical testing of outcome validity is possible. Additionally, as illustrated by our case studies, process tracing can be applied as well to augment validity testing. Thus both aggregate analysis and in-depth case analysis are appropriate applications of this hybrid model.

In order for the model to generate output, the exogenous inputs of a country expert are required, for the model cannot be applied without reference to country-specific information regarding the regime and opposition groups within a particular nation. However, the basic logic of regime response and the fundamental organizing concepts can be specified on a general and cross-national basis. The discussion of the organizing concepts follows, after which the logic of regime response is elaborated.

Values Associated with Instrumental Needs

In keeping with exchange theory propositions, it is essential to determine what values the regime pursues in its quest to satisfy its agenda of needs. Since, as mentioned previously, we view the process of fulfilling needs as theoretically equivalent to the process of acquiring control over values, and since we consider control over values as a more empirically based concept than fulfillment of needs, we find it useful to discuss the status of a particular regime relative to its control over an agenda of values. Indeed, if we can define values in relation to needs, then it is also possible to define needs in terms of values. To wit, when regime control over a value is weak, a need exists; when regime control is strong, the value becomes a tool or instrument through which outstanding needs might be fulfilled. During episodes of domestic political conflict, the regime draws upon those assets wherein it enjoys relative strength to use as tools in the struggle over value allocation control. Thus it becomes crucial to ascertain to what degree control over the values, hierarchically ordered just as needs are, has in fact been secured by the regime.

Drawing on the literature of Maslow, Lasswell, Davies, and others, we have devised a standard three-tiered hierarchy of values for use in the analysis of regime motivation. Each regime identifies values associated with **fundamental needs** it must control in order to function as a sovereign governing agent. Being basic to "life" for a regime, as control over these values is fundamental to control over the value allocation process within a society, they are considered to have the highest priority. Any threat to a regime's control over one of these would provoke immediate and serious response by the regime.

Critical to the ability of a regime to effectively govern a state with maximum longevity are the values associated with **domestic legitimacy needs**, which come next in the hierarchy. Strength in these areas allows the regime broader power to direct domestic value allocation activity. They are linked to the fulfillment of "legitimacy" needs because a regime that controls them is typically considered by the people the legitimate governing body within a state, thus fulfilling the regime's need for legitimacy/validation by others. When a regime loses control over these values, it loses legitimacy and may eventually lose the ability to govern with ease and efficiency if the governed withdraw support.

Control over values related to **international legitimacy needs** can similarly help the regime maintain its authority in the value allocation process. At the international level, one may in fact talk about two levels of the value allocation process—the first referring again to the allocation within the society, the second referring to value allocation within the system of nation-states. At this point in our analysis, we will continue to focus on values related to international legitimacy needs as they concern the first level. The function of international legitimacy in the societal arena stems from the broadened opportunities and assets available to the regime for use intra-societally when it has sufficient control over the values associated with such legitimacy.

A list of values relevant to the needs of political regimes appears in Table 3.1. Basic definitions for each value are also presented. The prioritization given in the table generally applies to most regimes. Variations are entirely possible. The basic principle underlying our prioritization parallels Maslow's notion of precedence: certain values are more directly related to the fulfillment of needs than others. Under Values Associated with Fundamental Needs, for instance, the physical survival of the regime would be immediately threatened by a loss of territorial integrity. Regaining this value then becomes of highest priority to the regime, while pursuit of all other values is either halted or relegated to a lower priority. Similarly, we argue that control over the policy making process, in conjunction with an efficient intelligence system, and control over the forces of coercive power within a society are all extremely important to any regime. Only after these are secured will a regime turn its attention to the legislature (if one exists) and the economy. As the last half century has documented, it is possible to govern for some period of time even with a disastrous economy and a strained executive-legislative relationship.

Table 3.1: Standard Priority List of the Instrumental Values That Are Associated with Fundamental Needs, with Basic Definitions

Values by Priority	Basic Definitions
Values Associated with Fundamental Needs	
(1) Territorial Integrity	Refers to the sovereignty of a nation, whether it is independent from other nations and whether is has control over established borders.
(2) Policy-making Procedure	The process by which official government policy is established, including directives, budgets, foreign affairs, and other executive duties, as outlined by the respective constitutions.
(3) Knowledge/ Feedback	Knowledge is the intelligence-gathering capabilities of the regime. Feedback is information fed the regime through various sources about domestic occurrences, opposition activity, economic trends, and that which influences regime decisions.
(4) Stable Military	The military includes any standing army, militia, auxiliary security forces, special forces, secret services, and such, as well as the domestic law enforcement community (local and national).
(5) Legislative Procedure	The process by which laws are drafted and passed.
(6) Stable Economy	The economy consists of all factors of production, the labor market, social infrastructural entities (e.g., utilities, public works), the money market, import/export markets, capital investment, and domestic commerce.

Values Associated with Domestic Legitimacy Needs

(1) Electoral Majority

Important for day-to-day politicking, and also best guarantees the regime a maximum term in office. A majority is defined differently for various constitutions. If a legislative body exists, it is determined by the votes/seats held by the regime's party. If such a body does not exist, the majority may be defined as a function of PAG constituencies loyal to the regime.

(2) Manipulation of Symbols

A rhetorical device used to convince, persuade, win election, justify actions, gain support, implement policy, consolidate power, discredit an opponent, exact concessions from the governed, and cover actual intentions. All regimes rhetorically manipulate symbols such as nationalism, culture, morality, tradition, defense, freedom, democracy, terrorism, capitalism, good, evil, imperialism, and so forth.

(3) Public Support

The term refers to the degree to which the general public rejects or accepts the regime's policies, ideology, or personalities. It may be measured by opinion polls, public cooperation, opposition success/failure with the public, voting habits, and/or resistance to policy implementation.

(4) Friendly Press

The press includes all media of public expression, whether newspapers, periodicals, radio, television, film, or theater. It may be free or controlled. The press (by choice, through affiliation, or under coercion) reports to the public on regime activities and expresses opinions on such.

(5) Cooperative Bureaucracy

A bureaucracy consists of all department, agencies, and commissions of the executive branch in the regime. It is responsible for domestic policy implementation, and for our purposes here, also includes local government bureaucratic institutions. It is the structure through which the regime is supposed to serve and govern the people.

(6) Ecclesiastical Endorsement

This the verbal and/or active support of religious leaders in a nation's dominant church(es) or religious groups, is such exist, for the regime.

(7) Communication

This is the two-way dialogue between opposition members and regime representatives. It does not involve intelligence gathering, but is a exchange of ideas, goals, principles, policies, or demands. It may lead to compromise or to co-opting of opposition members. It allows the regime to remain appraised of opposition goals, and can keep the conflict from turning militant.

Values Associated with International Legitimacy Needs

(1) International Recognition

The acknowledgment by other international actors that the regime leader is a legitimate domestic leader, an actor in the global political system, and/or the diplomatic representative of a people. Recognition may also include acceptance of a regime leader as a representative or chair of international bodies. Not all recognition is necessarily positive.

(2) External Support

This refers to allies, as in other states or international organizations. It is not necessarily a military ally, although it can be. It is also not necessarily an active support—a nation may profit by mere association in some instances.

(3) External Threat

All enemies, real or potential; all nations with which the regime has no diplomatic relations; non-domestic terrorist groups targeting the state; and ideological opponents as defined by the regime. Even allies can be called a threat if the regime declares the interests of the ally as contrary to its own in a given situation.

Similar considerations guided our ordering of values associated with domestic and international legitimacy needs. In the former, we sought to identify those values whose control would make the regime's task of governance the easiest: these became our higher priority domestic legitimacy values. For example, possessing an electoral majority makes the regime's job easier than if it did not have such a majority, even with, say, the endorsement of the press.

In the category of values associated with international legitimacy needs, we felt that recognition of the regime as being the legitimate voice for the nation by other nations was exceptionally important to most regimes. Such recognition is a barrier to acts which would undermine the regime's sovereignty. For years, the Hun Sen regime of Cambodia was isolated from the world because it was not recognized by the international community; it concentrated its international efforts on gaining that recognition, which then allowed it greater leverage in power sharing discussions with the Khmer Rouge and other groups at the international level. Next, the regime needs allies who can provide key support and even, at times, defense for the regime. Last, a regime needs enemies. This might seem counter-intuitive, but the presence of a tangible enemy can often assist the regime in its quest to control various other values (e.g., public support or a large military budget).

While we feel this specific prioritization is probably applicable to many regimes, we recognize that the unique composition of some regimes might alter this ordering. Therefore, at the discretion of a country expert using this model, values may be reordered within the three broad categories to more accurately represent the value agenda of the particular regime being studied. For example, in most Western nations, "ecclesiastical endorsement" (Value #6 in Domestic Legitimacy Needs) is not a high priority. However, in a nation such as Iran, this could be a truly significant value.

Further, it should be clear that the three broad categories of regime values are not intended to be strictly hierarchical. Rather, a step-like ordering should be visualized, in which lower priorities of one category may actually coincide with or overlap higher priorities of another. Therefore, while the category of Values Associated with Fundamental Needs is still the most important, its lowest priority element of stable economy (or whichever value the country expert determines should be last at this level) may not necessarily be more important than an electoral majority (or any other value chosen by the country expert), which has a high priority in the second main category of Values Associated with Domestic Legitimacy Needs. Where the overlap occurs depends again on the particular regime being considered. The model can therefore accommodate any conceptualization of a particular regime's value agenda.

Once the basic hierarchy has been established for a given regime, one must then determine the degree of regime control over each of the values.

This degree of control will serve as the basis for determination of patterns of regime strength and weakness, which information is vital in order to project regime response to opposition. To determine any given regime's relative control over a value, certain flexible guidelines have been established. These guidelines are not rigid definitions, but typologies to be used by the country expert in analyzing the strengths of the regime. We have designed the guidelines along three categories of strength: strong, moderately strong, and weak. It is important to the subsequent analysis for the country expert to determine into which category a regime falls regarding its control over each value. Country experts should refer to the definitions in Table 3.1 along with the guidelines in Appendix A.1 for producing strength calculations for the regime.

Knowing the regime's areas of strength and weakness is crucial in determining the regime's ultimate capacity to respond to opposition; however, this knowledge is not sufficient. One must also determine the threat to the regime posed by the opposition. This determination entails a detailed analysis of the sources of opposition within the society, their capabilities and activities. The following section explores what comprises such an analysis.

Opposition Group Characteristics and Threat

Two approaches are frequently used to typologize oppositions. The first attempts to identify "stock" kinds of opposition within society, such as the press, the church, the unions, the business sector, and so forth. The second classifies opposition according to a set of predetermined characteristics. In our view, the latter subsumes the former. Identifying basic dimensions of the opposition allows depiction of a wide variety of stock groups. We conceptualize this process as a survey of the "landscape" of opposition with which a regime must deal. Using this approach, the country expert's inventory of specific opposition groups is projected onto a theoretically dimensionalized grid. For example, two terrorist groups which may be lumped together using the "stock" approach may be distinguished according to their placement on this landscape/grid. One set of literature (for example, Hermann, Hermann and Hagan, 1987; Hermann, 1987; Hudson, 1984, 1988) classifies opposition in terms of its political proximity to the locus of policy decision-making. In accordance with this literature, we group opposition into four categories: within the primary advisory group to the regime leader (PAG); outside the primary advisory group but within the political system; outside the political system but within the society; and, in some cases, outside the society as part of foreign-based or outlawed opposition groups.

Each category represents the locus of political behavior for one or more groups. In some cases, each group is organized and acts as a separate group, thereby represented on the grid as a circle or locus of activity. However, some situations lead to the combining of these distinct groups, in which case distinction is no longer made between different groups. Because the essential question answered by the grouping is how proximate the actor is to being a member of the ultimate decision unit, cases where there are more than one group involved highlight the most active or the leadership group in the overall coalition of groups.

This classification scheme is based on the hypothesis that a decision-maker devotes the most energy to opponents closest to the seat of power since *ceteris paribus*, in theory, they would have greater access to the power resources necessary to effectively challenge the regime. In addition to this variable, however, three other variables add explanatory power in predicting potential threat: degree of organizational cohesiveness, degree of ideological salience, and group size.

Organizational Cohesiveness. Organizational cohesiveness is defined in terms of group structures and discipline. Hence a group splintered by feuding factions is a much less compelling opponent than one enjoying organizational discipline and freedom from divisions (see Hagan, 1988; Janda, 1980; our scale of cohesiveness is adapted primarily from Hagan). There are six basic levels of cohesiveness. They begin with being **operationally cohesive**, meaning that a group is disciplined and there is a high degree of regimentation under the uncontested leadership of a single person or group that has full decision-making autonomy. Slightly less cohesive are groups with **informal schisms**. That is, the group remains under the direction of an uncontested leader (individual or unified group of leaders), but decision-making autonomy of the leadership is occasionally constrained by policy differences within the membership of the organization so that action cannot be taken without some consultation with representatives of divergent viewpoints. Some groups will display **formal cliques** rather than just schisms. In this case, a group remains under the direction of an uncontested leader but divisions within the body of the organization are formally recognized with ad hoc caucusing agreements and policy decisions are not taken without formal consultation with the members of the group and these decisions are the result of consensus rather than ratification of a command decision. These schisms may be further formed into **institutionalized factions**, where the formal cliques of the group are represented by some sort of delegate within the leadership of the group so that activity among the group leadership must also proceed by a process of bargaining and consensus-building.

Groups experiencing cohesion problems may suffer serious splintering. Through this, the group is reduced numerically because members defect to set up rival organizations with an independent decision-making base. If

splintered sub-groups have formed within the last three months of the time period being studied, the cohesion is seriously weakened. The least cohesive group is one with no recognized group leadership. The group is a group in name only; there is no uncontested decision-making unit. Instead, several distinct organizations operate with informal rules of cooperation and coordination.

Ideological Salience. The concept of ideological salience contains two elements: the first is whether the opposition group's ideological cast is roughly congruent or recognizably dissimilar to the regime's; the second is determined by whether the opposition accepts current institutional practices for resolving domestic conflict or advocates their replacement. A group accepting neither the regime's ideology nor prevailing political processes constitutes, therefore, the most salient ideological challenge and would, *ceteris paribus,* pose a more formidable potential threat to the regime than a group that acquiesces to or accepts the regime ideology or its current political system (cf. Hermann, 1987).

An opposition actor with **high ideological salience** is marked by two distinct features: (a) it espouses an ideology that is either at one extreme of the political spectrum (if the regime has a centrist/moderate orientation) or clearly on the opposite side (left or right) of the spectrum (if the regime is clearly identified with one side or the other), and (b) it has called for the dismantling of the current institutional structure of the state during the regime's period of rule (including demands for a new constitution, appeals for popular revolution, or calls for a military coup). **Moderate ideological salience** is exhibited by groups that have one characteristic or the other, but not both. And a **low ideologically salient** group exhibits neither of the characteristics and is therefore in general agreement that the current regime is legitimate and useful, although perhaps not entirely infallible in policy formation.

The Formidability Index and the Landscape of Opposition. These three variables (proximity, cohesiveness, and ideological salience), supplemented by an estimation of group size,[4] allow construction of a qualitative formidability index for the range of opposition actors appearing on the socio-political landscape, as perceived by the regime. These variables also illustrate which landscape features are most striking to the regime. Individual country analysis becomes vital at this stage. As an example, Figure 3.3 illustrates our analysis of this landscape for Andreas Papandreou's regime in Greece in November 1985. (taken from Hudson et al., in progress)

---

4. Size is roughly determined by how many people a group can mobilize in its day to day operations to bring immediate pressure on the regime to reach its goals. One may look at how many members are registered if such records exist. How many seats a party holds in the legislature is also a gauge for some groups. The numbers in attendance at recent demonstrations may also give indications of size.

Figure 3.3: The Greek Political Landscape of Opposition According to Proximity, Cohesiveness, Ideological Salience, Size, and Activity, 1985-6.

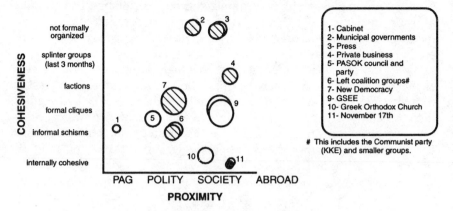

(NOTE: The size of the circles corresponds to the size of the group. Ideological salience is represented by the fills of the circles: high ideological salience is a black shaded circle; moderate ideological shading is a circe with diagonal lines; and low ideological salience is a blank circle. And finally, an active group is represented by a shadow. Groups engaged in "normal" activity have no shadow. Thus, five dimensions may be represented in this graph, and can be manipulated by a country-expert according to regime.)

Opposition Activity Levels. The formidability index, however, can only describe potential threat. To ascertain which opposition groups are most threatening at a given point in time, the level of opposition activity must be considered. Although groups in each "band" of proximity routinely engage in opposition activities appropriate to their location, groups expanding operations beyond their usual range have moved from "normal" activity to "intense" opposition.[5] Conceptually speaking, more intense activity raises the stakes for the regime by making it possible for a group to threaten higher-ranked values than it would normally be able to target. For Papandreou's regime in 1985, Figure 3.3 also offers a representation of activity levels. Table 3.2 suggests a range of behavior for opposition groups at normal and intense levels of activity that can be used by a country expert in making these determinations.

---

5. What is "normal" (standard, conventional, expected, routine) is to be determined by the country expert for the opposition and may well resemble Figure 5. The following should be considered in making that assessment: past record of regime propensity to apply direct or indirect tactics; record of cooperation with opposition groups; political philosophy (radical, liberal, conservative); regime's past tolerance for opposition; opposition's past ability to have dialogue with regime; past record of opposition activities that set precedent for expected behavior; and so on.

"Intense" is defined as activities surpassing those deemed standard by the country expert along the general lines of Figure 3.2, and might be determined by frequency with which said activities are highlighted by domestic free and controlled press.

Table 3.2: General Guidelines for Determining Normal and Active
Oppositions for the Range of Proximate Groups

Proximity	Normal Behavior	Active Behavior
Within Primary Advisory Group (PAG)	Generally supportive and acquiescent on matters of disagreement; some verbal disagreement on minor policy matter.	Verbal disagreement over major policy or leadership questions; splintering within group, possible quid pro quo arrangements or alternative proposals.
Within Polity	Rhetoric in line with party affiliation, alternative platforms and candidates highlight policy differences; inefficient policy implementation; general bureaucratic inertia; occasional discord.	Strident personal attacks question rule makers as well as rules; calls for censure, impeachment, or parliamentary vote of no confidence; attempts to circumvent or alter constitutional procedures allocating authority; boycott unnatural alliances across party lines; secession.
In Society	Rhetoric in line with traditional mandate of organization, spontaneous, small-scale protests and demonstrations; localized, symbolic work stoppages.	Rhetoric targeted at regime personalities challenging policy and policymakers; widespread coordinated protests or work stoppage; wide-spread civil disobedience; acts of violence.
Abroad	Rhetoric (more strident if from traditional enemy).	Strident rhetoric from traditional friends, open encouragement and support of domestic opposition efforts; new sanctions or interventions.

Threat Assessment

In summary, we have suggested three things about opposition and threat. First, the formidability of opposition actors can be assessed according to their proximity, cohesiveness, ideological salience, and size. Second, groups routinely participate in normal opposition activities, departure from which constitutes intense opposition. Thus activity level must be considered with formidability when determining which opposition groups pose the greatest immediate threat to a regime. Finally, intense opposition activity increases the range of values viewed as vulnerable from the perspective of the regime. Hence threat is also a function of the relative rank of the highest targeted value. *We assume, then, that a regime will direct its efforts against those opposition groups posing the greatest immediate threat in terms of formidability, activity, and level of value targeted.*[6] The above material

---

6. Keep in mind, however, that a non-targeted group may actually bear the brunt of regime response as part of an indirect tactic used by the regime. The model is capable of predicting such a move.

is combined into the variable "Threat Assessment," to be used with other key variables in figuring regime response.

As a general rule, normal opposition activity by any group does not threaten values associated with the regime's fundamental needs, but only affects those values related to domestic and international legitimacy needs as part of the typical give and take of political life. More formidable groups tend to target higher values at both levels of activity. However, some groups whose formidability is not great, such as terrorist cells, are able to target rather highly ranked values when they escalate activity.[7]

With the above information in hand, we may answer some crucial questions: What groups are in opposition? Which of them is considered most formidable? Which are active? And what is the highest value an active opposition group can realistically target? Answers to these questions permit projections of the most likely set of tactics the regime would employ according to the response logic discussed below.

Regime Response and Anticipated Value

To determine a particular regime's response to opposition, three pieces of information must be integrated: the Regime Strength/Weakness Profile across values associated with instrumental needs; the Threat Assessment for each opposition group identified; and the Anticipated Value for each possible regime response. The Regime Strength/Weakness Profile and the Threat Assessment were already introduced and are compiled primarily from the knowledge of the country expert. Discussion of the third ingredient, Anticipated Value of possible regime responses, follows. Unlike the Strength/Weakness Profile and Threat Assessment, the Anticipated Value is not derived from country expertise, but is rather a cross-nationally stipulated system of decision rules.

Before Anticipated Value can be analyzed in any detail, it is necessary to posit the universe of possible regime responses over which Anticipated Value is calculated. Every regime has at its disposal a palette of responses or tactics to counter opposition threat to the regime's needs. These responses draw upon the regime's value assets and they are available to the

---

7. It is difficult to say what normal activity is for a terrorist group such as November 17th, since they are considered terrorists for their threatening (intense) activity. In general, however, normal behavior for a terrorist organization, because of its distant proximity and ideological salience, is characterized by maintaining its existence and remaining elusive; by participating in petty, criminal activity (smuggling, establishing illegal bases, etc.); and by recruiting, indoctrinating, and training new members clandestinely. The groups may make statements from time to time to remind both public and regime that they are still "active," but they will save acts of violence for their intense opposition activity against the regime.

regime if certain strength requirements are met. Although the specific manner in which these tactics are implemented varies from society to society, regime to regime, and situation to situation, the basic palette remains essentially constant. We categorize them into four major groups: ignore, direct tactics, indirect tactics, and compromise, reflecting the degree to which the regime puts its control over the societal exchange system on the line in its efforts to counter opposition threat. Ignoring the opposition may involve less risk to regime control, at least in the short run. Direct tactics seek to eliminate the source of threat, again requiring no regime sacrifice over policy direction. Indirect tactics are designed to circumvent opposition demands for policy change. Indeed, all three of these categories can be seen as different types of avoidance behavior on the part of the regime. Only with compromise do we see the regime put its policies on the bargaining table in any meaningful sense.

Response Tactics

The first category, *ignore*, involves avoiding public comment on opposition activity and refraining from official punishment of and actual engagement with the opposition. We do not distinguish between two levels of application for *ignore*, but we identify three sets of circumstances in which the tactic is used. In the first, use of the tactic implies the regime does not regard opposition activity as threatening. In the second case, *ignore* becomes a synonym for regime paralysis (that is, the regime may not be able to use any other tactic or cannot initiate any viable policy moves). *Ignore* has no strength requirements.

In the third case, *ignore* is not a default, but is actively chosen for strategic reasons. The opposition may be threatening, but not overwhelmingly so. Strategic *ignore* is limited to extra-PAG groups; it is used to deny the opposition the legitimation it may be seeking, which legitimation would give the opposition greater ability to threaten higher values.[8]

A *direct tactic* is an action aimed directly at an opposition source by the regime. The response is not directed through any third party, but clearly affects the members of the opposition group, their properties, social position, finances, or families.

As either an attempt to circumvent direct confrontation with an opposition group or as a rational regime choice to use certain tools, an *indirect tactic* may be applied by a regime. For example, it may gather support for

---

8. Because this use of *ignore* is not a default, we identify expected gains and reductions in control over values for it (see Appendix B.2).

itself while overshadowing or discrediting the opposition—without mentioning the opposition—using, for example, a diversion.

Finally, *compromise* can work to the benefit or detriment of either party, and is characterized by the regime acknowledging opposition demands, offering certain concessions, and negotiating a mutually acceptable agreement at the lowest cost possible. The regime may sacrifice considerable power if the opposition is strong and demands much, but may also buy time through compromise to muster strength for a direct or indirect response to opposition activity.

Table 3.3 summarizes the list of more specific tactics. For operational definitions for each of the basic tactics at both levels of intensity, see Appendix A.2.

Anticipated Value

To determine which tactics a regime will most likely choose in a given instance, it is necessary to know more about the exchange value of the tactics. As alluded to earlier, it is assumed that tactic implementation will draw upon (or drain) the regime's strength in certain value categories.

Table 3.3: List of Specific Tactics at the Disposal of the Regime

Type	Tactic	Level of Application
Ignore		
	Strategic Ignore	Deny Legitimacy
Direct Tactics		
	Administer Punishment (AP)	(I) Harassment (II) Suppression
	Dispense Favor to Cooptable Members of Opposition (DF)	(I) Persuasion (II) Bribery
Indirect Tactics		
	Out-Persuade (OP)	(I) Highlight Differences (II) Denounce Opposition
	Dispense Favor to Non-Opposition Domestic Entities (DFNO)	(I) Natural Alliances (II) Unnatural Alliances
	Solicit External Assistance (SEA)	(I) Moral or Material Support (II) Direct Intervention
	Deflect/Eclipse (DE)	(I) Bluffs and Diversions (II) Commitful action
	Restructure Government (RG)	(I) Minor (II) Major or high profile changes
Compromise		(I) Minor concessions (II) Major concessions

However, the regime rationalizes the tactic choice expecting certain gains will accrue if the tactic is successfully applied, which gains would outweigh possible reductions. Also, response choice is a function of certain requisite regime strength levels in the values to be used as assets or tools. To extend the exchange analogy, one must have an adequate amount of "currency" (strength prerequisites) and be able to absorb the cost (expected reductions in control over certain values) in order to purchase the item needed or desired (expected gains in control over values).

For each tactic previously identified, then, strength requirements must be specified over all applicable values. Likewise, both the expected reductions and expected gains in control over values upon tactic employment must be outlined. One possible rendering of this information is correlated in the Anticipated Value Inventory for each tactic in Appendix B.2.

For example, consider the tactic *administer punishment*. At the lower level of application, if the regime successfully intimidates its opponents through relatively minor harassment techniques, it could expect to register moderate gains in control over several values. Monitoring and curtailing opposition activities reduce the amount of interference in regime affairs and increases the regime's policy-making maneuverability. Strength consequentially increases in policy-making procedure, knowledge/feedback, legislative procedure, and electoral majority. Also, since harassment will be implemented most frequently by the military and other related bureaucratic agencies, experience and familiarity developed in conjunction with tactic implementation will establish the precedent for a close working relationship and may result in a higher degree of bureaucratic loyalty to the regime on future occasions. Finally, silencing disruptive elements in society allows the regime, in some cases, to provide a more stable environment in which to direct economic activity.

On the other hand, the regime risks reduced control over certain values through these harassment techniques. In particular, the regime may experience losses in public support, friendly press, ecclesiastical endorsement, and communication. In other words, a regime's public image may be undermined by the stigma of somewhat oppressive and often visible acts. In addition, any dialogue the regime might have enjoyed with members of the opposition will likely evaporate in the face of these measures.

The higher level use of this tactic results in more significant potential reductions in a wider variety of values for the regime. Expected gains are also on average higher. This higher level is therefore riskier, but potentially more productive. Essential to remember is that anticipated values are just that—anticipated—and the regime is not guaranteed any set of results. Expected gains represent, then, a best case scenario for tactic application, and the expected reductions depict a worst case scenario. The regime chooses from the tactics for which greater net gains can be anticipated, which gains vary according to the circumstances.

WELDING THE ELEMENTS: THE LOGIC OF REGIME RESPONSE

With the three primary variable clusters outlined, it is now possible to present the logic of regime response choice. The slate of tactics described in Table 3.3 lies before a regime facing a given terrain of opposition activity, conceptualized along the lines of Figure 3.3. Which tactics are most likely to be chosen in response to opposition?

The answer is derived through a multistep inference process that is only partially formalizable. Components of the logic remain largely nonquantifiable which is not to say they are unpredictable or random in any sense. Patterns emerge, but are highly complex, as human reasoning defies simple analysis. The specification of this logic is the heart of any computational model. The following description of the regime response logic makes reference to the process illustrated in Figure 3.4.

Possibility and Tolerability

The first step is to determine which opposition group will be the primary focus of regime activity. As suggested, the group with the highest threat assessment will be the most likely candidate. In addition to the group's identity, it is important to determine which values are threatened by it, and of those, which is of greatest priority to the regime.

Once the most likely target group has been identified, the second step is to winnow out from the list of tactics those either *impossible* or *intolerable* to the regime. "Impossibility" is a relatively straightforward concept; given that each tactic requires a certain minimal amount of regime strength in various value categories, if a regime does not possess these requirements, the tactic is not possible for the regime to implement. As mentioned, the strength requirements for the tactics are presented in Appendix B.1.

The notion of intolerability is more complex to define and operationalize. Succinctly, a tactic is intolerable if expected gains are outweighed by anticipated reductions. A cursory glance at the Anticipated Value Inventory (Appendix B.2) might lead one to assume such an evaluation would be static over time. This is not the case, because anticipated gains and reductions must be correlated with the current regime strength/weakness profile that can experience volatile change.[9] Similarly, the priority of each

---

9. Anticipated moves from one level of strength to another in the strength profile scale will have variable significance for the regime. Noting that in our schema the minimum level of most tactic strength requirements is "moderately strong," it is more significant for the capacity of the regime to move from "weak" to "moderately strong" than it is to move from "moderately strong" to "very strong." Variable significance attends other possible moves from level to level as well. Regime strength judgments are to be provided by the country expert, using the guidelines presented in Appendix A.1.

Figure 3.4: Decision Calculus for Regime Response to Opposition

Step 1: Identify Target Group

| 1 | Which opposition group is to be targeted, according to the threat assessment (Formidibility and Activity) information? |

$\longrightarrow$

Step 2: Rule Out Infeasible Tactics

| 2A | List all tactics. |

| 2B | Of the tactics listed in | 2A | which are POSSIBLE, given current regime strength and the strength requirements for each tactic? |

| 2C | Of the tactics listed in | 2B | which are TOLERABLE, given the Anticipated Value Inventory and the current Regime Strength/Weakness Profile? |

Step 3: Task: Determine More Likely Tactics

| 3A | Rank the tactics listed in | 2C | according to their comparative gain/reduction ratios in column one. |

Tactic	Column 1

| 3B | In column 2, rank the tactics according to the criterion of strength abundance. |

Tactic	Column 1	Column 2

value on the regime's agenda may change over time. If gains and reductions in strength can be thought of in terms of a ratio, then any ratio less than one defines a tactic whose use would be intolerable to the regime.

More Likely and Less Likely

Once impossible and intolerable tactics have been eliminated, the set of feasible regime responses remains. The third, and most complex, step in the calculus is to determine which of these remaining tactics are more likely and which are less likely. Several considerations seem to us to be relevant at this point.

Comparative Gain/Reduction Ratio. If a ratio of anticipated gains and reductions is calculated for each feasible tactic, then assumably tactics with higher ratios would be more attractive to the regime than those with lower ratios. In our model, this comparison of ratios is the most significant factor considered in this third step of the inference process.

Strength Abundance. It is reasonable to assume, *ceteris paribus,* that a regime will prefer tactics that utilize its areas of greatest strength. Thus, if a regime has more than the minimum level of strength required in control over one or more of the values to use the tactic, the regime should find that tactic more attractive.

Appropriateness of Tactic Given Threat. A regime will tend to prefer tactics that, for a variety of reasons, appear to be a more appropriate match for the degree and type of threat faced. Such fine tuning can be captured in part by an analysis of the disaggregated measures comprising the threat assessment of the targeted opposition group. That is, by examining the targeted group's proximity, cohesiveness, ideological salience, size, highest targeted value, and current activity, the analyst may estimate which of the feasible tactics will seem more appropriate than others (see step 3C in Figure 3.4). Examples of how this may be done follow:

(1) In cases where formidability, activity, and priority of targeted values reach maximum levels, one would assume the opposition poses a very serious threat to the regime that would appropriately be met by a level two response.

(2) If the targeted group is within the regime's primary advisory group (PAG), the tactic of "restructure government" may be an appropriate option. This is not to suggest that this tactic is only appropriate when the opposition is in the PAG, nor that it is the only appropriate tactic when the opposition is in the PAG. This rule serves only to highlight the possible attractiveness of this tactic in the particular circumstance where the opposition group is in the PAG.

(3) If a tactic's use has resulted in a severe setback for the regime within the last year, the regime will avoid use of that tactic. Regimes do not like to replay their own most spectacular failures. Of course, we acknowledge the possibility that this rule may be suspended for certain ideologically rigid regimes as identified by the country expert.

(4) If a tactic offers particularly significant gains to the regime in the value category identified as the highest priority value targeted by the opposition group, this may incline the regime to its use.

(5) If the opposition's formidability is low, direct tactics will be more appealing, because they carry less risk to the regime when applied to less threatening groups. Again, certain cultural proclivities as identified by the country expert may mitigate against the application of this rule to certain regimes.

(6) If the targeted opposition group is operating only at its normal levels, the regime is, prima facie, facing less of a threat. In this case, the regime may differentiate between tactics that, on the surface, have similar gain/ reduction ratios. One notes in the AVI that certain tactics have shorter lists of expected gains and expected reductions than do others, but they can generate similar ratios. When the opposition is less threatening, tactics with lower risks could accomplish the same purpose as those with higher risks and could be chosen by the regime. Prime examples of high risk/high gain tactics that might be eschewed in this case are *deflect/eclipse* and *seek external assistance*.

(7) If groups of different ideological salience are intensely active at the same time, deflect/eclipse (both levels) becomes more likely because it offers an issue that renders ideological difference comparatively irrelevant.

General Regime Preference. Lastly, given that a regime seeks to minimize its loss of control over policy content and the policy-making process, it follows that a general preference ordering for types of tactics probably exists for a regime. For instance, direct tactics may be perceived as minimizing such regime loss, whereas major compromise may be seen as maximizing it. However, not all regimes are alike in their preference for and experience with direct and indirect tactics. Preference ordering over the feasible tactics should be determined by the country expert for the regime, taking into account the regime's structure, history of adherence to laws and human rights, and composition of its ultimate decision unit. In some regimes, use of direct tactics is legally difficult or culturally distasteful, whereas other regimes operating under different norms may turn to such tactics readily. The personality of a predominant leader may also be important to assess in this regard, as in this type of regime, the leader may act as if he or she were the final arbiter of social mores (cf. Hermann, 1984).

The general preference order of the regime completes the list of factors that help determine the probability of tactic use. Figure 3.4 shows how simultaneous consideration of these factors may be effected. Important to note is that the output of this decision calculus is not one tactic, but rather a short list of tactics whose pros and cons may be catalogued and compared. We have found, through successive runs of the model, that two or three tactics typically emerge as most likely, with a few others remaining feasible in addition to these. How these may be sorted through by the researcher, and what foreign policy effects can be anticipated with each tactic's use, are the subject of the remainder of this essay.

LINKING REGIME RESPONSE AND FOREIGN POLICY BEHAVIOR

Given the numerous possible regime responses to opposition, one should see different effects on foreign policy behavior, depending on which response is chosen. Some tactics have no foreign policy repercussions at all; for instance, a regime may choose to simply ignore insignificant opposition activity. No effects from this neglect would be apparent in foreign policy behavior. At the other extreme, foreign policy may be the primary tool with which the regime chooses to manipulate its opposition; under these circumstances the effect of opposition is direct, intended, and obvious. Between the two extremes lie more subtle, less direct, and usually unintended effects of regime response to opposition on foreign policy behavior. We hope to distinguish between these three circumstances later in the section.

The relationship between regime response and foreign policy is the second inference step (Figure 3.2) of the model. In this step, the output of the model (set of feasible tactics ranked according to the likelihood of use) is compared to hypotheses that link each tactic to change in the attributes of the regime's foreign policy behavior. To construct this step, we must identify basic attributes of foreign policy behavior that may be affected by various regime tactics. Although there are numerous attributes of foreign policy behavior in the literature of international relations (see Callahan et al., 1982), some are easier to link to the effects of regime response to opposition than others. We suggest five such dimensions.

Conflict/Cooperation. This dimension measures the direction and intensity of expressed feeling toward a foreign entity, accounting for whether that feeling is hostile, cooperative, or indifferent, as well as its degree of intensity. One could examine this dimension case by case or determine whether a regime's foreign policy behavior was gradually becoming more conflictual or cooperative over time. Numerous scales of conflict/cooperation exist in the literature (for example, see Azar, 1980; or Hermann, Hermann and Hutchins, 1982).

Commitment Level. This attribute determines the degree to which a regime's future behavior is constrained by its current foreign policy behavior. If the regime is issuing an ultimatum, signing a treaty, or actually transferring/allocating resources in response to a foreign policy problem, its behavior represents a higher commitment than, say, a mere verbal evaluation of the state of foreign affairs. One of the better designed commitment scales is explicated in Callahan, et al., 1982.

Initiation/Reaction. Also of interest is whether the acting regime is initiating foreign policy behavior or reacting to a foreign policy issue. Issues created or resurrected by the regime are usefully contrasted with a long-standing evolution of policy on a given international issue. For example, Greece under Papandreou resurrected fears of imminent military hostilities with Turkey in 1987, after the issue had by and large subsided by the late 1970s. Contrast this with his long-standing policy concerning Cyprus, which became reactive to any new moves by the Turkish government or Rauf Denktash (leader of the Turkish Cyprots).

Type of Recipient. Of special concern when foreign policy behavior is initiated is the type of recipient targeted: the regime may request assistance from a strong ally in dealing with internal opposition, or it may try to quell opposition at home by issuing provocative statements to enemies. Although knowledge of domestic opposition variables may not allow one to specifically identify a recipient, clues should emerge as to the *type* of foreign entity to be addressed. For example, nations may direct behavior towards international "Big Brother" figures when their landscape of opposition is configured in a certain way.

Level of Foreign Policy Activity. This attribute measures to what degree the regime is active in foreign affairs, usually determined by the quantity of foreign policy behavior (initiative and/or reactive) engaged in by the regime. As a regime becomes ever more preoccupied with internal dissent, overall levels of activity may decrease. On the other hand, certain types of opposition may encourage an increase in foreign policy activity. Events-based data sets such as WEIS and COPDAB are easily utilized to provide information on activity levels (see Fitzsimmons, et al., 1969; Azar, 1980).

Foreign Policy Behavior Effects

With foreign policy behavior attributes defined, we may now discuss how regime response to opposition may affect the values of those attributes. Important questions arise at this point concerning whether a foreign policy move is only normal behavior or a response tactic; and if a foreign policy move has positive domestic effects, whether it was a consciously applied tactic or simply the result of "normal" international behavior. The country expert plays a crucial role here in determining what is "normal behavior"—based on recent history, political ideology, and the situation. For example, when the Federal Republic of Germany joined the rest of the world in criticizing the United States for bombing Libya in 1986, its rebuke was not unexpected (despite being our ally). However, had Germany restricted trade with the U.S. over the incident, it would have been abnormal behavior, and a country expert would look for domestic political gains that might have been sought. Indeed, a foreign policy act should be suspected as originating as a tactic if the response represents other-than-normal foreign policy behavior according to the country expert's knowledge of past behavior. Evidence from current foreign policy research indicates that "policy decision makers relate foreign policy problems requiring immediate action to proposed solutions largely in terms of the domestic political ramifications" (Purkitt, 1990:23).

Some may posit that the tactical use of foreign policy may be a function of opportunity rather than calculated choice. Where foreign policy helps on the domestic front only because an opportunity has presented itself, we must remember that the model produces a set of "most likely" tactics, from which the regime will make its choice. If an external event seems most opportune to exploit and a tactic linked to the international sector is a "most likely" choice, there is no reason why a regime should not choose to capitalize on the issue. This is assumed in the model to be part of the decision process. Further, we do not believe a regime can use an international issue for domestic gain if it does not have the strength requirements to do so. The model should correctly determine if capitalizing on external events is possible and more or less likely.

If the country expert identifies a tangible shift from "normal" foreign policy behavior, thus leading us to investigate whether the regime is employing a tactic with foreign policy effects, we then need to delineate the nature of such effects. Some tactics result in tangential (spin-off) foreign policy effects—effects not consciously chosen or preferred by the regime, but those that follow naturally from use of the tactic. For example, a country embroiled in a civil war may find itself unable to keep up with a plethora of international meetings and conferences. This lowered international profile is not an effect specifically chosen by the regime, which may otherwise wish to continue as before. These effects may or may not come as a surprise to the regime.

Contrast this with consciously chosen changes in foreign policy. A regime may, in a calculating way, alter its foreign policy in direction or degree as part of tactic implementation. For example, if a regime infiltrates its neighbor's territory to eliminate opposition bases, foreign policy is part and parcel of tactic implementation. Effects are straightforward and discernible by the researcher.

As explained, the decision to *ignore* opposition activity should have almost no discernible effect on foreign policy behavior. If a regime feels no response to opposition is necessary, it will have no reservations about conducting foreign policy as usual. This does not suggest that the regime's external behavior will not exhibit change in the five descriptive variables outlined, but simply asserts that such change has virtually no relationship to domestic opposition activity. This logic should hold for both the default and strategic use of this tactic.

At some point, however, most regimes will lack sufficient control over values to be able to ignore threats posed by opposition groups. They may then attempt to acquire greater strength through the direct manipulation of foreign policy or the use of another tactic with foreign policy repercussions.

Like *ignore*, the direct tactic *administer punishment* level one (AP I) will likely have no effect on foreign policy due to its limited nature and exclusively domestic focus. However, an exception exists in cases where several distinct groups are operating in a coalition and include segments of opposition from abroad. If this is the case, possible harassment of these elements in an effort to cut the leadership's support base may result in some foreign policy effects (e.g. decrease in commitment; increase in negative affect; and decrease in international involvement). Likewise, administering punishment at the higher level (AP II) would naturally bring some international attention to the regime's actions. Specifically, this tactic could temporarily decrease the regime's international involvement and level of commitment as it concentrates efforts and resources internally.

The degree of decrease would be directly related to the degree of level two tactics being applied. For instance, if a nationwide crackdown were initiated that necessitated widescale jailings or military action, international activity would drop off sharply in the short-term for three reasons: (1) to allow the regime to isolate itself somewhat from international criticism; (2) to concentrate leadership efforts domestically; and (3) to allow for policy review, if necessary, before international activity is once again increased. China's leaders were quiet and inaccessible during the June 1989 massacre and immediately subsequent crackdown. Not until they felt in control through a policy of a continuing suppression movement did they entertain discussions with foreign diplomats.

Similarly, as activity decreases so does the level of the regime's international commitment. Participation in conferences, for instance, may be postponed or even canceled; promised financial aid or other payments could be withdrawn or delayed. The regime may condemn any foreign support of opposition as intervention in internal matters. In addition, foreign territory used as bases for opposition forces may be attacked or infiltrated. Thus, even though most of our hypotheses link AP II to indirect effects on foreign policy behavior, it is possible that under certain circumstances that direct and very obvious effects on foreign policy behavior may result.

The next tactic, *dispensing favor to co-optable members of the opposition* (DF), is more difficult to link to foreign policy behavior, as the tactic can be applied in so many ways. Indeed, at level one, we do not predict any real effect on foreign policy because the ideological co-optation of members of the opposition gives the regime breathing room to continue its policies virtually intact. At level two, however, there are at least three ways foreign policy behavior could be affected. First, if the regime is successful in co-opting opposition members through bribery or a significant quid pro quo, it may feel more confidence or strength resulting from the transfer of support or power from the opposition to the regime. With this greater confidence, foreign policy initiatives may increase as opportunities arise, especially if co-opted members represent a group acceptable to certain international actors, with whom the regime would like to have trade, dialogue, or better relations. In general, the regime would be less cumbered while operating in the international arena. Second, the increased confidence or strength could also result in greater commitment internationally—commitment to allies, to professed causes, to activities in progress elsewhere. And finally, the regime may be expected to exhibit an increase in intensity of affect, both negatively and positively, in communications with other international actors, as the tactic may have freed the regime to act less conservatively in all its dealings.

The first indirect tactic, *out persuade* (OP), may engender some possible foreign policy effects if external entities are somehow relevant to the issue at hand. Difficult to pin down unless the situational context is provided, OP at either level may have no effects, tangential effects, or may involve the calculated use of foreign policy. At level one, where rhetoric is applied to win favor, the regime may increase the intensity of its negative or positive affect on the international scene. Statements made to praise or criticize external entities will generally be more concise, clear, and substantial when the regime is trying to highlight differences between its own policies and those of its domestic opponents, with whom external actors may be linked or in conflict. Likewise, this increased affect intensity would be seen at level two, where the regime begins to assail the opposition on an ad hominem basis. The regime may censure the opposition's record vis a vis patriotism, morality, integrity, ideology and native intelligence. These attacks might produce increased initiatives abroad, as opportunity permitted, to garner international support for its condemnation of internal foes.

Dispensing favor to non-opposition domestic entities (DFNO) at level one would produce no foreign policy effects. Again, the regime is perhaps literally buying time to continue its policies intact. However, at level two, the same type of consequences as outlined for *dispensing favor to cooptable members of the opposition* would be observed. The opposition may not lose cohesiveness, because its members are not the targets of co-optation, but the regime would surely gain in strength and could potentially remove future support for the opposition by dispensing favor to other groups in the polity. Therefore, this results in confidence, strength, support, and perhaps even access to resources, depending on the structure of the economy. Thus, as with dispensing favor to the opposition, increased initiatives, greater commitment, and increased intensity of affect are potential foreign policy effects of applying this tactic.

Soliciting external assistance (SEA), by its nature, produces changes in the foreign policy attributes. Low level efforts increase the incidence of foreign policy initiative-taking, usually involving cooperative diplomacy with traditional friends—producing a generally higher level of foreign policy activity. However, at more intense levels, such as inviting armed intervention by another country, the regime can lose control over the course of foreign policy: in such a case the levels of activity and commitment decline, although the regime will likely continue cooperative gestures toward allies while engaging in conflictual behavior with enemies. Consequently and paradoxically, one may see more calculated effects at level one, and more in the way of tangential or spin-off effects at level two.

A regime choosing to employ *deflect/eclipse* (DE) as an indirect response to opposition activity has a wide range of options to pursue. Diversion of attention and support away from the opposition may or may not revolve around a foreign policy issue. If it does—that is, if circumstances offer an opportunity to divert to a foreign policy issue—one would observe increased levels of activity, an increase in initiative behavior, and greater intensity in public expressions of feeling, whether those expressions are conciliatory and cooperative or belligerent and conflictual. Used at more intense levels, the deflection tactic with a foreign policy flavor will cause the regime to increase its level of commitment in implementing that tactic. Note that the regime may choose an essentially positive diversion, such as concluding a major treaty; or may resort to a negative diversion, such as threatening war with a traditional enemy, in an attempt to regain control over the domestic situation.

When a government removes lower-ranking officials in an attempt to appease domestic opposition (restructure government), little effect on foreign policy usually results. The key decision makers concerned with foreign policy making (such as the Foreign Minister or Secretary of Defense) are by definition high ranking officials, unaffected by such a lower level "house clearing." In contrast, a reorganization of the government at level two could have profound effects on foreign policy if such key figures were removed. For instance, there might be a resulting change in the pattern of international commitment, if not an actual decrease, depending on the type of change in personnel. On the other hand, a level two reorganization may still have no effects on foreign policy if only officials with no connection to foreign affairs are targeted. The most we can say in this case is that an important shake-up of the government will likely begin a period of caution in governmental policy making circles, which may affect foreign policy by lowering the regime's overall level of international commitment.

If a regime *compromises* with an opposition group, unfortunately little can be said about effects on foreign policy behavior for two reasons. First, the compromise may or may not involve an issue with foreign policy ramifications. In the former case, the effect on foreign policy behavior would be direct. In the latter, it is possible that no perceptible effect on foreign policy behavior would result. Second, in the absence of country-specific information about the policy preferences of the regime and the opposition groups, it is virtually impossible to tell what the substance of the compromise will be. Only when that substance is known can the effects on foreign policy behavior be gauged.

Referring to Figure 3.5, we can see that our conceptual journey is complete. We have moved from country specific information on regimes and opposition groups to a cross-national inventory of tactics and their likely effects on the regime's agenda and its foreign policy behavior. Table 3.4 represents what we would consider as counting against the model's worth as an analytical tool. Because the model involves some very complex relationships, one must understand that such a negative vote cannot automatically render the model useless. On the contrary, it might lend information for the improvement of the model or permit others to build on the foundation we have laid here. If our model were seen as part of the process of the cumulation of knowledge in this subject area, we would be encouraged.

Several tasks remain for future research in the area of domestic opposition. Foremost among these is to tie specific model parameters to the theoretical literature. Though fundamental concepts and organizing principles of the model are rooted in theory, the theoretical justifiability of numerous operational procedures could legitimately be called into question. For example, weighting of values associated with regime needs or the step function used to tabulate gains and reductions bear further scrutiny. Furthermore, a more concrete understanding of the effects of each tactic on regime foreign policy behavior is needed. As Starr and Most (1989) point out, foreign policy analysis studies must cope with policy substitutability; one can achieve the same goals with different policies and vice-versa. Empirical testing of the model using detailed inputs from country experts

Table 3.4: Conditions for Falsification

Condition	Count Against
Of the very likely tactics, regime only uses some	NO
Of feasible tactics, regime uses no very likely tactics	YES (minor)
The regime uses impossible or intolerable tactics	YES (major)

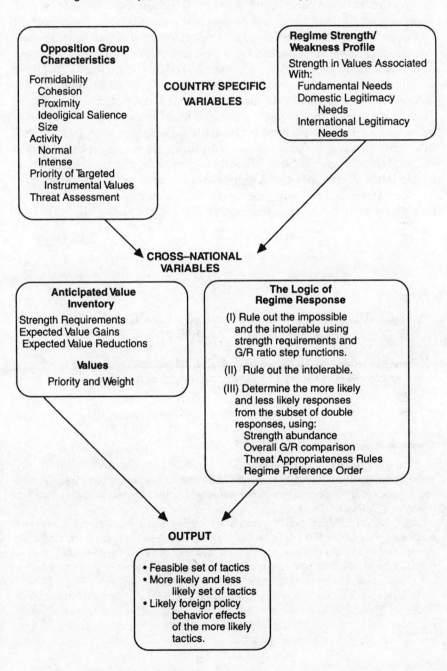

Figure 3.5: Representation of the Domestic Opposition Model.

Opposition Group Characteristics

Formidability
  Cohesion
  Proximity
  Ideoligical Salience
  Size
Activity
  Normal
  Intense
Priority of Targeted
    Instrumental Values
Threat Assessment

COUNTRY SPECIFIC VARIABLES

Regime Strength/ Weakness Profile

Strength in Values Associated With:
  Fundamental Needs
  Domestic Legitimacy
    Needs
  International Legitimacy
    Needs

CROSS–NATIONAL VARIABLES

Anticipated Value Inventory

Strength Requirements
Expected Value Gains
Expected Value Reductions

Values

Priority and Weight

The Logic of Regime Response

(I) Rule out the impossible and the intolerable using strength requirements and G/R ratio step functions.

(II) Rule out the intolerable.

(III) Determine the more likely and less likely responses from the subset of double responses, using:
  Strength abundance
  Overall G/R comparison
  Threat Appropriateness Rules
  Regime Preference Order

OUTPUT

• Feasible set of tactics
• More likely and less
    likely set of tactics
• Likely foreign policy
    behavior effects
    of the more likely
    tactics.

will therefore play a crucial role in the evolution of this domestic opposition model, and we have begun this task (Hudson, Sims, Murdock, and
Thomas, in progress). Finally, as in an actual game of chess, it is important
to see domestic political struggles not only at the level of particular moves,
but also at a more dynamic level as a series of moves and countermoves.

Despite the ground still to be covered, we feel the model as currently
constituted represents a real advance in the effort to understand the
linkage between domestic politics and international politics. Though the
model presented here may not be optimal in all senses of the word, it can
be seen as a workable prototype of that ideal: concrete theory instantiated
in an empirically falsifiable model. With Rosenau, we assert that "a wide
range of theories can be built out of these materials, and nothing inherent
in the latter determines the design, elegance, and utility of the former.
These qualities must be supplied by the analyst, which is what makes the
task of theory building awesome and challenging" (1980: 168).

APPENDIX A.1

GUIDELINES FOR DETERMINING REGIME STRENGTH
OVER VALUE ELEMENTS

These guidelines do not represent exclusive definitions, but flexible typologies
to be used by the country expert in analyzing the strengths of a give regime.

VALUES ASSOCIATED WITH FUNDAMENTAL NEEDS

Territorial Integrity

STRONG: Firmly established borders are maintained peacefully by a relatively
small force capable of handling border traffic and controlling infiltration. Borders
are recognized by the international community; any disputes are minor and do not
disrupt control of the border.

MODERATE: Established borders are maintained in general peace, despite
tensions and occasional unrest over border disputes, by a fairly large force capable
of controlling most traffic and infiltration. Borders are recognized in the international community, but perhaps not by all actors. The possibility of invasion or
secession exists, but is not imminent.

WEAK: Borders are not firmly established and are disputed through violent
clashes with neighbors or secessionists. They are only tentatively maintained by
military forces prepared for armed conflict, and are not necessarily recognized by
most (if any) actors in the international community.

Policy Making Procedure

STRONG: The leadership is cohesive and possible opposition elements in the PAG are either weak or non-existent.

MODERATE: The regime may occasionally be blocked on policy issues, but maintains the ability to act as it wishes in most cases. The leadership is not always cohesive, and opposition elements within the PAG apply consistent pressure and influence on the regime's decisions and actions.

WEAK: Regime policy is often disputed and altered to meet demands of the opposition. The regime may even be dominated by fractious elements within the PAG. The regime leadership is fragmented and often unable to produce definitive policy because of internal debates.

Knowledge/Feedback

STRONG: The regime has a well-established system for intelligence gathering that provides accurate feedback to it. The regime also has access to several other sources for information, which are loyal to the regime and accurate in their reporting.

MODERATE: The regime has an established system or agency for intelligence gathering that produces generally reliable information to the regime. The regime has only a limited number of other sources for information, which may not always prove loyal or accurate.

WEAK: The regime may or may not have an established intelligence gathering system or agency. If so, it is poorly developed and unable to provide reliable reports to the regime. If no system exists, the regime must rely on other sources, whose loyalty and/or accuracy cannot be determined. Disinformation is a great danger, as is the overall lack of information, which problems could isolate and/or cripple the regime leadership.

Stable Military

STRONG: The military is either highly institutionalized and loyal to the government system or well-organized and indoctrinated to be loyal to a specific individual in the executive office. Either condition allows the military to be used by the regime, but not against it. Military officers are generally satisfied with their status and treatment. They may be either politically neutral (with little influence on domestic politics) or fully active as a key supporter of the regime.

MODERATE: The military has either pledged loyalty to the executive office or a specific individual in power; this loyalty is not necessarily firm and could shift if the military is displeased with the regime. The military is generally not neutral military leaders are courted for their support. The military cannot always be trusted to implement regime policy. Nevertheless, it is sufficiently loyal at the time to be used as a tool when needed.

WEAK: The military has not pledged its loyalty to the regime, or if it has so pledged, it is not completely loyal. It has been known to revolt or sponsor coups, and is politically active. The military may be factionalized, and may be openly dissatisfied with the government and/or the government's treatment of the military. Troops may receive indoctrination from opposition groups and cannot be trusted by the regime to enforce policy or remain stable. In fact, the military may be used against the regime by an opposition group.

Legislative Process

STRONG: The legislature may be a rubber-stamp body which ratifies all decisions of the ruling party; or it may contain a majority representation of the ruling party that would allow the regime to sponsor and pass legislation favorable to its desires. The regime has a good working relationship with its party members, such that they support its policies in legislative decisions.

MODERATE: If a traditionally rubber-stamp legislature, the body begins to exhibit some signs of autonomy or opposition. In a multiparty legislature, the ruling party may have the greatest representation, but not a majority. Opposition groups may support regime legislation, but expect support in return. This inhibits the regime from sponsoring and passing its own legislation without compromise or modification.

WEAK: Traditionally rubber-stamp legislatures demand a greater role. Multiparty legislatures are led by a majority of the opposition which is often not cooperative with the executive. Or, the ruling party governs through a coalition of various parties, which do not agree on legislation and often dispute it during the legislative process, making it very difficult for the ruling regime to receive favorable legislation or influence the process.

Stable Economy

STRONG: Industrial and GNP growth increase steadily. Fluctuations in currency value, inflation, and unemployment are deemed insignificant and within acceptable range. The economy is diversified and resilient when faced with sectoral setbacks. Strikes and other labor disputes are minimal. International debt is manageable and does not consume a significant portion of the GNP, or it does not exist. A skilled labor pool exists and forms a significant proportion of the workforce in industrialized countries. In non-industrial societies, unskilled labor is not seen as an obstacle to development. Less than 10 percent of the GNP is spent on the military.

MODERATE: Industrial and GNP growth are not in decline and may increase somewhat. Inflation may be above 10 percent, as is unemployment, with labor disputes affecting productivity in some sectors. International debt is a burden inhibiting investment and growth, but is not unmanageable. Skilled labor is available, but unskilled labor poses an impediment to further growth. Markets are vulnerable to world commodity prices and are often dependent on overseas trade for success. A moderate trade deficit may exist. More than 10 percent of the GNP is spent on military concerns.

WEAK: Imports exceed exports by a wide margin. Industrial and GNP growth rates are stagnant or declining. Hyperinflation may exist. International debt is high and may exceed GNP levels. Skilled labor, natural resources, technology, and capital are scarce. Vulnerable economics, such as single-commodity export markets are the rule of thumb. Natural disasters at times derail the economy. The economy is often agriculture-based and/or lacking in industrial production. Social problems (population, infrastructure) prevent economic investment. Underemployment is high.

VALUES ASSOCIATED WITH DOMESTIC LEGITIMACY NEEDS

Electoral Majority

STRONG: In multiparty legislatures, the regime possesses a majority with a comfortable margin. This value may drop out of assessments of regimes where multiparty legislatures do not exist.

MODERATE: The regime may possess a majority, but by a narrow margin. Or, the regime does not possess a majority and operates through a strong coalition.

WEAK: The regime is in office, but does not possess a majority, having either lost it or operating through a less-than-secure coalition. The regime is possibly subject to a vote of no-confidence, power struggles, or dissent. It is not fully capable of controlling the government.

Manipulation of Symbols

STRONG: Regime has great credibility and legitimacy with the public, whether or not the public supports the regime's policy positions. The resort to using symbols by the regime will have an immediate and unifying effect. The regime's manner of manipulation will ensure that the effect does not wear off quickly.

MODERATE: The regime is either not credible or is unable to maintain the mobilization provided by the symbol manipulation for very long.

WEAK: The regime is completely incredible and no mobilization of public unity results from any attempt at manipulation by the regime.

Public Support

STRONG: While this value is difficult to measure, some indicators are useful. Public opinion polls show the public views the regime and/or its policies with favor. Protests and demonstrations are few. Anti-government movements are isolated and find no haven among the citizenry. Public policy is implemented with a minimum of public resistance. Public interest in and respect for regime leaders is high.

MODERATE: Public opinion polls are favorable in some areas, but not in others. Dissent, protests, and demands may be increasing. Derogatory and sarcastic references are made to the regime. Limited clashes over policy implementation may occur. Anti-government movements gather support from certain segments of society.

WEAK: The regime faces widespread public expressions of distrust, anger, and disapproval through polls, protests, demonstrations, and even civil disobedience. Calls for resignation are voiced; opposition groups take advantage of this displeasure with the regime and increase their activities. The regime might need to maintain loyalty through state security forces and/or violence.

Friendly Press

STRONG: The regime controls the press and allows no opposition voice in the media. Or, in a society with a free press, the press often publishes information favorable to the regime. In this case, the press is generally respected and trusted and a good working relationship exists between the press and the regime.

MODERATE: The regime-controlled press is being undermined by legal or illegal opposition press, or the controlled press pushes for some freedoms. If a free press exists, it frequently publishes unfavorable information about the regime, resulting in less cooperation between it and the regime, and poorer public relations for the regime.

WEAK: A supposedly controlled press breaks with the regime and prints negative information about it. Alternatively, a free press constantly assails regime leaders and policy, and does not have a working relationship with the regime.

Cooperative Bureaucracy

STRONG: The bureaucracy implements regime policy as planned without intentional hindrance, and is supportive of regime goals. It may even engage in illegal or borderline activity if called upon to do so.

MODERATE: The bureaucracy implements regime policy for the most part, but may be liberal in interpretation of intentions and can impede execution if the policy is distasteful to the bureaucrats involved. The bureaucracy is not afraid to protest regime policy and will act in some cases in self-interest.

WEAK: The bureaucracy is either incapable (through poor organization, corruption, lack of support or training, or lack of funding) or unwilling to implement regime policy without very liberal interpretation of policy goals. Self-interest is a prime motivator in bureaucratic action. The bureaucracy deliberately hinders policy it disagrees with, thus undermining the regime's authority.

Ecclesiastical Endorsement

STRONG: The regime leadership receives direct support from the state church, if such exists. In states without an official church, major religious organizations announce their approval of a regime (through public communiques, letters, personal appearances, and such) and recommend their members' support. In some cases, use of church facilities is offered to the regime.

MODERATE: The regime is not opposed by the state church, but also does not receive direct support. In the absence of a state church, major groups support the regime in general based on principles, values, political ideology, and the like, but will not actively endorse regime leaders. At the very least, key religious organizations do not favor opposition groups over the regime. In cases where religion is suppressed, no major opposition to this regime stance is noted.

WEAK: Key religious organizations denounce the regime or refuse their cooperation when asked for it. They may actively support and aid opposition groups. In states where religion is oppressed and ecclesiastical endorsement means little, religious groups and individuals may demonstrate against the lack of religious freedom and may foment future dissent.

Communication

STRONG: The regime has an open channel open for discussion with opposition members, which channel is actively used by both sides. The regime works to keep this channel open, as does the opposition by its rejection of rigid or violent positions.

MODERATE: A channel exists for discussion between the regime and opposition groups; however, the channel is not often used. Contacts are lost or are unreliable or without authority to speak on behalf of the parties involved. Confusion about messages received or sent may be commonplace.

WEAK: If a channel of communication exists, it has fallen into disuse. Or, a channel does not exist at all. Communication of ideas and goals must travel through indirect sources and is subject to distortion, which an lead to frustration, violence, and various other troubles. Either the regime is unwilling to speak with an opposition group, or that group ignores regime overtures, or some other circumstance hinders direct discussion.

VALUES ASSOCIATED WITH INTERNATIONAL LEGITIMACY NEEDS

International Recognition

STRONG: The regime enjoys wide international recognition and exchanges ambassadors with a majority of United Nations members. The regime leader is welcomed internationally. No counter-regimes are supported by other nations.

MODERATE: The regime has recognition from a majority of UN members, and exchanges ambassadors with most. But ambassador-level relations may not be established with a major world power. The lack of recognition may be due to ideological conflicts with the regime leadership, and may not imply open enmity. The leadership is generally accepted in international bodies.

WEAK: The regime may lack recognition from a majority of United Nations members and may face calls for UN action against regime. Other nations may support insurgency movements against the regime. The regime likely lacks relations with one or more major powers, and may be isolated internationally. Regime leadership is often not included in international conferences or is avoided by others at such gatherings.

External Support

STRONG: The regime enjoys positive relations with states who are willing to either enter into an alliance (economic, political, military) with the regime, or are willing to extend aid, verbal or diplomatic support, or both. The regime leadership is welcome to visit other nations and is often invited to do so.

MODERATE: The regime enjoys stable relations with states who are willing to forge agreements and cooperate on a limited basis. Aid, diplomatic support, or both, may be offered but not without conditions. Regime leaders are welcome to visit other nations, but may not be invited. Support from other nations is often tentative, rather than automatic, and can be less than enthusiastic in a given situation.

WEAK: The regime has few allies and lacks good relations with one or more major powers. Most states may seem hesitant to enter into agreements with the regime, while others are simply enemies of the regime. Diplomatic relations may be established, but are not necessarily friendly. Aid may be available, but not without conditions.

External Threat

STRONG: The regime is able to capitalize on any real or potential threat to galvanize domestic support, to impose unpleasant measures on society (austerity, martial law, other restrictions) without revolt, to increase military expenditures, or to draw attention away from opposition groups and any domestic problems. Any real threat is not so great as to endanger sovereignty or provoke war.

MODERATE: The regime is able to use any real or potential threat to call for domestic support, to call for legislation on drastic measures, and to increase military expenditures. While the regime may enjoy short-term success with these measures, it does not have the ability to extend them indefinitely. A real threat may be severe enough to pose a crisis for the regime or lead to war.

WEAK: The regime is unable to manipulate any potential threat for domestic political gain, either because no threat exists, or past attempts to use potential threat failed and the people are skeptical, or because the domestic problems completely overshadow potential threat.

APPENDIX A.2

Tactic Definitions

Ignore—This involves avoiding public comment on opposition activity, and refraining from official punishment of and actual engagement with the opposition. It does not imply the regime is unaware of or disinterested in the opposition. While there are not two levels for this tactic, there are three sets of circumstances in which it is used. In the first situation, the choice of ignore reflects the regime's attitude that opposition activity is not threatening. The regime is not inactive, but is not reacting to opposition behavior.

In the second case, **ignore** is a synonym for regime paralysis. That is, if a regime is incapable of attempting any other tactic because it lacks the strength requirements to do so, its paralysis may be manifested as **ignore**, since no viable policy initiation emanates from the regime.

In the third case, **ignore** is no longer a default tactic, but is actively chosen by the regime for strategic reasons. The opposition *is* threatening, although not overwhelmingly so. Indeed, we limit the applicability of this tactic to extra-PAG opposition. In addition, the opposition is seeking legitimation, as it has not enjoyed that previously—the opposition may not have even existed previously. The regime ignores this type of opposition in order to deny it the legitimation is seeks, thus hopefully keeping a lid on this group's ability to threaten values associated with regime needs. This is the only set of circumstances for which we identify expected gains and reductions in control over values.

(DT) Direct Tactics—an action aimed directly at opposition source by the regime in obvious reaction to opposition activity. The applied response is not directed through any third party, but clearly affects the leaders and members of the opposition group, including their families, properties, social position, or finances.

(IT) Indirect Tactic—a tactic that avoids direct confrontation with an opposition group. Choosing an indirect tactic need not connote regime weakness, as it may merely signify a conscious regime choice to use certain tools and not others. For example, even a very strong regime may gather support for itself while discrediting the opposition—without mentioning the opposition—by taking advantage of an opportunity to divert public attention to some international problem that has fortuitously presented itself.

(Comp) Compromise—This tactic represents a separate category of regime response to opposition. Unlike the previous three categories, where the regime—through a variety of means—avoids having to budge on important policy matters to which the opposition objects, the regime signals through compromise its willingness to alter its policy position.

Direct Tactics

(AP) Administer Punishment—Either through the military, police or other appropriate bureaucratic sources, the regime directly punishes the opposition source for its activity. At the lower level (AP I), this includes harassment, and at the higher level (AP II), involves widespread suppression. **Harassment** includes such specific measures as patrolling buildings when opposition meetings are held; threatening opposition sources within the government with removal or scandal; allowing police to physically strike, but not kill, leaders and opposition members; and the withdrawal of certain social privileges (travel rights, housing, or employment). **Suppression** involves the widespread jailing of opposition leaders; withdrawing a group's legal status; destroying, banning or confiscating publications; disbanding meetings; and isolating the opposition from open society. Even more extreme measures such as assassinations, thuggery by government-sponsored paramilitary organizations, civil war, and even genocide may occur.

(DF) Dispense favor to cooptable members of opposition group—This is designed to weaken the support base of the opposition from within, thereby reducing cohesion and therefore threat. At its lower level (DF I), **co-opting** involves the ideological persuasion of group members to agree with the regime's position. It may also involve publicly identifying certain members of the opposition as having ties to or a post with the regime, fomenting dissent within the opposition's ranks. Bringing co-opted opposition members into the government allows the regime to exercise greater control over their actions and words. At the higher level (DF II), **bribery or a significant quid pro quo** is used by the regime, which offers money, favors, employment, or a reprieve from harassment to opposition members in exchange for their defection. It may be used to recruit opposition members to engage in illegal activity for the regime against the opposition (wiretapping, theft, etc.).

Indirect Tactics

(OP) Out-Persuade—This is used to compete for public support against the opposition. As substantial political power is gained in most regime-types through public support, this can be an important, often used tactic. It is indirect because it seeks to undermine the opposition through the public. At its lower level (OP I), **highlighting the differences** between the regime's interests/policy and the opposition's objectives is used to gain public favor. Naturally, the regime attempts to shed favorable light on its position while discrediting that of the opposition. The differences may not only be at the level of actual policy, but also concern for style, conduct (ethics), or long-term goals. At the higher level (OP II), the regime may choose to publicly **denounce** the group or an individual as treasonous or criminal. Rather than choosing between viewpoints, the public is now faced with an ideological judgment, and specific policies are by and large removed from discussion.

(DFNO) Dispense Favor to Non-Opposition Domestic Entities—This is designed to consolidate power and capabilities necessary to counter opposition threats. Favors, typically, are perquisites or privileges that the regime may dispense at will. These favors are never linked to core ideological or policy positions that the regime wishes to maintain. Therefore, a favor is given without sacrifice of policy content or control that is of interest to the regime. If such were the case, we would have moved to the realm of compromise. At the lower level (DFNO I), the regime establishes natural allegiances with legitimate favor recipients in the nation. These entities might include business leaders, prominent social figures or organizations, think tanks and universities, unions, ethnic or religious groups, and other organized and legal constituencies. We call these **natural allegiances**, and distinguish between natural and unnatural allegiances on the basis of the regime's risk in even talking to a group. If the risk is non-existent, we say the contact is natural or legitimate. If the risk is tremendous (if Israel's Shamir were to meet with the PLOs Arafat), the contact is unnatural or illegitimate. The dispensing of favor to legitimate recipients includes legal moves such as appointments to positions, coalitions, commissions, contracts, projects, grants, legislative favors, and so forth. The natural friends may be publicly praised, highlighted in press releases, offered financial assistance, or openly petitioned for advice or cooperation. Favor dispensation may also include unpublicized low-level illegal activity—such as excessive gratuities paid for nominal services, jobs unethically obtained, or unfair favoritism in the private sector.

At the higher level (DFNO II), a regime may find it desirable to engage in **unnatural allegiances**. One example might include higher risk favors to legitimate recipients. This may include financial schemes, economic intervention on behalf of the friends, PAG appointments that favor friends for the purpose of gaining power (not based on political qualifications), and legal irregularities. Also at this level, a regime may dispense favor to illegitimate recipients. As with legitimate recipients, this favor may be legal or illegal, but unlike in the case of legitimate recipients, even legal favor is purposefully never publicized by the regime. For example, criminal figures may be co-opted to carry out certain tasks; businessmen with shady reputations may be asked to participated in projects or coalitions otherwise inaccessible to them; and unions under attack for questionable practices may be given concessions over business interests.

(SEA) Solicit External Assistance—As most regimes have foreign allies, they may seek moral or material support from them in order to gain strength domestically. They may also solicit assistance from international organizations, such as the United Nations, if they can link their problems to an external threat. At the lower level SEA I), depending on the threat, a regime may only seek verbal approbation for itself or condemnation for its opposition. Yet, this request may also entail seeking financial assistance to ease economic problems that might appease an opposition source. A regime may seek material support for its armed forces as a way to offset opposition strength. At the higher level (SEA II), when the opposition threat seems more severe, the regime may ask its allies or other international bodies to intervene in its domestic affairs—either militarily, diplomatically, or economically.

(DE) Deflect/Eclipse—This tactic may also be called diversion because it involves regime attempts to divert attention away from the opposition and/or its activity. Alternatively, the regime simply overshadows the opposition with a higher profile concern. At the **lower** level (DE I), the regime may use propaganda to divert public and/or bureaucratic attention away from any opposition challenges. For example, the regime may choose to remind constituents and opponents alike about various threats to national security hovering over the nation; it may use public campaigns to draw attention to a social issue NOT addressed by the opposition. The regime may even engage in short-term bluffing. The regime may even attempt to draw attention from opposition concerns by appearing to take drastic measures in a policy field not related to current opposition demands. This ploy is designed to focus attention immediately on the regime's initiative, and is distinguishable from an actual policy move in that it generally lacks resolve and is short-lived. Nevertheless, such actions and all other level one deflections are more propaganda ploys than anything else.

Higher level tactics (DE II), however, represent a difference in degree. Rather than bluffing or enacting short-lived policies, the regime may implement specific economic, diplomatic, or even military policies that require the allocation of significant regime resources. If sufficient external threat is available, the regime may choose to engage in military conflict. Alternatively, with the help of allies and adversaries, the regime may engage in more positive activity by holding summit meetings, settling disputes, signing accords, or initiating joint projects. The goal is to capture attention and defuse the opposition through significant policy initiatives.

(RG) Restructure Government—In our particular use of this term, we are not referring to instances where the regime purges the ranks of the PAG as a way of dealing with proximate opposition. Those cases would appropriately be seen as examples of administering punishment, which is a direct tactic. As an indirect tactic, restructure government includes cases where the regime sacrifices certain of its own members—who are not in the opposition to the regime—for the sake of appeasing opposition forces. Though a restructuring of the government may take place within the context of compromise with the opposition, often it is the result not of a dialogue with the opposition, but a desire to placate it without having to actually compromise on policy content. For example, an unpopular Minister of Economics may be sacked—only to be replaced by someone with nearly identical views on economic policy. A minor (RG I) restructuring could include low-profile personnel resignations (forced or voluntary); the creation of minor commissions or agencies to research or investigate opposition concerns, or to provide new administration for problem programs; and/or minor organizational changes. Major (RG II) restructuring could entail critical constitutional changes; high-profile personnel resignation or dismissals; a significant cabinet reshuffling; the creation of major bureaucratic agencies to administer new or old programs; large-scale criminal or civil investigations into the activities of government personnel; and so forth.

(Comp) Compromise—Typically, but by no means in every case, this indicates the regime lacks the strength to maintain its authority through use of the other tactics. Minor compromises (COMP I) are used to stall for time, appease less radical opposition elements, defuse crisis situations, and set a framework for further dialogue when necessary. At the minor level, the regime sacrifices relatively little; but, as that could represent a major victory to the opposition (thereby settling the matter), it can be a powerful tool. Such small settlements can lend to regime credibility and strengthen the regime against further opposition. A major compromise (COMP II) is used to salvage a regime, avert disaster, or avoid revolt and war. It is the last resort tool of the regime for which other options are not viable, and represents a greater degree of sacrifice for the regime. What constitutes an acute sacrifice depends on the regime, but would generally include the loss of control (strength) in one or more of the values associated with fundamental needs.

APPENDIX A.3

Coding Rules for Opposition Characteristics

Proximity

Four spatial levels for potential opposition activity, each representing the locus of political behavior for one or more groups; in essence the question is how close the actor is to being a member of the ultimate decision unit (see Hermann, 1987).

(1) **Within Primary Advisory Group (PAG):** This group is drawn from cabinet and/or minister level officials appointed by the leader. It does not, however, include all such officials. Instead, the country expert identifies which posts have been the most prestigious in recent history as well as the appointees who oversee the departments/ministries clearly linked to the fulfillment of the regime's needs. Individuals who have the leader's ear but who are not members of the polity are not included because they have no authority to make decisions. The PAG is unlikely to include more than eight or ten people.

(2) **Outside the PAG but Within the Polity:** If the state has a unitary regime, this includes only non-PAG members of the government, elected members of the national representative assemblies (usually organized in parliamentary parties or similar coalitions), and higher level national civil servants. If it is a federal state, this includes the above plus regional governments (executives and legislatures) and highest level civil servants.

(3) **Outside the Polity But Within National Society:** This category may include a plethora of potential agents. The key characteristic of this group is that they do not hold a formal position in any state institution, although they may be represented by individuals within such institutions and usually lobby public officials for their interests. However, they have no public statutory authority at either the national or regional level.

(4) **Outside the National Society** (Foreign Based): This category includes two basic groups of actors. The first are those individuals or groups who are legally barred from entering and residing in the country because of their political beliefs. These opponents are allowed no legal representation within the polity or national society of the country under study. It should be noted that although barred from residence, they still may in fact reside inside the nation's boundaries. The second group refers to actors whose ultimate decision unit is located in another country and who cannot respond to state directives without the approval of that foreign-based decision-maker. Examples of this include some multinational corporations, some churches, and perhaps a few terrorist organizations. This category does not include foreign governments nor their officially recognized diplomatic emissaries in the country—certainly some foreign governments represent a genuine threat to some regimes, but the dynamic of that relationship lies beyond the purview of our framework.

Ideological Salience

The concept of ideological salience contains two elements: whether the opposition group's ideological base is roughly congruent or recognizably dissimilar to the regimes; and whether the opposition accepts current institutional practices for resolving domestic conflict or advocates their replacement.

(1) **High Ideological Salience:** (a) The actor espouses an ideology that is either at one extreme of the political spectrum (if the regime is of a centrist-moderate orientation) or clearly on the opposite side of the spectrum (if the regime is clearly identified with one side of the right-left spectrum); and (b) the actor has called for the dismantling of the current institutional structure of the state during the regime's period of rule (This could include calls for a new constitution, appeals for popular revolution, or requests for a military coup.).

(2) **Moderate Ideological Salience:** Either (a) or (b), but not both.

(3) **Low Ideological Salience:** Neither (a) nor (b).

Cohesiveness

Organizational cohesiveness is defined in terms of group structures and discipline. Hence a group splintered by feuding factions is a much less compelling opponent than one enjoying organizational discipline and freedom from divisions (Hagan, 1988). There are six basic levels of cohesiveness.

(1) **Operationally Cohesive:** The group is disciplined and there is a high degree of regimentation under the uncontested leadership of a single person or group that has full decision-making autonomy.

(2) Less Cohesive—**Informal Schisms Within the Group:** The group remains under the direction of an uncontested leader (individual or unified group of leaders), but decision-making autonomy of the leadership is occasionally constrained by policy differences within the membership of the organization so that action cannot be taken without some consultation with representatives of divergent viewpoints.

(3) Less Cohesive—**Formal Cliques Within Group:** the group remains under the direction of an uncontested leader but divisions within the body of the organization are formally recognized with ad hoc caucusing agreements, and policy decisions are not taken without formal consultation with the members of the group and these decisions are the result of consensus rather than ratification of a command decision.

(4) Less Cohesive—**Institutionalized Factions Within Group:** the group has the same characteristics listed in #3; in addition, divergent factions within the group are represented by some sort of delegate within the leadership of the group so that activity among the group leadership must also proceed by a process of bargaining and consensus-building.

(5) Less Cohesive—**Splintered Sub-Groups Within Last Three Months:** the group has been reduced in numerical size within the last three months because of the defection of members who have set up their own rival organization with an independent decision-making base.

(6) **Least Cohesive:** No Recognized Group Leadership: the group is a group in name only; there is no uncontested decision-making unit, instead several distinct organizations operate with informal rules of cooperation and coordination.

Size

There are various questions that are asked when determining the size of a group. Some of them are listed here. How many people can a group mobilize in day to day operations to bring immediate pressure on the fulfillment of the regime's needs? How many registered members are with the group, if registration exists? How many seats do they hold in the parliament, if a legitimate political organization? How many have joined any recent demonstrations? Categories are difficult to determine because of differences in population sizes and other variables, but the graphic representation of the size is depicted in either small, medium, or large. The country expert will determine which category the group belongs in given the answers to these questions and any other related questions that are pertinent to the situation.

APPENDIX B.1

STRENGTH PRE-REQUISITES FOR TACTIC APPLICATION

While many values would be useful and helpful in securing maximum gain, there are only a few that are necessary for a regime to even apply the tactic. This is a list of the **minimum** strength requirements for a regime to apply a given tactic. And the regime must have **moderately strong** control in the listed values to apply the tactic. A **weak** showing is unacceptable, and makes use of the tactic impossible.

TACTIC	STRENGTH PRE-REQUISITES	JUSTIFICATION
STIG	none	by definition
AP I	a) policy-making procedure b) knowledge	a) to order punishment b) to know targets and monitor effects
AP II	a) stable military b) manipulation of symbols c) external threat d) cooperative bureaucracy	a) in control, will not escalate, and will execute orders b) to justify actions to public and constituents c) to blame for opposition, and justify severity of punishment d) to implement longer-term punishment, to effectively hinder opposition members
DF I	a) policy-making procedure b) communication c) manipulation of symbols	a) to authoritatively co-opt opposition member b) to have dialogue with cooptable individuals c) to convince and persuade

TACTIC	STRENGTH PRE-REQUISITES	JUSTIFICATION
DF II	a) policy-making procedure b) knowledge c) cooperative bureaucracy d) communication	a) to avoid obstacles to bribing and other defined tactics b) to find suitable contacts in opposition for bribery or quid pro quo c) to participate in dispensing favor d) with those targeted members of opposition
OP I	a) manipulation of symbols	a) as propaganda tool in public campaign of issues
OP II	a) policy-making procedure b) manipulation of symbols c) external threat d) external support	a) to make it a matter of gov't policy that opp. group is denounced b) in propaganda campaign c) to link opp. group to for strong denunciation d) that continues to support, as legitimacy for action
DFNO I	a) policy-making procedure b) cooperative bureaucracy	a) to dispense favor without hindrance b) to participate in favor granting (jobs, etc.) without hindering regime
DFNO II	a) policy-making procedure b) cooperative bureaucracy c) knowledge	a) to act, legally or illegally without serious challenge b) to participate in activity without hindering, and to facilitate illegal activity c) to monitor targets, to gain unnatural friends, to engage in illegal activity
SEA I	a) external support b) international recognition c) policy-making procedure	a) must be there to seek b) to retain international legitimacy during action c) to initiate diplomatic procedure with other nations or groups

TACTIC	STRENGTH PRE-REQUISITES	JUSTIFICATION
SEA II	a) external support b) international recognition c) policy-making procedure d) legislative procedure e) cooperative bureaucracy f) manipulation of symbols	a) there to be sought b) to retain legitimacy during activity, especially when intervention is called for c) to initiate and oversee cooperation with external support source d) to gain legislative permission or acceptance for external assistance e) to implement necessary programs as required by intervening party or regime during external assistance f) to use in propaganda to justify actions
DE I	a) external support b) manipulation of symbols c) policy-making procedure d) external threat	a) for positive interaction that would deflect attention b) to persuade parties to consider other matters c) to initiate low-level diversion activity d) for propaganda and/or negative interaction
DE II	a) stable military b) manipulation of symbols c) international recognition d) policy-making procedure e) external support f) external threat	a) when military diversions are used, to remain in control, and not revolt b) to justify actions, gain public support c) to retain legitimacy if action is negative or to use in creating positive interaction for diversion d) to sign treaties, declare war, implement new programs e) as back-up in war, to sign agreements with, for stability f) to war with, to threaten war, to blame, to agitate
RG I	a) policy-making procedure b) knowledge	a) for authority to make changes b) to monitor inner-gov't opposition, to strategically target positions or policies that pose least threat to regime

TACTIC	STRENGTH PRE-REQUISITES	JUSTIFICATION
RG II	a) policy-making procedure b) legislative procedure c) knowledge d) stable military e) electoral majority f) manipulation of symbols g) cooperative bureaucracy h) international recognition i) external support	a) to carry out restructuring without hindrance b) to keep from losing position upon restructuring and to gain necessary legal permission to make changes c) to monitor and target d) to keep from revolting when change occurs e) to have necessary votes for any constitutional changes f) justification/propaganda g) to not impede changes h) to retain legitimacy despite action, or to make change without intervention i) to lend to international recognition
Comp I	a) policy-making procedure b) manipulation of symbols c) communication	a) to initiate process and make agreements b) to explain and justify action c) to know opposition goals and reach a compromise
Comp II	a) policy-making procedure b) legislative procedure c) communication	a) to initiate process and finalize agreements b) to gain support for compromise, and push for any legislation necessary to meet terms of agreement c) to have dialogue with opp. group, and reach a settlement.

APPENDIX B.2

ANTICIPATE VALUE INVENTORY

TACTIC	EXPECTED GAINS	EXPECTED REDUCTIONS
STIG	Policy Making Procedure* Stable Military Legislative Procedure Stable Economy Electoral Majority Manipulation of Symbols* Public Support Friendly Press Ecclesiastical Endorsement External Support	Policy Making Procedure Knowledge/Feedback Stable Military Legislative Procedure Stable Economy Electoral Majority Manipulation of Symbols Public Support* Friendly Press* Cooperative Bureaucracy Ecclesiastical Endorsement Communication* External Support

TACTIC	EXPECTED GAINS	EXPECTED REDUCTIONS
AP I	Policy Making Procedure Knowledge/Feedback Stable Military Manipulation of Symbols Cooperative Bureaucracy	Public Support Friendly Press Ecclesiastical Endorsement Communication
AP II	Policy Making Procedure* Stable Military* Cooperative Bureaucracy* Electoral Majority* Manipulation of Symbols* Friendly Press	Stable Economy Stable Military Territorial Integrity Knowledge/Feedback Public Support* Friendly Press* Ecclesiastical Endorsement* Communication* International Recognition* External Support
DF I	Stable Military Policy Making Procedure Legislative Procedure Manipulation of Symbols Friendly Press Cooperative Bureaucracy Ecclesiastical Endorsement	Cooperative Bureaucracy
DF II	Policy Making Procedure* Legislative Procedure* Stable Military Knowledge/Feedback*	Electoral Majority* Manipulation of Symbols* Public Support* Friendly Press* Cooperative Bureaucracy* Ecclesiastical Endorsement* Communication
OP I	Legislative Procedure Public Support	Public Support Manipulation of Symbols
OP II	Policy Making Procedure* Legislative Procedure* Public support* External Threat Friendly Press* Electoral Majority* Cooperative Bureaucracy*	Electoral Majority Manipulation of Symbols* Public support Friendly Press Cooperative Bureaucracy Ecclesiastical Endorsement Communication* External Support

TACTIC	EXPECTED GAINS	EXPECTED REDUCTIONS
DFNO I	Policy Making Procedure Knowledge/Feedback Stable Military Legislative Procedure Electoral Majority Cooperative Bureaucracy Ecclesiastical Endorsement	Public Support Friendly Press
DFNO II	Policy Making Procedure* Knowledge/Feedback* Stable Military* Legislative Procedure* Stable Economy* Electoral Majority Cooperative Bureaucracy External Support External Threat	Stable Military Stable Economy Electoral Majority* Public Support* Friendly Press* Cooperative Bureaucracy* Ecclesiastical Endorsement* Communication* External Support
SEA I	Policy Making Procedure Stable Military Stable Economy Public Support Cooperative Bureaucracy	Manipulation of Symbols Cooperative Bureaucracy Public support Friendly Press Ecclesiastical Endorsement Communication External Support
SEA II	Stable Military* External Support* Stable Economy* External Threat*	Stable Economy* Territorial Integrity* Stable Military* Policy Making Procedure* Electoral Majority* Public Support* Friendly Press* Cooperative Bureaucracy* Ecclesiastical Endorsement* Communication* Manipulation of Symbols* External Support* External Threat* International Recognition*
DE I	Policy Making Procedure Legislative Procedure Manipulation of Symbols Cooperative Bureaucracy	Manipulation of Symbols Public Support Friendly Press Ecclesiastical Endorsement External Threat External Support

TACTIC	EXPECTED GAINS	EXPECTED REDUCTIONS
DE II	Territorial Integrity*	Policy Making Procedure
	Policy Making Procedure*	Stable Military
	Knowledge/Feedback*	Stable Economy
	Stable Military*	Legislative Procedure
	Legislative Procedure*	Manipulation of Symbols*
	Stable Economy*	Public Support*
	Manipulation of Symbols*	Electoral Majority*
	Electoral Majority*	Friendly Press*
	Public Support*	Cooperative Bureaucracy*
	Friendly Press*	Ecclesiastical Endorsement*
	Cooperative Bureaucracy*	Communication*
	Communication*	External Support*
	Ecclesiastical Endorsement*	
	External Threat*	
RG I	Policy Making Procedure	Manipulation of Symbols
	Knowledge/Feedback	Electoral Majority
	Legislative Procedure	Public Support
	Stable Military	Friendly Press
	Public Support	Cooperative Bureaucracy
	Friendly Press	Communication
	Cooperative Bureaucracy	
	Communication	
	Ecclesiastical Endorsement	
	External Support	
	External Threat	
RG II	Policy Making Procedure*	Stable Economy
	Knowledge/Feedback*	Stable Military*
	Stable Military*	Knowledge/Feedback*
	Legislative Procedure*	Electoral Majority*
	Stable Economy	Manipulation of Symbols*
	Electoral Majority*	Public Support*
	Public Support*	Friendly Press*
	Friendly Press*	Cooperative Bureaucracy*
	Cooperative Bureaucracy*	Ecclesiastical Endorsement*
	Communication*	Communication*
	Ecclesiastical Endorsement*	External Threat
	International Recognition	
	External Support	
	External Threat	

TACTIC	EXPECTED GAINS	EXPECTED REDUCTIONS
Comp I	Policy Making Procedure Knowledge/Feedback Legislative procedure Stable Economy Electoral Majority Public Support Friendly Press Cooperative Bureaucracy Communication	Electoral Majority Public Support Friendly Press Cooperative Bureaucracy Communication
Comp II	Territorial Integrity Policy Making Procedure Stable Economy* Manipulation of Symbols* Communication*	Territorial Integrity Knowledge/Feedback Stable Military Legislative Procedure* Stable Economy Electoral Majority* Manipulation of Symbols* Public Support* Friendly Press* Cooperative Bureaucracy* Ecclesiastical Endorsement* Communication* External Support International Recognition

* Denotes that the expected gain or reduction in strength will be severe (or take more than one step). That is, there will be a greater jump or decrease in control over that value, depending on the success or failure of the application of the tactic.

4

Neither Compromise nor Compliance

INTERNATIONAL PRESSURES, SOCIETAL INFLUENCE,
AND THE POLITICS OF DECEPTION
IN THE INTERNATIONAL DRUG TRADE

H. Richard Friman

The United States is at "war" with countries exporting cocaine and heroin in the 1990s, just as it was at war with exporters of cocaine in the 1980s, of heroin and marijuana in the 1970s, of marijuana in the 1960s, of alcohol during the 1920s and early 1930s, and of cocaine and opium and its derivatives from the early 1900s to the late 1930s (Taylor, 1969; Brecher, 1972; Musto, 1973; Simmons and Said, 1974; Bruun, Pan, Rexed, 1975; Walker, 1981). The need for recurrent drug wars often against the same countries—such as Columbia, Mexico, and Peru—and the same drugs, however, suggests that victories have been the exception rather than the rule (Walker, 1981; Bagley, 1988; Nadelmann, 1988; Tokatlin, 1988). Yet, despite this track record, American strategy has consistently relied on the use of external pressure to attempt to force drug-exporting countries to cooperate with the United States (Office, 1989).

As suggested by societal and state-centered theoretical approaches to the study of foreign economic policy, however, the logic of American strategy may be flawed (Ikenberry, Lake, Mastanduno, 1988). Specifically, both approaches contend that policy makers in target countries are likely to face domestic as well as international pressures. Although noting specific conditions under which domestic factors may hold sway, scholars from both approaches have suggested that policy makers seek to reconcile the dictates of contending pressures. Building on these arguments, Robert Putnam (1988) has noted that rather than simply complying with either domestic or international pressures, policy makers turn to strategies of compromise. In contrast, this chapter argues that as contending pressures increase, policy makers in target countries are more likely to turn to strategies of domestic and/or international deception.

This chapter, therefore, seeks to challenge the American premise that international pressure leads to cooperation as well as the theoretical debate concerning the domestic and international sources of foreign policy. It does so by exploring the American premise against two counter arguments: 1) domestic political pressure determines the extent to which policy makers comply with the demands of other countries; 2) policy makers respond to increases in contending international and domestic pressures with deception rather than compromise or compliance.

The first section derives the three hypotheses from debates in the international political economy literature. The second section offers a preliminary test of the hypotheses against two cases drawn from the first American drug war. The final section discusses the tentative implications of the chapter's findings for the theoretical analysis of foreign policy formulation and for the substantive area of American drug policy.

INTERNATIONAL PRESSURES, DOMESTIC POLITICS, AND DECEPTION

An extensive portion of the international political economy literature has sought to identify and determine the relative importance of international and domestic sources of foreign economic policy. The result has been the emergence of a basic premise that policy makers face both international and domestic pressures, and considerable debate over the impact of such pressures.[1] Commenting on the latter, Putnam (1988, 430) has accurately noted that theoretical development at this international-domestic nexus remains a primary research task for the literature. This section draws on the scholarly debate to derive three broad hypotheses concerning the dynamics of foreign policy formulation in target states.

H1: *External pressure on target states leads to their cooperation with the sanctioning state.*

This hypothesis, which basically restates the American premise, draws on realist and neorealist arguments concerning the dynamics of the inter-

---

1. The literature here is extensive. For example, see Krasner (1976; 1978; 1983), Lake (1988a), Keohane (1984), Keohane and Nye (1977), Gourevitch (1986), Katzenstein (1978a; 1985), Ikenberry et al. (1988), Shannon (1989), Rogowski (1989), and Milner and Yoffie (1989).

national system.[2] As argued by Kenneth Waltz (1979), states exist as the primary actors in an international system distinguished by anarchy—the absence of a supranational authority to guarantee the security and independence of the system's members. To ensure self-preservation, states turn to the pursuit of power. Although concerned with absolute power, states, according to Joseph Grieco (1990, 36-49), place greater emphasis on relative gains and losses. More precisely, states act as "defensive positionalists" avoiding steps that will undercut their power relative to that of other states in the international system. In this sense, the dynamics of international anarchy can inhibit cooperation among states. If a cooperative arrangement—defined by Grieco (1990, 22) as states turning to the voluntary adjustment of their behavior "to reach some mutually beneficial outcome"—is likely to undercut a state's relative power, the state will choose not to participate.

Drawing on classical realist arguments, however, Robert Keohane (1984, 73-74, 248) notes that choice in international relations is usually not a "purely voluntary" act. Decisions made where states are "equal in power or...their actions...are unconstrained" by fears of external coercion are rare. States are more likely to make choices in the context of constraints stemming from the relative power of other states.[3] Thus, although states may prefer not to enter into arrangements that adversely affect their relative power, they may be pressured into doing so when faced with the threat or actual use of force from stronger states.

For example, Hans Morgenthau (1973, 521) has argued that to resolve the conflicting objectives of different states, policy makers can turn to two forms of external pressure—diplomacy and force. The means of diplomacy consist of persuasion, compromise, and the threat of force. Morgenthau posits that the intelligent strategy in gaining foreign compliance from a target state, short of exercising force, is to combine all three. As argued by Waltz (1979, 113-14), "the constant possibility that force will be used limits manipulations, moderates demands, and serves as an incentive for the settlement of disputes." Waltz also notes that the competitive nature of international politics suggests that states will at times need the cooperation of others to achieve self-preservation (i.e., in turning to balancing or in preventing others from aligning against you). In order to keep this option open, states "socialize" themselves to the system: "conforming to common international practices even though for internal reasons they would prefer not to" (Waltz 1979, 127-28).

---

2. Given the chapter's substantive focus on the American premise, I explore those "international" arguments that appear to lend theoretical support to U.S. drug strategy.

3. For detail on the neoliberal challenge to realist arguments on international cooperation, see Keohane (1990:1-20, 158-79).

From the standpoint of analyzing foreign economic policy, however, the utility of the argument that external pressure leads to cooperation is partially undercut by a systemic-level focus that treats states as like and cohesive units. For example, Waltz's stated intent is to develop a systemic-level theory of international politics rather than a unit-level theory of foreign policy (1979, 95-97). Similarly, Grieco (1990, 24) takes a systemic-level focus to defend realism from the systemic-level counterarguments raised by neoliberal institutionalism as to the dynamics of international anarchy. Although both Waltz and Grieco acknowledge that states have internal as well as external considerations, they do not analyze the former in a systematic manner. By arguing that states conform to international practices over internal considerations, Waltz implicitly assumes that policy makers are able to ignore domestic pressures. In contrast, Grieco (1990, 24) notes the potential for constraints on policy makers stemming from "domestic political institutions and dynamics." Yet, by arguing that state actions are primarily based on considerations of relative power, Grieco discounts how policy makers in target countries would balance international and domestic considerations.

H2: *Domestic political pressure determines the extent to which policy makers cooperate with the demands of other countries.*

The second hypothesis draws upon societal and state-centric arguments concerning the domestic sources of foreign economic policy (Ikenberry, et al. 1988, 7-14). As argued by Peter Gourevitch (1984, 1986), for example, policy choices are not solely determined by a country's relative position in the international system. Although international pressures can suggest specific policy alternatives, policy choices are primarily shaped by domestic factors. Of these, the interplay between ruling politicians and changing coalitions of societal forces and their representative associations are the most important. Gourevitch (1986, 64-65, 222-38) posits that to gain and/or maintain domestic political support, ruling politicians will select those policy alternatives that reflect the preferences of dominant societal coalitions. The international economic situation of specific societal groups shapes their preferences and, in turn, the demands of their representative associations (Gourevitch, 1984; Milner, 1988). In contrast to realist arguments, therefore, policy makers in target countries are likely to comply with international pressures when faced with strong societal pressure for such a stance and resist such compliance when faced with strong societal pressure to do so.

Although societal groups can directly affect politicians through electoral pressure, state-centric approaches suggest that not all policy makers are politicians especially in countries with strong bureaucracies. More important, scholars such as Stephen Krasner (1978) and Peter Katzenstein (1978b) have demonstrated that elections are only one channel of access to the policy making process and not necessarily the channel providing societal groups with the greatest influence over that process. The structure of state institutions—specifically the fragmentation of state power and authority across such institutions—as well as institutional arrangements linking state and society (Katzenstein's "policy network") determine the number and nature of the channels of access to the policy making process available to societal interest groups. Thus, although dominant interest groups are unlikely to be ignored by policy makers, societal strength alone is not sufficient to determine policy. Societal interest groups must also gain access to those state institutions—in part by gaining the support of those officials staffing said institutions—able to influence the policy making process (Friman, 1990).

One difficulty with this combined approach, however, is that like its component parts, it discounts international pressures (Ikenberry, et al. 1988, 7-14; Putnam 1988, 430-33). More precise, the hypothesis reflects an implicit assumption that domestic pressures can under specific conditions force policy makers to act in a manner that precludes a conciliatory response to international pressures. For example, Gourevitch (1986), Krasner (1978), and Katzenstein (1978b) all acknowledge that policy makers face international and domestic pressures. By recasting international pressures as sets of policy options that may or may not have the support of dominant societal coalitions, however, Gourevitch's work suggests that societal groups determine whether policy makers follow or contradict international pressure. For Krasner's statist approach, the more fragmented a state's structure, the greater the likelihood that central decision-makers will simply be forced to comply with the dictates of strong societal interest groups. Although Katzenstein's original work on domestic structures (1978b) illustrates the same problem as Krasner's statist approach, his more recent work on "small states" suggests that for certain types of countries, at least, international pressures set parameters within which societal forces must act. In larger states such as the United States, Great Britain, France, Germany, and Japan, however, domestic dynamics still appear to be able to override international pressures (Katzenstein, 1985).

H3: Policy makers respond to increases in contending international and domestic pressures with deception rather than compromise or compliance.

This hypothesis starts from the assumption that policy makers will seek to respond to both domestic and international pressures. States are organizations consisting of differentiated institutions and holding primacy of place within a given territory as the center or focal point of political relations. As such, states lie at the juncture of domestic and international pressures (Skocpol 1979, 30-32; Mann 1987, 112; Nordlinger 1988, 881-84). The task of responding to these pressures is made more complex by the rarity of states acting as cohesive units. As argued by Putnam (1988, 432), in addition to the conflicts between the executive and the legislature that characterize most advanced industrial states, divisions usually exist within the executive itself. More broadly, the primary state officials in a given issue area—hereinafter referred to as policy makers—can face varying degrees of input from other state officials into the policy making process. Thus, policy makers are by virtue of their position "directly exposed" to societal, state, and international pressures and, in turn, "have a special role in mediating" such pressures.

Societal pressures on policy makers can consist of the electoral costs of ignoring dominant coalitions of societal interest groups and/or the costs of ignoring threats to the country's domestic economic, political, and social stability stemming from such groups. Elected policy makers rely on direct electoral support while politically appointed policy makers rely on indirect support. Policy makers falling into neither of these categories, such as career bureaucrats, are likely to place more emphasis on domestic stability. Political stability, for example, refers to state-societal interaction through institutionalized channels rather than street demonstrations or violent protest. Economic stability refers to considerations such as economic growth, low unemployment and inflation while social stability includes considerations such as the health of the domestic population (Downs, 1957; Gourevitch, 1986; Putnam, 1988; Swank, 1988).

Where interest groups turn to institutionalized access channels aside from the electoral process, by contrast, state pressure comes into play as well. Within democratic countries, and to a lesser degree in nondemocratic countries (Comisso, 1986; Tyson, 1986), the institutional structure of the state is fragmented such that channels exist for societal interest groups and their state supporters to influence the policy making process. Although greater degrees of fragmentation of state power and authority across state institutions offer a greater potential for interest groups to influence state policy, such groups must still capture or gain the support of those portions of the state that lead to binding influence over the policy making process (Frieden 1988; Friman, 1990). More precisely, state pressure can include state officials exercising oversight or control over the financial resources available to policy makers, holding the legislative initiatives of policy makers hostage, and, at the extreme, exercising their authority to dictate policy over the opposition of policy makers.

The presence of societal and state constraints, however, does not imply that all countries are able to act in such a way that fully contradicts international pressures nor are policy makers, their country's ability aside, always willing to do so. International pressures refer to the severity of threats and/or actions invoked by a sanctioning country against a target country. These threats and actions can include the exercise or threat of military force, the exercise or threat of economic sanctions, and the exercise of diplomatic sanctions. It is important to note, however, that not all target countries necessarily face these threats. Specifically, the options of international pressure available to sanctioning countries are not always viable in a given dispute. For example, the relative political-military and economic capabilities of the sanctioning and target countries can shape the ability of the latter to ignore specific international pressures (Hufbauer and Schott, 1985). Yet, recounting Waltz (1979), those target countries that ignore international pressures can place prospects for future cooperation at risk including potential assistance in dealing with other aggressors. Similarly, Putnam (1988, 434) notes that the choice of policy makers to simply ignore international pressures in favor of domestic considerations can lead to international costs such as foregoing the prospect of current and future cooperation by other countries (including the sanctioning country) across an array of issue areas.

The assumption that policy makers are unlikely to completely act contrary to either international or domestic considerations—by turning to full compliance with the demands of the sanctioning country or the demands of dominant societal groups—still fails to answer the question of *how* policy makers will respond to international and domestic pressure. Putnam (1988, 435-41) contends that policy makers seek to mitigate pressures through compromise: choosing the policy that falls in the range of acceptability of both the contending groups that comprise the policy maker's domestic constituency and the policy maker's counterparts in international negotiations.[4] Yet, for the reasons noted above, granting domestic and international actors that which they will reluctantly accept rather than that which they ideally want entails political costs. Policy makers may be able to reduce these costs through side payments (concessions) aimed at easing the extent of domestic and/or international pressures. Yet, opportunities for side payments are not always possible nor do ready compromises always exist.

The third hypothesis contends that rather than compliance or compromise, policy makers are more likely to turn to deception—the "deliberate concealment or misrepresentation of truth with intent to lead another into error or disadvantage"—to bridge domestic and international pressures (American 1969, 342). In this context, strategies of deception rely on cheating and the use of ambiguity. First, policy makers can cheat on existing

---

4. Putnam is not alone in arguing that policy makers seek to reconcile contending pressures and do so with strategies that partially meet the dictates of both. For example, see Milner and Yoffie (1989) and Evans (1989).

formal and informal agreements and arrangements by violating their specific provisions. Second, policy makers can negotiate ambiguity into formal and informal agreements and arrangements to facilitate action contrary to their intent. David Yoffie (1983, 26-28, 31-34) has focused on how developing countries use cheating and ambiguity to counteract protectionist pressures in developed countries. In this chapter, by contrast, I propose the broader existence of a politics of deception that can be used by developed and developing target countries alike as a strategy for dealing with international and domestic pressures.

Deception has been relatively understudied in a systematic manner by the literature on foreign economic policy. For example, game theoretic analyses of international cooperation as well as portions of the regime literature address the issue of states cheating on agreements with each other and the need for international frameworks to inhibit such action. This literature, however, devotes little systematic analysis to either the issue of states turning to ambiguity with the intent to deceive or the domestic-international dynamics that lead to international deception (Keohane, 1984; Oye, 1986; Keohane, 1989). Due to a systemic focus, this literature also does not address the potential for policy makers in target countries to aim deception at domestic as well as international actors. Similarly, despite incorporating a unit-level focus, neither Gourevitch (1986), Krasner (1978), nor Katzenstein (1978b, 1985) discusses deception as a strategy for responding to domestic and/or international pressures.

Deception enables policy makers in target countries to appear to turn to compromise or compliance. Policy makers reduce the costs of compromise or compliance by misleading domestic and/or international actors into believing that they have each gained more than is actually the case. The inherent contradiction of turning to deception, however, is that the policy is ultimately untenable. As the deception is discovered, policy makers are increasingly placed back in the initial position of having to deal with contending pressures. In addition, they may also face a backlash of retaliation—domestic and/or international—in response to the deception coming to light. Domestic and international actors may tolerate deception but only up to a certain point. For example, Putnam (1988, 434) notes that in the two-level game of policy makers seeking to balance domestic and international pressures "players (and kibitzers) will tolerate some differences in rhetoric between the two games but in the end" policy must be consistent. Yoffie (1983, 32-33) also argues that countries can turn to cheating as long as it is kept within "tolerable levels." Once this point is passed, policy makers may face greater pressures than they started out with.

The bottom line and attractiveness of a strategy of deception as an alternative for policy makers, however, is that the costs of deception in contrast to the immediate costs of compliance or cooperation come due sometime in the future. Moreover, as argued by Jon Elster (1985, 7-8), the typical "time preferences" of individuals tend to "attach less weight to future consumption or utility than to present." In effect, policy makers trade long-term costs for short-term gains. Game theoretic arguments on iterated games, by contrast, contend that individuals are less likely to discount the future and defect from cooperative arrangements—and thereby gain a reputation for defection—if they must deal with the same players in the future (Haggard and Simmons 1987, 504-6). Yet, this argument assumes that the defection is discovered by these players. More precise, defection in a game-theoretic sense, and the adverse effects of defection, would not occur until the deception is discovered and, to borrow from Yoffie (1983, 32-33), exceeds the level of tolerance of those international and/or domestic actors exerting pressure on policy makers.

NEITHER COMPROMISE NOR COMPLIANCE

This section offers a preliminary test of the three hypotheses against two cases drawn from the first war on drugs waged by the United States. Although real differences exist between these historic cases and contemporary drug problems, the former illustrate the initial implementation and foreign reaction to the American premise. As such, they provide an ideal starting point for testing the American premise against the two contending hypotheses. Moreover, they suggest a pattern of how policy makers respond to contending pressures that lends support for additional research into the dynamics of deception. Methodologically, these cases rely on process-tracing. Through secondary sources and archival data, the case studies trace the decisions by policy makers in target countries to determine the extent to which societal, state, and international pressures were actually reflected in specific policy choices (Aggarwal 1985, 38-39).

Beginning in the early 1900s, the United States and Great Britain were the two major powers that shaped the parameters of international regulations on the trade of drugs of abuse and addiction. More important, the British—as the largest producers and traders of opium through colonial holdings in India—bore the brunt of American pressure. Domestically, British policy makers faced pressure from pro-and anti-opium forces as well.[5]

How did British policy makers respond to international and domestic pressures?[6] In 1906, domestic pressure led to a formal British condemnation

---

5. British policy makers on the issue of the international drug trade during the period of the two case studies consisted of the Secretaries of State for Foreign Affairs, India, and the Colonies, the Director of the Board of Trade, and the Prime Minister.

6. Due to the focus of this article, I do not systematically address why U.S. pressure emerged. Although important, several historians have addressed this issue in detail including Musto (1973), Stein (1985), and Taylor (1979).

of the opium trade and a pledge for its elimination. In response to U.S. pressure, British policy makers agreed to participate in the Shanghai Opium Commission of 1909 and the Hague Opium Conference of 1911-12 aimed at controlling the international drug trade. Rather than compliance or compromise, however, process-tracing reveals that these British responses were all tainted by deception.

CASE I: United States Versus Great Britain: 1906-09

Although both Americans and the British had been active in the opium trade to China during the 1800s, Great Britain dominated the trade. The East India Company and later the British Crown utilized a monopoly over the production and sale of Indian opium to generate revenues for India's colonial government estimated at $50,000,000 annually. As a result, efforts by the Chinese government to halt the opium trade were met with strong British opposition—as seen in the Opium War of 1839 and the legalization of opium imports under British pressure in 1858. Although the United States government formally withdrew support for American involvement in the opium trade to China during the 1880s, by the early 1900s the British government had not followed suit (Owen, 1934; Stelle, 1941; Lowes, 1966; Stein, 1985).

Concerned that the United States was being shut out of China by the British and the Japanese, and facing domestic pressure from missionaries, reform organizations, prohibition groups and their Congressional supporters, American policy makers began to exert pressure on Great Britain. The initial diplomatic overtures in 1905 and 1906 were limited to suggestions for international treaties to prohibit "the sale of intoxicants and opium to all uncivilized races" (Taylor 1969, 28-30; Musto 1973, 24-29; Stein 1985, 29-48). On October 17, 1906, however, the U.S. Ambassador approached the British Foreign Secretary on the idea of a joint international commission to investigate the Far Eastern opium trade. The positive British response the following month to the idea of such an investigation, however, had less to do with American pressure and more to do with changes in Britain's domestic politics (Taylor 1979, 24-25; Musto 1973, 29; Stein 1985, 50).

Domestic Politics. Domestic support for the Crown's stance on the opium trade had traditionally come from individuals who "were or had been in the employ of the government of India, or were responsible for defending its policies in the Commons" (Stein 1985, 14-15). In contrast, societal pressure from organized interest groups opposed to British policy, and state pressure on the behalf of such groups, did not emerge in noticeable force until the establishment of the Anglo-Oriental Society for the Suppression of the Opium Trade (SSOT) in 1874 (Johnson 1975, 309, 320). By 1888, anti-opium forces had grown to include the populist Christian Union for the Severance of the Connection of the British Empire from the Opium Traffic, the Women's Anti-Opium Urgency Committee, the Friends' Anti-Opium Committee for Suffering, the Edinburgh Committee for the Suppression of the Indo-Chinese Opium Traffic, and the Anglican Anti-Opium Committee. In 1894, the strength of the anti-opium alliance was increased further by the establishment of the Representative Board of the British Anti-Opium Societies (BBAOS) linking the individual associations (Johnson 1975, 310; Stein 1985, 9-10, 16).

The SSOT's combination of extensive organization and financial resources contributed to its impact on the British political debate. From 1874 to 1893, the SSOT's influence increased as it garnered the support of Liberal and some Conservative Party members of Parliament. In 1891, the SSOT with strong backing from Liberal members of parliament had pressed for a parliamentary resolution to declare the opium monopoly system in India "morally indefensible" and call for its elimination. Cabinet—especially top officials in the India, Foreign, and Colonial Offices—and Conservative Party opposition, however, led to the resolution's defeat. The following year the potential for state pressure on the behalf of anti-opium forces appeared to have increased with the electoral victory of the Liberal Party. Yet, although three SSOT members became part of the new cabinet under Prime Minister William Gladstone, the Secretary of State for India as well as the majority of the cabinet remained opposed to suppressing the opium trade (Owen 1934, 311-14; Johnson 1975, 307-10; Stein 1985, 9).

Concerned over potential cabinet resistance to a renewed attempt at the 1891 resolution, SSOT supporters in Parliament introduced in 1893 what they saw as a compromise resolution calling for the establishment of a Royal Commission to study how the opium trade could be suppressed in India and England. Faced with what appeared to be rising state pressure on behalf of anti-opium groups, Gladstone did not ignore the resolution but instead proposed an alternative compromise. Backing an amendment proposed by the India Office, Gladstone called for a Royal Commission that would only study the medical, revenue, and regulatory aspects of the opium question in India and England. Gladstone's proposal took advantage of the fact that the initial proposal by the SSOT had focused more on establishing a Royal Commission than the scope of the commission's inquiry. Since the SSOT proposal had mentioned India and England but not China, Gladstone's compromise ruled out a focus on the impact of the Indian trade on China. In addition, the questions of the morality raised in the 1891 resolution failed to appear in the commission's focus. Despite opposition by the SSOT to Gladstone's "compromise," the measure passed in Parliament with strong Conservative Party backing and a split Liberal Party vote (Owen 1934, 313-17; Johnson 1975, 307-10).

As the commission conducted its investigations over the next two years, British policy makers were essentially insulated from domestic pressure. SSOT representatives had approved the membership of the commission and had come to assume that the eventual report would support the anti-opium cause. Much to the dismay of the SSOT, the other associations of the newly formed BBAOS, and their state supporters, however, the commission's findings released in 1895 were "almost a total vindication of the Indian government and a direct refutation of many anti-opium claims." The influence of anti-opium forces was undercut further by the electoral victory of the Conservative Party in June 1895. Moreover, although Gladstone had simply been opposed to the SSOT's demands, the new Prime Minister, Salisbury, had served as the Secretary for India and "was strongly pro-opium" (Owen 1934, 328-29; Johnson 1975, 310-16). For the next ten years, the combination of limited state pressure on their behalf due to the Conservative Party presence in Parliament and views at odds with those of British policy makers resulted in anti-opium forces having little impact on shaping British policy.

The general election of 1906 marked a clear turning point in domestic pressure on the opium issue. Capitalizing on public dissatisfaction with Conservative Party rule, anti-opium forces again threw their support behind Liberal Party candidates. Organizations such as the SSOT relied on foreign criticism of British opium policy (including the report of the United States's Philippine Opium Committee) and the proliferation and apparent success of legislated opium prohibition in other countries such as Japan to bolster their arguments for change. In addition, the anti-opium groups linked their support to formal pledges by candidates "to support the anti-opium cause in Parliament." The "landslide" victory by the Liberal Party included 250 such candidates (out of a total of 333 seats won). More important, the new cabinet was distinguished by its anti-opium views including those reputedly held by the Secretary and Undersecretary for India. In May 1906, anti-opium supporters in Parliament reintroduced a version of the 1891 resolution declaring "the Indo-Chinese opium trade morally indefensible" and requesting that the government "take such steps as may be necessary for bringing it to a speedy close." In contrast to years past, the resolution was supported by the government and "passed unanimously" (Owen 1934, 333-35; Taylor 1969, 25; Johnson 1975, 316-17).

Although the resolution was a major concession to the members of the BBAOS, it was neither a case of domestic pressure determining state policy nor a simple compromise. As is evident in the testimony on the resolution in the House of Commons, the language of the resolution still left British policy makers with considerable leeway to act contrary to the intent of the anti-opium forces. Speaking before the House of Commons prior to the resolution's passage, the Secretary for India, John Morely, had noted the decline in the relative importance of opium revenue to the Indian government as well as the finding of the U.S. Philippines Commission that the financial gains from opium could not compensate for the "evil" of its use. More important, Morely argued that although he was unwilling to support opium prohibition, he would be "willing to restrict Indian production if the Chinese government would suppress poppy cultivation and its use" (Owen 1934, 330; Johnson 1975, 317; Stein 1985, 20-22). These statements as well as government support for the parliamentary resolution were taken by the anti-opium forces as a sign of a shift in British policy towards ending the opium trade and the Indian monopoly.

The conditional nature of Morely's interpretation of the parliamentary resolution, however, revealed a distinction between the positions held by British policy makers and by the anti-opium forces. Whereas the latter saw the opium trade as immoral and in the past had demanded its unconditional suppression, the former were not willing to accept the loss of a market, however immoral, to either domestic Chinese production or alternative foreign sources such as Persia or Turkey. Despite this distinction, anti-opium groups and their parliamentary supporters did not alter the language of the resolution. In 1895, anti-opium forces had focused so much on gaining a Royal Commission that they neglected aspects of the Commission's scope. Eleven years later, these forces appeared to have made a similar error. In focusing on gaining a government admission that the opium trade was immoral and should be ended, they left it up to the government to interpret how this was to be accomplished (Johnson 1975, 316; Stein 1985, 22).

Rather than turning to immediate suppression, British policy makers placed the burden of ending the trade on China. In September 1906, the Chinese government released an imperial declaration pledging renewed efforts against the opium problem including new regulations aimed at restricting opium use and a proposal for a ten year phased reduction of opium imports. The latter was accepted by the British government in 1907 (Stein 1985, 22).[7] The resulting Ten Year Agreement called for an annual reduction in Indian opium exports by 10 percent of the average annual export. Following a three-year trial period (1908-1910) to determine the patterns in imports and China's success in curtailing domestic production, the Agreement was to be renewed for another seven years (Taylor 1969, 22).

As Morely had argued, the relative importance of opium to India was slowly decreasing, thus, phasing out the opium trade over a ten year period would reinforce an ongoing trend rather than introducing new dislocations through rapid suppression. Since the base period was set at the higher 1901-

---

7. Based on State Department sources, Taylor (1969:22) argues that the British through the Indian government had made overtures to the Chinese about cutting exports as early as 1905. Johnson (1975:318) argues that the idea of a gradual suppression over ten years had been advanced by a number of people including the head of the SSOT (Joseph Alexander) as early as 1895.

1905 average rather than a narrower, more recent base, the immediate impact of the reduction would be lessened on the Indian government and those individuals involved in opium production and trade. Moreover, as revealed to frustrated Chinese officials in 1910, the British were basing the annual reductions of 10 percent not on 10 percent of the average total Indian exports for 1901-1905 (67,000 chests) but on 10 percent of the exports taken by China during this period (51,000 chests). Relying on ambiguity negotiated into the agreement, British policy makers had interpreted the agreement to call for annual reductions of 5,100 chests per year as opposed to 6,700 chests per year. By 1910, therefore, the British would still be allowed to export 51,700 chests of opium from India, essentially 700 more chests than the Chinese had imported *prior* to the Ten Year Agreement.[8] Finally, if China failed to curb consumption and production during the probationary period, a task made more difficult by the availability of Indian opium, Britain was no longer bound by the agreement.

International Pressure. The timing of events in 1906 suggests that rather than forcing the British into international cooperation on controlling the international drug trade, pressure from the United States played an extremely limited role in gaining British compliance with the idea of an international investigative commission. As argued by Taylor (1969, 25), the U.S. proposals of October 1906 for an international investigation of the opium issue would "most likely have been ignored or rejected" if it were not for the steps taken by China to impose control at home and the "anti-opium agitation in Great Britain." Although British policy makers agreed to the U.S. proposals in 1906, to divert attention from India the British added the conditions that China's domestic opium production be considered and that British participation would hinge on the participation of other major powers invited to participate in the commission. Almost two years later, with the Ten Year Agreement in place by January of 1908 and domestic pressure essentially mollified, however, British officials took steps to effectively remove the Indo-Chinese opium trade from the commission's agenda.

Efforts by the United States to expand the number of conference participants and the death of China's Empress Dowager delayed the onset of the Shanghai Opium Commission until February 1909 (Lowes 1966, 112-14; Taylor 1969, 49-52; Musto 1973, 35). Taking advantage of the delay and the upcoming British decision necessary to extend the Ten Year Agreement in 1910, however, the British Foreign Office had instructed Sir John Jordan,

8. This analysis is based on full reprints of original British Foreign Office files on opium and related drug issues from 1910 to 1941 (Scholarly Resources, 1974). References to specific files from this collection will hereinafter be cited by sender, recipient, date, and file number. For example, see Mr. Max Mueller to Sir Edward Grey, April 20, 1910, No. 45; India Office to Foreign Office, June 9, 1910, No. 64; Grey to Mueller, June 17, 1910, No. 76.

Britain's minister in China, to obtain an "expression of satisfaction" from the Chinese Foreign Ministry on the Agreement. Not surprisingly, Jordan's success raised concerns in the United States that American efforts to build an international consensus on a more restrictive solution to the opium problem would be wasted. Responding to urgent American entreaties, the British Foreign Office assured U.S. officials that China's satisfaction did not preclude discussion of the Indo-Chinese opium trade (Taylor 1969, 4-65).

Although the British appeared to be bowing to American concerns, this was not the case. Immediately prior to the Commission meetings, the British delegation had sent an emissary to the viceroy of Nanking with a different message. Citing the statement of satisfaction from the Chinese Foreign Ministry, the emissary noted the British intent to prevent discussion of the Ten Year Agreement at the Shanghai Commission (Taylor 1969, 64-65). This proved to be the case once the commission hearings began. Resolutions introduced by the U.S. delegation affecting the Indo-Chinese opium trade were either severely modified or simply rejected by the British delegation. In addition, citing the Chinese "expression of satisfaction" the British Delegation refused to allow the Shanghai Commission to discuss the Ten Year Agreement (Taylor 1969, 67, 69-74; Stein 1985, 54). Since the United States needed British cooperation to salvage the Shanghai Commission as the first international conference on the international drug trade, the American delegation chose not to reveal the British deception. As a result, the United States ended up with a Shanghai Commission whose nonbinding resolutions sanctioned the British program of gradual suppression of the opium trade.

Case II: United States Versus Great Britain, 1909-11

After the experience at Shanghai, American policy makers shifted their efforts to convening an international conference capable of producing a binding international agreement on controlling the opium trade. Although the initial U.S. proposal for such a conference was received by British policy makers in September 1909 and domestic pressure calling for British compliance with the proposal emerged in March 1910, formal British acceptance of the proposal did not come until September 1910. Moreover, rather than complying with the American proposals or turning to a simple compromise, British policy makers again turned to deception.

The U.S. proposal contained a number of provisions that British policy makers found objectionable. The British position during the Shanghai Commission had been that since different countries faced different drug situations, uniform regulations and control efforts as well as foreign review of existing drug treaties made little sense. In addition, such steps would infringe on the phased reduction of the Indo-Chinese opium trade. The conference proposed by the United States, however, included these very points that the British had sought to avoid in 1909. Not surprisingly, the initial communications between the British Foreign Office and the India Office, Colonial Office, Board of Trade and the colonial government in India revealed strong opposition to the American proposals.[9] From the standpoint of the British Secretary of State for Foreign Affairs, Sir Edward Grey, however, it was better to have a deciding voice within an international conference than to "stand out alone and obstruct the convening of the proposed conference." He, therefore, called for an interdepartmental meeting to discuss the British response to the United States.[10]

Domestic Pressure. Grey's position reflected slowly increasing domestic and international pressure. Domestically, during 1908 and 1909 the Ten Year Agreement and British participation in the Shanghai Commission had served to quiet societal interest groups. This situation had changed in 1910. With the end of the three year trial period for the Ten Year Agreement and the active quest by United States for a new international conference, societal pressure reemerged. As early as February 1910, representatives from six anti-opium groups including the BBAOS and the SSOT began to demand that the government shorten the time frame of the Ten Year Agreement. State pressure on behalf of anti-opium forces, however, was less extensive than that seen in 1906. In March 1910, Theodore Taylor, leader of the anti-opium faction in Parliament merely questioned the government as to its willingness to shorten the Ten Year Agreement. The Foreign Office reply to Taylor as well as to the anti-opium groups simply noted that since the Chinese government had not "expressed a desire to reopen the question," the British government would not be considering such a change.[11]

On the issue of an international conference, by contrast, societal pressure and state pressure were both limited. During 1910, appeals to British policy makers by anti-opium forces focused more on the China question than the American proposal. Pro-opium forces, consisting of individual British opium merchants in China (such as E.D. Sassoon and Co.) and business interests represented by the China Association, followed a similar pattern. For example, although the China Association notified the Foreign Office of its opposition to the intrusion of the United States in the bilateral arrangements between Britain and China, the Association's greater concern was to

---

9. Stein (1985:61-63); India Office to Foreign Office, March 24, 1910, No. 29, April 6, 1910, No. 36; and Colonial Office to Foreign Office, May 3, 1910, No. 44, May 14, 1910, No. 50.
10. Stein (1985:62-63); and India Office to Foreign Office, July 1, 1910, No. 3.
11. London and Edinburgh Anti-Opium Organizations to Foreign Office, February 12, 1910, No. 12; Professor Caldecott to Sir Edward Grey, February 10, 1910, No. 11; Foreign Office to India Office, February 21, 1910, No. 15; Question asked in the House of Commons, March 10, 1910, No. 21; Foreign Office to Caldecott, March 11, 1910, No. 22; and Caldecott to Foreign Office, March 21, 1910, No. 25.

obtain government assistance in preventing new import levies in the Chinese provinces.[12] Unsurprisingly, state pressure calling for British participation in a new international conference never reached the level of parliamentary resolutions. Speaking before the House of Commons in March 1910, Taylor simply asked for the status of the British government's response to the U.S. proposal. Similarly, during 1911 state pressure consisted primarily of questions raised in the House of Commons as to the date of the Hague Conference. The reply of Foreign Office officials was either that no date had been set or that the conference would occur sometime in 1912.[13]

International Pressure. The deciding factor in the British decision to respond to the United States regarding the Hague conference appears to be more international than domestic. On June 8, 1910, the U.S. Ambassador, Whitelaw Reid, notified Grey of the preliminary acceptance of the U.S. proposal by six countries including Germany, Japan, and the Netherlands and urged the British to do the same. Two days after Reid's request, the Foreign Office passed on a copy of the note to the other executive departments and began to make arrangements for the interdepartmental meeting noted above.[14] The drafting and approval of the formal reply to the United States delayed the British response until September.[15] Further pressure from the United States, however, appeared to be delayed by British intimations that a reply was forthcoming and that the British were interested in addressing problems of morphia and cocaine.[16]

On September 17, Grey finally notified Reid of the formal British position on the Hague Conference. Grey specifically noted that the British government would be "ready...if satisfactory assurances can be given to them on certain points...to take part at a proper time in a conference" to give "effect" to the "resolutions of the Shanghai Commission." These assurances included the following. First, all conference participants must be willing to fully discuss the "restricting of manufacture, sale, and distribution" of morphia and cocaine as well as opium. Second, participants also were to engage in preliminary studies collecting data on the domestic production and trade patterns in these drugs. Third, the Ten Year Agreement and other existing

---

12. For example, see China Association to Foreign Office, June 24, 1910, No. 87; India Office to Foreign Office, June 27, 1910, No. 88; and China Association to Foreign Office, July 11, 1910, No. 18.
13. Question asked in the House of Commons, March 10, 1910, No. 20, March 28, 1911, No. 92, June 1, 1911, No. 194, August 17, 1911, No. 75.
14. Foreign Office to India Office, June 14, 1910, No. 72, July 6, 1910, No. 10; India Office to Foreign Office, July 1, 1910, No. 3, July 6, 1910, No. 12, July 11, 1910, No. 17; Board of Trade to Foreign Office, July 2, 1910, No. 6, Foreign Office to Board of Trade, July 6, 1910, No. 8; and Foreign Office to Colonial Office, July 6, 1910, No. 11.
15. Foreign Office to India Office, July 27, 1910, No. 34; India Office to Foreign Office, August 3, 1910, No. 46; Board of Trade to Foreign Office, August 18, 1910, No. 64, August 31, 1910, No. 69; and Colonial Office to Foreign Office, September 5, 1910, No. 73.
16. Reid to Sir F. Campbell, August 8, 1910, No. 54.

treaties between Great Britain and China "should be excluded from consideration by the conference." Fourth, the British were not prepared to discuss the American proposals for allowing searches of naval vessels, restricting the uses of flags by naval vessels, or establishing an international body to implement agreements reached at the conference.[17] On October 14, Reid conveyed the acceptance of the British conditions by the U.S. government.

Taylor and Stein have argued that the British insistence on the inclusion of morphia and cocaine was intended as a deceptive tactic to delay the onset of the Hague Conference. Taylor (1969, 90-91) cites the ongoing negotiations between China and Great Britain over the Ten Year Agreement and the need to delay the conference until the negotiations were resolved. Stein (1985, 64-65), in contrast, argues that by shifting the conference's scope to cocaine and morphia, British policy makers would be able to draw international attention away from the British colonies and the opium trade. More important, the Germans and Japanese, past supporters of the United States during the Shanghai Commission, would be less likely to both rush into an international conference and, once the conference began, to align with the United States due to their involvement in morphia and cocaine production and trade.

The irony of these arguments is that British policy makers did turn to deception but not in the manner or for the reasons noted by the authors. In contrast to Taylor's argument, the United States accepted the British condition that the Ten Year Agreement and all British treaties with China would be removed from the conference agenda. Moreover, the British Foreign Office files suggest that British policy makers were not concerned with any type of linkage between the ongoing negotiations over the Ten Year Agreement and the pending Hague Conference. In contrast to Stein's argument, Britain and Germany were the two largest exporters of morphia. Broadening the focus of the conference would, therefore call more rather than less attention to Great Britain. In addition, by early 1910 British policy makers were being pressured by local authorities in the crown colonies to do something about the morphia and cocaine trade and growing problems of addiction. Unilateral British action to restrict the morphia trade, however, would merely open the foreign market to competitors such as Germany and, to a lesser degree, Japan.[18]

The key to the British deception lies in the acceptance by the United States of the position that the British government had to receive "satisfactory assurances...on certain points" before it would participate in the conference.[19] Since British policy makers would be the ones to determine if such assurances had been made, the United States had unwittingly placed

---

17. Grey to Reid, September 17, 1910, No. 80; and Stein (1985:62, 65-66).
18. Colonial Office to Foreign Office, January 1, 1910, No. 2, February 8, 1910, No. 10, May 3, 1910, No. 44, May 14, 1910, No. 50; and Board of Trade to Foreign Office, May 12, 1910, No. 49.
19. Grey to Reid, September 17, 1910, No. 80.

Britain in control of determining when the Hague Conference would meet. As noted above, Grey's logic in participating in the conference was to have the "deciding voice" within it. Since the British were primarily interested in restricting German morphia and cocaine exports, they could delay the conference until the Germans complied—ideally the Germans would even be pressured to do so by the United States—with the British conditions.

This proved to be the case. In October 1910 Reid informed Grey that the resolutions adopted by the Shanghai Commission in 1909 were evidence that the British conditions on morphia and cocaine had already been "satisfactorily" met. Resolution 5 of the Commission had called on the delegates to urge drastic measures to deal with the morphia trade. From the U.S. standpoint, the combination of informal discussions on cocaine during the commission and the call for drastic action on morphia also implied that governments were willing to take drastic steps against cocaine as well.[20] Grey replied to Reid, however, by simply restating the position agreed to earlier by the United States that Great Britain's participation in the Hague Conference was conditional, and by inquiring as to the extent to which "steps have been taken to obtain the assurances desired from the other Powers" that these conditions had been met.[21] Less than two weeks later, Reid informed Grey that the Netherlands government as host to the conference had notified the United States that it was making the British conditions known to the other countries invited to the conference. In December 1910, Reid notified Grey that other countries had been informed of the British position.[22]

From December 1910 until October 1911, the onset of the Hague Conference was delayed as the United States, the Dutch, the Germans, the Japanese, the Portuguese, the French, and the British attempted to sort out the extent to which other countries had met the British conditions.[23] Frustrated with the delay, in April American policy makers again sought to increase diplomatic pressure on the British this time by announcing the names of the U.S. delegates to the Hague Conference. Grey responded the following month by noting correspondence from the Netherlands that Germany, Portugal, and Japan, were unable to meet the condition of severe restrictions prior to the conference. Grey informed Reid that since these countries were going to be absent, it again made sense to delay the conference.[24]

---

20. Reid to Grey, October 4, 1910, No. 95.
21. Stein (1985:66-67); and Grey to Reid, November 3, 1910, No. 123.
22. Reid to Grey, November 15, 1910, No. 133, December 22, 1910, No. 162.
23. Grey to M. van der Goes, December 1, 1910, No. 144; Foreign Office to Board of Trade, January 23, 1911, No. 19; Foreign Office to India Office, January 23, 1911, No. 20; India Office to Foreign Office, January 25, 1911, No. 24; Grey to Baron Gericke, January 31, 1911, No. 28; Grey to M. Cambon, January 31, 1911, No. 29; F. Campbell to M. Manoel, January 31, 1911, No. 30; and Grey to H. von Kuehlmann, March 22, 1911, No. 86.
24. Reid to Grey, April 18, 1911, No. 114; and Grey to Reid, May 4, 1911, No. 143.

American policy makers then turned to pressuring Germany, Portugal, and Japan to comply with the British conditions and to pressuring Great Britain to agree that its conditions had been met.[25] On July 29, the German government informed the British government that in response to the inquiries of the United States, Germany agreed "in principle" to the British conditions although due to domestic legislation it would not be able to "enter for the present into binding international agreements" on the sale of morphia and cocaine.[26] On August 3, Reid informed Grey that the United States had acquired pledges from France, Germany, and Japan that the British conditions would be met by October 1 and that "Portugal would make every effort to do so."[27] Following efforts to obtain final assurances that the Germans would indeed have the necessary information on the morphia and cocaine trade collected prior to the conference, Grey notified Reid on September 6 that the British government was ready to participate in the Hague conference as soon as Germany, Japan, Portugal, and France informed the Netherlands government that they were ready.[28] On October 2, having the necessary assurances, the Netherlands government proposed December 1, 1911 as the starting date for the conference. On October 21, its conditions as originally laid out over a year ago finally being met, the British government agreed.[29]

Conclusion

Since the early 1900s, American policy makers have operated from the basic premise that external pressure on target countries could lead to their compliance in the war against drugs of abuse and addiction. This premise, however, is grounded in a realist theoretical tradition that discounts the role of domestic pressures and, in turn, the potential that such pressures can lead to outcomes other than compliance. The counter argument that foreign policy formulation in target countries is shaped more by the demands of

25. The extent to which these countries turned to deception as well is addressed in the broader research project from which this chapter is taken.

26. Note Communicated by Count Metternich, July 29, 1911, No. 45.

27. Reid to Grey, August 3, 1911, No. 53.

28. Foreign Office to Board of Trade, August 9, 1911, No. 59; Colonial Office to Foreign Office, August 14, 1911, No. 67; India Office to Foreign Office, August 16, 1911, No. 72; Grey to Reid, August 19, 1911, No. 80, September 6, 1911, No. 109; Reid to Grey, August 20, 1911, No. 87; Foreign Office to India Office, August 23, 1911, No. 89; and Grey to Baron Gericke, September 5, 1911, No. 104.

29. M. van der Goes to Grey, October 2, 1911, No. 131; Board of Trade to Foreign Office, October 10, 1911, No. 139; India Office to Foreign Office, October 14, 1911, No. 144; Colonial Office to Foreign Office, October 17, 1911, No. 145; and Grey to M. van der Goes, October 21, 1911, No. 148.

societal groups and their state supporters than by international pressures, however, is also incomplete. As noted by Putnam (1988, 460), instead of turning to international or domestic compliance policy makers seek to "reconcile" contending pressures. The research question addressed in this chapter is how such reconciliation is brought about. In contrast to the emphasis on compromise found in Putnam's discussion of "two-level games," I have suggested that policy makers are more likely to respond to increases in contending pressures through domestic and/or international deception.

To what extent did British policy makers turn to deception rather than compliance or compromise during the first American drug war? Ethan Nadelmann's (1990) important work on "prohibition regimes" notes the success of moral entrepreneurs in anti-opium organizations such as the SSOT in forcing the British government to reverse its opium policy in 1906. In addition, Nadelmann (1990, 505, 508-9) notes the success of U.S. influence in establishing a drug control regime beginning with the Shanghai Opium Commission in 1909. Process-tracing focusing on the influence of societal, state, and international pressures on the policy making process, however, reveals the that these "successes" were all tainted with deception. Ambiguity in the 1906 declaration, for example, allowed British policy makers to act contrary to the intent of societal and state backers of the resolution—as seen in the content and track record of the Ten Year Agreement. Cheating in 1909 allowed British policy makers to mislead the United States as to the scope and future influence of the Shanghai Opium Commission until it was too late. Moreover, ambiguity in the British pledge to participate in the Hague Conference allowed British policy makers to mislead the United States as to the onset, scope, and leadership of the conference.

From a theoretical standpoint, these findings suggest ramifications beyond the analysis of drug policy. Specifically, in addition to the strategies of compliance and compromise already addressed by the literature, this chapter proposes an analytical focus on strategies of "deception." The argument that policy makers turn to deception is not new. Journalistic works on foreign policy that incorporate conspiracy theories of deception abound (see Woodward, 1987; Wright, 1987). Yet, scholars of foreign policy, especially those of foreign economic policy, appear to have swung the pendulum towards the other extreme of refusing to acknowledge that policy makers can and do turn to strategies of deception. This chapter calls for a middle ground—the systematic analysis of the politics of deception.[30] The theoretical benefits of such a focus fall across an array of foreign policy issues and lie in the potential for gaining insights into what James Scott

---

30. My argument here draws heavily on a similar critique raised by John Orman (1980, 4-5) concerning the literature on presidential secrecy and deception. Orman also calls attention to the data needs and potential pitfalls of such a focus.

(1990) has termed the "hidden transcript," the actual preferences and behavior of actors beyond their official public stance, and the impact of this transcript on foreign policy.

The arguments raised by this chapter offer a starting point for further research systematically analyzing the role of deception in foreign policy formulation. In brief, the chapter has suggested that policy makers turn to deception for pragmatic reasons. In the context of increases in contending domestic and international pressures for compliance, strategies of deception appear to offer policy makers an alternative with lower short-run costs than either compliance, or compromise. As contending pressures for compliance increase, this analysis suggests that policy makers are more likely to turn to deception.

Yet, these pragmatic calculations may also be based on aspects of contending pressures more specific than those noted above. First, the case study on the Shanghai Commission suggests that policy makers may be more likely to turn to cheating where the domestic and/or international mechanisms for monitoring and enforcing compliance are weak. At the same time, however, despite weak international institutions from 1906 to 1991, British policy makers only cheated in their commitments to the United States in 1909. Second, and in contrast, British policy makers appeared to make greater use of deception through ambiguity in dealings with societal, state, and international actors throughout the two periods under analysis. The cases suggest that the "room for disgression" (Goldstein 1988, 182-83) accorded to British policy makers in responding to the demands of anti-opium forces and their parliamentary supporters on the 1906 declaration and to the demands of American policy makers concerning the Hague Conference may have facilitated the turn to such strategies.

Pragmatic calculations may also be based on considerations in addition to those raised by contending international and domestic pressures noted above. As in Putnam's model of the two-level game (1988, 456-57), this chapter relies on the implicit, simplifying assumption that policy makers primarily act as brokers between international and domestic pressures. Relaxing this assumption to allow for policy makers having their own interests, creates a "three-level game" in which policy makers seek to reconcile their interests with the pressures outlined above. As argued by Eric Nordlinger (1981, 14, 31-37), these preferences can stem from external (societal) and internal (state) sources. In contrast, other theorists, including Theda Skocpol (1985, 9) and David Lake (1988b, 36-38), have emphasized international considerations of relative economic and political-military power. The case studies suggest that the preferences of British policy makers were shaped by domestic as well as international sources. Moreover, these preferences appear to have increased the costs of turning strategies of compliance and compromise relative to strategies of deception.

Archival records of correspondence between British policy makers and between these policy makers and societal groups and foreign officials reveal a receptiveness to the economic arguments of pro-opium forces (Scholarly Resources, 1974; Stein, 1985). For example, despite the limited influence of such forces in Parliament after 1906 (Johnson, 1975; Stein, 1985), officials from the Foreign, India, and Colonial Offices as well as the Board of Trade were receptive to the appeals of commercial opium traders and the China Association concerning the economic ramifications of the Ten Year Agreement and China's behavior under the agreement. These records also suggest an internationally-rooted opposition to compliance or compromise with the demands of the United States and anti-opium forces concerning the Shanghai Commission and Hague Conference. Specifically, policy maker preferences appeared to be shaped by concerns with British colonial holdings—and the impact of the opium trade on those holdings—as a vital component of Britain's influence abroad. Moreover, these preferences were shaped by "considerations of relative advantage" (Lake 1988b, 37) over Britain's economic competitors, especially Germany. These findings suggest the need for more systematic analysis of the dynamics of the three-level game in explaining foreign policy formulation.

Finally, from a policy standpoint, the chapter suggests that the recurrent problems with those target countries "cooperating" with the United States in the drug wars of the 1980s and 1990s may reflect the tendency of policy makers in such countries to turn to deception rather than compromise or compliance. As noted, the context and targets of first drug war waged by the United States differ from those of the current war. Yet, like their British counterparts of the early 1900s, policy makers in those developing countries currently targeted by the United States face the dilemma of contending pressures on the drug issue. Moreover, these pressures, appear to be much greater than those of the early 1900s.

As in the early 1900s, the short-run solution for policy makers in target countries faced with increases in contending pressures would appear to be the politics of deception. In contrast to diplomatic threats, policy makers in target countries now face specific threats of economic and military sanctions from the United States. Domestically, these policy makers face mobilized, economically and militarily powerful, societal groups with a stake in the drug trade and access to state institutions (Walker, 1981; Bagley, 1988; Nadelmann, 1988). Although, as noted, policy maker preferences and the more specific aspects of contending pressures may also shape pragmatic decisions, at first glance the costs of full compliance with either the United States or domestic drug cartels would appear to be highly prohibitive. A similar argument could be raised for policy makers in target countries turning towards strategies of compromise during "wartime."

To date, American drug strategies have placed more emphasis on gaining the compliance of target countries through international pressure and less emphasis on addressing the ways in which foreign policy formulation in such countries is also shaped by factors such as appeals and pressures from societal interest groups and their state supporters. Until this emphasis is shifted, the drug war waged by the United States is unlikely to lead to either compromise or compliance. Moreover, if such responses appear to emerge they should be viewed with caution. As in the early 1900s, policy makers in target countries faced with contending international and domestic pressures will be more likely to engage in the politics of deception.

5

Grassroots Activism as a Factor in Foreign Policy-Making

THE CASE OF THE ISRAELI PEACE MOVEMENT

Tamar Hermann

THE LINKAGE BETWEEN PUBLIC OPINION AND FOREIGN POLICY-MAKING

The function of public opinion[1] in foreign policy-making has varied over the years and from one political context to another. In many political settings, even democratic ones, the linkage between the two has been quite weak; in others, it has been much more salient. And yet, research into the factors which bring about such variations remained fairly limited and unelaborated until the early 1970s.[2] Over the past two decades, however, the issue has drawn growing scholarly attention; a shift initially spurred by the Vietnam War and the fierce public protest it stirred.

The growing salience of public opinion regarding foreign matters is also manifested by the frequent surveys carried out in many states by specialized governmental agencies.[3] Although the direct impact of citizens on foreign policy decision-making still appears quite low, it may well be that a bilateral or even multilateral pattern of influence has been established: increasing public vigilance has heightened the responsiveness of politicians and raised the interest of scholars and pollsters; at the same time the

---

1. For a discussion of the complexity of the term "public opinion" and the methodological problems it raises, see Everts (1990) and Russett (1990) chapters. 1, 4.
2. The literature on the linkage between public opinion and foreign policy formation is too large for a detailed enumeration. Some outstanding works on the subject are however: Almond (1950), Key (1961), Caspari (1970), Mueller (1973); Page and Shapiro (1983), Russett (1990), Eichenberg (1990).
3. On the use of such governmental surveys in the Reagan era see Russett (1990) 17–18.

higher attention of the latter three is likely to have strengthened the citizens' sense of competence and power. However, as these mutual processes have been almost simultaneous, it is difficult to distinguish the dependent and independent variables from one another.

Scholarship on the relationship between public opinion and foreign policy making has proceeded along two routes: normative and empirical (Avaroanel and Hughes 1975, 47). The normative perspective questions the very desirability of grassroots interest and involvement in these highly sensitive issues. Although classical democratic theory points to the central role of the active citizen, it contains no categorical assertion that public opinion should dominate all aspects of statesmanship. Still, it is expected that citizens at least be allowed to participate in setting the agenda for national deliberations.[4]

Empirical research has attempted to assess the public's degree of participation in foreign affairs. Most studies have found that, even in times and places in which an increase of grassroots participation occurred in other socio-political areas (such as civil rights, women's equality, or environmental preservation), public interest and involvement in foreign affairs has remained relatively low except in cases where citizens perceive a direct personal stake in events abroad. Several explanations regarding the public's low interest, participation, and hence impact have been put forward. The first emphasizes public apathy, a condition caused by the widespread feeling that foreign and security issues are too remote from the everyday life of average citizens and too complex for them to grasp. Indeed, surveys carried out in the United States during the 1960s showed that 70 to 90 percent of the respondents were not interested in foreign policy matters at all and had rather limited and unstructured knowledge about them (see, e.g., Robinson, Rusk, and Head, 1968). Surveys carried out in West Germany in the 1970s reflected much the same tendencies (see, e.g., Merritt, 1973). Another prevalent school of thought, known as "mood theory", suggests that not only is the public relatively disinterested, but its views are highly unstable and wavering. Public opinion regarding foreign issues is often based upon uninformed sentiments and prejudices (Almond,

---

4. A prevalent hypothesis is therefore that democratic states, in which the public is expected to be more involved in the decision-making process, would be, by this very virtue, more peaceful than authoritarian ones. This hypothesis has not yet been empirically confirmed. However, positive correlations between internal instability and engagement in conflictual foreign policies have been observed, as have negative correlations between such policies and major intra-governmental opposition. (See, e.g., Geller, 1985.) Russett indicates that the industrialized, democratic states of the northern hemisphere actually constitute, among themselves, a vast "Zone of Peace" since World War II. At the same time he points to the fact the mechanisms which maintain this peace are not effective when these democracies deal with non-democratic states (Russett, 1990, ch.5).

1950). The normative implication of this approach is that public attitudes and preferences cannot serve as the basis for a stable and rational foreign policy. At the same time, however, these attributes may allow policy-makers to manipulate public opinion by using emotional means of persuasion.[5]

A third type of explanation emphasizes linkages between citizens' attitudes regarding the realm of foreign policy and their social location (see, e.g., Galtung, 1964). A small group at the social center allegedly formulates policy—in most cases of a conservative but pragmatic nature—and transmits it to a larger group, which is located at its immediate periphery. Here the policy is interpreted and the message is dispatched to the masses at the remote periphery. This theory, too, assumes that those who are located at this periphery have only limited knowledge, interest, or critical ability and therefore passively accept the message from above.

All of these explanations have one premise in common: they estimate the public's potential and practical access to the decision-making process to be generally low. At the same time, none of them actually suggests that policy-makers can ignore the publics' feelings completely (see Merritt, 1975). And indeed, even those taking the elitist position admit that politicians, in democratic as well as in authoritarian states pay at least some lip service to what seems to be the will of the people. It is also quite obvious that leaders everywhere try to manipulate public opinion in various ways in order for their policies to gain domestic legitimization and bolster support.[6]

This central point has been further developed and elaborated in recent studies, most of which emphasize the major influence of domestic political structures on the level of attention and responsiveness of political elites to grassroots reservations and demands. Thus, for example, Russett attributes the prolonged peace in the Western hemisphere to the restrictions imposed on Western political leaderships by the rejection on the part of their respective publics of the use of force as a mechanism for realizing the national interest in disputes between representative, democratic states (Russett, 1990).

The original somewhat crude differentiation between the public's access to foreign policy matters in democratic and authoritarian regimes has also been refined. Different democratic structures seem to allow for varying degrees of public involvement in foreign policy-making. By presenting various opportunities for the public to exert influence on the coalition

---

5. This claim requires qualification. When the public has already been emotionally swayed to one side, the leaders may find it difficult to change direction, even if they are convinced that such a turn-around is unavoidable in light of new external circumstances. See, e.g., George (1980).

6. An interesting analysis of this circular process in Israeli politics may be found in Kies (1975).

building process among elite groups, different democracies encourage different amounts of grassroots indirect influence on the shaping of their respective national foreign policies (Risse-Kappen, 1991). The manipulation of citizens by their leaders in open societies is also found to be more problematic than assumed in the past, as nowadays the media supply audiences with much information and detailed analyses of the international arena. This in turn leads to the formation of better informed and more stable foreign policy opinions on the part of citizens and renders their views less amenable to manipulation from above. (see, e.g., Hurwitz, 1989).

Recent research on activist segments of the public also suggests a greater scope for societal influence than previously assumed. Studies such as *Mobilizing for Peace* (Rochon, 1988) or *A Winter of Discontent* (Meyer, 1990) explicate the entangled relations between the active and organized part of the public and the authorities. They also demonstrate that, although activists rarely achieved the direct goals they strived for, their very activism in a sphere traditionally closed to the public changed the latter's position vis-à-vis the authorities.

The normative and empirical perspectives reviewed above cannot be separated, however, because political participation is to a great extent derived from the broader normative system. The linkage between the two is most conspicuous and crucial when, for various reasons, certain segments of the public overcome their apathy and begin to take hesitant steps to express views on matters that are usually considered to be the exclusive domain of the political elite. In such cases, norms approving public involvement are indispensable, as they legitimize the new grassroots activity. Where there are no such norms, those who express overt dissatisfaction with official foreign policy are often condemned by the authorities as subversive, reviled by the mass media as unpatriotic or even as traitors, and consequently ostracized by their fellow-citizens.

But such prohibiting norms can be changed, usually after interested individuals or groups openly contest them. Peace movements have often constituted such a vanguard. In the past few decades peace activists, particularly in the West, have challenged the prolonged pariah status imposed upon them by norms which delegitimized open criticism from below of national foreign policies. They confronted, in an unprecedented and direct although mostly non-violent manner, the establishments in charge of foreign policy-making as well as the norms legitimizing their exclusive authority to do so. Although most recent peace campaigns have failed to achieve their direct goals, such as nuclear disarmament, the discussion which follows suggests that they have had considerable success in bringing about major modifications in the general attitude toward grassroots involvement in the realm of foreign policy.

The Flourishing of Peace Activism

The rejection of war on religious and ethical grounds has been a widespread phenomenon in the West for almost two thousand years now (see Brock, 1972). Still, pacifism has always been a minority position. Typically, political elites and the general public not only stigmatized pacifists as utopians, but also denounced them as a kind of fifth column that helped the enemy from within by challenging the rationality and morality of decision-makers and impairing national unity in times of external conflict. Actually, pacifist criticism of the prevalent violent modes of domestic and international behavior has served as a par-excellence example of deviation from the norm that defines interstate relations as the exclusive domain of the rulers. Peace activists, in most cases politically and socially located on the remote periphery, presented a fundamental challenge to the national leadership by questioning its moral right (or, later on, its political mandate) to resort to violence.

In view of the horrors brought about by modern warfare and the "conversion" of most modern peace movements from absolute and religious pacifism to more circumstantial and politically oriented versions, it has become more difficult to delegitimize such demands for change. "Pragmatic pacifism" has therefore taken root in the Western political arena in the last thirty years or so, contributing greatly to a redefinition of the boundaries of the discourse on national foreign policy formation (Rochon 1988, 205-208). The spectacle of hundreds of thousands demonstrators, all ordinary citizens, marching through the streets of London, Bonn, Amsterdam, and other major European cities in the late 1970s and early 1980s, demanding that their governments object to the implementation of NATO's decision to deploy new nuclear missiles, provided unmistakable evidence that a profound modification had occurred.

The increasing activism of Western peace movements in the late 1970s and early 1980s and their growing public appeal and political salience (no matter how transitory) should be interpreted then primarily as the transcendence of a collective cognitive barrier; so should the subsequent emergence of similar movements in other regions of the world. Only in the second place should the growth of these movements be interpreted as a manifestation of flourishing anti-war sentiments at the grassroots level. Indeed, the worldwide expansion of peace activity served less as a cause of the noticeable rise in the public's awareness of defense problems (Rochon 1988, 207) than an outcome of that new vigilance. Surveys indicate that an increase in the public's attentiveness to foreign policy and security matters started before the ground-swell of peace movements that followed NATO's twin-track decision of December 1979.[7] A number of studies, however, suggest that peace campaigns, such as the American antiwar movement during the Vietnam era (see e.g., Wittkopf and McCormick 1990, 3) or the U.S. nuclear freeze campaign of the 1980s (Finn 1985, 163), have been self-reinforcing.

Other sources of the rise in grassroots activity concerned with foreign policy issues must be considered. It is possible the higher ranks of the political hierarchy themselves have contributed, probably unintentionally, to the occurrence of such changes. The question here is thus: under what circumstances do elites, which have delegitimized, either on normative or pragmatic grounds, overt grassroots manifestations of discontent regarding foreign policies, begin to tolerate, or even to approve of such an open collision of ideas? Furthermore, does such a modification always indicate a positive trend, that is, growing maturity and democratization of the system, or may it also be a sign of alarm that indicates the leadership's internal disintegration? In the latter case the contenders within the elite may try to gain power by undermining the authority of the present leaders using the masses as their proxy.

An increase in citizen vigilance may also be the outcome of basic social changes. A rise in the average level of education, greater public access to information arising from increased exposure to a pluralized mass media, or fluctuations in the economic situation or in occupational distribution may afford more free time or available resources, with the result that individuals are able to shift from passive to active modes of political participation.[8] Where no such fundamental social changes are observed, however, a sudden increase in the public's involvement in political issues that were formerly neglected may indicate a crisis of confidence—that is

---

7. In September 1979 (three months before Western anti-nuclear activism reached its climax in the wake of NATO's twin-track decision), 40% of the respondents in a German nationwide survey replied "yes" to the question, "Are you interested in foreign policy?". One year later 47% gave the same answer. Only 19% replied "no" to this question in the survey of 1979 and even fewer (16%) chose this option in 1980 (Noel-Neumann, 1981, 410). In 1979, only 31% agreed with the statement, "foreign policy is too complicated; one can hardly understand what is going on"; even fewer (15%) agreed that "foreign policy is not interesting for the individual citizen" (ibid., 411). These findings certainly differ from those of most surveys of the 1960s and even the 1970s, which concluded that the average citizen was apathetic about foreign policy. Nevertheless, it remains unclear whether this apparent rise in the public's attentiveness caused the intensification of peace activism or was caused by it.

8. Socio-demographic surveys of the activists in Western peace movements and in the Green Parties have disclosed that about half of their membership consists of youngsters, unemployed workers who get allowances from the government, retired persons, students or homemakers—in other words, people whose time is not very tight and whose economic activity is quite limited (Alber, 1989, 204). These findings go hand in hand with the theory regarding the cultural shifts caused by the economic changes typical to the post industrial era, shifts which in turn produce higher grassroots political participation, see Inglehart (1990).

mounting distrust in the leaders' capacity for rational deliberation. An unprecedented urge to influence the course of foreign relations may also derive from a deterioration of the central collective ideology or from the emergence of contradictory interpretations of its core notions.

Other inputs may seem self-evident sources of normative as well as pragmatic changes in the patterns of public involvement. For example, a sharp increase in an external threat, drastic transformations in international surroundings, or a fundamental change in foreign relations may render questionable the basic postulates of the ongoing official policy. The noticeable increase in (Jewish) peace activism in Israel in the late 1970s and early 1980s, as well as the political salience and relative legitimacy it has gained present an intriguing example of the practical and normative modifications that are under discussion here. The case study that follows is an almost classical combination of all the above mentioned causes leading to growing public involvement in the debate about the desirable direction of national foreign policy. Contributing factors include: an aggravation of the rivalries inside the collective ideological framework (Zionism), and hence a decline in the unanimity regarding its basic imperatives; a period of political transition following a change of the party in power (from Labour to Likud); a widespread distrust and apprehension concerning the proficiency of the new party in power; the growth of articulate cohorts of young people with a deep sense of self-confidence and competence, who, unlike the older generation, do not hesitate to challenge the wisdom of the political elite; a perceptible prospect of fundamental change in relations with the external environment (the Arab world, as demonstrated by the Sadat peace initiative); and the indirect or even subconscious impact of the American antiwar movement in the 1960s and the European antinuclear movements of the 1970s.

THE ISRAELI CASE STUDY: A GENERAL OUTLINE

The complexity of Israel's foreign relations, and especially the negative nature of its interactions with the Arab world created, even before the establishment of the state, a special "state of mind" among its Jewish citizens dominated by a constant and all-encompassing concern about foreign policy and security issues.[9] Fierce debates about the right way to deal with regional conflicts and continuing dependence on foreign powers have sharpened the country's collective sensitivity to these aspects of politics while elevating them above all other issues. The perception of a

---

9. On the Israeli public belief structure regarding national security matters, see Arian (1989).

hostile environment has contributed much to the crystallization of a world view that emphasizes the negative attitude toward the state of Israel on the part of most relevant actors in the international arena.

These circumstances have produced a fundamental national consensus on the indispensability of military superiority as well as a sense of limited political flexibility (see Horowitz, 1985; Barzilai, 1987). Such basic notions and the common perception of the country's limited freedom of action in the international arena sometimes attain the level of a "siege syndrome": the boundaries of discussion concerning Israel's foreign and security doctrine are then defined as too crucial to be debated in the street. Nevertheless, Israeli citizens have always demonstrated a significantly higher level of attentiveness toward foreign and security affairs than those observed in most Western countries (Kies, 1975; Arian, Talmud, and Hermann, 1988).

These strong pressures for conformity, typical of a small and threatened society have been intensified by the general commitment to one dominant ideology, namely Zionism. As the national revival movement, Zionism criticized the passivity of the Jewish people in the diaspora. The change that Zionism demanded was the "normalization" of the Jewish existence: not only the return to the land of the forefathers, but also the politicization of the people, including the formation of a defense force (see, e.g., Harkavi, 1986: Shapira, 1988). A combination of these ideological imperatives, and Arab hostility, invested the Israeli military forces with an aura of "savior of the nation". For years it also protected policy makers from fundamental criticism. Although disagreements between doves and hawks persisted,[10] both camps acknowledged the importance of domestic support for decision-makers when they encountered challenges from the external enviroment.

Moreover, the widely accepted notion of the Israeli-Arab conflict as a zero-sum game created a cognitive condition in Israel that has facilitated the adoption of a rather rigid "political realism" which emphasizes the inherent contrast among national interests and almost obliterates the possibility of regional cooperation and a long-lasting peace. The deep-rooted belief that the state is in a no-choice position has also produced a fundamental perception of shared destiny as well as a high level of individual preparedness to sacrifice one's life, not to mention one's money and time, to defend the collective enterprise. This civic characteristic has facilitated official attempts to denounce reservations concerning the official policy, and especially peace activism, as an expression of personal egotism and cowardice, or even of disloyalty to the state.[11]

---

10. This division is in some ways parallel to the left-right split in Western politics. However, most political scientists agree that in Israel the crux of the matter is the debate on national security policy rather than socio-economic issues.

11. An extreme example of such criticism of the peace activists by Israeli political leaders is

Restraints on the emergence of a genuine domestic opposition to Israel's official foreign policy were reinforced by another characteristic of the Zionist movement, and later, of Israel's political system: authoritative paternalism. Until the late 1960s, the general course of influence and control undoubtedly flowed "from the top down" (Lehman-Wilzig, 1990). Almost every aspect of public life in Israel, including most of the economic, educational, and health systems, have been directed and controlled by the authorities. It is therefore not surprising that foreign policy, which is the most visible activity of every government, was in this troublesome context left almost totally in the hands of the politicians. Up to the mid-1970s, Israel's political elite was extremely successful in manipulating public opinion regarding these issues. In retrospect it is quite clear that even when foreign policy decisions contradicted widespread public convictions, all eventually gained general approval and support (see. e.g., Kies, 1975). For years, then, the Israeli public accepted without too many reservations most steps taken by the authorities in foreign and security affairs, as they seemed to be faits accomplis the only substitute for war, or, in the most critical situations, the sole means of avoiding catastrophe.

The Israeli political system is characterized by several historic cleavages. Most relevant here is the rift between the Labour camp and the Revisionist one, which first emerged in the mid-1920s. More than once, clashes between the core parties in these camps approached an open break; in the late 1930s and early 1940s, when the conflict was over relations with the British mandate during the struggle against Nazi Germany;[12] in the mid-1940s, when the dispute concerned whether to agree to the partition of Palestine; and immediately after the creation of the state, when the new government, headed by Labour, was eager to prove it was in full control

---

Ben Gurion's sarcastic reply to Natan Hofshi, one of the leading figures in the tiny Israeli pacifist movement, who was also a member of the Mapai party, which Ben Gurion then headed. Hofshi warned in the party conference of 1950 against what he considered to be the growing militarization of the Israeli mind and policies following the War of Independence, and Ben Gurion responded: "If Natan Hofshi from Nahalal says: 'I will not go to war, I am against any bloodshed,' I think no one should force him to. Even if the enemy will stand at the gates of the state or of Nahalal...It would be against his convictions...However, I could not imagine what would have happened if some Arab hooligan would have actually entered Nahalal and started butchering the children there. Would Natan Hofshi just say: 'No, I read Tolstoy now, I refuse to shed any blood'?...I think we should not make such people go to war, however, neither can I say that Natan Hofshi is one of the guardians of the state" (Ben Gurion, 28.4.1950).

12. The Labour camp, which at the time constituted the mainstream of the Zionist movement and the establishment, advocated a temporary suspension of the continued national liberation struggle against British rule for the duration of the war against Nazi Germany. The Revisionist minority argued that the Jews living in Palestine should continue fighting the British as if the Nazis did not exist, and at the same time participate in the military campaign against Germany as if there were no clash with the British.

while the Revisionists were still hoping to preserve at least some of the autonomy they had held in the pre-state era. However, where the external relationships or negotiations of the pre-state political body or, later on, of the state itself were concerned, both sides were usually careful to present a unified facade to the outside (much like the Jewish communities in the diaspora have done for ages). Episodes of inter-party disagreements over external affairs were often concealed while dealing with foreign adversaries and sometimes even while negotiating with allies.

This policy has been accompanied by the disposition of the political elite to confine essential debates to the horizontal level—that is, to leaders of the party in power and those who are heading the opposition. The vertical dimension has been almost disregarded. The public at large, including the rank and file of the main parties, has been minimally involved in the processes of deliberation and decision-making. Public involvement was encouraged only when the exchange of ideas between the elites of the parties had reached a dead end. Such an incident occurred in 1951-1952, when the Revisionists recruited the masses to protest against the Labour government's decision to accept reparations from West Germany. Many in Israel condemned this exceptional tactic as "cheap populism", which bore fascist connotations. The Israeli political system has been truly bottle-necked when it comes to grass-roots involvement (see Lehman-Wilzig, 1990).

ISRAELI PEACE ACTIVISM AS AN INDICATOR OF CHANGING ATTITUDES

The influence of these norms, and the modes of operation derived from them, are best demonstrated by the prolonged and rather hostile reaction of Israel's political elite (in both camps) and the wider public toward the small peace groups that have emerged since the mid-1920s.[13] The clash between these peace groups and the political mainstream originates to only a limited extent from the essential contradiction between their respective political programs. An equally important reason for the continued rejection and condemnation of peace activity lies in the activists' tendency to overlook the "exclusivist" norm that the leadership has tried to implant, and the public's willingness to accept this norm out of a sense of uncertainty in the face of a complex reality.

---

13. For a detailed analysis of the Peace Covenant and the peace groups discussed hereafter see Isaac (1976).

Conflicts of this kind were the basis of many objections to the early Israeli peace groups and forced them to remain semi-sectarian and isolated. This was the fate of the Peace Covenant (*Brit Shalom*),[14] The League for Jewish-Arab Rapprochement (*Ha'liaa Le'hitkarvut Ve'shituf Yehudi-Arvi*), the Union (*Ihud*), and the Israeli Peace Committee (*Va'ad Ha'shiom Ha'Israeli*). On the rare occasions when national leaders agreed to examine the peace groups' suggestions or plans, they stipulated in advance that they would do so only if the part in future negotiations.[15]

Although most Israeli peace activists acknowledged the government's authority to formulate official foreign and defense policies, they emphasized their civic-democratic right to take part in the preliminary debate and to promote alternatives, usually before a final decision was made, but sometimes even afterward. Each of the peace groups has exercised this right. Some of them, however, stretched it further: when they failed to gain domestic support they applied for assistance to powerful Jewish organizations in the diaspora and sometimes even to foreign officials. In some cases, they tried to arouse international public opinion by publishing their views in the foreign press.[16] Most often, such tactics not only failed to accomplish the desired results, but also alienated the majority of the Israeli public from all peace activity as such. These tactics also stigmatized the demand to influence foreign policy-making as one which put the united national image in danger and placed Israeli security in jeopardy.

---

14. This first peace group, many of whose members were on the faculty of the new Hebrew University, dared in the late 1920s to stand up against the official objective of the Zionist movement to create a Jewish majority in Palestine. Instead it advocated the constitution of a binational state. Moreover, its members argued that, the regional conflict had been caused, at least partially, by the Zionists brushing aside the fears and interests of the Arabs. These assumptions, which presented a clear antithesis to the mainstream Zionist doctrine, have been shared by most of the peace groups that succeeded the Peace Covenant, and have continued to be at the heart of the difference between them and the representatives of the prevalent political ethos.

15. For example, in 1937 the group named "Kedma Mizraha" succeeded in establishing some promising contacts in Egypt. Moshe Sharet (then director of the political department of the Jewish Agency) agreed to find out whether these contacts could be of any real political use, on the condition that the initiating group would keep out of future negotiations (Sharet, 1971, 130).

16. The most striking example of an Israeli peace group trying to prevent the implementation of official policy by seeking help from the outside occurred in March, 1948. The group, Ihud, was headed by Jehuda L. Magnes (the chancellor of the Hebrew University and a fervent activist for a binational solution in Palestine) and the eminent philosopher Martin Buber. After having failed to prevent the Zionist establishment from accepting the partition plan, Ihud sent a cable to Warner Brown, the American representative to the UN Security Council, urging him to adhere to his suggestion to establish a new external mandate in Palestine despite the Zionists' demand for a sovereign Jewish State. (A copy of the cable is in Magnes' personal papers, in the Central Archive of the Jewish People, Jerusalem, file no. P3/2565).

Attitudes did not change much even in the late 1960s, when, following the 1967 War, a new type of peace group, The Movement for Peace and Security (*Ha'tnus Le'shalom U'bitachon*), was established. The Movement's main aspiration was to build a grassroots public barricade, which would block what its founders considered to be the government's deterioration into chauvinism and annexationism (Isaac, 1976). This aim could be attained only by a change in the earlier semi-sectarian mode of operation. The initial objective, therefore, was the creation of a large, popular movement. But this aspiration was not realized. As in the case of earlier peace groups, the hard core of the movement remained fairly exclusive: most of its active members were university professors. professionals, writers, and journalists.[17] They were largely urban, of European (Ashkenazi) origin, and politically, they all stood somewhat left of center. The establishment largely ignored the Movement, considering it a kind of late "youth rebellion" by a segment of the second generation who were frustrated by the fact that the first generation still occupied most leadership positions, and indeed, the emergence of the movement could be interpreted as an internal struggle of power between the then ruling elite and its immediate challengers, both of whom came from the same upper classes.

Such an interpretation may have been reinforced by the Movement's super-cautiousness not to shake the foundations of the system. Its members expressed their deep concern about the future of the country in the face of an erosion of its moral standards, brought about by the occupation of the West Bank, Gaza, and the Golan Heights. Still, they emphasized that they were proud and loyal Israeli citizens as well as confirmed Zionists. Moreover, they made clear from the very beginning of their activity that the Movement was not intended as a challenge to the overall political system. They did not question the capacity of the authorized decision-makers to formulate a reasonable foreign policy. On the contrary, at least in the initial stage stretching from late 1967 until early 1969, the Movement endeavored to carry on a "constructive debate" intended to strengthen the more dovish components of the government.[18] The Movement was also careful to use only moderate and generally approved modes of persuasion, forgoing mass demonstrations and, needless to say, more caustic measures like civil disobedience. Its activity was therefore restricted to holding open meetings, circulating and signing petitions, calling press conferences, and

---

17. Most Israeli peace activists are, like their European and American counterparts, more highly educated and articulate than the average citizen. An education profile of Western peace activists and some of its implications may be found in Opp, 1989, 195–196. For their Israeli counterparts, see Hermann, 1989, 336–338 and 346–348.

18. At the time, a "national unity government" had been constituted just before the outbreak of the 1967 war. This government encompassed almost all Israeli parties. There was, therefore, practically no significant parliamentary opposition. (For a short but interesting discussion of the importance of the opposition in foreign policy-making, see Appleton, 1975).

writing open letters to the government, most of them published in the local press in order to prove the genuine patriotism and the nonconspiratorial character of the Movement.

The original political recommendations of the Movement for Peace and Security were also rather modest. To start with, it accepted the official definition of the 1967 War as defensive and, hence, as justified. Accordingly, its principal slogan was "yes to security, no to annexation!". Furthermore, the Movement did not demand Israel's unilateral or complete withdrawal from the West Bank, Gaza, or the Golan Heights, but accepted the government's demand for considerable border revisions. It did take a stand against the legal annexation of the occupied territories, for alleviating the harshness of the military rule there, and for an official declaration that Israel was willing to confer with the leaders of the Arab states—all of this provided that Israel's security demands were first met.

The restrained criticism and relatively moderate methods did not produce the desired outcome, i.e., general legitimization and support. Despite the objective (although limited) coverage by the media and the basically positive response of certain segments of the population, the Movement's political momentum stagnated. The War of Attrition, which reached its climax in 1969, rallied the entire nation, citizens and leaders alike around the flag. The collective disposition, created by the prolonged tension and aggravated by the daily casualties along the Suez Canal, was to excoriate any overt criticism of the National Unity government's performance, condemning it as sabotage of the national defense effort. Without a base to stand on, the Movement reacted, as often happens in such cases, by voicing its criticisms more radically than before. The result was public outrage, which brought about a vicious cycle of increased radicalization and condemnation, until the Movement gradually declined in the early 1970s. It left behind deep disappointment and bitterness on one side, and anger and mistrust on the other. Still, the seeds of grass-roots active involvement in the realm of foreign and defense policy had been sown.

It was therefore not unexpected that a new peace movement, Peace Now (Shalom Achshav), emerged less than a decade later. And yet, in light of the past, Peace Now attained a surprising degree of public support and even a modicum of official recognition.[19] Can this departure with the past be explained solely by the unique character and policies of the new movement or had the political environment itself shifted? Again, most of the individuals involved in the new movement came from the same, specific, sociopolitical background: they, too, were highly educated, urban, Askenazi, and somewhat to the left of center in their political convictions. Like their

---

19. For detailed analyses of the evolution of Peace Now, see Bar On (1985) and Hall (1986). Elon (1990) contains a short retrospective description.

predecessors, they were not absolute pacifists and defined themselves as Zionists whose basic loyalty was to Israel as a Jewish state. They had no anti-system predisposition whatsoever. Furthermore, a comparison between the platform of Peace Now and that of its closest predecessor, the Movement for Peace and Security, reveals no significant differences. It seems logical, therefore, to suspect favorable for that the circumstances of the late seventies were more favorable for grassroots criticism of official policy than in earlier periods.

Several sources nourished the growth of the embryonic peace initiatives that began to emerge after the 1973 War and later developed into Peace Now. The first of these was mounting dissatisfaction on the part of certain segments of the public toward the government's apparent indifference to or disregard of new opportunities for reconciliation between Israel and its neighbors. Secondly, the new peace initiatives had been motivated, somewhat paradoxically, by the accomplishments of the ultra-nationalist movement called The Bloc of Faithful (Gush Emunim). Although at the opposite end of the political spectrum, this success suggested that a new era had opened for extra-parliamentary activism in Israel.

The third source was the unprecedented change of the party in power in 1977. The accession of the Likud (the contemporary version of the pre-state revisionists) and Labour's new role in the opposition had at least two effects. One was the realization that it is possible for the people to replace a failing leadership. This recognition undoubtedly increased the Israelis' sense of political competence as well as their attentiveness to the political debate. The other effect of the transition was the maturation of real inter-party competition over the conduct of national affairs, and thus for public support. The Labour party, which in the past had fought most of the extra-parliamentary groups, because they appeared to challenge its hegemony, now encouraged such grass-roots opposition, perceiving the activists as potential allies in its campaign against the new Likud government.

The fourth source of the unprecedented public participation in the 1978 effort by Peace Now to influence the course of official policy, was the impression shared by many that the Israeli-Egyptian negotiations, initially the source of so much hope, had arrived at a dead end because of the Israeli government's rigidity and obstinacy. Indeed, Peace Now originated in what is now known as the "Officers' Letter," which criticized Israel's response to Sadat's initiative.[20] The original letter was signed by about 350

---

20. The letter, which was actually a petition, was written in February 1978. A number of army reserve officers, many of them in elite combat units, warned Prime Minister Begin not to establish new Jewish settlements in the occupied territories, an action that would impede the peace process. The letter also argued that a smaller Israel at peace was preferable to a greater Israel constantly at war. The signers added that, because this interpretation did not seem to be shared by the government, they had begun to lose confidence in the absolute justice and sincerity of the Israeli posture.

reserve officers. After it had been sent to the Prime Minister's office it was released to the public and garnered unexpected support and popularity. In less than a week, over 250,000 additional signatures were collected. Clearly, the letter expressed an authentic dissatisfaction with the government's performance and a strong demand for a change in policy. The potential for a mass protest movement was evident.

In the spring and summer of 1978, Peace Now organized numerous well attended demonstrations, petition-signing campaigns, and other mass expressions of concern about the future of the peace negotiations. The political leadership became aware that this time the protest was on a scale which could neither be ignored nor easily denounced. Prominent activists were therefore invited to meet with the prime minister and the minister of foreign affairs, both members of the Likud. Although the talks were fruitless, due to an absence of common ground, the very invitation implied some governmental recognition. Labour, the leading opposition party, was more supportive, though party leaders hesitated to openly identify with the movement due to uncertainties over public reaction.

Unlike its predecessors, Peace Now received considerable financial and logistic support from the left-of-center parties through their affiliated bodies, mainly the Kibbutzim. In contrast to the past, moreover, media coverage of the movement was both intensive and sympathetic right from the beginning. News reports presented the image of a successful movement, providing an important boost to Peace Now's credibility even while sometimes producing an exaggerated impression which aroused false hopes.

Peace Now mounted a large demonstration in September 1978, just before Prime Minister Begin left for the Camp David summit. Huge placards urged Begin to be flexible and to show goodwill in order to continue the momentum toward peace. The demonstration was attended by roughly one hundred thousand people, including, for the first time in Israel's short history, several delegations of Jewish communities from the diaspora. Its concluding statement of intentions declared that if Begin failed to fulfill its expectations, his return home would be met by massive protest. This episode represents one of the relatively few cases when Peace Now initiatives appeared to have some direct effect on policy. In an interview some years later, Begin admitted that Peace Now's warning rendered him somewhat more compliant when dealing with President Sadat and President Carter (Elon 1990, 94).

The outbreak of the Lebanese War in 1982 was a critical point for the government, because it presented in the most severe manner the problem of what kinds of public protest are proper and permissible in such a situation. Opinions on this issue were divided and the debate caused deep splits within Israeli society in general and the peace movement in particular. The vast majority of peace activists shared the public's conviction that protest should be delayed until the war was over. Peace Now declared that it strongly opposed the decision to wage the war and regarded it as a serious mistake. Nevertheless, it reminded its members of their supreme civic obligation to obey a decision that had been taken by a legitimate authority even though they rejected its substance. And indeed, contrary to the expectations of many, the movement was quite slow in joining the protest against the war, much less in serving as its spearhead. Thus, the collective mind set that had prohibited public protest against such governmental decisions in the past, and against which the peace activists had always struggled, resurfaced as soon as the first shot was fired.

However, a vocal minority led by a new small peace group, There Is a Limit (Yesh Gvul) declared that citizens in a democratic society always have the right and even the obligation to express their disapproval with actions of the authorities. Furthermore, if no satisfactory response is forthcoming, radical methods, such as mass demonstrations or a refusal to fight, are morally and politically justified even though the soldiers are still in the field. This splinter group argued that, by denouncing civil disobedience, the majority of the peace movement had betrayed its mission and therefore was just as responsible for the outcome and damages of the war as the government (Melzer, 1985).

Peace Now found it extremely difficult to deal with this radical internal opposition, since it was not able to convince the public that its own policy possessed internal logic and consistency. Its response therefore consisted of a somewhat unbalanced mixture of actions; some were intended to prove the movement's patriotism and political responsibility, while others were meant to reinforce its position as the leader of the peace camp. Because this combination caused bewilderment and a critical loss of support, neither of these aims were attained.

The decline of Peace Now since the mid-1980s, the ideological splits inside the peace movement, and the rise of numerous (up to 70 in 1989) smaller but more radical peace groups which appeal to specific and limited segments of the public,[21] reduced the potential of the Israeli peace movement to become an established force in the national political arena. The message of the peace movement has apparently been rejected by the majority of Israelis and has no reflection in official foreign policy. Nevertheless, the breakthrough of 1978-1985 and the limited but ongoing peace protest since then have broadened the circle of active participants in the

---

21. A typical example of such peace groups is Ad Kan (literally, Enough Already), which brings together some dozens of university professors, mostly from Tel Aviv, who protest mainly against the harsh measures taken by the Israel authorities to quell the Palestinian uprising.

national security debate (which has intensified considerably since the outbreak of the Intifada in late 1987). The changes produced by the highly visible peace protests of the late 1970s and early 1980s are felt simultaneously at two levels: that of the political leadership and that of the general public. At the first level, memories of the flourishing peace activism of those years remind politicians that the Israeli public might again try to change the national discourse and play an active role in drawing the boundaries within which foreign policy is formulated. Recalling their past disregard toward similar activities. the close attention Israeli leaders nowadays pay to initiatives taken by the peace activists (e.g., the furious reactions to the visit of the peace movement's delegation to the United States in mid-1991 in order to encourage President Bush's peace plan for the Middle East) offers evidence of the elite's higher sensitivity toward the potential for grassroots mobilization.

Moreover, few of those familiar with Israeli political dynamics would deny that even though the domestic opposition to the Lebanese War was rather unpopular and often condemned, it marked a turning point in the traditional public compliance with the government's decisions and acts in the realms discussed here. The strong pressure from below on the government to investigate the Israeli involvement in the massacre of the Palestinian refugees in Sabra and Shatila in the fall of 1982 was perhaps the most obvious example of such effective public discontent. There is also good reason to believe that the vociferous antiwar protests of 1982-1984 played a role quite similar to that of the antiwar movement in the United States during the Vietnam era. It may well be that an Israeli "Lebanese syndrome" has developed, somewhat comparable to the "Vietnam syndrome" which for two decades contributed to the reluctance of American officials to engage in prolonged or controversial military interventions abroad (Sobel, 1989).

On the second level, peace activism contributed, in direct as well as indirect ways, to the creation of a sense of political competence on the part of Israeli citizens. This observation goes hand in hand with the findings of more general studies of Israeli grassroots political activism in the late 1970s and early 1980s, an era which is correctly defined by some scholars as "the age of protest normalization" (Lehman-Wilzig 1990, 40-42). Empirical support for this hypothesis is provided by a survey conducted in Israel in 1987 which points to an unexpectedly high public political self-confidence accompanied by a surprisingly low faith in the political elite.[22] For example, in response to the question, "To what extent do you understand enough about security issues to be able to express an opinion?" 79 percent

---

22. This information was made available by Professor Asher Arian, Director of the National Security and Public Opinion Project, Jaffee Center for Strategic Studies, Tel Aviv University.

of the respondents said that they had enough knowledge to express an opinion. Only 21 percent answered "to a small extent" or "not at all". The question, "Whose opinion should be taken into account regarding the future of the territories?" was answered as follows:

Israel Defense Force generals	43.0%
The public	29.5%
Likud leaders	10.0%
Professors of political science	8.0%
Alignment (Labour) leaders	7.0%
Rabbis	2.5%

In addition, certain traditionally passive segments of the Israeli population have become politically active since the emergence of the peace movement. The most striking example is the participation of women. For many years. Israeli women had been motivated primarily by their feminine commitment to their families and by the notion of the woman as the ultimate origin of nurture and compassion in the nation. These dispositions inhibited Israeli women to a greater extent than men, from expressing dissatisfaction and disapproval with official policy. Protest was considered not only a mark of poor citizenship, but a kind of betrayal of natural feminine and maternal attributes. Moreover, because Israeli women serve in the army only as noncombatants, most of them consider themselves, and are considered by many men as poorly informed with regard to security and military matters, and thus ill equipped to take part in debates regarding war and peace. But these attitudes have changed somewhat in the past few years. More Israeli women than ever are now active in peace groups. A dozen or so womens' groups, militantly campaigning for peace, have emerged in the past decade, enriching and enlarging the debate on these crucial matters.[23]

---

23. Some of the women's groups are quite mainstream; others present fairly controversial postures. The "Israel Women's Peace Network" [Reshet Nashim Israeliot Lemaan Ha'shalom] is a good example of the first type. It is a coalition of several nonpolitical service organizations, which attempt to enable Palestinian and Israeli women to meet and discuss the need for a mutual recognition of human rights on both sides. The radical type is exemplified by the "Women in Black" [Nashim Be'shahor]. Every Friday afternoon, groups of women dressed entirely in black demonstrate at busy intersections in ten or more Israeli cities and towns. This organization calls for an end to the bloodshed, for a start of peace talks with the Palestinians as represented by the PLO, and the creation of an independent Palestinian state in the occupied territories.

CONCLUSIONS AND GENERAL APPLICATIONS OF THE CASE STUDY

The Israeli peace movement's loss of momentum over the past few years should not be taken then as evidence of a return to the previous situation, where public initiatives regarding foreign policy and security matters were virtually unheard of. While the direct impact of grassroots protest on foreign is difficult to measure in the Israeli case, as in and others, it serves as a rather promising starting point for identifying the factors that encourage, or discourage, public awareness and vigilance.

It seems likely, for instance, that the formative period of a political entity is not favorable to self-initiated and authentic grass-roots activism, because at that time the political elite strives to gain full control of the nation's political dynamics. Moreover, at that point, the national leadership tends to regard any challenge to its dominance in policy formation as an expression of opposition to its very authority. In other words, a political entity must reach a certain level of maturity and stability before open debate on the most crucial national issues, especially those involving foreign and security affairs, can be easily tolerated or accepted.

A strong collective conception of external threat also seems to facilitate the national leadership's efforts to limit the number of participants in debates over the basic postulates of its foreign policy. Nevertheless, in cases where national security problems become chronic and the on-going policy does not seem to bring about any positive outcome, the government's claim to sole authority and its demand for total public support, gradually loses its impact. At that point, the public begins to doubt the ability of its leaders to resolve the impasse. The more articulate and educated segments of the society are especially reluctant to accept the leadership's demand for exclusive control and consequently try to promote alternative solutions. In addition, social groups that, for one reason or another, are basically alienated from the established socio-political order, or have gradually become so, are more likely to be either totally indifferent to political developments or, alternatively, to challenge overtly the very political wisdom, moral standards, or ruling skills of the incumbent decision-makers.

Apparently, major shifts in long standing and formerly unchallenged foreign and security policies may draw growing public attention to these normally remote matters and stir grassroots activism in support of or against the new direction taken by the authorities. Much like the NATO "twin-track" decision of 1979 disturbed and annoyed so many Western citizens already accustomed to detente, by invading Lebanon in 1982, the Israeli decision-makers also deviated from its traditional defensive military orientation and in doing so opened an unprecedented nation-wide debate about the basic features of national security policy.

The case study presented here shows that the public's interest and active involvement in foreign policy-making may well be fostered by mounting rivalries within the political elite as well. A divided leadership is usually both unwilling and incapable of maintaining a unified facade. The citizens are presented then with contending political alternatives, supplied with much more information than in times when the upper echelons of power are united, and hence become more attentive than usually to political debate. Moreover, the contending parties often try to strengthen their respective positions by mobilizing public support. In order to gain such support from below the politicians pay, or pretend to pay, more attention to grassroots reservations and demands while also cooperating more enthusiastically with extra-parliamentary movements which challenge the ruling party.

In addition, a fervent domestic opposition may be the outcome of generational change. For example, if political socialization occurs in times of war, when the leaders are looked upon as the nation's saviors, the "war children" when they grow up, are not likely to be very critical of decision-makers. Another case is that of a society which has absorbed large waves of immigrants. These immigrants tend to be indebted to their adopted country; hence, they develop a strong sense of personal loyalty toward its authorities. These emotions may assuage, for many years, any reservations concerning the government's performance. The next generation, however, consisting of young people, native-born, who acquired their political consciousness in a relatively stable and sheltered environment, is more likely to express dissatisfaction with the leadership. This inclination to scrutinize the political elites is reinforced by higher levels of education and economic status, both of which enable individuals to pay more attention to public issues.

The Israeli case also suggests a process of "democratization" in policy-making (in terms of the number of participants, but not necessarily in the course that they advocate), has occurred during the past few decades in regions other than the United States and Europe. Such a widening in the scope of discourse seems to have taken place even in political contexts that, due to subjective or objective reasons, have long been fairly inhospitable to grass-roots demands for participation. This process is frequently motivated by "imported" ideas. In many countries the political ethos tends to reject such "imported" behavior out of a strong inclination to emphasize the uniqueness of the national situation, but it is quite obvious that the growing demand for a greater popular voice, not only in Israel but also in Eastern Europe and elsewhere, has been influenced by the information, disseminated mainly by the mass media, about the burgeoning of citizens' initiatives in Europe and the United States.

A final observation concerns the ultimate normative effect of grassroots movements. Since, in most societies, the postulates of official foreign policy appear to be in accord with those of the right and the more conservative forces, the drive for participation that is aimed at a change in national policy comes mostly from the left and liberal circles. However, the breakthroughs achieved by this kind of activism have a momentum of their own. Thus, breaches in the normative barrier may in the future serve as openings through which opposite or quite different grass-roots demands will be introduced—for example the demand from below for a more aggressive national posture in international affairs. The impact of a social movement, peace movements included, should not be assessed then only by its desired outcomes: i.e., the realization of the movement's concrete demands or its ability to survive. Perhaps to a greater extent, it depends on the imprint, desired or undesired, that such activity leaves on the normative system of the political body and on its approved or unapproved operational codes.

PART TWO

Societal Approaches

6

Domestic Imperatives and Rational Models of Foreign Policy Decision Making

Douglas Van Belle

Foreign policy decisions lie at the intersection of domestic and international politics. Nations must not only act within the spectrum of constraints and opportunities defined by the dynamics of the international system (Kaplan, 1957; Waltz, 1964; Modelski, 1983; Thompson, 1983; Doran and Parsons, 1980) and those defined by their nation's capabilities to act within that system (Bueno de Mesquita, 1981; Huth and Russett, 1984; Organski and Kugler, 1980). The leaders of those nations must also act within the spectrum of constraints and opportunities defined by their own nation's domestic political structure (Allison, 1969; Putnam, 1988). That is, the foreign policy decision maker must answer to a domestic audience that includes supporters, agents responsible for enacting policy, critics of the leadership, and most importantly, challengers for the leadership position.

When domestic political considerations are not included in the study of foreign policy, researchers are limited to developing a set of necessary, but not sufficient, conditions for foreign policy decisions based on the structure of the international arena and the attributes of the state. Excellent examples of this type of study abound (Bueno de Mesquita, 1981; Huth and Russett, 1984; Organski and Kugler, 1980). This kind of explanation is vital, in that it can establish the limits that the international arena and the attributes of the state impose upon the leader's menu of available choices; however it is incomplete in that it does not pursue domestic political constraints on that menu of choices and neglects the domestic forces that motivate the decision maker (Russett and Starr 1989, 21-25).

The goal of this project is to go a step beyond the externally oriented models and incorporate the domestic political forces into a domestic imperatives model of foreign policy decision making. This will be accomplished by avoiding the assumption that the national interest is the rational goal of foreign policy decisions and replacing it with the assumption that the best interest of the leader is the goal that drives the rational pursuit of foreign policy. Such a model is expected to be at least complementary to externally oriented models, providing insights into cases that the projections of externally oriented models have difficulty explaining. To what degree the domestic imperatives model actually challenges the externally oriented models is a question that needs to be addressed empirically through the rigorous application of the model. For this project, a general model of the best interest of a democratically elected[1] leader of a relatively open regime will be built, and then a specific model of United States foreign policy decisions will be constructed. The project will conclude by taking a cursory look at two cases chosen as plausible examples of the model's implications and conclusions.

Scholars have produced works that bridge this artificial estrangement of the two political arenas and include domestic politics as a force influencing the leader's foreign policy choice. Of particular note are the works of Allison (1969) and Putnam (1988). Allison applies three different conceptual models to explain the events of the Cuban Missile Crisis. Two of these models, the organizational process model and the bureaucratic politics model, are built around the limits that the domestic political structure of the country imposes upon foreign policy. These menu-defining limits are beyond those that were delineated by the state-centric, rational-actor (realist) models of the time, in that they included state processes such as the fight for budget shares and the inertia of bureaucratic organizations as part of the foreign policy decision making process.

Putnam (1988) presents a project that is particularly interesting in the way it depicts the interaction between the two political arenas. Putnam focuses on cooperative behavior such as negotiation, and with his simultaneous-game conception of the negotiation process (domestic and international), he assembles an insightful analysis of how both games are played against each other by the chief negotiators in an attempt to maximize political gains in both arenas. Thus, the international-level game is used as leverage to overcome obstacles in the domestic game, and the threat of agreement-nullifying opposition in one player's domestic game is used to maximize the concessions of other players in the international game. Several of Putnam's ideas transfer easily into a study of conflict situations,

---

1. Of particular importance to the modeling exercise is the question of where the leader's support is generated. It is assumed that the leaders of non-democratic countries have domestic political structures that are fundamentally different than those of democratic regimes. Thus, even though the general idea of domestic imperatives is applicable to undemocratic regimes, this exercise will not address them.

particularly the use of the international level of politics as a tool for attaining goals in the domestic political arena.

Recently, there has been an increase in the number of projects that have explicitly addressed the domestic sources of foreign policy. The increase is marked by the *Journal of Conflict Resolution* devoting an entire issue (June, 1991) to articles addressing the interaction of domestic and international politics, and the increase of articles appearing in other journals. These articles address the relationship between internal politics and various aspects of external relations, such as Gaubatz's (1991) discussion of electoral cycles and war; the role of democratic structure and conflict (Morgan and Campbell, 1991; Risse-Kappen, 1991); the role regime type, more generally, plays in conflict (Maoz and Abdolali, 1989; Kilgour, 1991); how extensive the relationship is between internal and external politics (James and Oneal, 1991; Marra, Ostrom and Simon, 1990; Barnett, 1990). These articles all recognize, or explicitly measure an empirical relationship between domestic and international politics, and many of them examine the mechanics of how the interaction occurs. This project attempts to tackle the puzzle from a more theoretical direction, beginning with a few assumptions about the fundamental drives behind policy and attempting to develop a deductive explanation for the interrelationship between the two political arenas.

DOMESTIC PRIMACY

Proposition I: The domestic political arena will take precedence over the
                 international political arena.

I begin with the assumptions that: (a) the leader attempts to pursue, rationally, his or her best interest; (b) the leader of a state is responsible for the major policy decisions in the international political arena; and (c) s/he is then held liable in the domestic political arena for the results of these policy decisions. It is then a short step to postulate that the needs of the leader and the nature of domestic political liabilities define the criteria for rational choice. The condition of domestic accountability, therefore, is the link between the domestic and international arena. In order to discuss the nature of accountability, it is first necessary to establish the needs of the leadership. For the model presented here, the argument is that the primary goal of a rational leader is to maximize his or her domestic political support. Thus, the immediate goals of both domestic and foreign policies are means by which the leader's primary goal of maximizing domestic political standing can be attained.

This argument for the primacy of the domestic arena is not without precedent. Previous works have focused on the leader's desire to remain in office. The researchers working with the Inter-Nation Simulation had a bottom line of domestic support that the players must maintain in order to remain in control of their respective nations (Guetzkow 1963, 24-29). Putnam (1988, 457), makes a similar statement in his article, arguing that it is reasonable to presume that the leader "will normally give primacy to his domestic calculus...not the least because his own incumbency often depends on his standing at level II (domestic)."

Theoretically, a strong desire to remain in office is based upon the value of holding the leadership position. The leadership position has a great deal of value, both to the person holding it and to those who would challenge the leader for that position. It does not matter why the position is valuable to a leader; s/he must remain in control of the position in order to exploit the value inherent in it. A leader must retain the position in order to realize the drives that Downs (1957, 30) identifies, "desire for power, prestige and income, and ... love of conflict."

Even if one assumes that the leader is completely altruistic and is only holding the office to attain some unselfish end, s/he must retain the position in order to utilize the resources of the leadership position to direct the government to implement policies that will attain those selfless goals. Since the primary threat to incumbency arises in the form of challengers from the domestic arena, the leader will try to maximize her domestic support and thus minimize the ability of domestic challengers to threaten her position. In some cases, such as a second-term U.S. president, any argument that links the desire to remain in office directly with the decisions of the leader becomes tenuous. An alternative is to focus on the power aspect of domestic political support. In the case of the United States Presidency, a significant portion of the power of the president has been clearly linked to the domestic support of the President as it is measured in the presidential approval ratings. (Light, 1982; Lowi, 1985; Simon and Ostrom, 1988; Neustadt, 1990.)

Thus, the second theoretical justification for positing the primacy of domestic standing is the interaction pattern between domestic support and the ability to act on behalf of the state. Domestic standing is the measure of support from the domestic power bases. It is the support of these power bases—whether they are other elected representatives, financial leaders, bureaucrats, military organizations, or whatever—that gives the leader the ability to act on behalf of the state. The power bases are either the actual mechanisms of action, e.g. the military, or they control access to the means through a function performed as a check on power, e.g. the budgeting power exercised by Congress. This ability to act, to pursue goals or to resolve issues, is what then enables the leader to maintain or to gain domestic support. The domestic power bases react to the outcome of the action, positively, negatively or neutrally, and their support for the leader and his policy choices fluctuates accordingly.

A leader who is careful to make decisions that augment, or at least do not adversely affect, his domestic standing will continue to be able to direct the resources of the state towards the attainment of goals or the resolution of issues. Conversely, a leader who pursues actions or allows situations to persist that harm her domestic standing soon ends up with too little support or too much opposition to direct efficiently the resources of the state in the pursuit of policy. Political paralysis ensues, and s/he would be unable to implement policies that might improve that low standing. This motivation for maximizing or maintaining domestic standing is immediate and constant; it works in concert with the episodic and occasional incumbency motivation.

Relating the concept of domestic primacy to foreign policy decision-making leads to the conclusion that the leader does not choose among foreign policy options through an objective rational calculation of what is best for the state as a whole. Instead, the leader attempts to decide rationally which option is either least likely to harm her domestic standing (risk-minimizing rational behavior) or most likely to enhance it (gain-maximizing rational behavior). The desire of the leader to remain in office, combined with the desire to maintain the utility of that office, makes political concerns in the domestic arena dominate the political concerns in the international arena.

Depicting Domestic Support

Proposition II: In a nation with a multiplicity of power bases, the distribution of political support will approximate a normal curve.

In every state the composition of the power bases and the distribution of political power among them is different, but there is always a multiplicity of power bases. Examples could include military leaders, party leaders, institutional leaders, religious leaders, business interests, voting coalitions, individual voters, interest groups academics, and others. The nature of this distribution of power affects the leader's ability to win or lose support, and consequently, it affects the strategies the leader uses to gain or maintain support.

In a nation with a multiplicity of power bases, a few domestic power bases would be either fanatical supporters or diehard opponents of a particular leader. These power bases would be represented at the extremes of the spectrum by the tails of the bell curve. The direction of their political support, for or against a particular leader remaining in office, would be difficult to alter. The majority of domestic power bases would then be in the center of the spectrum, represented by the peak in the bell curve. The power

Figure 6.1: Support Distribution Depiction

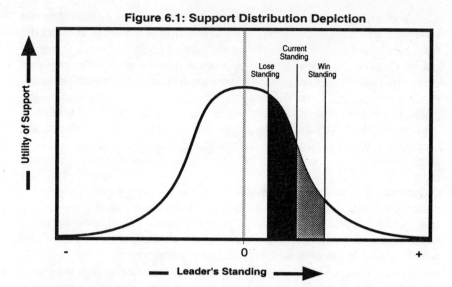

bases in the center would be basically neutral, though they might lean slightly towards or away from supporting any particular leader. Their support would be alterable, meaning it would vary as these moderate power bases reacted to different actions or policy options and it could be won or lost by the leader. The exact shape of the curve, and where each power base fell along the spectrum would vary from leader to leader, but the overall shape of the distribution should be similar for all leaders.[2]

A hypothetical representation of this curve is presented in the Support Distribution Depiction of Figure 6.1. Each point along the curve is the amount of support located at that particular point along the easiest-to-most-difficult spectrum, while the area under the curve represents the sum total of domestic support available. The total amount of domestic support for a leader at a specific domestic standing equals the area under the curve between the negative extreme and a vertical line representing his standing. If the leader has the support of exactly 50% of the domestic power bases, then exactly 50% of the area beneath the curve would be between the negative extreme and the line representing his current standing. This position upon the graph would be at the apex of the normally-distributed curve and is represented by a vertical line at zero on the scale.

---

2. The assumption of a unimodal normal curve is a particularly strong one. It must be noted that for different distributions of domestic support, such as a polarized bi-modal depiction, different expectations concerning the relationship between risk-propensity and domestic standing would be generated.

Two fundamental aspects of political behavior can be drawn from this representation of domestic support. If a leader is secure in office (above 0 on the scale) s/he should be risk-averse. If the leader is weak in office (below 0 on the scale) s/he should tend towards more risk-acceptant behavior. The logic of this reasoning can be shown most easily in the graphic figure: a vertical line is drawn indicating the current domestic standing of a leader that is well above the zero point. Then a certain amount of standing is put at risk, indicated by a vertical line representing the higher standing of the leader if the risky policy succeeds and one equally distant in the negative direction for the failure of the policy.

The area under the curve that is trapped between each of the potential standings and the line representing current standing, respectively, represents the amount of support that could be won (gray area) and the amount of support that could be lost (black area). A simple visual inspection shows that the area of the black figure, representing the amount of support that could be lost, is significantly greater. This comparison illustrates a political law of diminishing returns for leaders with support greater than 50%. For a leader who is in danger of losing control, however, his standing will be on the opposite side of the curve's apex. The relative amount of support to be won or lost for a certain amount of risk will be reversed.

Thus, such a leader should be more willing to take risks, because for a certain amount of risk, s/he has more to win than to lose. Thus, assuming a multitude of domestic power bases and a centralizing trend away from fanatic support for an individual leader or fanatic opposition, modeling the pattern of support leads to two conclusions: a rational leader who is secure in office will be risk-averse; a leader with a low level of support will be more risk-acceptant.

UNCERTAINTY AND RISK

Proposition III: Risk can be minimized by shifting the context of the decision and the criteria for choice out of the international political arena and into the domestic political arena.

Few would dispute the inclusion of risk as an integral part of the foreign policy decision-making process, but introducing it into a model also poses some problems. Milburn and Billings (1976) provide an excellent source of concepts and relationships concerning risk, which are relevant to the theoretical model-building project. Risk is a complex construct. It is a product of uncertainty in the decision making process combined with the possibility that negative consequences might result from the decision. Risk has two fundamental components: uncertainty over the probability of negative consequences and uncertainty over the size of those negative consequences. Increasing the degree of uncertainty concerning either or both aspects of the negative consequences increases the decision maker's perception of risk.

Uncertainty can be conceptualized as the absence of perfect information for the decision maker (Milburn and Billings, 1976). The degree of uncertainty is then how much information is lacking, or how far the decision maker is from obtaining perfect information. For the foreign policy decision maker, the international arena is awash in uncertainties. The information that the leader receives from the international arena is limited in scope; it has been filtered and distilled by several different people; it must often cross societal and linguistic barriers; it is typically inferential in nature; and occasionally, it will be outright fiction. This lack of reliable information translates into greater degrees of risk regarding both the possibility of negative consequences and the possible size of those consequences.

The domestic political arena creates fewer uncertainties. Indeed, the leader can be assumed to be an expert concerning the domestic political arena. The leader is, by definition, the most recent champion of the domestic political arena. Also, the greater amount and reliability of information concerning the domestic arena contributes to a reduction of uncertainty and a lower perception of risk. Applying this reasoning to our modeling project, it is plausible to conclude that a leader will be able to predict the domestic political consequences of both the success and failure of a policy more accurately than s/he will be able to predict its actual success or failure. Thus, a risk-averse leader can minimize the uncertainties involved in foreign policy decision making by planning for the worst case scenario in the international arena (policy failure) and selecting the policy option with the most favorable domestic response to the failure of the policy. This strategy of decision shifts the context of the decision so as to minimize uncertainties and risk.

The leader thereby moves the decision out of the international arena, where uncertainty and risk abound, by assuming that the policy will fail. Then the risks involved with the possibility of failure or negative consequences are no longer relevant to the decision. The leader makes the decision in the context of the less uncertain domestic political environment and assesses the probability as well as the size of positive or negative domestic response to the policy failure. The magnitude of the expected negative consequences in the international arena is only important in its effect upon the domestic response.

Depicting Domestic Response

Proposition IV: Policy options can be categorized according to the expected
domestic responses to policy success and policy failure.

Domestic response has two components, direction and magnitude. The
direction of domestic response can be defined as the gain or loss of domestic
support due to foreign policy actions, while the magnitude of domestic
response can be defined as the size of the positive or negative response. This
two-component definition of domestic response corresponds directly with
the two component definition of risk (See Gallhofer and Saris, 1979). The
possibility of negative consequences corresponds with the possibility of
negative domestic response and the size of the possible consequences
corresponds with the magnitude of the possible negative response. Here
only the direction of the domestic response will be modeled; the magnitude
of domestic response, how much gain or how much loss, will be introduced
later.

Foreign policy actions are defined as the decision either to announce or
to implement a change in foreign policy. Conversely, inaction is defined as
the continuation of current policy. The domestic response to either action or
inaction can be categorized as harmful, neutral, or beneficial to the leader's
standing. S/he can lose standing, stay the same, or gain in standing. In
modeling the direction of expected domestic response, these possibilities
can be represented as a continuum of expected domestic responses from
harmful up through beneficial. This spectrum is then divided into three
hierarchical regions that represent from top to bottom the categories beneficial, neutral, and harmful.

This division creates two important thresholds. The Prevent Harm
threshold is at the point where the direction of the domestic response is
expected to shift from being harmful for the leader's standing to being
neutral; keeping the domestic response above the threshold prevents harm
to the leader's standing. The Enhance Standing threshold is at the point
where the direction of the domestic response is expected to shift from being
neutral to being beneficial; keeping the domestic response above this
threshold enhances the leader's domestic standing.

Using a spectrum and thresholds to describe the direction of domestic
responses rather than the three categories of beneficial, neutral, and harmful, permits the modeling of uncertainty about the outcome. Distance from
a threshold, above or below, represents certainty of the direction of response, not the magnitude of the response. If a leader is certain that the
response to policy failure will be harmful to his standing, the expected
direction of the response to the failure of the option is a great distance below
the prevent harm threshold. If the leader is uncertain whether policy failure

Figure 6.2: Expected Domestic Response Preference Ordering

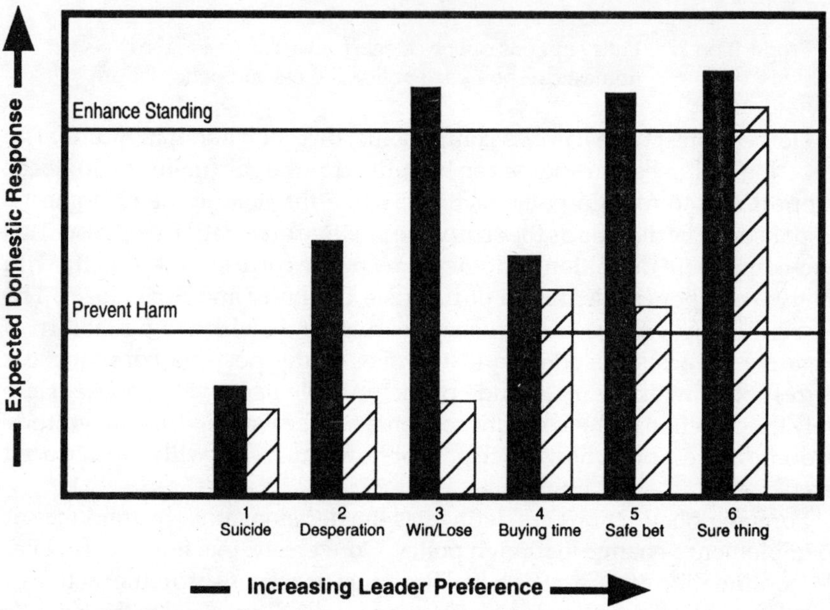

will be in the harmful or neutral direction, then the expected direction of the response to the failure of the option is very close to the prevent harm threshold.

In the following graphic models of policy choices and decision making the vertical axis is divided into the three regions, Harmful, Neutral, and Beneficial, by the two horizontal thresholds, Prevent Harm and Enhance Standing. Policy choices are represented in this model by how their success or failure will affect the leader's domestic standing. If the response to policy failure can always be expected to be lower than the response to success, then six different types of foreign policy options can be defined by noting where their expected domestic reactions fall in relation to the three regions and the two thresholds mentioned above. These six types of responses are represented graphically in the Expected Domestic Response Preference Ordering Figure (see Figure 6.2).

In this figure, each of the six policy options is represented as a pair of vertical bars, the top of which represents the location on the spectrum representing the direction of domestic response. The top of the black bar represents the expected response to the success of the policy option, and the top of the gray bar represents the expected response to the failure, or worst-case outcome of the policy. All six possibilities for expected reaction are presented here, and using the assumption of a leader who is in good standing and is risk-averse (avoid risk first, maximize gain second), the leader's preferences for the policy options can be rank-ordered in the graph, from least preferred on the left (Option 1) to most preferred on the right (Option 6).

A descriptive label can be given for each of the six options for clarity. The two lowest ranked options, (1) Suicide (2) Desperation, should be either nonexistent or exceedingly rare as policy choices, occurring only by profound miscalculation on the part of the leader. *Suicide* represents a form of domestic political suicide that a rational leader would be expected to avoid, with the domestic response to both failure and success in the harmful category, below the prevent harm threshold, it harms the leader's standing no matter what the outcome of the policy choice. The second lowest option, Desperation, would be nearly as bad, with the value of success above the prevent harm threshold and the value of failure below. A leader choosing a desperation option would be risking harm if the policy fails just to gain a neutral response if the policy succeeds.

(3) *Win/Lose*, with the response to success being beneficial and the response to failure being harmful, represents the option that was originally modeled in the bell-curved, domestic support model in Figure 6.1. The leader is risking a loss of domestic standing in an attempt to gain domestic standing. (4) *Buying Time* is an option where both potential responses are in the neutral region. No standing is being risked but there is no expected gain for policy success.

The rank ordering of *Win/Lose* and *Buying Time* might be reversed if the leader is highly risk-prone; however, that is only expected to occur in cases of extreme and immediate domestic threat to the leader. As noted earlier, the assumption made in modeling the risk-averse leader is that s/he would avoid risk by avoiding the potential of harm to her standing first and seek gain by maximizing the potential enhancement of her standing second. Thus, a risk-averse rational leader would choose option 4 over 3 based on the expected response to failure, grey bar, while a risk-acceptant rational leader would prefer option 3 over 4, based on the expected response to success, the black bar. Extending this criteria to the rest of the categories, the preference ordering for all of the other options would remain the same.

The last two options, like the first two, are also fairly self-explanatory. A (5) *Safe Bet* has an expected response to failure that is above the prevent harm threshold, and the expected response to success that is above the enhance standing threshold, so if policy success does occur, it is expected to be beneficial, but a failure is not expected to be harmful. The last category (6) *Sure Thing* has both of the potential domestic responses above the enhance standing threshold, so no matter what the outcome, the response should be beneficial.

To summarize, assuming that there are three potential domestic responses to the outcome of policy choices and if the response to the worst case outcome of a policy will always be lower than the response to success, there are six categories into which potential responses can be divided. Using the assumption of a risk-averse leader, the preferences among those categories can be established. These categories and the preferences among them can then be used to develop models of rational decision.

THE BOUNDED GAIN MAXIMIZER MODEL

Proposition V: A risk-averse leader will choose the policy option that is
                  expected to provide the best possible domestic response to
                  the failure of the policy.

The bounded gain maximizer model rests upon the assumption of bounded rationality where the leader attempts rationally to choose the option with the highest utility from a limited menu of options. Again, for modeling purposes, the magnitude of those utilities, how much is to be gained or lost, is not included in the model, but it will be included at a later point. This model is graphically represented in Figure 6.3.

The bounded nature of the model is a result of the limited menu of alternatives and the limited time for consideration. The time line of the model runs from left to right across the bottom of the model, and it begins when the foreign policy subject or foreign policy situation is introduced to the decision maker. This point occurs when the domestic response to inaction on a foreign policy issue falls below the harmful/neutral threshold. Inaction is considered to be the default policy choice (i.e., no change in policy on the issue), and it is represented as the initial choice.

Inaction continues to be the policy choice until a policy alternative is discovered that has an expected domestic response to policy failure that is in a higher category than that of inaction.[3] In the graphic model, the utility of inaction is below the Prevent Harm threshold; therefore, inaction is harming the domestic standing of the leader. The first acceptable alternative introduced to the leader is the option labeled C, a Buying-time option. It has an expected utility for both success and failure above the Prevent Harm threshold. Thus, even if the policy fails, as the pessimistic leader fears, it is better for the leader to choose this option than to do nothing.

---

3. Basing the choice on the expected response to failure is an aspect of risk minimization where the leader avoids the uncertainties of the international arena and minimizes risk by assuming the policy will fail and planning based on that assumption. It is assumed that the leader is rational in risk taking and will avoid any risk that is not explicitly tied to a potential payoff.

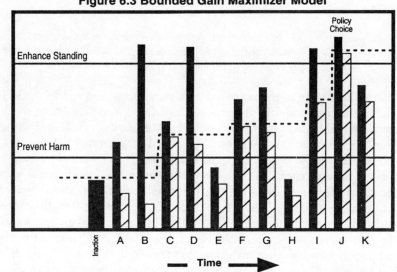

Figure 6.3 Bounded Gain Maximizer Model

The proposal and consideration of options will continue right up to the moment that the decision must be made, announced and implemented. During this time the policy choice will continue to be changed as better options, options of a higher leader preference, are discovered. Options that are poorer are passed over. In the model this mechanism for choosing policy is represented by the double-dashed line that jumps as better options are found. The line begins at the level of the default policy, inaction, shifts to option C, a Buying-time policy, then it shifts to option F, a Buying-time policy with a higher value for failure, then to option I, a Safe-bet, and then to J, a Sure-thing. Finally, when decision making time runs out, the option to be implemented will be the last one that has been chosen. This is represented in the model by the last jump in the dashed line (option J).

If no Buying-time or better option has been discovered, the choice will default to the best win-lose option. If none of those options have been found, a desperation option might or might not be chosen depending on the importance of the issue and the specific risk-prone propensities of the specific political actor. A rational actor, no matter how risk-prone, should never choose an option that is perceived as a suicide option.

RATIONAL SATISFICER MODEL

Proposition VI: A risk-averse, satisficing leader with constraints upon the
menu for choice, will choose the *first* option presented that
is expected to prevent harm even if the policy fails.

An alternative to the bounded gain maximizer as a model of decision
making is the model of the rational satisficer, a management model of
decision making that is usually applied to the managers of large businesses
(Simon 1976, intro xxix, 80-88 and 240-250). The difference between the two
models lies in the definition of rational choice. In classical rational actor
theory, rational choice is characterized as being choices directed towards
the most efficient, cost-benefit achievement of goals (Downs 1957, 4-8),
while rational choice for the satisficer is the first option that meets a
sufficient, or satisfactory, condition. The first good enough option will be
the option chosen (Simon, 1976). Thus, the satisficer abandons the idea of
maximizing and attempts to just do good enough. It can also be modeled in
the same fashion as the previous bounded gain maximizer model (see
Figure 6.4). Using the earlier characterizations of the leader, the sufficient
condition for rational choice should be the prevention of harm to the
domestic standing of the leader, or the first Buying-time or better option
found.

The model is presented graphically in Figure 6.4. In the model, option C
(a Buying-time option) is found and the consideration of alternatives for
dealing with the harmful issue ends. The leader's decision-making resources are then immediately directed towards the next crisis on the
agenda, or the next harmful issue. The reasoning behind the model centers
around the conceptualization of the leader as a person who, by virtue of
tremendous responsibilities, is faced with a shortage of decision making
resources, such as time or information, and is unable to pursue decisions all
of the way out to the best solution. S/he deals with this shortage, not only
by accepting the first satisfactory option considered, but also by dealing
only with crisis situations, i.e., situations that s/he is forced to deal with.

The crisis-only aspect of the model is represented here (and in the
rational actor model presented earlier) by starting the time line when an
issue forces itself into the decision-making arena. That is, the default policy
of inaction, the continuation of current policy on that issue, becomes
harmful or eminently harmful to the domestic standing of the leadership. If
this crisis manager concept is applied in an unreserved manner, it would
mean that the only issues that would be decided would be issues that have
forced themselves into the spotlight.

The rational satisficer model for foreign policy decisions explains more
than the bounded rational actor model. It can show why the leader seems
to behave in an immediate, reactive, stimulus-response manner rather than

Figure 6.4 Limited Option Satisficing Decision Model

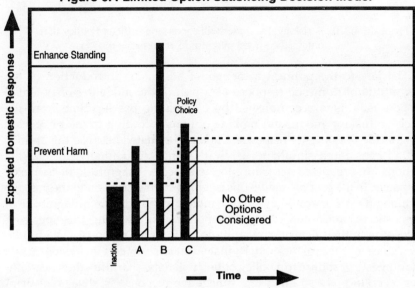

a long-term, planned and strategic manner. This type of behavior occurs because s/he only deals with the hottest issue (Allison 1969, 711). It gives a hint as to why non-optimal solutions might be chosen, because the non-optimal options are good enough. It also provides an angle from which some concerns regarding the premature cognitive closure of leaders in crisis situations can be addressed. Leaders are not shutting off the rational consideration of options too soon. Instead they have found a buying-time or better option and they are trying to move on to the next crisis. It also offers a mechanism for explaining why current policies (defined as inaction in the model) tend to have a momentum that defies rational choice criteria. If the issue does not appear to pose a threat to the leader's standing, or if it is not the hottest issue, or if no Buying-time or better option can be found, then the leader will not address the issue.

The rational satisficer appears to bring the description of the decision-making process one step closer to reality, but both of these models still share a common shortcoming. They represent the options considered as being individually evaluated and sequentially presented to the leader. A more accurate model of the foreign policy decision maker may be to view the options considered by the leader as a fairly broad set of foreign policy options all considered simultaneously.

THE POLITICAL ACTOR MODEL

Proposition VII: A risk-averse leader will choose the sufficient policy that
entails the lowest magnitude of domestic response.

The key to the political actor model lies in the introduction of the
magnitude of domestic response as a part of the modeling of potential
responses. This is accomplished by eliminating passing time from the
decision making model and ranking options according to their expected
magnitude of domestic response. Time is eliminated because the options
are all considered simultaneously rather than sequentially. Instead the
options are organized according to the expected magnitude of domestic
response. In the graphic model this is represented by replacing the passage
of time on the horizontal axis of the model with increasing magnitude of
domestic response and placing the policy options along this spectrum
according to their expected magnitude of domestic response. The fundamental assumption of the model is that no matter how certain a leader is that
the domestic response to a policy option will not be harmful, the uncertainties of politics are so great that a negative response is always a salient
concern of the leader. Thus, if given a set of alternatives, a leader will choose
the sufficient policy (Buying Time or better) that entails the lowest magnitude of potential domestic response, just in case the domestic response is
negative. This assumption is merely an extension of risk minimization.
      The risk of negative consequences is minimized through the assumption
of policy failure and the setting of an expected neutral response to failure as
the minimum sufficient condition for policy choice. Although this strategy
minimizes the probability aspect of risk, it does not address directly the
value aspect of risk, i.e., the size of possible negative consequences. By
choosing the sufficient condition with the lowest expected magnitude of
domestic response, the value aspect of risk is also minimized.
      The model resulting from the minimization of this aspect of risk is
represented graphically in Figure 6.5, where the magnitude of domestic
response for option A is less than option B, which is less than option C, etc.
When the leader considers action on an issue because the inaction option
has become harmful to his standing, s/he begins with the menu option that
is expected to create the lowest magnitude of domestic response and
considers whether or not it will be sufficient to prevent harm to his domestic
political standing. If s/he does not expect it to be sufficient, s/he moves to
the next lowest option. This process continues until a Buying-time or better
option is found with the minimum possible magnitude of domestic response. In Figure 6.5, this option is C, the one with the lowest magnitude of
expected domestic response that also prevents harm to the leader's standing no matter what the substantive outcome (success or failure).

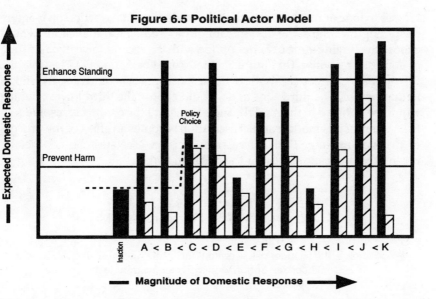

Figure 6.5 Political Actor Model

This model offers insight into phenomena that the simple rational actor model cannot. It gives a possible explanation of why policies that almost never succeed, such as trade sanctions, continue to be used by leaders. Trade sanctions carry a low level of domestic liability[4] (which is the magnitude of potential harm a policy might cause in the domestic political arena) and even though they almost always fail to accomplish their stated goals (Lindsay, 1986), they do present the image of action to the domestic power bases. This useless action, i.e., action expected to fail, can prevent the harm to the standing of the leader that inaction was causing. The leader then hopes that the situation will correct itself or fade from urgency with the time that has been bought, thus, the label Buying Time for the option. It buys the leader time for the issue to resolve itself or for the issue to be lost in the passage of time.

This model also gives a new perspective from which to look at escalation in conflict situations. If an issue involving conflict with another nation

---

4. Domestic liability is the amount of harm a policy could potentially do if the domestic response to the policy were negative. This is different from the magnitude of domestic response in that liability refers only to the negative possibility of the magnitude of domestic response, and it is different from salience in that salience is the operationalization of the magnitude of domestic response for a regime with relatively free news media. Liability is used so that in subsequent modeling exercises, the concept can be transferred when referring to non-media related liabilities like alienating bureaucratic supporters in a system dominated by political power struggles.

refuses to fade or resolve itself, then the leader must take action on it again. Assuming that the same option cannot be used again, the leader would choose the Buying-time or better option with the second lowest magnitude of domestic response. (In Figure 6.5 that would be option D.) Presumably, this option's greater magnitude of domestic response would raise the stakes in the conflict. The third time s/he would choose the third lowest (which would be option F in the model), and so on, until the conflict is resolved. In the context of this model conflict escalation becomes an effect of the process of decision-making. Each successive decision escalates the conflict by raising the domestic stakes for the decision maker.

RISK ACCEPTANCE AND THE POLITICAL ACTOR MODEL

Proposition VIII: The more risk-acceptant the leader, the more likely s/he will choose an option with a greater magnitude of domestic response.

Returning to the attitudes that the leader holds toward risk, the question arises: how can this model account for a leader who is more risk-acceptant? The answer should be found in the relative levels of uncertainty that exist along the different aspects of the decision process. The idea of a risk-acceptant leader does not exclude the concept of risk minimization; instead, the difference lies in increased emphasis put on potential gain. It follows logically that the leader's acceptance of risk in pursuit of gain should occur in the area of least uncertainty, which allows for the pursuit of maximum gain while incurring the smallest possible increase in risk. In areas of the decision-making process where there is a great deal of uncertainty, such as the probability of policy success or failure, the decision-making emphasis should still be upon minimizing risk. In the areas of least uncertainty, such as the domestic response, the decision-making emphasis should shift to maximizing possible gains.

Relating this reasoning to the model means that the major difference between a risk-averse and a risk-acceptant leader should be found along the axis representing the magnitude of domestic response. The uncertainties in the prediction of policy success or failure in the international arena are so great that the assumption of policy failure should still hold, and a neutral or better response to policy failure should remain as the minimum condition for policy choice, but, keeping in mind that any policy could result in a negative domestic response, a leader in a position to be more risk acceptant should be willing to accept a greater magnitude of domestic response in return for a greater possibility of a gain in domestic support. In Figure 6.5, therefore, a risk-acceptant leader would move further up the scale of expected magnitude of domestic response in search of a policy with the possibility of a beneficial outcome. A risk-acceptant leader might choose option D over option C. If the leader is extremely risk-acceptant, option I or J might be chosen.

Breaking down domestic response into its components and looking at the direction and the magnitude separately adds insights that appear to bring the full impact of the domestic political arena into the foreign policy decision-making process. The next steps in the model building process are to operationalize domestic response in a form that represents a specific nation, in this case the United States, and then model it dynamically in terms of the costs of inaction and the expectations for response to policy choices.

THE EXPECTATION OF ACTION

Proposition IX: The domestic response to issues in general will be an expectation of action; this expectation will be embodied in a call for the leader to resolve the problem at the root of the issue.

The "expectation" of action proposition is a representation of the domestic response to issues in general. An issue is considered to be a matter of national scope or consequence, and the leader is considered to be the individual responsible for dealing with these matters. The expectation of action is no more than the expectation that the leader should fulfill his or her responsibilities. Various methods of measuring the call for action could be pursued, including opinion polls, letters to-the-editor, and public demonstrations.

Regardless of how it is measured, the call for action on a particular subject is usually mixed, with different power bases calling for different policy responses by the leader. Any link between a particular call and a particular course action would be tenuous at best, because the calls of different portions of the nation's total power base may cancel each other out by demanding opposite responses (i.e., threaten vs. reassure). Theoretically, however, it is possible to think of the call for action as the aggregate demand for the leader to pursue the single goal of resolving the problem at the root of the issue rather than as a demand for the leader to take a specific action.

Empirically, the call for action is more likely to be mixed for issues concerning negotiation or cooperation with foreign nations. Domestic power bases on all sides of the issue will compete to define not only the goal to be pursued, but also the nature of the problem that needs to be solved. In situations of conflict between nations, the issues are more clear-cut. Even though there will still be competition to define the specific course of action, there is a clear—though often vaguely-defined—goal of victory that the majority of the power bases share. This shared goal should aggregate itself into a more uniform demand for the leader to take action in pursuit of the commonly desired goal.

For example, when students in Iran took American hostages, they instigated a conflictual foreign policy situation between the U.S and Iran. In the U.S., the domestic call for action was clear, and the decision situation was clearly one of presidential dominance (Rosati, 1981). Presidential involvement is high enough so that s/he can be considered the dominant decision maker, and s/he is least constrained by organizational processes, such as those delineated in the bureaucratic politics and organizational politics models (Rosati, 1981; Allison, 1969). In this conflict situation it was the president's decision to make; there was a clear opponent (Iran); and there was a clear victory condition (win the release of the hostages). Even though specific calls for action may have differed, there was a common thread among them. It emerged as a call for the leader to act towards the common goal of victory, the resolution of the issue, through the release of the hostages.

DOMESTIC RESPONSE AND SALIENCE

Proposition X: The direction of the domestic response to inaction, whether it is harmful, neutral or beneficial, will be directly related to the importance of the issue.

The importance of an issue determines the direction of the response to inaction for that issue. The aggregate domestic call for action should be relatively constant across different issues, and across time for an individual issue. Despite the constant expectation of action, inaction on an issue that is of insignificant concern to the domestic power bases cannot be harmful to the leader's standing. Conversely, inaction on a highly important issue, one that is of great concern to the domestic power bases, is almost certain to be harmful to the leader's standing. The more important the issue becomes, the more certain it becomes that inaction is harming the leader's domestic standing. As the issue becomes less important, it becomes less likely that it is harming the leader's standing.

Operationally, fluctuations in the importance of the issue can be tied to the salience of the issue. The work by Iyengar and Kinder (1987) suggests that in the United States the news media sets the agenda for the public by defining what should be considered important. They demonstrate that the importance individuals place upon an issue fluctuates in response to the amount of coverage the issue receives in the television news media. They also demonstrate that while the importance varied, the individual's policy position and basic attitudes on the issue remained unaltered. In their study, a correlation of survey data from several sources and the content of the news casts occurring in the same time frame show a strong relationship between the most important issue facing the nation and the amount of coverage that issue received. They also tested this relationship experimentally and reached the same conclusion. Therefore, a good measure of the public importance of an issue in the United States should be its salience in the news media.

In addition to the direct relationship between salience and public importance that Iyengar and Kinder describe, the salience of an issue can also be linked to the leadership's perception of the issue's importance. Since direct communication between domestic power bases in the United States is often limited, the leader and the domestic power bases use the media as a means of communication and the amount of coverage should reflect the amount of communication being attempted. The news media become the leader's window on the reactions of domestic power bases to events. Domestic power bases use the news media to state positions, voice concerns and otherwise communicate their needs and expectations to the leader; the leader uses the news media in a similar way to communicate back to the domestic power bases. This indirect communication increases the attention that both the domestic power bases and the leader give to the issues in the news media, enhancing it as an indicator of an issue's importance.

One objection that might arise in any attempt to link news media coverage to the decision-making of a leader is that the government, and the leadership in particular, create a great deal of the source material for the media. The leadership can influence the level and tone of news coverage and thus influence the domestic importance of issues. Works by scholars such as Bennett (1988) and Edelman (1977) have focused on this aspect of public information dissemination and its effects.

While acknowledging the strength of the premise that the President plays a primary role in setting the agenda for the media, it is important to make a distinction between the influence of the President and the assumption of control. The President does not decide which covered issues will capture the attention of the public nor can s/he remove an issue from the media. Instead, his role is one of manipulating the salience of issues through actions and statements in order to shift as much attention as possible towards issues that can be handled in a manner which reflects positively on him.

It should also be pointed out that most of the information produced by the government on foreign policy subjects is generated in response to an occurrence that has already captured attention. The example of President Reagan's relationship with the press lends credibility to the thought that even declining to provide information to the media on such foreign policy events can create as much media coverage as does providing information.

In the United States, therefore, the media coverage is the reporting of a mixture of created events and spontaneous events. The balance of these sources of media coverage as well as the leadership's efforts to influence the content and the amount of coverage will be included below in the modeling of the two types of foreign policy decisions.

TYPES OF FOREIGN POLICY DECISIONS

There are a universe of organizational schemes to categorize foreign policy decisions (McClelland, 1961; Hermann, 1972). In the construction of the three rationality models, the default foreign policy choice is the continuation of current policy, i.e., inaction. If we categorize foreign policy change by looking at the context which motivated the leader to choose action over the default choice of inaction, then two categories of foreign policy decisions can be identified.

The first, which has been implicitly used in the building of the model, is the Management Decision. In this category, the change in foreign policy is made as an attempt to directly manage an issue that has become a crisis. The issue has thrust itself into the domestic awareness and gained a high level of domestic salience, making the domestic response to inaction clearly harmful to the leader's standing and forcing the leader to take action. The second category is the Opportunity Decision, a foreign policy decision made to generate salience and shift the public's attention away from a harmful issue or issues. In the opportunity decision the leader cannot, or does not deal with the troublesome issue and uses a foreign policy event that reflects favorably upon the leader to redirect the attention of the domestic power bases.

Management Decisions

In a predominantly open society, such as the United States, management decisions should account for the vast majority of the foreign policy decisions made. The concept of a management decision also coincides with the rational satisficer model of an overworked manager who only deals with the most pressing foreign policy situation. To understand the mechanics and the concepts behind management decisions, it is necessary to look at an issue's salience decay patterns, its salience threshold, and how salience, through its relationship to the importance of an issue, should be related to the costs of inaction. (see Figure 6.6).

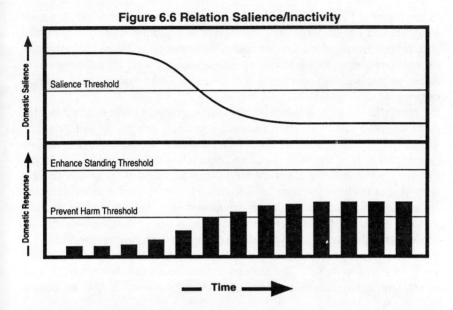

Figure 6.6 Relation Salience/Inactivity

In the Salience/Inactivity model (Figure 6.6) the domestic salience of an issue is represented by the dark curve that begins in the upper left edge of the top half of the figure, dropping and leveling off as it moves to the right. If salience is measured as the amount of news coverage an issue gets, it starts out near or at its highest point, which is when something dramatic (usually an event beyond the control of the leader such as a coup, a speech by foreign official, etc...) has caused the issue to explode into the domestic awareness. If there is no further action reinforcing the salience of the issue, it holds this high level of attention for a short time and then the amount of news coverage that the issue receives begins to fall off. The salience of an issue continues to fade over time until the curve flattens out and a minimum level is reached where its further decay is extremely slow. Over time, a second event related to the first event, such as a policy action by the domestic leadership, may cause a second jump in salience level. The decay process will then begin again from the new level set by the second jump.

The salience threshold line in the model represents the point where the level of domestic salience shifts between where inaction is harmful to the standing of the leader (above the line) and where the issue can be safely ignored by the leader (below the line). This relationship is shown graphically by comparing the upper and lower half of Figure 6.6. As time passes, the level of salience fades, while the value of inaction rises. When the salience falls below the salience threshold, the value of inaction rises above the Prevent Harm threshold. For an individual foreign policy situation, the level of this threshold might shift to some degree over time, but any shifts in the threshold level, especially after the situation has persisted for some time, should not be large and the threshold should remain fairly stable throughout the incident. Under relatively stable conditions, the potential domestic response to inaction correlates inversely with the salience of an issue, as the salience increases the direction of the domestic response decreases.[5]

Using this model of salience decay, we can graph hypothetically how the domestic response to inaction varies in conjunction with the salience (see Figure 6.6) and how that translates into a dynamic decision making model (see Figure 6.7). If the salience of an issue never rises above this salience threshold, then the issue does not need to be addressed. If the salience of the issue does rise above the threshold, then the leader is faced with a dilemma. If the leader does not take action, the default policy of inaction will continue to harm him until the salience of the issue fades below the threshold line. If the leader does take action by making a change in the foreign policy directed towards the entity or nation involved, then the domestic perception switches from inaction to action. The domestic response shifts from harmful to neutral or perhaps even beneficial. However, two other things also occur:

1. The salience of the issue takes a sharp jump upward with the announcement or demonstration of action by the leader. This increases the initial benefit to the leader, because the beneficial perception of action is also coupled with a jump in issue importance; however, the length of time needed for the issue to fade below the threshold line and the salience level at which the issue will level off have both been increased.

2. The perception of action fades back to inaction over time. If the perception of action fades before the salience falls below the threshold, the response to the issue will shift from beneficial, or neutral, back to harmful.

The size of the jump in salience resulting from the leader's action should be directly related to the magnitude of the domestic response that the policy choice entails. The higher the magnitude of the response, the larger the jump in salience.[6]

Thus, when an issue thrusts up above its salience threshold (i.e., becomes harmful to the leader's standing), the leader can weather the storm and hope the issue fades quickly. Or s/he can take action and face the possibility that the resulting boost in salience might cause its minimum salience level (the

---

5. This assumes that the issue is a troublesome one that the leader is expected to handle, i.e. there is a call for action.

6. This does not depend on whether or not the issue is harmful. The salience and the mamagnitude should covary regardls of the benefit or harm of the issue, though after the decision the leader might be expected to attempt to reduce the salience of a harmful issue and bolster the salience of a favorable.

level at which the curve flattens and further decay is very slow) to rise above the threshold. The perception of action might then fade back to inaction while the issue does not fall back below the threshold salience level. In such a case, a second action would be necessary.

The second action taken on an issue should have a few characteristics that distinguish it from the first. The most clearly ascertainable should be an increase in the magnitude of the domestic response. If the leader chose the policy option with the lowest expected magnitude of domestic response on the first choice and now must make a second choice, the second choice should be the choice with the next lowest expected magnitude of domestic response. Thus, as noted earlier, when issues must be addressed again and again, the magnitude of the domestic response should increase with each return to the issue.

It is doubtful that in an open society, such as the U.S., or even in a closed society, a leader would be able to suppress directly or lower forcefully the salience of an already salient issue, but the salience of an issue can nonetheless be manipulated. There are always several issues in the domestic arena, all contending for a relatively finite amount of news media coverage. The amount of coverage that different issues receive can be thought of as a zero-sum, or nearly zero-sum relationship between several competing issues. The salience of any one issue can be manipulated downward by enhancing or bolstering the salience of one or more competing issues. This near zero-sum relationship leads to the discussion of the second type of foreign policy decisions.

Opportunity Decisions

Decisions of opportunity are primarily characterized as decisions made on non-salient or low-salience issues. Decisions on low-salience issues can have two possible forces driving them. Either the leader acts to prevent an issue from becoming harmful or the leader acts to distract attention from another persistent and unresolvable issue. While it is possible that a decision on a low-salience issue is the result of a leader's foresight, that conceptualization does not fit well with the overworked-manager model of the leader. Therefore, if it does occur, it is probably a rare event.

It is more in step with the overworked-manager model of the leader to posit that low-salience foreign policy decisions are examples of the use of foreign policy as a tool to achieve other ends related to the leader's standing. This idea is not new. Machiavelli proposed that wars should be used as a means to quell domestic unrest. In its purest form, a decision of opportunity occurs when the leader is faced with a situation where an issue (either domestic or international in nature) has forced itself into the decision arena.

The leader either cannot, or does not, wish to address it directly, and the salience of the harmful issue either will not fade below the threshold salience or persistently returns.

The leader then searches for an issue to bolster dramatically, in an attempt to lower the salience of the harmful issue. When a foreign policy issue is chosen as the means to accomplish such an end, that decision is an opportunity decision. Consequently, a way to think of opportunity decisions is to look at them as one of the available choices for handling a management decision on another issue. Opportunity decisions should ideally be characterized by the following:

1. The initial salience of the subject should be very low while the salience of a harmful issue should be very high.

2. The policy chosen should have a high expected magnitude of domestic response so it captures the headlines in the media, or there should be a concerted effort by the leadership to enhance the magnitude of the response, or both.

3. There should be some justification or precedent for the instigation of a conflict, such as a long-standing conflict or a triggering event.

A graphic representation of the opportunity decision is presented in Figure 6.7 where the salience of the issue of decision is compared with the salience of the harmful issue. The upper-half represents the harmful issue and the lower-half represents the salience of the issue of the opportunity decision. The large jump in salience of the opportunity decision causes a decline in the level of salience of the harmful issue, but the opportunity issue fades quickly and the harmful issue remains above the salience threshold. Thus, an effort either to bolster the salience of the opportunity issue or to undertake a second action occurs (represented by the second jump in salience). This time the harmful issue falls below the salience threshold for a time, but threatens to return, and the opportunity issue is now a potentially harmful issue.

For several reasons, decisions of opportunity should be fairly rare. There is the risk that if a conflictual policy option is pursued, the opponent will react much more forcefully or much more powerfully than expected. There is the very real possibility of creating two issues of damagingly high salience where there was previously only one. The risk involved is the most important reason for expecting opportunity decisions to be rare. The risk involved in a policy option involves both the direction of the expected reaction and the magnitude of that reaction. Uncertainty in predicting the reaction of the domestic power bases does not allow the complete elimination of the possibility of a negative, or harmful response. Thus, the greater

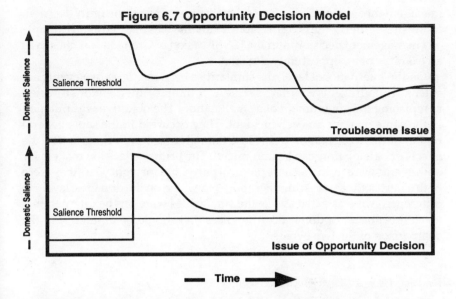

Figure 6.7 Opportunity Decision Model

the magnitude of the domestic response, the greater the possible harm to the leader's domestic standing (the greater the size of the possible negative consequences) and the greater the risk.

This reasoning can be tied back into the decision-making model and operationalized through the attitude towards risk held by the leader. As discussed in the model of domestic support, the leader should only become a gain-maximizer or a risk-avoider when her domestic standing is low. Thus, one of the necessary conditions for an opportunity decision is a low domestic standing. Other necessary conditions are: a harmful issue that the leader is unable or unwilling to resolve; a triggering event or historic conflict that can be used as an issue of opportunity; and the availability of a policy option that has a high expected magnitude of domestic response.

EXAMPLES: THE PANAMA AND GRENADA CASES

Two cases have been chosen as examples to illustrate the plausibility of hypotheses derived through the propositions of this modeling exercise. Two major criteria were used in choosing these cases. First, an effort was made to find cases in which the differences in the structural constraints and effects of the international arena could be minimized. Second, it was necessary to find one example of a case that illustrated a predominantly management decision and one case that illustrated an opportunity decision. Using these criteria, the U.S. invasion of Panama was selected as an example of a management decision, and the U.S. invasion of Grenada was chosen as an example of an opportunity decision.

On the international level, the similarities between these two events are extensive. Both events were large-scale, U.S. military interventions directed at replacing the government of a small nation. The objective was pursued in the same manner for each incident. They occurred in the same general region of the world. They were close enough together in time so that the effects of passing time can be minimized. The primary decision makers for both events were from the same political party, and for eight years they were both a part of the same Administration. However, on the domestic level the differences were as extensive as the similarities were on the international level. It is this set of domestic differences that should be of interest in the comparison of the two events.

Panama, 1989: A Management Decision

Taken as a single, isolated event, the invasion of Panama conforms to the management decision hypothesis that foreign policy decisions are made in an effort to manage the salience of a troublesome issue. Shortly before the invasion, two events, the declaration of a state of war with the U.S. and the killing of an American serviceman, hit the news media and caused a spike in salience (Vanderbilt, 12-89). Panama became a high profile foreign policy issue, which made inaction on the issue harmful to President Bush's standing. President Bush responded by implementing a change in policy. The invasion caused a huge rise in salience, coupled with an image of action, and it resolved the troublesome issue. This positive result, combined with the high salience, drove President Bush's domestic standing, as measured in a job approval poll (Gallup, Jan. 90), to its highest level.

Stretching the time frame to include the events that occurred over the course of the previous year, the support for the model grows stronger. The incidents in December that immediately preceded the invasion were the third set of incidents in Panama in that year to gain a high level of salience (Vanderbilt, 5-89; Vanderbilt, 10-89). In May, 1989, the Panamanian election fiasco, including the beating of the opposition candidates, grabbed enough attention to hold the lead story on at least one of the network newscasts for eight days straight (Vanderbilt, 5-89). In October, the failed coup attempt held the most network time for a foreign policy event for seven days, and it held the lead story for three of those seven days (Vanderbilt, 10-89).

In the television and press media, both of those earlier events were equated with the failure of previous policies to obtain the stated goal of driving Noriega from power. Also, the wording of the coverage of both

incidents equated current policies with inaction even though severe economic sanctions were in place and efforts to isolate Noriega diplomatically
were ongoing. Thus, with both previous incidents there was a rise in
salience coupled with the perception of inaction. Both incidents also created
a low-risk foreign policy reaction from the White House. After the first
incident an increase in American troop strength in the Canal Zone was
announced (NYT 5-12-89, 1), and new diplomatic measures were undertaken. After the second incident, the implementation of a three-million-
dollar, covert operation to oust Noriega was made public (NYT 11-17-89, 3).

The Noriega/Panama issue conforms well to hypotheses from the model.
President Bush held a high level of domestic standing throughout the entire
incident (Gallup, 1989), and he acted in a manner that avoided risk to his
domestic standing. He reacted only after a rise in salience, and he avoided
options with a high level of domestic liability until he ran out of low risk
options.

Grenada, 1983: An Opportunity Decision

An example of a political actor making an opportunity decision can be
found in President Reagan's choice to invade Grenada in, 1983. From the
framework of a state-level, rational actor model it is difficult to explain the
invasion, although thorough efforts have been made (Adkin, 1989, Burrows, 1988, Shahabuddeen, 1986). A much simpler, and possibly stronger,
argument lies within the framework of the opportunity decision model. In
the opportunity model, the invasion of Grenada was prompted by the need
to direct domestic attention away from an issue that had proven itself to be
both unresolvable and detrimental to President Reagan's domestic standing. That issue was the Lebanese civil war and the U.S. role in it, including
the stationing of Marines in Beirut.

Figure 6.8 shows the weekly totals of television network news salience of
Grenada and Lebanon for the 40 weeks prior to the invasion. The salience
levels are measured in minutes as recorded in the Vanderbilt Television
News Abstracts, with the time for the lead story weighted by a factor of 1.5.
A quick look at the figure shows that as far as long-term salience goes,
Lebanon was by far the more salient issue. Combined with that high level
of salience was a strong domestic opposition to the stationing of the Marines
in Beirut and a profound lack of anything that could be labeled an accom-
plishment. The strong spikes in coverage corresponded to primarily negative events, such as terrorist attacks that victimized the Americans stationed
there (Vanderbilt, 5-83 through 10-83). This pattern re-occurred several
times during the weeks before the invasion, but the key event happened just
a few days before the invasion of Grenada. On Sunday, October 23, 1983, the

Figure 6.8 News Coverage Compared for Grenada and Lebanon

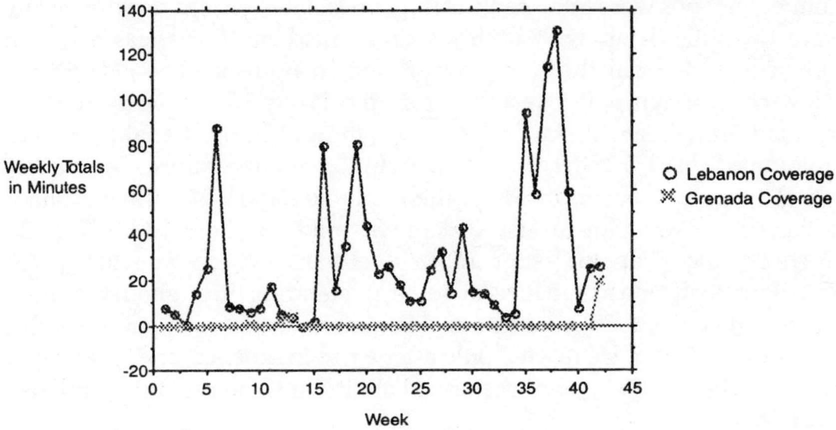

Marine barracks were bombed and over 200 American soldiers lost their lives. The two networks that had national news casts that evening each devoted over 20 minutes out of the approximately 24 minutes available to the coverage of the tragedy (Vanderbilt, 10-83); the content was far from flattering for President Reagan. Two days later The United States invaded Grenada.

The daily salience pattern (see Figure 6.9) shows the network coverage measured in the same manner as in Figure 6.8 with the amount of coverage measured in average-per-newscast in order to avoid problems with the weekends, where there are often only one or two of the networks producing a national news program. This figure covers the two weeks before and after the invasion. Of particular interest is the affect that the invasion of Grenada had upon the coverage of the Beirut bombing. The tremendous drop in coverage of the bombing, two days after the bombing, coincides with the tremendous surge in the coverage of Grenada.

In the bottom half of Figure 6.9 is the decay curve of the shooting down of the KAL airliner over the Soviet Union, an incident that occurred in relative isolation from other news grabbing events. Comparing this more gradual decline with the sharp drop for the Beirut issue, it is easy to see that the sharp drop in coverage is probably not natural. Combining that with the theoretical ground work laid earlier, it is reasonable to conclude that the invasion of Grenada and the massive media coverage it generated caused the sharp drop in salience for the Beirut bombing. Thus, if the Grenada invasion was an opportunity decision, it was successful. It replaced the salience of a troublesome issue with that of a successful issue.

The invasion of Grenada is consistent with what is expected of an opportunity decision, just as the invasion of Panama was consistent with the

Figure 6.9 Daily Salience Pattern between Grenada and Lebanon

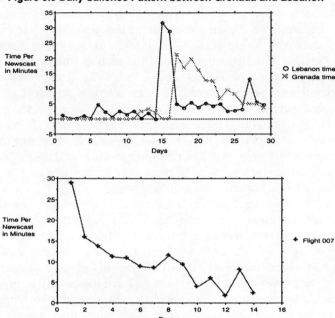

expectations for a management decision. Grenada had a low level of salience, while a troublesome issue had a high level of salience and could not be resolved. The choice of an invasion was of a highly dramatic and media-grabbing nature, and there was a concerted effort made to enhance level of coverage and the positive aspects of the coverage. There was a triggering event, the killing of the Grenadan leader, and a justification, the protection of American students in residence on the island. The outcome of the event is consistent with what the model predicts the goal of the opportunity decision would be. Also consistent with the modeling hypotheses is the level of President Reagan's domestic support, which (as measured by Gallup Polls) was very low and had been very low for a considerable length of time. Opportunity decisions are decisions of high risk for the political actor and low levels of domestic support should make a leader more acceptant of risk.

CONCLUSION

There are additional aspects of each case that lend further support to the notion that the overriding goal of the decision maker was not the strategic considerations for the United States as a whole. Instead, the goal was a set of rational, strategic considerations regarding the domestic political arena.

In the Panama case, the announcement of the implementation of a covert action is an oxymoron at the least and, if taken at face value, it borders on the unbelievable. It is difficult to believe that such an announcement would enhance the chance of the success of such an activity. If taken in the context of a rational state actor, it could be interpreted as an effort to unsettle Noriega, or to get him to direct limited resources towards protecting himself from such an action. But if these or similar objectives were the true goal of publicly releasing such a policy, it seems reasonable to believe that there would be more effective ways to accomplish such a goal. Those other means would include an effort to make Noriega truly believe that such an activity was actually being planned and implemented.

Taking the announcement in the context of the model of a domestic political decision maker, it is much easier to explain such an unusual choice of action. The oxymoron of an overt/covert action is not some convoluted effort to unsettle Noriega or to reassure other potential coup leaders. It is instead a direct effort to create a low-risk image of foreign policy activity for the domestic power bases. Covert actions have the quality of invisibility. There should be no way to observe their preparation or the workings of such an action. By announcing such a covert operation, the leader is creating action, but it is an invisible action. No one can follow its implementation, no one will know if it succeeds or fails, and no one knows if it really even exists.

Thus, it is the perfect buying-time foreign policy option. It creates the pure image of activity with no concrete activity for the media to cover. As far as media coverage and domestic standing is concerned, it is a completely risk-free option that has the positive value of shifting the domestic perception from inactivity to activity. This characterization is especially true if there is no actual covert action being implemented.

In the Grenada case, one indicator of overriding domestic political imperatives is the manner in which the press coverage of both the Lebanon and Grenada incidents was handled. The White House avoided generating anything, such as official statements, that could increase the news media coverage of the Beirut incident. On the day after the bombing there were seven pages of the New York Times, including the entire front page, devoted to the coverage of the incident. Of that seven pages, only four sentences, the entirety of President Reagan's statement on the issue, was attributed to the White House (NYT 10-24-83, 8). It wasn't until two days after the incident that a short press conference was held by a White House official.

The exact opposite is true of the Grenada invasion. The White House made every effort to provide information to the press on the Grenada invasion, and access to non-government sources was restricted as much as possible (NYT 10/27/83, 1). President Reagan's initial announcement of the invasion was over three times as long as the statement he made on Beirut, and press conferences on the invasion abounded. The transcript of Secretary of State Shultz's press conference alone took up a solid page of text in the *New York Times* (10-26-83, 13), and items such as aerial reconnaissance photos were made available to the press. Direct access by the press was not allowed until most of the fighting was over (NYT 10/27/83, 1). The handpicked few allowed to go were flown there by the government and they were only allowed to stay for a few hours (NYT 10/28/83, 13).

A second point is that the final decision to invade Grenada was made just a few short hours after the President was informed of the devastating bombing in Beirut (Adkin, 1989), although the plans had been drawn up earlier in the week. Even if the bombing had not occurred, other incentives to generate a distraction existed. The long-standing and extremely negative press regarding the stationing of troops in Lebanon was one incentive. Domestic opposition, including congressional attempts to use the War Powers Act to force the withdrawal of the Marines, was also strong enough to expect an attempt to generate a distracting, high-profile, foreign policy action such as an opportunity decision.

With these cases, I have tried to establish the plausibility of domestic political imperatives as an influence upon foreign policy decision-making. The next step is to operationalize and empirically test the implications of the model. This model might provide a framework to examine when nations will and will not act upon the opportunities defined by their strength or positions within the international system. One way to use this model of domestic imperatives is to re-examine analyses of decisions to initiate war, which focused upon capabilities or alliances within the international system to explain these decisions (Bueno De Mesquita, 1981; Huth and Russett, 1984; and Lebow and Stein, 1987). In that way the domestic imperatives model's relationship to these externally oriented models can be established. The domestic political imperatives model should provide an insight into the forces that drive foreign policy decisions in those cases where nations acted contrary to the expectations generated by the balance of power or deterrence models, but the model might also explain, albeit with a different causal explanation, the instances when nations acted as the external models predicted they should.

7

The Conflicting Roles of American Ethnic and Business Interests in the U.S. Economic Sanctions Policy

THE CASE OF SOUTH AFRICA

Elizabeth S. Rogers

I n 1986, the United States Congress passed a comprehensive and stringent economic sanctions bill, directed at the Republic of South Africa,
overriding President Reagan's veto by a vote of 313 to 83 in the House and
78 to 21 in the Senate. This was the culmination of over twenty years of anti-
apartheid pressure in the United States. This chapter will examine the
influence of domestic interests on U.S. economic sanctions policy toward
South Africa. This is a particularly interesting case because specific, easily
identifiable interests existed on both sides of the issue. Business interests
opposed the imposition of economic sanctions against South Africa. In
favor of sanctions were a racial/ethnic interest, Black Americans, backed
up by a loose coalition of church groups and students. To students of
interest groups and foreign policy, this would appear to be a David versus
Goliath contest. However, another interesting feature of this case is that, as
in the biblical story, the policy outcome favored David (Black interests) and
not Goliath (business interests).

The importance of organized domestic interests in shaping United
States foreign policy was increasingly recognized in the 1970s and 1980s
(Hughes, 1978; Skidmore, 1992). This chapter examines one particular set
of circumstances in which a foreign policy issue involved competing
domestic interests. Furthermore, both the costs and the benefits of policy
were, in this case, concentrated domestically on specific, easily identifiable
groups. The significance of this derives from the argument that policy

making will differ in situations where the domestic costs and/or benefits of a policy are concentrated on specific, easily identifiable interests from those circumstances in which the domestic costs and/or benefits are spread diffusely throughout the population.[1] Situations in which domestic interests are lined up on both sides of an issue are especially interesting because they are more difficult to predict than those circumstances in which domestic interests are aligned on only one side of an issue. For example, if domestic interests will bear disproportionate costs should a given policy be enacted, and no domestic group(s) will reap disproportionate benefits, then one would hypothesize that leaders will be reluctant to enact this policy. The opposite is true if the benefits will be concentrated domestically, but the costs will not. Predictions are less clear cut when both the domestic costs and benefits are concentrated. However, even here certain hypotheses can be put forward.

Where specific and easily identified interests are set against one another, the policy outcome will vary with the distribution of power between them. If the balance of power is symmetrical, one could expect the lobbying effects of each side to cancel out, leaving policy-makers with considerable freedom of action. An asymmetrical balance, on the other hand, will favor the more powerful lobbying coalition. Three factors determine influence levels: resources, issue salience and coalition unity. These factors are influenced by the nature of the specific issue at hand. This can lead to unexpected outcomes, where normally weak groups are better able to match their special assets to the conditions of a particular issue environment than groups which are generally considered more powerful.

Thus, in this case, we find that Blacks, a group generally considered of marginal influence in foreign policy-making, managed to achieve an advantageous balance of power vis á vis important business interests. Though Black political resources remained limited, they reached an historic high in the mid-1980s. The high salience of the South African issue led to energetic lobbying efforts while the absence of serious conflicting interests or ideological perspectives allowed for a high level of unity. Although the potential resources available to business were great, they were not fully mobilized in this battle due to the limited salience of the sanctions issue for most business groups. Moreover, since the economic interests and potential options varied across those firms with business dealings in South Africa, the anti-sanctions coalition proved deeply divided. Following a brief historical review of U.S. policy toward South Africa, these conclusions will be substantiated by examining the strengths and weaknesses of each side in the sanctions debate.

---

1. This theory is in the tradition of Lowi (1964) and Wilson (1973: especially chapters 15 and 16).

U.S. Relations Toward South Africa: 1870–1986

Historically, the United States has maintained friendly relations with South Africa. While officially, the U.S. did not approve of the apartheid system introduced in 1948, it remained, in the midst of the Cold War, unwilling to condemn or take action against South Africa because of that nation's anti-communism (Noer, 1978; Foltz, 1978; Nyangoni 1981, 1-12).

The 1960 incident at Sharpeville in which sixty four people were killed focused worldwide attention on apartheid and marked the beginning of South Africa's international isolation and the emergence of economic sanctions as a continuing UN issue. In August 1962 the UN General Assembly requested that member states break diplomatic relations with South Africa, "sever shipping and air links and boycott South African trade" (Doxey 1987, 47). A year later, in August 1963, the Security Council imposed much more limited sanctions. An embargo on arms sales passed with abstentions by Britain and France. A trade boycott was rejected. Differences between the Security Council and the General Assembly have persisted.

Like the UN Security Council, U.S. policy makers have been reluctant to sanction South Africa. Evidence of mixed signals and a reluctance to impose sanctions can be found from the early 1960s through a 1987 veto in the Security Council of a mandatory sanctions package similar to that enacted in October 1986 by the Congress over President Reagan's veto.

In the 1950s and 1960s U.S. foreign direct investment (FDI) in South Africa grew steadily. Under the Kennedy administration, policy toward South Africa hardened slightly as relations with the emerging nations of Black Africa assumed importance. The U.S. became more vocal in its denunciations of apartheid, while remaining fundamentally opposed to using economic sanctions. Small steps taken included canceling a recreation stop at Capetown for the aircraft carrier *Franklin D. Roosevelt* and preventing the IMF from buying South African gold priced above thirty five dollars an ounce.[2]

When the Nixon administration came into office, National Security Advisor Henry Kissinger reviewed U.S. policy toward southern Africa. This led to National Security Study Memorandum 39 (NSSM 39) which recommended that the U.S. make a greater effort to work with the current rulers in the region. NSSM 39 also explicitly rejected the use of economic sanctions, against Portugal or South Africa "because they are likely to be ineffective and because they could lead to a U.S. military involvement in

---

2. The former was a congressionally led effort and also resulted in a new policy of refueling ships at sea. See Hufbauer and Schott (1985: 347). For a brief summary of U.S. policy toward Africa from 1946 to the mid-1980s, see Rothchild and Ravenhill (1987: 393–429).

their enforcement" (Cohen and El-Khawas 1975, 45). Evidence of this approach can be seen in the U.S. voting record in the UN, and in the passage of the Byrd amendment.[3] Only one new sanction against South Africa was imposed during the Nixon, Ford, Kissinger years, and it resulted from a congressionally led effort.[4]

In the mid-1970s, faced with mounting domestic pressure from the Congress, American Blacks, and others, Kissinger reluctantly began to shift the direction of U.S. policy. The Carter administration accelerated this trend. The Soweto riots in 1976 and Steve Biko's death in 1977 focused attention on South Africa and brought about new measures.[5] Also, an important development occurred in the private sector with the creation in March 1977 of the Sullivan principles, a code of conduct for companies operating in South Africa. However, the administration set limits as to how far it was willing to go. National Security Advisor Brzezinski stated:

> We are opposed to the use of mandatory trade embargoes as a political instrument except in the most exceptional cases. It is important, moreover, that we retain flexibility for the future, should developments in South Africa warrant further U.S. or international response.

Even Andrew Young, the administration's most outspoken critic of the South African regime, expressed opposition to corporate disinvestment stating that, "the free market system can be the greatest force for constructive change now operating anywhere in the world."[6] These mixed signals gave rise to charges that Carter's changes were more of style than of substance and that policy toward South Africa was confused and lacking in clear direction.

The Reagan years further highlighted the contradictions in U.S. policy toward South Africa. Assistant Secretary of State for African Affairs, Chester Crocker, presented the administration's policy which became known as "constructive engagement." This approach aimed to bring about change in

---

3. In the UN General Assembly, the U.S. began to vote against resolutions rather than abstain from them as it had in the past. The Byrd Amendment allowed precious metals including chromium to be imported from Rhodesia. The Carter administration later worked for and obtained the amendment's repeal. See Daoudi and Dajani (1983: 84)

4. Pressure from the Congressional Black Caucus resulted in a temporary halt of shipments of nuclear fuel to South Africa in 1975. See Hufbauer and Schott (1985:52–53).

5. The U.S. barred the shipment of nuclear materials in 1977 because of South Africa's refusal to sign the Non-Proliferation Treaty. Shipments of materials to the South African military and policy were banned in 1978, and the size of the military attache's staff in South Africa was reduced. In 1979 Eximbank loans were restricted by Congress to firms with fair labor practices. See Hayes (1987: 10).

6. Also, President Carter "at one point referred to South Africa as a stabilizing force: and Vice President Mondale spoke of South Africans as "good friends." *South Africa: Time Running Out* (1981:362) and Danaher (1984: 42).

South Africa by maintaining economic ties and quietly working behind the scenes through diplomatic channels to encourage moderate elements. The administration argued that the U.S. would have more leverage this way than it would by breaking ties as advocates of economic sanctions urged. Indeed Reagan reversed several of the mild steps that had been taken against South Africa.[7]

In 1985, faced with the prospect of strong congressionally led sanctions, Reagan announced his own milder economic sanctions package. Sales of computers and nuclear technology were restricted, as was the import of Krugerrands. Also, loans to the South African Government, or entities owned or controlled by it, "except for loans and credits which would improve the welfare of those disadvantaged by apartheid" were prohibited (Hayes 1987, 11). The administration's hopes of preventing further sanctions were dashed as domestic pressure continued to mount, generating bipartisan support in Congress for a tougher economic sanctions bill that passed in October 1986 over Reagan's veto. This legislation prohibited imports of South African uranium, coal, iron, steel, armaments, and agricultural products. Exports of petroleum products, arms, nuclear technology, and computers were also affected. New investment and bank loans were banned, and landing rights for South African planes in the United States were canceled (U.S. News 28 July 1986, 25; Hilton 1986, 24).

U.S. policy toward South Africa since World War II has been characterized by the tensions between an East-West, containment outlook and a desire to maintain distance from South Africa's apartheid system. Historically, the executive branch has been most concerned with maintaining friendly relations with South Africa because of its strong anti-communist stance, while the Congress has taken the lead in urging that stronger measures be taken against South Africa until apartheid is abolished.

The Influences of Domestic Costs and Benefits on Policy Formation

It is clear in the South African case that two quite different, easily identifiable domestic interests stood to bear disproportionate costs and benefits from the imposition of sanctions. They are American Blacks on the benefit side of the equation and U.S. multinational corporations (MNCs) on the cost side. While the costs to business were economic in nature, the

---

7. The embargoes on nuclear shipments and the sale of many non-military goods to the South African military and police ended. The number of military attaches sent to South Africa increased, and on the diplomatic front, South Africa was allowed to open new consulates in the U.S. During the first three years of the Reagan presidency $28.3 million in military goods was exported to South Africa. Danaher (1984:64,67), and UN Centre on Transnational Corporations (1984:16).

benefits that accrued to Blacks were emotional and social. In the literature, there is a clear contrast in the perceived efficacy of the two interests in the foreign policy arena. While Blacks have historically been uninvolved and more recently viewed as ineffective, there is a school of thought that considers business interests to have disproportionate influence in shaping U.S. policy. Critics of U.S. foreign policy point to specific incidents such as United Fruit in Guatemala in the 1950s and ITT in Chile in the 1970s as examples of corporate influence in the foreign policy arena (Williams, 1969; Kolko 1969, 156, 163) This view, taken to its extreme, is stated by William Domhoff:

> American foreign policy during the postwar era was initiated, planned and carried out by the richest, most powerful and most international-minded owners and managers of major corporations and financial institutions. None of the factors that are often of importance on domestic issues—Congress, labor, public opinion—had anything but an occasional and minor effect on foreign policy. (Hughes 1978, 157) (1969, 25)

Less sweeping claims regarding the significant influence of business interests on foreign policy formulation have been advanced by other scholars (Schattschneider, 1960; Bauer, Poole and Dexter, 1977). This analysis of South African economic sanctions will demonstrate the need for revision of the generalizations in the literature on Black interests and suggest limitations that reduce the effectiveness of business interests.

Domestic Interests That Benefit from Sanctions:
Black Americans and U.S. Policy Toward South Africa

Anthony Lake (1976, 71-72) has described the Black community as "the only anti-apartheid group with a natural interest in Africa which also had political clout." In fact, while white students, members of church groups, and labor unions participated in the Free South Africa Movement, the leadership was Black. Given this, it is then somewhat surprising to discover the paucity of scholarly writing on the role of American Blacks in shaping U.S. policy towards South Africa. It is clear that one explanation for this is the comparative lack of influence historically exerted by Black Americans over U.S. foreign policy. In large part, the reason for scholarly interest in ethnic groups such as Polish, Greek, and Jewish Americans is that these domestic interests have significantly affected U.S. foreign policy toward the areas of the world which interest them. There is less evidence of this with respect to Black Americans. Daoudi and Dajani (1983, 206) refer to the "low priority of African issues for US liberals and blacks." Anthony

Lake (1976, 71) states that, "although statements by individual black leaders on southern Africa were given some weight by American officials, the black community as such paid little attention on African issues." Inexperience often meant that Black interests were disorganized, unaware, or unprepared, thus preventing them from acting as an effective lobby.[8] Jake Miller (1979, 246) stated this view most succinctly: "Regardless of the reason, it can be said that the influence of Blacks in foreign policy-making is virtually nonexistent."

Martin Weil (1974, 109) presents three criteria necessary for an ethnic interest to influence U.S. foreign policy: "(l) an electoral threat, (2) a lobbying apparatus, and (3) a successful appeal to the symbols of American nationhood." An examination of Weil's three factors will demonstrate that in the case of South African sanctions, Blacks were an effective interest. First, however, the question of past Black ineffectiveness on foreign policy must be briefly addressed.

Historically, a lack of Black interest and influence in foreign policy matters is easily understood given the unique position of Blacks in American Society. No other race or ethnic group was forced to immigrate to this country, and certainly no other domestic interest experienced slavery and its long aftermath of injustices. During the 1950s and 1960s American Blacks entered the political arena and successfully influenced policy. Not surprisingly their efforts were concentrated on the immediate domestic policy problems they faced. Civil rights issues received top priority. Success in these arenas was, in fact, a prerequisite for the exercise of influence over U.S. foreign policy. Also, Black leaders feared that taking strong stands on foreign policy issues might "interfere with their domestic goals."[9] This helps to explain why Blacks were not a major force affecting U.S.-Rhodesian and U.S.-South African policy in the 1960s and early to mid-1970s.

It was not until the mid-1970s that significant time and resources could be devoted to foreign policy issues. In particular, Weil's first criterion for influence, a Black electoral threat, was present for the first time. The closeness of the 1976 presidential election and the fact that Black support provided Carter with the margin of victory was seen as evidence of the importance of the Black vote. In addition, U.S. policy towards Africa shifted during the Carter administration in the direction desired by Black

---

8. For an account of the problems Black Americans encountered in attempting to affect U.S. policy with respect to the Byrd amendment in 1972, see Lake (1986:231–233).

9. For example, Kenneth Longmyer (1985:11) notes that Black leaders were concerned that Martin Luther King's criticism of the Vietnam War would create problems with the Johnson administration. This argument that foreign policy activism would hurt the domestic agenda was raised again in the 1980s regarding the sanctions movement.

Americans. Also, for the first time Blacks such as Andrew Young and Donald McHenry were appointed to prominent foreign policy positions. This convinced many that Black influence was on the rise (Payne and Ganaway 1980, 588-97).

While, historically Black registration and voting rates have fallen below those for the voting age population as a whole, this was less true during the mid-1980s, when sanctions legislation was passed, than in earlier or later periods. The highest percentage of Black voter turnout between 1972 and 1988 was reported in 1984. Also, in 1984 more Blacks were registered to vote than at any time since 1972 (Stanley and Niemi 1990, 80). Jesse Jackson's 1984 presidential campaign and the voter registration drives that accompanied it were a major reason for this. Thus, minority voting power (the "Rainbow Coalition"), and the Black electoral threat in particular, were very prominent in the mid-1980s. The fact that South Africa was said to be the only foreign policy issue members of Congress raised with their Black constituents reinforced perceptions of Black political clout (Longmyer 1985, 12). If elected officials perceived that Blacks cared about this issue and might cast votes collectively on that basis, then whether or not the threat actually existed becomes less important.[10]

Indeed, statements by Black leaders suggest that they are united in their firm opposition to apartheid, and in their support for strong U.S. economic sanctions against South Africa. Longmyer (1985, 13) suggests that this unity goes beyond the sanctions issue. He states that members of the Congressional Black Caucus (CBC) "are far more likely to agree and to vote alike on foreign-policy questions than Democrats in general."

The second criterion for influence is a lobbying apparatus. The lack of an effective lobby has been cited as one of the reasons Blacks were unsuccessful in their attempts to shape U.S. policy toward Rhodesia. Again, the timing of events (in the 1960s and 1970s) provides an explanation for the absence of a successful Black lobby. However, with respect to South Africa in the 1980s, Blacks were organized and worked effectively both within the government and outside of it. Within the government, the Reagan administration's policy of constructive engagement and its outspoken opposition to economic sanctions precluded influencing policy via the executive branch. Therefore, Blacks concentrated their efforts on getting sanctions legislation through the Democratically controlled Congress. Within the Congress, the Congressional Black Caucus (CBC) spearheaded anti-apartheid sanctions efforts. The CBC was founded in 1971 and by the mid-1980s had members with considerable seniority and positions on key

---

10. For a discussion of perceptions that Blacks provide an electoral threat, see Spanier and Uslaner (1982:142).

committees, including William Gray (D-Penn) who chaired the House Budget Committee.[11]

In 1984, CBC chair Julian Dixon (D-Calif.) added a provision to IMF legislation which prevented the United States from supporting new IMF loans to South Africa unless apartheid was ended. A key factor behind the CBC's success in getting sanctions imposed in 1985 and 1986 is that while members disagreed as to how severe sanctions should be, they were able to put their differences aside in order to get a bill passed. In 1984, CBC members introduced 15 separate pieces of economic sanctions legislation in the House, but ultimately united behind one bill (H.R. 1460) sponsored by William Gray (Longmyer 1985, 10; Dixon 1984, 14). The success of this bill in the House and of weaker legislation in the Senate forced President Reagan to introduce his own mild sanctions in 1985, in an effort to thwart the tougher congressional package. However, Reagan's success was short-lived. In 1986 Congress passed stronger economic sanctions legislation over his veto.

Anti-apartheid efforts outside the government were led by TransAfrica. This organization was founded by Blacks in 1977 to lobby for Black policy positions on African and Caribbean issues. By 1985 TransAfrica had ten thousand members and a four hundred thousand dollar annual budget (Longmyer 1985, 10). Beginning on Thanksgiving day 1984, TransAfrica director Randall Robinson organized a small sit-in at the South African embassy in Washington. The sit in and subsequent arrest of the participants spawned the Free South Africa Movement. This movement was led by Robinson and a core group of volunteers, the Southern Africa Support Project. Although its leadership was Black, the Free South Africa Movement was a national coalition of Blacks and whites including: students, church groups, and labor unions (Wilkins, 1985, 29; Longmyer 1985, 10). Beginning with that Thanksgiving day in 1984, the Southern Africa Support Project continued to maintain and organize daily protests in Washington at the South African embassy. Through local chapters of TransAfrica, protests were held at consulates and dealers of Krugerrands in twenty seven other cities around the country. The protests and arrests were well publicized–in part because they often involved celebrities.[12] These Black-led efforts kept apartheid and economic sanctions in the limelight, forcing members of Congress and the executive branch to confront the issue.

---

11. In the mid-1980s CBC members committee assignments included: the House Committee on Foreign Affairs, its Subcommittee on Africa, and the House Appropriations Subcommittee on Foreign Affairs among others. Dixon (1984:29).

12. By mid-1985 over 1800 people had been arrested in Washington. Celebrity protestors included singers Harry Belafonte and Stevie Wonder, Arthur Ashe, the children of Jimmy Carter and Robert Kennedy, Sen. Lowell Weicker (R-Conn.), and 18 members of the House of Representatives. Wilkins (1985:30).

There is a clear coincidence of timing between the protests and demonstrations organized by TransAfrica and the Free South Africa Movement and action by U.S. leaders. Southern Africa Support Project member Roger Wilkins notes that within one month of the beginning of the movement, President Reagan issued what was at that time his toughest condemnation of apartheid. Also, in his first public statement as chair of the Senate Foreign Relations Committee, Richard Lugar (R-Ind.) spoke at length on South Africa (Wilkins 1985, 31). In addition, like any effective interest group, TransAfrica was working with the CBC and others in Congress who supported their position. The Free South Africa Movement also lobbied Congress intensively to pass sanctions legislation 1985 and 1986. At the same time, they launched public education campaigns throughout the country (Wilkin 1985, 31, Dixon 1984, 13). This pressure helped create the two thirds majority necessary to override the president's veto of sanctions legislation in 1986.

Finally, in addition to an electoral threat and a lobbying apparatus, Weil (1974, 315) states that to achieve influence, an ethnic interest must make "a successful appeal to the symbols of American nationhood." Apartheid is a perfect issue for this purpose as it is in direct opposition to basic American values of freedom, justice, and equality. By couching the issue in these terms, Black leaders were able to achieve widespread support for their positions.

Ganaway and Payne (1980, 598) noted during the Carter administration that, "there is a convergence between general American foreign policy interests in Southern Africa and Black demands. The congruence between American ideals and Black concerns has increased the ability of Blacks to influence U.S. Southern African policy." While congruence with the Reagan administration was certainly absent, it is true that significant segments of U.S. society, including church groups, students, and labor unions mobilized behind the Black position on South Africa. By a 5 to 1 ratio, the American public sympathized with South African Blacks rather than with the South African government. However, this sympathy did not automatically translate into a desire for action. In 1985, responding to the question, "What should the U.S. do?," 44% of the public said don't get involved while only 16% favored sanctions. This was not in line with elite opinion, which was more likely to oppose U.S. business involvement in South Africa than the public at large.[13] Overall, this data suggests that Black critics of South Africa could count upon general public sympathy for their cause, but still faced public skepticism about the use of sanctions as the appropriate tool for bringing about change.

---

13. According to a 1982 Chicago Council on Foreign Relations study, elites, by a ratio of 79 to 45%, were more likely than members of the mass public to favor a more active U.S. role in opposing apartheid. Schneider (1987:54, 61–62).

Black leader Jesse Jackson also made South Africa an issue in his 1984 presidential campaign, further focussing national attention on apartheid and U.S.-South African relations. He attacked the Reagan administration's constructive engagement approach and proposed instead establishing closer ties with those in South Africa working to end apartheid. Jackson (1984, 8) stated that, "My administration would bring to bear the full range of diplomatic and other resources at its command to encourage change in this positive direction." Jackson's candidacy provided the sanctions effort with momentum and helps to explain the imposition of economic sanctions on South Africa within a year of the 1984 presidential election.

The impact of the media is often raised as a partial explanation for the imposition of strong economic sanctions in the mid-1980s when such sanctions had not been possible in the 1960s and 1970s after dramatic events like the Sharpeville massacre and the Soweto riots. Certainly media (and especially television) coverage of events in South Africa was much more extensive than it had been in previous decades. Desmond Tutu's Nobel Peace Prize, the suppression of anti-apartheid protests in South Africa, the continuing controversy between the Reagan White House and Congressional demands for a tougher South African policy, and the creative public protests mounted by anti-apartheid groups in the United States generated increased coverage of the South African situation. Moreover, the presidential candidacy of Jesse Jackson focused attention on apartheid and U.S.-South African relations. Although media coverage of South Africa did increase, this did not supplant the successful efforts of Black leaders and the organized Black-led movement for sanctions. It should be noted that not all leaders of the Free South Africa Movement were happy with the media's coverage. Wilkins (1985, 29) stated that, "the press has under-reported the demonstrations and has consistently misinterpreted them."

The question of Black influence on US-South Africa policy is a complicated one. Until the 1980s, the consensus in the literature was that Black influence was minimal. However, since that time perceptions have changed. James Barber and Michael Spicer (1979, 399) argue that "Even if the Western governments wanted to downgrade the South African sanctions issue, it is likely that they would only have a limited success. The concern over racial issues within their own societies...will persist." Margaret Doxey (1987, 94) refers to the vigorous support Black Americans gave to congressional Democrats advocating a new South Africa policy in 1985. A combination of the Black electoral threat, the efforts of Black organizations inside and outside of the Congress, and the appeals of Black leaders for a change in U.S. policy resulted in "Black America's most successful attempt to alter U.S. foreign policy" (Longmyer 1985, 5; also see Wright 1985, 4-5). As the domestic interest that would most obviously benefit from the imposition of economic sanctions against South Africa, Blacks mounted and led a multidimensional, multi-racial campaign in support of sanctions that to date stands as their most comprehensive attempt to influence U.S. foreign policy. It is important to note that no comprehensive sanctions package followed dramatic events in South Africa at Sharpeville and Soweto in 1960 and 1976, in the period before Black interests in the U.S. were organized around foreign policy issues. Given that the South African case represents the first major, successful Black foreign policy influence attempt, the future effectiveness of this interest is uncertain. The potential has long been recognized. Writing in the mid-1970s, Anthony Lake (1976, 285) stated that:

> In the long run, in the absence of dramatic events in southern Africa which force a policy change, the direction U.S. policy takes will depend heavily on the black community here. It is the only American group with both the inherent motive and the political means of forcing such a shift. The development of black consciousness about African issues will be a key in deciding the pace of pressure on the government.

The interesting question for the future is: Are South African sanctions an anomaly or a harbinger of future Black influence on U.S. foreign policy toward Africa and the Caribbean?

DOMESTIC INTERESTS HURT BY SANCTIONS: U.S. MULTINATIONAL CORPORATIONS

The major U.S. interest hurt by the imposition of economic sanctions was American business and specifically U.S. multinational corporations (MNCs) doing business in South Africa. Business interests had clear reasons to organize and lobby against economic sanctions. Those MNCs most deeply affected should lobby hardest. The disproportionate influence attributed to business in the foreign policy arena by the literature has already been noted. Given the strength of business interests, one would expect that they would be able to prevent the imposition of sanctions.

In fact, of course, this proved not to be the case. This apparent anomaly can be resolved by examining the special features of the South Africa issue that worked against business influence. Barry Hughes (1978, 212-213) has suggested three conditions under which business interests are likely to be successful. The issue must involve economic matters which attract little public interest and involvement, the decision-making process must stretch over a lengthy time period, and the relevant groups or coalition of groups must be internally united in its stand.

Only one of these conditions existed in this case. The decision was made over a considerable period of time. However, the existence of an opposing interest and media coverage kept South Africa in the public eye. Also, business interests were not united in firm opposition to economic sanctions. MNCs with no investment in South Africa were not willing to expend time, money, and political capital on this issue. Since only approximately one percent of U.S. FDI was in South Africa, business interests did not stand to lose too badly overall even if they were required to cease doing business in South Africa—something the economic sanctions in 1985 and 1986 did not mandate. While some MNCs were significantly affected by sanctions and worked hard to prevent their imposition, the business community as a whole failed to mobilize around this issue. Even many firms with interests in South Africa either opted out of the battle, due to limited stakes, or preferred to seek ways of eluding or living with sanctions rather than lobby strenuously against them.

How have MNCs responded to the divestment movement and the prospect of economic sanctions? They have taken one of three possible actions regarding their South African operations, disinvesting fully, partially, or not at all.[14] MNCs generally determine which of the above three options to select based on one of three reasons: business considerations, domestic pressure in the U.S., and moral considerations. Those MNCs whose economic stake in South Africa was greatest were least subject to domestic pressure, least likely to disinvest, and most likely to lobby against U.S. policies which would restrict their activities. Conversely, those with a smaller economic stake were more inclined to disinvest fully or partially and less likely to actively oppose sanctions.[15]

In order to evaluate accurately MNC actions it is necessary to establish criteria for measuring which companies are most deeply affected by sanctions. The multinationals most affected were those consistently making a profit on their South African investments, and those with significant fixed assets which could not be easily transferred.[16] For MNCs in this situation, leaving South Africa, or even curtailing activities, is unlikely to be viewed as a sound business practice. Thus, it is these companies that would be most likely to oppose sanctions strongly. For industries whose assets are mostly liquid and easily transferable, one might expect a different ap-

---

14. The terms disinvestment and divestment are often confused. Disinvestment, as used here, refers to the withdrawal of capital from South Africa. Divestment refers to the sale of stock in companies doing business in South Africa.

15. Regardless of which option corporations selected, they universally condemn apartheid. Its restrictions and the unrest it causes are considered bad for business. Also, there is some evidence that South African Blacks link capitalism and apartheid. This could have negative consequences for U.S. business interests when majority rule occurs. Hauck (1986:2–3, 6–7).

16. Easily transferable refers to the ability to use assets for purposes other than those for which they were created. For example, some plant and equipment could be used or easily converted to manufacture a variety of products, and some is only suitable for the manufacture of one specific good.

proach. An examination of the activities of specific MNCs in South Africa in the last decade provides considerable support for this hypothesis.

In South Africa, U.S. FDI grew steadily from the 1940s into the early 1980s, and as of 1984 U.S. subsidiaries outnumbered those of all other countries (UN Panel of Eminent Persons... 1986, 24; Danaher 1984, 50). Until the mid-1980s, American based MNCs deliberately avoided political involvement in South Africa. The argument was that it would be inappropriate and probably counterproductive for foreign businesses to meddle in internal political affairs. South African companies should represent only business interests to the government. Another argument for non-involvement was that U.S. businesses could best bring about change by providing an integrated, model workplace which adhered to the Sullivan principles rather than through political channels.

However, the growth of the divestment movement in the U.S. and proposed sanctions legislation forced businesses to reevaluate their position of non-involvement. In the mid-1980s, the American Chamber of Commerce (AMCHAM) in South Africa was "undergoing an internal struggle over what its main mission should be at a time of growing disinvestment pressure in the United States" (Hauck 1986, 16). The split concerned whether AMCHAM's strategy to diffuse the sanctions movement should be to "organize and coordinate lobbying actions to be taken by the South African business community in the United States," or "to lobby for changes in government policy in South Africa" leaving U.S. lobbying up to the home offices (Hauck 1986, 16). The latter strategy was adopted. This decision meant one less group lobbying in the U.S. It was also a risky strategy because to ease the disinvestment pressure, AMCHAM had to do more than issue statements and take out advertisements in newspapers. It needed to produce satisfactory results which, given the high expectations of the U.S. anti-apartheid movement, was not likely, at least in the short term. Influence is especially problematic because there is a history of animosity between the mostly English business community in South Africa and its Afrikaner political leaders. Indeed, P.W. Botha has been described as the first modern era prime minister willing to listen to non-Afrikaner views (Hauck 1986, 19–20).

Perhaps the industry least likely to be deeply affected by economic sanctions is banking. Assets are extremely liquid and readily transferable. Also, banks are naturally reluctant to lend to countries in political turmoil. Thus, in a general sense, the goals of the divestment movement in the U.S. were compatible with what bankers would consider sound business practices.[17] In fact in 1985, banks began refusing to renew short term loans to

---

17. However, domestic pressure did in some instances force actions which would not otherwise have been taken. For example, Citicorp's decision to leave South Africa was a direct result of New York city's divestment policy. See United Nations, Transnational Corporations In South Africa... (1986:53).

South Africa. This led to pressure on South Africa's foreign exchange reserves and the decision to suspend foreign debt repayments (UN Panel of Eminent Persons... 1986, 53). Also, at this time, new loans were prohibited as part of the 1985 Reagan sanctions package. However, while bank loans to the public sector declined in the 1980s, private sector borrowing increased. This was particularly troubling because the South African government could borrow from the private sector (UN Panel of Eminent Persons... 1986, 51-54). Thus, U.S. banks may have unintentionally lent money to the South African government.

Perhaps the strongest statement objecting to sanctions for purely business reasons was made by IBM chairman John F. Akers: "We are not in business to conduct moral activity, we are not in business to conduct socially responsible action. We are in business to conduct business."[18] IBM was in fact making a profit in South Africa. Its share of the South African computer market was twice that of its nearest competitor (Felder 1986, D22). In addition, IBM did not manufacture products in South Africa. Therefore, it did not face the problem of selling fixed assets. This not only made disinvestment easier, but it also made IBM less vulnerable to fluctuations in the South African economy and political turbulence. Thus, IBM's outspoken opposition to sanctions and the company's unwillingness to disinvest is easily understood.

In light of this, IBM's decision to disinvest partially is at first puzzling. Given that business was good, and the company felt no moral obligation to leave, the third possibility—domestic pressure in the U.S.—bears closer examination. In fact, there are clear indications that this was an important consideration. Chairman Akers (Felder 1986, 1) acknowledged that IBM was "feeling the economic impact of pressure from groups in this country opposed to the South African Government's policy of apartheid, or racial discrimination." In fact, although profitable, IBM's business in South Africa was only a very small part of its total operations. IBM's sales in South Africa accounted for less than one half of one percent of its worldwide total. The combination of domestic protest and small investment made the "hassle factor" too great for IBM. Even here, however, it should be noted that by partially disinvesting IBM hoped to quiet its critics while still making money in South Africa. IBM's decision to disinvest and the manner in which this was done suggest that the company determined that it made better business sense to appease U.S. domestic interests at the risk of losing a very small percentage of its business than to stand firm in South Africa, receive negative publicity, and possibly lose U.S. sales.[19] This is consistent

---

18. Akers made this statement in the Spring of 1986. Ironically, by the following October, IBM had announced its intention to disinvest. Felder (1986: D22).

19. In addition to allowing their products to be sold in South Africa, it has been reported that IBM loaned money to its South African buyer which financed the purchase. Hayes (1987:27).

with the argument that those most deeply affected will lobby the hardest against sanctions. Ultimately, IBM was not going to be badly hurt by economic sanctions affecting its business in South Africa. Thus, both IBM's initial opposition to sanctions and its partial disinvestment under pressure are consistent with expectations.

Companies with a large investment in fixed assets such as oil, mining, and automobile manufacturing were most likely to oppose sanctions. Automobiles serve as an example of an industry with significant fixed assets in South Africa that nonetheless began withdrawing from South Africa prior to the imposition of U.S. economic sanctions.

All three major United States auto makers manufactured in South Africa at one time. Chrysler decided to leave in the late 1970s as part of a global retrenchment in the face of financial difficulties. Ford and General Motors (GM) stayed until the mid-1980s when they too began to disinvest. GM chairman Roger Smith "indicated that the sanctions being imposed on South Africa by the United States Government were part of the decision to withdraw."[20] However, it is also clear that the auto industry in South Africa was losing money. The South African economy went into a recession in 1981 which stretched through the remainder of the decade. This depressed the auto industry which had been growing at a steady rate of 4.7% annually from 1970 to 1981.[21] One reason for the industry's decline is the particularly devastating effect of the recession on South African Blacks. The automobile market was already considered saturated for whites in 1981. Half of the white population owned a car while the ratio for Blacks was one in fifty. With the recession continuing, losses mounting, and political turbulence increasing, GM chose to disinvest. Chairman Roger Smith stated (Holusha 1986, D30) that the company did not see the situation "turning around in the near future." GM's action could thus be described as cutting its losses. The longer the economic and political situation in South Africa remained bad, the less GM could hope to sell its assets for, and the harder it would be to find a buyer.[22] Also, by partially disinvesting (selling a majority interest in their subsidiaries), Ford and GM retained an easy avenue by which to return to South Africa should the climate become more favorable. Chrysler

---

20. Also, Timothy Smith, director of the Interfaith Center on Corporate Responsibility, stated in discussing GM's disinvestment decision, "The fact is, G.M. was facing pressure from some significant investors." Holusha (1986: 1, D30).

21. From 1981 to 1986, GM failed to make a profit in South Africa, and its market share dropped from 10% to 7%. Eleven hundred workers were laid off in the fifteen months prior to the decision to disinvest. Because its labor force was 60% Black, GM was reluctant to implement wage and benefit cutbacks which would almost certainly gave resulted in negative publicity. Cowell (1986: D22).

22. At the time GM announced its decision to disinvest, it was the second largest U.S. employer in South Africa. Like IBM, it was reported that GM provided a loan to finance the purchase of its subsidiary by the South African buyer. Hayes (1987:27).

began with partial disinvestment before finally selling its last shares in Sigma Motors to the South African corporation, Anglo American.[23] Thus, despite significant fixed assets, the auto manufacturers were willing to, at least partially, leave South Africa. Ultimately, they were harder hit by the problems of the South African economy than by proposed economic sanctions. Leaving South Africa was a sensible business decision. Under the circumstances, it is not surprising that auto manufacturers did not vigorously oppose sanctions.

One would expect a company making a profit and with significant fixed assets in South Africa to be hardest hit by a comprehensive economic sanctions package. MNCs in this position should have mounted the strongest opposition to sanctions. Goodyear provides a good example. The company has a long history of involvement in South Africa. It began selling tires in South Africa in 1916 and manufacturing them there in 1947. In the mid-1980s, Goodyear had a $100 million investment in South Africa, including a $20 million plant expansion completed in 1985. Like GM and IBM it ranked among the ten largest U.S. employers in South Africa in 1986. Goodyear's South African operations were consistently profitable. Indeed, profit margins there have been described as "among the best it achieves in any country" (Kessler 1985, 24). One of Goodyear's principal concerns was that economic sanctions would affect technology transfers or new investments that would make it difficult for them to remain competitive in South Africa. Also, disinvestment, Goodyear argued, could mean that foreign competitors such as Dunlop might take over their market share, and quite possibly their plants (Kessler 1985, 25-26). Thus, not only would Goodyear lose a profitable operation, but their competitors would gain in the process. Therefore from a business standpoint, it is not surprising that Goodyear chose to remain in South Africa and opposed the imposition of economic sanctions.

Unlike many MNCs, Goodyear was willing to speak publicly about its decision to remain in South Africa, and its opposition to sanctions. Goodyear maintained that it was a force for change in South Africa and could have more influence by staying than by leaving. As evidence, the company pointed to its record in South Africa which included: high Sullivan principle compliance ratings, six million dollars given to Black education and employment programs, equal pay for equal work before the Sullivan principles mandated it, and non-whites supervising whites at its plants.

---

23. Ford's actions provide an example of partial disinvestment in which the U.S. multinational maintains "significant interest in the new company. Ford merged with AmCar to form the South African Motor Company of which AMCar owned approximately 60%, and Ford 40%." UN Panel of Eminent Persons... (1986:44). For the Chrysler figures see UN Centre on Transnational Corporations (1984:54).

Also consistent with the Sullivan principles and the AMCHAM approach, Goodyear's managing director made public appeals for an end to apartheid (Kessler 1985, 25–26). What separated Goodyear from other companies profiting in South Africa was their willingness to publicly discuss their operations in South Africa and their opposition to sanctions. According to Kessler (1985, 24–25), at a time when other companies were shunning the limelight, Goodyear allowed reporters to sit in at corporate meetings, interview executives, and examine documents. However, while company executives were united on remaining in South Africa, Kessler (1985, 26) reported that there were divisions regarding the direction U.S. policy should take. With more to lose than many MNCs, Goodyear was willing to do more. Yet, these internal divisions regarding appropriate U.S. policy and the fact that the sanctions were not as stringent as they might have been, combined to prevent Goodyear from taking stronger action.

This examination of business interests and their effect on U.S. economic sanctions policy making toward South Africa provides support for the hypotheses previously stated. Business interests did campaign against sanctions. However, because a relatively small number of businesses would be affected, and most of those not seriously, business interests did not oppose sanctions as aggressively as they might have. Also, several of Hughes' criteria for successful influence by economic interests were not met. The issue was economic and the decision was made over a long period of time, however businesses were not united behind the issue, and the issue was kept in the public eye. Thus, although the executive branch was sympathetic to the concerns of MNCs operating in South Africa, it is not surprising that economic sanctions against South Africa were imposed in the mid 1980s. The existence of a competing domestic interest that would benefit from the sanctions made their imposition even more likely.

CONCLUSION

One indication of the importance of specific domestic interest groups in influencing the changes in U.S. policy toward South Africa is the fact that public opinion on South Africa remained virtually unchanged for the eight year period from 1978 to 1986. According to thermometer ratings done by the Chicago Council on Foreign Relations, South Africa's mean temperature was 46 degrees in 1978, 45 degrees in 1982, and 47 degrees in 1986 (Reilly 1988, 50). Led by Blacks, a domestic movement built momentum, pressuring both the private sector and the federal government to impose sanctions against South Africa. Disinvestment grew during the 1980s until at one point between January 1985 and the first quarter of 1986, 48 firms left South Africa. This was the period when domestic pressure was at its peak

(Hilton 1986, 24). In many instances, these companies were performing poorly.[24] The rising tide of domestic pressure for sanctions in the U.S. coincided with a recession in the South African economy. The moderate nature of the sanctions meant that business interests were not affected as adversely as they might have been. Also, only approximately 1% of U.S. foreign direct investment is in South Africa.[25] Therefore, business interests did not launch an all out campaign to defeat the proposal. MNCs did oppose the sanctions. However, because a small number of businesses were affected in small ways, the opposition was confined to public statements and advertisements. AMCHAM's strategy of working within South Africa also diverted resources that might have been spent on lobbying in the United States. Thus, although the literature has traditionally considered business interests to be strong and powerful, in this case because their interests were not seriously affected, big business was not the strongest domestic interest involved.

Blacks were the domestic interest most deeply affected by the South African sanctions issue and the policy outcome reflected their interests. Blacks organized and mounted a campaign for the imposition of economic sanctions. Through organized protests and sit-ins, TransAfrica and the Free South Africa Movement kept the issue in the public eye for several years. Within the Congress, the Congressional Black Caucus sponsored and worked effectively for the passage of economic sanctions legislation. Thus, the imposition of economic sanctions on South Africa in 1986 demonstrates that Blacks can effectively influence U.S. foreign policy and that business interests are not always successful, even when their views coincide with those of the President. This case provides support for the theory that the domestic distribution of costs and benefits influences U.S. economic sanctions policy making. It also provides a framework for assessing the balance of power among contending coalitions. Where costs and benefits fall on different groups, their relative influence can be predicted by examining resources, issue salience and coalition unity. Significantly, resources alone are a poor predictor of power. The other two variables depend greatly upon the specific issue environment. Since issue characteristics will affect mobilization and unity, groups with modest resources can

---

24. This was especially true in the early 1980s when a UN study found that, "Reductions in the investment or outright divestments, where they have occurred, have generally been explained by commercial rather than political factors." UN Centre on Transnational corporations (1984: 7–8). See also Kaempfer, Lehman, and Lowenberg (1987).

25. Kaempfer Lehman and Lowenberg (1987:14) argue that if other more serious and costly forms of sanctions such as physical disinvestment—"the closing of American owned factories and other capital in South Africa. . . or the actual removal of currently emplaced capital goods"—are considered then, "the counter-pressure by affected firms would rise as the cost of such a policy rises above the cost of financial disinvestment." See also Rothchild and Ravenhill (1987:394).

sometimes outmaneuver more substantially endowed groups. Ultimately, other similar cases must be examined to determine the extent to which the conclusions reached here can be generalized.

8

The Politics of National Security Policy

INTEREST GROUPS, COALITIONS, AND THE SALT II DEBATE

David Skidmore

Over a quarter century of research has brought forth a vast corpus of scholarship on the domestic sources of American foreign policy. For sheer bulk, this body of work is particularly impressive in the areas of public opinion, bureaucratic politics and leadership psychology. By contrast, the accumulated literature on the influence of organized societal groups over U.S. foreign policy decision-making remains remarkably thin.

The paucity of research on foreign policy interest groups stems from the assumption that such groups are politically marginal. To gauge the persistence of this view, one need only compare Lester Milbrath's (1967, 240) two decade old conclusion that the "impact [of interest groups] on foreign policy is slight at best" with Joseph Nye's (1986, 116) more recent appraisal: "By and large, the influence of such groups [on U.S. Soviet policy] is limited."

While there exists a rich tradition of research on group influence in domestic affairs, foreign policy-making has been viewed as a separate realm, standing apart from the messy factional politics of the domestic sphere. In contrast with the "stable structure of interest groups" seeking to influence domestic policy, the foreign policy interest group structure has been described as "weak, unstable, and thin rather than dense" (Wildavsky 1966, 10). These assumptions are not universally held. Many aspects of foreign economic policy are thought susceptible to group influence and some ethnic lobbies, it is often acknowledged, carry weight with respect to particular issues. It is safe to say, however, that most scholars consider core national security policies largely beyond the sway of interest group politics (e.g., Rourke 1990, 239–41; Kegley and Wittkopf 1987, 276–89).

This chapter argues that such a sharp delineation between the role of interest groups in domestic and foreign affairs is unjustified. This distinction may have held descriptive accuracy during the depths of the Cold War when a broad consensus surrounded U.S. foreign policy. Yet the ideological rifts over America's role in the world which emerged in the wake of the Vietnam war have eroded loyalty to a singular version of the national interest and given rise to occasionally intense group conflict over central features of U.S. national security policy. If this growth in the density and intensity of interest group mobilization and conflict has been overlooked by most scholars, so has the impact of these developments on the making of national security policy. While the influence of such groups should not be exaggerated, the relatively open, democratic nature of the American polity and the growing role of Congress in foreign policy-making in recent decades has allowed for greater access and impact on the part of interest groups than is commonly supposed.

After a brief discussion of the literature on interest groups and national security policy, we examine the debate over ratification of the SALT II treaty, arguing that interest group politics played a crucial role in the entire process at both the Congressional and Executive levels. We conclude by offering more refined hypotheses about the conditions under which foreign policy interest groups might effectively pursue their goals.

INTEREST GROUPS AND NATIONAL SECURITY POLICY

The notion that national security policy-making is exempt from interest group influence rests upon claims about the nature of the issue area as well as the structure of the decision-making arena. Security issues fail to evoke group conflict, it is argued, because they involve national rather than group interests: "The essence of interest group activity is group advantage. But private group advantage is difficult to calculate in the security policy arena; we are all more or less advantaged or disadvantaged collectively" (Cohen 1983, 224). Even where particular groups do perceive their special interests at stake and are motivated to influence such policies, they face the problem that they have no presumptive legitimacy to speak on behalf of the national interest (Jensen 1982, 137–38).

These issue related obstacles are magnified by the institutional structure of national security decision-making. Important choices are made at the apex of the state, among the President and his close advisers. Congress is routinely deferential on national security issues while the relevant bureaucracies possess less independence from Presidential oversight than their domestic policy equivalents. By design, this structure insulates key decision-makers and provides private groups with few avenues of access (Hughes 1978, 188, 217).

Interest groups may seek to place external pressure on Presidents and strengthen their claim to speak for the nation through public persuasion. Yet the relevant literature holds out little hope that such groups can succeed in swaying broad public opinion. Presidents have much readier access to the media, possess a more plausible claim to speak for the national interest and benefit from the public's presumption that they are more fully informed than their critics (Milbrath 1967, 250).

The institutional claim is the strongest, for it suggests that even if groups do mobilize around national security issues, their chances to exert influence are slim. Yet this depiction of a centralized and insulated decision-making system stands in stark contrast with prevalent descriptions of the American state drawn from the fields of comparative politics and international political economy. From the perspective of writers in these fields, the American state is "weak" as compared with the "strong" states of countries such as France or Japan (Krasner, 1978; Katzenstein, 1976). While strong states feature highly centralized authority and a low degree of vulnerability to societal pressures, weak states are characterized by diffused or divided authority and the ready access they allow to societal groups. An important consequence of state weakness is that it forces political authorities to place a premium on coalition building, within both the government and the society at large (Risse-Kappen and Muller, 1990).

The United States belongs in the weak state category by virtue of the open, democratic character of its political system, the shared authority among its three branches of government and its decentralized bureaucratic system. While the institutions created to manage U.S. national security may be less open and more centralized than those responsible for domestic policies, some observers have nevertheless pointed out that the national security apparatus remains relatively fragmented and subject to societal pressures (Lowi, 1979; George, 1980, Nincic, 1990). The growing role of Congress in managing foreign policy during the past two decades has only accentuated these characteristics (Crabb and Holt, 1980; Spanier and Nogee, 1981; Zeidenstein, 1978). These considerations suggest that institutional structure should pose far less an obstacle to interest group influence than many observers have claimed.

This leaves the argument that national security issues, by their very nature, fail to evoke group interest or activity. Stephen Krasner (1978, 70) asserts that "A state that is weak in relation to its own society can act effectively in the strategic arena because its preferences are not likely to diverge from those of individual societal groups."

If, indeed, all significant social groups viewed security issues through the prism of a single and apparent national interest, then state strength or weakness would remain untested and, therefore, irrelevant. As is widely recognized, some security related issues are clearly not viewed in this way by all important groups. Issues such as defense spending or the imposition of economic sanctions involve distributional dimensions or vary in salience across groups. In these cases, the "national interest" and the interests of various groups often fail to coincide.

Yet these exceptions do not generally reach to the core assumptions or the central directions of U.S. national security policy. Does national security in this broader sense evoke societal unity or at least deference to the state? It is widely accepted that something approaching a societal consensus backed U.S. policy during the deep Cold War of the fifties and early sixties. Whether the U.S. state was weak or not, under these conditions, Presidents faced few societal constraints on their powers because the politics of consensus did not give rise to group mobilization or opposition.

Yet this condition may have represented more an aberration than the norm. The Cold War consensus rested upon two pillars. International hegemony made it possible for the U.S. to use its abundant resources and global dominance to escape difficult choices and to satisfy the demands of many domestic interests simultaneously. In addition, the ideological chasm dividing East and West was never so wide as during this period. Beginning in the late sixties, however, the relative decline of U.S. power sharpened the trade-offs among groups and across foreign commitments while failure in Vietnam and the loosening of the Cold War bloc system lessened faith at home in the ideological basis of America's Cold War strategy. These changes robbed national security issues of their heretofore unitary and consensual nature.

Indeed, data on elite and public opinion indicate that the post-Vietnam era witnessed the emergence of pervasive ideological splits over U.S. national security and foreign policies (Rosenau and Holsti, 1984; Schneider, 1983). It is not surprising, therefore, that the same period brought an unprecedented explosion in the number of foreign policy interest groups and in the scope and intensity of their activities, as the following case study will suggest.

No longer able to manage foreign policy on the basis of consensus, political leaders became dependent on the support of partial coalitions. Organized along the liberal/conservative dividing lines which emerged after Vietnam, these alliances became increasingly coherent and well organized as the decade of the seventies progressed (although asymmetries existed between them, as we suggest below). This political environment of contestation exposed the long hidden structural weaknesses of the American state in the national security realm and rendered Presidential management of foreign policy increasingly problematic.

The political evolution of the foreign policy interest group structure was not divorced from trends in the broader domain of interest group politics. The literature on interest groups in the field of American politics (see

Loomis and Cigler, 1986; Loomis, 1986; Hrebenar and Scott, 1990; Mahood, 1990; Schlozman and Teirney, 1989; and Berry, 1989) suggests five important trends over the past two decades: (1) The absolute number of interest groups has grown dramatically. (2) Public interest groups, organized on ideological bases, have grown even more rapidly than traditional groups which typically reflect narrow material interests (e.g., labor unions, trade associations, etc.). (3) The activities of interest groups have expanded beyond lobbying or campaign contributions to include new techniques for raising money, mobilizing members or participants and swaying public opinion. These include the sophisticated uses of the media and direct mail. (4) Interest groups have increasingly worked in league with like minded groups through both long term and ad hoc coalitions. (5) The decline in political party organizations and the decentralization of power in the Congress have enhanced the influence and role of interest groups in articulating societal demands.

Each of these changes is mirrored in our discussion of the role of interest groups in the SALT II debate, further suggesting that distinctions between the politics of domestic and national security issues have been exaggerated by many commentators.

SALT II AS A TEST CASE

The debate over ratification of the SALT II treaty serves as a useful test case to gauge the validity of our assertion that interest groups can indeed play an influential role in the making of U.S. national security policy. We argue that interest group pressure, along with related domestic political factors, placed important constraints on Presidential control of national security policy-making during the Carter years and, more specifically, help explain heavy Congressional resistance to the SALT II treaty.

Why this particular case? SALT II offers a useful test because there existed three major reasons to expect that group interest and influence should have been low in this instance.

First, the SALT II treaty represented a key component of U.S. national security policy during the late seventies. It impacted such crucial issues as arms control, military spending, and U.S.-Soviet relations. If such a clearly central pillar of U.S. security policy engendered division and group mobilization rather than unity around a common national interest, then a key tenet of the traditional wisdom is called into question.

Second, we might expect interest group opposition to be ineffectual with respect to a policy which so clearly reflected a high Presidential priority. The institutional strengths of the Presidency might be expected to overwhelm interest group opponents.

Third, we might expect Congress to be relatively immune to interest groups pressure if the legislative branch is, for institutional reasons, more deferential to Presidential prerogatives on national security issues than on other sorts of policy matters. This expectation should be strengthened by the fact that Congress has traditionally been reluctant to challenge Presidents on major treaties. Indeed, SALT I passed the Senate by an overwhelming majority despite the fact that, according to most observers, its terms were less favorable to the U.S. than those of SALT II. With respect to SALT II itself, moreover, President Carter proved especially assiduous in consulting Congressional leaders during the negotiation and drafting of the treaty. Despite all of this, of course, SALT II faced stiff Congressional resistance. This anomaly again suggests that we should look beyond institutional factors for an explanation. In particular, the interest group mobilization which took place between Congressional consideration of the SALT I and SALT II treaties helps to explain their different fates.

If, despite these apparent obstacles, we find that interest groups did indeed play a significant role in the ratification process and that their opposition to the treaty contributed to Carter's inability to obtain quick and easy approval, then further research into the impact of interest groups on national security policy more generally would seem warranted. Once it has been established that national security policy is not immune from effective interest group intervention, then the next step is to identify the conditions under which group advocacy is most likely to prove influential. While recognizing that any generalizations drawn from a single case must remain tentative, we attempt, in our conclusion, to draw such lessons from the SALT II experience.

THE STRUCTURE OF INTEREST GROUP COMPETITION IN THE CARTER YEARS

We can learn a great deal about the direction of policy change in the seventies by examining the constraints placed upon Presidential choice by the foreign policy interest group environment. To do so, we must examine both the coalitional patterns which joined or divided various groups and the balance of power among them.

The domestic politics of U.S. foreign policy during the seventies was driven by the competition between two opposed coalitions. The first bloc was based upon a loose and rather awkward alliance between internationally oriented business interests and liberal activists, many of whom first entered politics as critics of the Vietnam War. Despite some glaring differences between them, both elements of this coalition supported the reform of America's Cold War policies, Detente with the Soviet Union and a broadening of the nation's foreign policy agenda.[1]

The high point of liberal mobilization came with the Presidential election of Jimmy Carter, who embodied both popular skepticism about the Vietnam War and U.S. interventionism abroad as well as the interests of internationalist business groupings, such as the Trilateral Commission where Carter received his training in foreign affairs.[2] Carter's liberal internationalist orientation stressed the need to cope with declining U.S. power by reducing U.S. commitments in peripheral areas, sharing burdens more evenly with friends and allies and seeking accommodation with adversaries. In the security field, this translated into lower defense spending and arms sales, preventive diplomacy along with the avoidance of military force in the Third World, and the expansion of Detente and arms control with the Soviet Union.[3]

Pitted against this liberal coalition was a conservative bloc built around an alliance between the traditional Cold War establishment and the emerging New Right. The former included figures from the military-industrial complex, managers of the national security apparatus and Cold War intellectuals. The New Right was a popular, largely middle class movement which arose in reaction to the welfare state, high taxes and liberal social and moral permissiveness. Although primarily domestic in origin and focus, the New Right viewed U.S. withdrawal from Vietnam, Detente and liberal policies toward the Third World as signs of a self-imposed retreat from American global power and leadership. These concerns increasingly pulled the movement toward deeper involvement in foreign policy issues (Peele, 1984; Crawford, 1988).

While popular disillusionment with the Vietnam War worked to the advantage of liberals during the early seventies, the conservative coalition proved the stronger and more cohesive of the two as the decade progressed. Below, we examine this growth of conservative strength as well as the effects an asymmetrical interest group environment had on Carter's efforts to gain Senate ratification of SALT II.

CONSERVATIVE MOBILIZATION

The conservative mobilization of the seventies took place in the wake of a series of sudden and unprecedented challenges to the dominance of the

---

1. On business alignments toward U.S. foreign policy during the 1970s, see Ferguson and Rogers (1980).
2. On the Trilateral Commission, see Sklar (1980) and Gill (1990).
3. For a discussion of Carter's early policies, see Skidmore (forthcoming).

Cold War paradigm in American foreign policy. Early in the decade, traditional Cold War policies lacked any coherent organizational sponsor in American politics. George McGovern's Presidential nomination signaled the centrality of anti-war critics within the Democratic Party while a Republican President pursued openings toward the world's two largest communist powers.

The Cold War establishment found itself placed on the defensive by this erosion of popular and elite support for traditional policies. Two events created the political space for a conservative counteroffensive. The end of direct U.S. military involvement in Vietnam reduced the salience of the peace issue and allowed room on the nation's political agenda for criticisms of America's overall security posture. In addition, Watergate first distracted Nixon from the complex game of triangular diplomacy and finally discredited and removed the architect of detente from office altogether. Conservatives responded to these opportunities by mobilizing elements of the old Cold War establishment while simultaneously seeking out new allies.

The result was a proliferation of conservative pressure groups. Some grew from the traditional Cold War establishment and were dominated by former military officers, past State or Defense Department appointees, businessmen and union officials tied to large military contractors, and academic foreign policy or defense specialists. This core constituency augmented its strength through cooperation with the more ideologically oriented and broadly focused groups of the emerging New Right.

As the most prominent element of this coalition, the Committee on the Present Danger (CPD) deserves special attention. Evolving from a series of discussions among its founders between 1974 and 1976, the Committee's membership read like a Who's Who list of the traditional foreign affairs establishment. According to Max Kampelman (1984, xvi), it was decided that "the principal qualification for membership would be expertise and experience in the areas of foreign and defense policy...we would concentrate on inviting persons who had held top posts in State, Defense, and Treasury, as well as senior figures in appropriate departments at leading universities around the country."

Approximately 150 such notables initially joined the Committee. Roughly one third had previously held government posts and many, including Paul Nitze, Eugene Rostow, David Packard and Dean Rusk, had long been highly influential members of the Cold War establishment.[4] The Committee's

---

4. Other familiar names among the founders were Henry Fowler, Lane Kirkland, Charles Walker, William Colby, John Connally, Arthur Dean, Douglas Dillon, Andrew Goodpaster, Leon Keyserling, Charles Burton Marshall, Matthew Ridgeway, Paul Seabury, Maxwell Taylor, Edward Teller, and Bertram Wolfe. For a full list of the CPD's initial membership, see Troyler (1984, 5–9). On the Earlier CPD, see Wells (1979, 141–51) and Sanders (1983, 51–48).

name was taken from that of a similar group which had pressed for a posture of global containment.

While individual members often testified before Congress, the Committee eschewed formal legislative lobbying in favor of activities designed to sway public and elite opinion. The CPD cultivated extensive contacts in the press, sent members on speaking tours and prepared a series of statements on contemporary issues concerning defense, arms control, and U.S.-Soviet relations. The first such statement, issued the day following the 1976 Presidential election, declared that "The principal threat to our nation, to world peace, and to the cause of human freedom is the Soviet drive for dominance based upon an unparalleled military buildup" ("Common Sense..." 1984, 3).

In the coming years, the CPD acted as a foreign policy establishment in exile. The Committee enjoyed a coup of sorts very soon after its founding. CPD members had asserted that the National Intelligence Estimates prepared annually by the CIA understated the Soviet danger. Stung by these criticisms, outgoing President Ford took the extraordinary step of appointing a 'Team B' of conservative defense and foreign affairs experts from outside the government to prepare a report which would parallel the CIA's normal efforts. Dominated by leading CPD members, 'Team B' produced a draft considerably more pessimistic about Soviet capabilities and intentions than that prepared by the CIA's regular 'Team A'. According to one insider account (Pipes 1976, 34; also see Sanders 1983, 197–204), CIA Director George Bush subsequently intervened in the dispute by ordering 'Team A' to "substantially revise its draft" to produce "an estimate that in all its essential points agreed with Team B's position." By enhancing the intelligence community's sensitivity to conservative criticism, it seems likely that this episode played a role in the increasingly alarmist tenor of intelligence estimates regarding Soviet defense spending during the 1970s. A reappraisal conducted by the CIA in 1983 concluded that the Agency had previously failed to detect a significant slowing in the rate of growth in Soviet defense spending from 1976 onward and that its estimates tended to overstate the Soviet threat (Holzman 1980, 100; Cox, 1980; Gelb and Halloren, 1983; Smith, 1983; Garthoff 1985, 794–800).

CARTER AND HIS EARLY CRITICS: EARLY SKIRMISHES

The incoming Administration soon dampened the CPD's enthusiasm over the success of 'Team B'. Ignoring the CPD's lengthy list of suggested candidates for top foreign and defense posts (Sanders 1983, 180), Carter appointed a host of liberal foreign policy intellectuals; many relatively young and most critical of previous U.S. involvement in Vietnam.[5] Unable

---

5. Among these were Paul Warnke (arms control), Marshall Shulman (Soviet Union), Andrew

to ignore conservative sentiment altogether, however, Carter crafted a strategy for dealing with his opponents which shifted between confrontation and accommodation, with the latter tactic playing a more prominent role as time went on.

Conservatives won an early skirmish when their opposition forced Carter to withdraw his nomination of Theodore Sorensen, a former Kennedy adviser and Democratic liberal, for directorship of the Central Intelligence Agency. A more significant debate emerged over Carter's nomination of Paul Warnke for the job of chief SALT II negotiator. Contending that Warnke held overly dovish views, a number of conservative groups formed the Emergency Coalition Against Unilateral Disarmament to oppose his Senate confirmation.[6] By challenging Warnke, conservatives put Carter on notice that the liberal direction of his declared policies would not go unchallenged.

The Senate ultimately confirmed Warnke's appointment after a heated debate. But, as Henry Jackson had predicted (Sanders 1983, 209–10), the number of favorable votes for Warnke fell below the two thirds majority that would be needed to approve any treaty which Warnke might eventually negotiate. This placed pressure on Carter to adopt a tougher negotiating stance and consequently contributed to his ill fated decision to seek deep, comprehensive nuclear force cuts in SALT negotiations with the Soviet Union during the Summer of 1977.

After the close vote on Warnke's nomination, Carter moved "to bring some of his critics into the policy-making process. Henry Jackson, a hardliner generally regarded as the Senate's leading SALT expert, was invited to the White House to advise the president directly and to submit his own SALT proposals in writing" (Destler 1978/79, 48). Carter's subsequent proposal incorporated the provisions for deep cuts in Soviet heavy ICBMs favored by Jackson.

The Soviet rejection was swift and harsh when Secretary of State Vance presented Moscow with Carter's "comprehensive proposal" along with a fallback position which contemplated only minor variations on the proposals agreed to in the Vladivostok Accords. The Soviets criticized Carter's new package as too one-sided in favor of the U.S. and a serious departure from the assumptions underlying previous negotiations. The fallback proposals were rejected as well for offering no progress on the agreement reached at Vladivostok (Marder, 1977; Talbott 1979, 38–78).

Young (UN), Leslie Gelb (Politico-Military Affairs), Richard Moose (Africa), Richard Holbrooke (East Asia), Anthony Lake (Policy planning), and Patricia Dean (Human Rights). On the critical reaction of the conservative Democrats to Carter's appointments, see Evans and Novak (1977).

6. Warnke was criticized, in particular, for two articles he wrote (1975, 1976–77) during the mid-1970s in which he warned against exaggerating the Soviet threat.

Jackson's role in shaping Carter's early arms control proposals was accompanied by other White House efforts to appease the powerful Senator. Secretary Vance agreed in October, 1977 to meet with Jackson's Armed Services Subcommittee on Arms Control every two weeks. Carter also reappointed General Edward Rowney, at Jackson's urging, as the representative of the Joint Chiefs of Staff to the U.S. SALT delegation (Platt 1982, 169–70). Rowney later resigned from the negotiating team and thereafter denounced the final accord.

Carter narrowly survived yet another early skirmish, this time over his cancellation of the B-1 Bomber. In his memoirs, Carter (1982, 81) refers to the B-1 lobby as "one of the most formidable ever evolved in the military industrial community" and recalls that "there was tremendous pressure on Congress to go ahead with plans for an entire fleet" of new bombers.[7] Though Congress narrowly upheld the decision to cancel production (the House vote was 202 to 199), Carter's victory proved neither complete nor lasting. By continuing to fund research and development, Congress allowed the B-1 program to remain alive through 1981, when a new President revived production.

COPING WITH THE CRITICS: FROM ACCOMMODATION...

Despite, or perhaps because of, these early confrontations between the White House and its critics, Carter began to shape an accommodationist track in his dealings with conservatives. The President took pains, for instance, to provide conservatives outside of the government with access to top officials. Though Carter apparently hoped to co-opt some of his critics and thereby alleviate the political pressures on his Administration, it seems likely, in retrospect, that this accommodationist strand of Carter's strategy only helped to accelerate the insinuation of conservative influence over policy while doing little to free the Administration from outside pressures.

Carter's efforts at accommodation were evident in the preparation of PRM 10, a global strategic review he ordered shortly after taking office. Following the Team B precedent, a group of predominantly conservative outside consultants was asked to join with an interagency team of staffers in preparing the study. Unlike Team B, these outsiders were to work directly with the official task force rather than prepare a separate report. But since this arrangement resulted in repeated conflict, the final report

---

7. On the role of interest groups in the B-1 debate, see Lanouette (1977, 1991); Adams (1988); and Hampson (1989, 170–76).

was split into two sections. The first, dealing primarily with political issues, was written in a pessimistic tone by the team of outside experts. The second, focusing on defense requirements, was composed by a more liberal Pentagon team and called for a relatively modest defense program based upon more optimistic assumptions. The result was a confusing and inconsistent statement which did little to add clarity to the direction of Carter's foreign and defense policies (Smith 1977; Sanders 1983, 244–47).

Carter's sensitivity to conservative opinion was further reflected in an incident which occurred in August of 1977. Stung by criticisms contained in a recently published CPD statement entitled "Where We Stand On SALT II", Carter invited members of the CPD's executive committee to the White House where he pleaded with them to tone down their attacks on the Administration. In return, Carter promised the group greater private access to top Administration officials including Carter's National Security Adviser, Zbigniew Brzezinski, and Secretary of Defense, Harold Brown (Sanders 1983, 247)

... To Retreat

Conservative criticism nevertheless abated little. The CPD ("Countering..." 1984, 179) charged Soviet leaders with the aim of "impos[ing] an imperial system dominated by the Soviet will". Complaining of the Administration's "unwillingness to compete with the Soviet Union and to hold its drive in check", the CPD ("The 1980 Crisis..." 1984, 171–72) warned that "Pursuing a policy built on illusion, we have been adrift and uncertain while the Soviet Union expanded its power and empire on every continent and on all the seas."

Finding a growing echo in Congress and the media, these criticisms appeared to have an impact on public perceptions. Popular approval for Carter's handling of foreign policy sank from 48% in July, 1977 to only 22% in July of 1978 ("Opinion Roundup" 1979, 29). A Gallup Poll (Gallup 1979, 213) taken in July 1978 revealed that 43% of those surveyed disapproved of the way Carter was handling U.S.-Soviet relations while only 34% approved. In 1974, a poll conducted for the Chicago Council on Foreign Relations showed that over twice as many respondents believed that the U.S. spent too much on defense as thought the government spent too little. By 1978, the proportions had reversed with 32% now convinced that the U.S. spent too little on defense compared with 16% who felt the country spent too much (Rielly, 1975 and 1979). These trends heightened Carter's desire to toughen up his image as a means of restoring domestic support and accelerated his shift toward more conservative and confrontational policies.

Despite his campaign promise to cut defense spending, Carter proposed a 3% increase in his initial State of the Union address and later prodded other NATO countries to go along with similar increases. In addition, 1978 brought tighter restrictions on trade with the Soviet Union involving the transfer of sensitive technologies (Sanders 1983, 252–53). Carter also stepped up his criticism of human rights abuses in the Soviet Union; a move described by Carter aide Hamilton Jordan as an effort to shield the President from right wing attacks: "One of the first impressions the American people have of their new President is that he's been tough with the Soviets on human rights...And in terms of the SALT talks, it provides a good argument against those who later on might accuse him of being soft on the commies, to be able to point back to an experience when he was really tough on the Soviet Union" (Quoted in Spencer 1988, 38–39). Several days before a March, 1978 speech at Wake Forest University in which Carter took a harsh line toward the Soviet Union, Zbigniew Brzezinski, Carter's National Security Adviser, remarked that Carter's tougher rhetoric was designed to "prove we weren't soft" (Quoted in Sanders 1983, 250). Samuel Huntington (1984, 279), at the time a Brzezinski's aide, later recalled that "The positive response" to Carter's Wake Forest speech "encouraged White House political advisers to believe that a strong defense was good politics." Carter soon found another occasion to lambast the Soviets in an address at the Naval Academy in June.

In September, 1978, Marshall Shulman (1979, 223), Vance's Soviet expert, openly acknowledged in Congressional testimony that domestic constraints limited the Administration's ability to halt the deterioration in U.S.-Soviet relations:

> The blurring of popular understanding of the limitations of 'detente' contributed to a sense of disillusionment and anger...A measured and effective reaction to the military and political competition from the Soviet Union has been made more difficult by the persisting post-Vietnam apprehension that the United States may be seen as lacking sufficient will and resolution.

The SALT II Debate

It was in this atmosphere that negotiations over SALT II neared a successful conclusion in early 1979. Mired in controversy over both domestic and foreign issues, Carter's ability to fend off inevitable attacks on the approaching treaty stood in serious doubt. Public approval of Carter's overall performance fell to 30% (Garthoff 1984, 741). An early June survey (Smith, H., 1979b) showed that only 36% of the public approved of Carter's handling of foreign policy issues. Yet this paltry level of public support was only symptomatic of more fundamental ills weakening Carter's ability to guide the nation's foreign policies.

Carter's costly Panama Canal victory hurt rather than helped him with respect to the looming battle over SALT II. Politically moderate Senators who had voted with Carter on the Canal treaties, such as Republican Howard Baker, were wary of once again defying the right wing (On Baker, see Spanier 1985, 211). Conservative groups not only proved their ability to mobilize public sentiment in the earlier battle, but also succeeded, during the 1978 mid-term elections, in punishing Senators who had sided with the Administration on the Canal treaties. Moreover, the Panama experience taught conservatives that Carter could be forced into concessions in a tough Congressional battle (Moffett 1985, 176).

SALT II's prospects were also weakened by the widely held belief that the Soviet Union had achieved overall military superiority vis à vis the U.S. and that the Soviet drive for military dominance continued unabated in the face of U.S. passivity. The CPD ("What is...?" 1984, 12–13) cultivated these perceptions by arguing that "Neither Soviet military power nor its rate of growth can be explained or justified on grounds of self-defense." By mid 1979, a plurality had come to accept the CPD's claim of Soviet military superiority. In a poll (Smith, H., 1979b) taken in early June, 43% agreed that the U.S. was "not as strong" as the Soviet Union compared with 11% who believed that the U.S. was militarily stronger. These perceptions allowed critics to effectively argue for higher defense spending while attacking SALT II for "ratifying", as Senator Sam Nunn (Quoted in Burt, 1979d) put it, an existing nuclear imbalance.

PARTISAN CONFLICT

The final signing of the SALT II treaty thus took place in the context of a weakened Presidency, a fearful and insecure public, and an active and well-organized conservative opposition. This atmosphere precluded the possibility that debate over the treaty might focus narrowly on its merits. SALT II became a lightening rod; attracting bolts of criticism from those who found themselves at odds with Carter's larger foreign and defense policy agendas.

The growing partisanship of the foreign policy debate provided a measure of Carter's domestic vulnerability. Early 1979 brought an extraordinary meeting of 95 top Republican officeholders, including 26 Senators, at which it was decided that the Party should "abandon its traditional bipartisanship in foreign policy and make overall Soviet conduct a key issue in negotiating and considering a new strategic arms treaty." Referring to

Republican Senator Arthur Vandenberg who had championed a bipartisan approach to foreign policy during the post-World War II period, Senator Howard Baker stated that "Vandenberg was right in his time, but I think we're right in our time." With only two dissenting votes, the group passed a resolution "accusing the Carter administration of having let American military power decline and of having ignored 'Soviet aggressiveness'" (Quoted in Clymer, 1979)

Leading Republicans launched an even harsher attack against the Administration less than a month later when the Republican National Committee charged that "The failure of this Administration in national security is enormous." The Republicans compared Carter's program with the appeasement policies pursued by British Prime Minister Neville Chamberlain toward Hitler's Germany during the 1930s. Finding an "eerie parallel" between the two situations, the Committee stated that "Once again we witness a Chamberlain-like government's fervid hopes that a dictatorship's good behavior will compensate for its own inadequacy. Yet these hopes are based more upon an obstinate denial of unpleasant facts than honest and realistic evaluation of the Soviet buildup." According to the *New York Times* (Weinraub, 1979), Bill Brock, the Republican National Committee chairman, "made it clear that the Carter Administration's defense and foreign policies...would serve as key issues in next year's Presidential elections."

THE OPPOSITION MOBILIZES

This growing polarization between Carter and his critics and the increasingly conservative public mood foretokened a bruising ratification battle. Sensing SALT II's vulnerability, conservative interest groups mounted massive direct mail, media, and lobbying campaigns.[8] The Committee on the Present Danger spent $750,000 in its efforts to derail SALT II even before the treaty was announced. Executive Committee and Board members testified on 17 different occasions before Senate committees during consideration of the treaty and participated in 479 television and radio programs, press conferences, public debates, briefings of influential citizens, and major speeches on arms control and defense. The Committee distributed over 200,000 pamphlets and reports (Sanders 1983 264). The Committee's key role prompted one government spokesperson (Quoted in Kurkowski 1982, 153) to comment that "The interest groups on the right shaped the terms of the SALT II debate. In the community of experts, the Committee on the Present Danger was the most influential..." Similarly,

---

8. For information on many of the groups discussed below, see Watson (1990).

Cyrus Vance (Quoted in Scheer 1983, 37), in 1982, remarked that "There is no doubt that the Committee on the Present Danger had a great deal to do with undermining SALT."

Still, as the intellectual wing of the anti-SALT coalition, the CPD's greatest contribution was to issue reports critical of the treaty written by noted arms control and defense experts. The task of mobilizing grass roots opposition fell to other groups whose activities were coordinated through an ad hoc umbrella organization called the Coalition for Peace Through Strength.

Launched under the auspices of the American Security Council in the Summer of 1978, the purpose of the Coalition, according to its co-chair Paul Laxalt (Quoted in Sanders 1983, 225), was to gather together "some of the most prestigious names and groups in the defense community to build a formidable organization dedicated to the adoption of a national strategy for peace through strength." The promotion of "peace through strength" translated into a campaign of criticism aimed at the SALT negotiations as well as vigorous calls for higher defense spending.

The Coalition was three-pronged. By the time SALT II came before the Senate, it included 191 Congressmen among its members, a figure which later swelled to 204. Another arm included well known conservatives outside of the government, some of whom provided organizational leadership and carried out the Coalition's day to day activities. Falling under this wing were 2,500 retired generals and admirals. The Coalition also helped coordinate the activities of 106 affiliated organizations (Neal, 1979; Kurkowski 1982, 134; Sanders 1983, 226, 264).

In addition to its coordinating role, the Coalition independently spent $2.5 million and organized a 150 member speakers bureau. The Coalition's central importance in the anti-SALT II drive was revealed in January 1979 when "a House Armed Services subcommittee used a luncheon given by the organization to release an official report opposing SALT" (Neal, 1979).

In April, the Coalition issued its own sixty–two page report criticizing the treaty accompanied by a news conference featuring a number of former defense officials and retired military officers. The report ("Excerpts...", 1979; also see Burt, 1979c) argued that "The most important reason for rejecting SALT II is that it is a symbol of defeatist policies which have led to phased surrender by the United States as it retreats around the world in the face of Soviet aggression."

One of the most effective anti-SALT groups was the American Security Council (ASC), a long time champion of high defense spending with strong ties to leading military contractors. ASC boasted over 200,000 dues paying members and an annual budget of $4 million. The Council spent $3 million opposing SALT II and sent out 10 million pieces of mail. It produced and distributed three films dealing with defense, nuclear weapons and arms control prior to and during the SALT II debate. The SALT Syndrome, which like the other two included appeals for money and memberships, showed 600 times on local stations and netted 50,000 new members for ASC. The other two films were shown a total of 1,800 times. The group's speaker program, featuring retired military officials such as Maj. Gen. George Keegan and Lt. Gen. Daniel O. Graham, reached 800 audiences (Charlton, 1977; Lanouette 1977, 1991; Kurkowski 1982, 133, 48136–39; Sanders 1983, 264–65).

With an enormous 325,000 dues paying members and an annual budget of $3 million, the American Conservative Union (ACU) also brought considerable resources to bear in its attempt to derail SALT II. The ACU organized a grass roots campaign centered around its 42 state affiliates. It also sent one million pieces of mail and produced as well as distributed two anti-SALT films. One of these showed on 300 stations and brought contributions of $450,000 (Kurkowski 1982, 126–32). Yet another group, the Conservative Caucus spent $1 million and sent 5 million pieces of mail (Sanders 1983, 264–65).

As a direct result of these efforts, many Senators found themselves awash with constituent mail expressing opposition to ratification. In a survey (Kurkowski 1982, 244) of fifty five Senate staffers, 44% reported that mail ran strongly against ratification while 36% said mail ran slightly against the treaty. Only 2% reported that mail ran strongly in favor of SALT II.

The thrust of the opponent's arguments against SALT II had less to do with the treaty's specific terms than with the overall direction of the Administration's foreign and defense policies. Senator Jake Garn declared that "I intend to make this a debate on the whole strategic and defense policy of the United States" (Quoted in Mohr, 1979). Treaty foes rejected the symbolism of cooperating with the Soviets on arms control at a time when conservatives viewed the Soviet threat as growing. Senator Henry Jackson (Quoted in "Jackson Calls...", 1979) darkly suggested that Senate passage of SALT II would be "appeasement in its purest form."

Above all, conservatives feared that, by reinvigorating Detente, SALT II would lull the public into a sense of complacency and undercut support for a vigorous defense buildup. CPD member Paul Nitze (Quoted in Congressional Digest 1979, 205) counseled the Foreign Relations Committee that "the Senate must first resolve the question of whether, in times of increasing danger, including military danger, it is wise to let down our guard or whether it is time to pull the country together for the major effort that is required on many fronts." Nitze worried that "To accept the case that is being made for the Vienna terms, with all its fallacies and implausibilities, can only incapacitate our minds and wills for doing the things necessary to redress the strategic imbalance."

THE LIMITS OF INTEREST GROUP SUPPORT FOR SALT II

Private interest group supporters of SALT II lacked the resources and the high degree of organization possessed by opponents. The principal group to lobby on behalf on the treaty called itself Americans for SALT (AFS). Led by Townscend Hoopes, former Under-Secretary of the Air Force, and Charles Yost, former chief delegate to the United Nations, along with other prominent political notables, AFS helped coordinate the efforts of various pro-treaty groups. It functioned, however, only partially autonomously from the White House. The Administration played a role in the group's formation and helped direct its activities from behind the scenes (Spanier 1985, 212). The major purpose of American's for SALT was "to do the sort of hard political organizing that cannot by done by Government employees" (Quoted in Roberts, 1979). Yet the group's plans included spending only $200,000, far less than any of the major groups working against the treaty (Burt, 1979a). One staffer (Quoted in Kurkowski 1982, 81) reported that "It was hard to raise money." AFS suffered from other disabilities as well. Three top ranking staffers were fired during the first six months after the group's founding and some in the Senate considered the group lacking in credibility owing to its close ties to the White House (Kurkowski 1982, 85).

Business support for SALT II was expressed through the American Committee on East-West Accord which featured notables such as Donald M. Kendall (President of PepsiCo Inc., a firm active in exporting to the Soviet Union), George Kennan, John Kenneth Galbraith, Jeremy Stone, Fred Warner Neal, Robert Schmidt, Carl Marcy, and Jerome Wiesner among its 145 founding members (Hallenberg 1990, 15).

One third of the Committee's funding came from firms actively involved with East-West trade (Kurkowski 1982, 73). According to co-director Carl Marcy (Quoted in Lanouette 1977, 1987), the committee

> was first formed... in 1974, because of concern over the Jackson-Vanik amendment to limit U.S.-Soviet trade. Then last year [1976] we shifted our focus to keeping the country from slipping back into the cold war syndrome. Most of the members believe that we can't make headway in arms control unless we have normal business and cultural exchanges and we can't make headway in business unless there's progress on arms control.

The Committee's principal contribution to the campaign for SALT II was a half hour film which showed on over 300 local television stations, reaching an estimated 90 million people. Background materials were also mailed to 4,000 editors and community leaders (Lanouette 1977, 1987; Kurkowski 1982, 73–74). Liberal activist organizations also worked on behalf of SALT II. The Disarmament Working Group and the Coalition for a New Foreign and Military Policy coordinated the efforts of numerous peace groups (Lanouette 1977, 1985, 1990). Due to ideological differences, however, coordination between these groups and the elite-centered organizations discussed above was weak.

Despite their work on behalf of SALT II's ratification, the enthusiasm these groups brought to the task was often tempered by philosophical reservations. Many peace activists favored speedy efforts at total nuclear disarmament and considered SALT II a timid and disappointing step in that direction. While negotiations on the pact were still underway, F. Raymond Wilson (Quoted in Lanouette 1977, 1985), chairman of the Disarmament Working Group, predicted that "When the terms of the treaty come out, we will probably be pretty unsatisfied, but it needs to be ratified as a step to SALT III, which, supposedly, will be much more a step to disarmament." Jeremy Stone, a prominent arms control advocate and director of the Federation of American Scientists, drew considerable attention for his criticisms that SALT II did not go far enough (Kurkowski 1982, 101–108).

The effectiveness of most liberal groups was hampered not only by their own qualms about the treaty, but also by shoestring budgets. Bob Brammer (Quoted in Lanouette 1977, 1985), a Disarmament Working Group staff member, conceded that "Letter writing is the bottom line, the bread and butter for every issue, especially because we don't have an awful lot of money to spend." The fate of one such group is illustrative. Modeled after Common Cause, an organization known as New Directions sprang up in the mid-seventies with the goal of building grass roots support for a reorientation of U.S. foreign policy. The group drew up ambitious plans for campaigns revolving around a number of issues, including SALT II. The group's founders hoped to use the battle over the Panama Canal treaties as a vehicle for building a mass base of supporters and contributors, much as New Right groups were successfully doing at the time. The hoped for financial contributions failed to materialize, however, and New Direction's efforts in support of SALT II were hampered by debts incurred due to the failure of its earlier direct mail campaign (Kurkowski 1982, 115; Hogan 1986, 110).

Despite the considerable number of groups involved, interest group support for the SALT II treaty proved relatively inconsequential. Not only did private group foes of SALT II far outspend supporters,[9] but supporters were divided by ideological tensions and their efforts were less effectively coordinated than was true of their conservative counterparts.

---

9. As of March , 1979, one survey (see Stuart 1979, 1, 7) found that SALT opponents had outspent supports by a margin of 15–1.

These political realities dictated Carter's strategy for gaining treaty approval. Given the asymmetrical interest group environment which it faced along with precarious levels of popular support for both Detente and arms control, the Administration choose to soft-sell the SALT II treaty (Platt 1982, 162–63). Hoping to "appeal to skeptics in the Senate", Carter aides began "to publicly maintain that the treaty will neither transform the basic character of Soviet-American relations nor make significant improvements to the country's strategic arsenal unnecessary. Indeed, an important part of the Administration's case for the agreement is that it will allow the United States to deploy several new weapons in the 1980's". Carter placed much of the weight of his pitch for SALT II on "the military and political dangers of a failure to impose some constraints on the future growth of the two nations' strategic arsenals" (Burt, 1979b; also see Burt, 1979e).

The cautiousness of the Administration's approach was apparent in Secretary of State Vance's testimony (Reprinted in Congressional Digest 1979, 202) on behalf of the treaty before the Senate Foreign Relations Committee: "We do not suggest that SALT II will by itself carry us to a new world of prosperity and peace...Nor do we suggest that if SALT is not approved, we could not survive." The treaty would, however, make "an important contribution to maintaining a stable strategic balance" and "enable us to broaden the work of arms control." As for Detente, SALT would "help us to fashion a balanced relationship with the Soviet Union in which we build on areas of mutual interest, but do not let the benefits of cooperative measures blind us to the reality of our continuing competition."

Vance and Defense Secretary Harold Brown argued that SALT II represented an improvement over SALT I since, unlike the earlier agreement, it provided for equal limits on both sides. The Administration defended SALT II's verification provisions as fully adequate and stressed that the treaty "impose(s) on the Soviet Union significant restraints that balance those it imposes on us..." (Congressional Digest 1979, 208). Finally, Carter cited the support of the Joint Chiefs of Staff and America's NATO allies as indications that the treaty adequately served U.S. and Western security interests. These arguments failed to hold early public support. Momentum clearly favored the treaty's critics. While initial polls showed high public approval for SALT II, a series of surveys taken during 1979 revealed a steady deterioration of popular approbation. The Administration's position weakened as the debate over SALT II exposed the public to criticisms of Carter's policies toward U.S.-Soviet relations and the military balance between the two powers.

A Gallup poll taken in mid-March, 1979 showed that those aware of the treaty favored Senate ratification by a ratio of 3-1. Yet by late June public support for the treaty had narrowed to a ratio of 5-3. By late September, after months of heated campaigning by both supporters and opponents, public attitudes had completed a remarkable turnaround: a small plurality of informed respondents now expressed opposition to the ratification of SALT II.[10] Part of the public's skepticism toward SALT II grew from a fundamental distrust of the Soviet Union and lack of faith in the U.S. ability to verify Soviet compliance with the treaty—both themes stressed by anti-treaty groups. In one survey (Smith, H., 1979b), 47% of those polled did not expect the Soviet Union to live up to the treaty terms. Public attitudes toward U.S. defense requirements had also hardened by this time. Whereas a plurality felt that military equality with the Soviet Union was an adequate basis for U.S. security in July, 1978, by October, 1979, according to an ABC News/Harris survey, 49% had come to believe that U.S. military superiority was a necessity as compared with 43% who supported equality alone (Platt 1982, 159).

These trends provided a measure of the continuing ideological potence of the message carried by anti-treaty groups as well as their success in disseminating their views. Comparing the American Committee for East-West Accord with the Committee on the Present Danger, for instance, one study found that the latter was much more effective than the former in gaining press coverage of its views and activities.[11] David Kurkowski's survey (1982, 292) of nineteen Senate staffers found that 63% believed anti-treaty groups were more effective than pro-treaty groups in influencing public opinion. Kurkowski (1982, 288) concludes that the treaty's failure can be traced in part "to a steady decline in public support for SALT and the creation of a negative political climate. The interest groups opposed to the treaty contributed to this climate. And in this regard, the anti-treaty groups can be said to have won the battle for public opinion."

This dramatic erosion of public support only sharpened the political dilemma faced by moderate Senators who privately supported SALT II but feared the political consequences of doing so publicly. For the Administration, the negative trend in opinion increased its desire to find ways of defusing charges that it was "soft" on the Soviets.

In this climate, Carter's only hope for treaty passage was to devise some package of concessions which could sway the substantial body of publicly

---

10. Gallup (1979, 123, 195, 272). These results were confirmed by other surveys. See also Lanouette (1979, 1564); Kurkowski (1982, 284–91); and "Opinion Roundup: SALT Support Shaky" (1979, 40).

11. From 1977 through 1979, the Committee on the Present Danger or its spokespersons were mentioned 98 times in the *Washington Post* the *Christian Science Monitor*, and the *New Orleans Times-Picayune*. These papers mentioned the American Committee on East-West Accord only 23 times during the same period. See Hallenberg (1990, 19–22).

uncommitted Senators. Carter resisted significant revision of the treaty's terms for fear that changes might require renegotiation with the Soviets and perhaps doom the treaty altogether (Burt, 1979f).[12] Carter instead sought support by offering concessions on various defense programs and policies. One result, ironically, was that arms control became the lever by which conservatives succeeded in prying greater military spending from the Administration.

One of Carter's first moves was to remove Paul Warnke as head of the Arms Control and Disarmament Agency. At Brzezinski's suggestion, Warnke was replaced by the more conservative George Siegnious, a retired military general, who, it was hoped, would provide a better defense of SALT II (Garthoff 1984, 818).

Carter's eagerness to appease the right led to a significant political miscalculation during the Fall of 1979 when he strenuously objected to the presence of a Soviet military brigade in Cuba. Carter seized upon the issue as a response to critics who charged the Administration with leniency toward Soviet misbehavior. The Administration's reaction contrasted sharply with its handling of a similar episode a year earlier when the Soviets shipped a squadron of MIG-23 fighter-bombers to Cuba. In that instance, Carter played down the significance of the shipment; thereby avoiding an international crisis or prolonged domestic debate over the issue. When the Soviet brigade was discovered, however, the Administration decided to dramatize its importance. One aide (Quoted in Burt, 1979g) explained that "This time, with SALT at stake, we felt we had to come out swinging." As it happened, the effort backfired when Carter was forced to concede that the Soviet troops were advisers who had long been stationed in Cuba without American objection and found that the U.S. had no reasonable means for bringing about their withdrawal (Garthoff 1984, 828–48; Smith 1986, 213–216). During the campaign for the treaty, Carter came under pressure from a number of crucial Senators to adopt a tougher U.S. defense posture in return for their support on SALT II. These demands were particularly intense over the issue of strategic force modernization. (Franck and Weisband 1979, 290–91). In June, Carter responded by proposing $40 billion in funding for the deployment of MX missiles and later announcing a new mobile basing plan for the weapons (Spanier 1985, 214).

---

12. Yet the Administration took pains to consult with Congress while negotiations were underway. In one White House aide's view, "I don't believe there's another issue of foreign policy where there's been more consultation." Twenty-six Senators along with forty-six Representatives, drawn from both parties, attended the Geneva negotiations. In several instances the Administration held out for additional Soviet concessions as a result of pressure from key Senators. The White House hoped, apparently in vain, that extensive Senate involvement in shaping U.S. negotiating positions would lessen opposition to the treaty's ratification. See Smith, H. (1979a).

Another concession to political realities was Carter's attempt to reassure SALT skeptics that he intended to pursue a hard line in future arms control negotiations. In September, Carter issued Presidential Decision (PD) 50 which outlined a new set of arms control guidelines. Prepared by Brzezinski's staff without the knowledge of Arms Control Director George Seignious, PD 50 committed the Administration to a more conservative stance toward ongoing and future arms control efforts. Its stringent negotiating guidelines were designed to protect existing and future military programs. The *New York Times* (Burt, 1979h) reported that the new directive was intended to "deemphasize the role of arms negotiations in foreign policy" and give "military considerations greater weight in arms control planning for future talks." This shift was prompted in part by domestic political constraints. According to one aide, the Administration hoped that the new guidelines would lead to "less controversial accords" (See also Garthoff 1984, 746).

Carter also came under tremendous pressure to increase military spending faster than the planned rate of 3% real growth per year. In late Summer, the Administration acquiesced when the Senate added $4 billion to the 1980 defense budget. Sam Nunn and other Senators also called upon the Administration to commit itself to real increases in defense spending of 5% for 1981 and 1982. Nunn, whose views on defense were influential among Democrats, linked his SALT II vote to substantial military budget increases (Burt, 1979d; Burt, 1979i). In a September appearance before the Senate Foreign Relations Committee, Harold Brown hinted that the Administration might be willing to contemplate future increases in defense spending beyond the 3% level. In late November, senior Carter aides engaged in private negotiations with Nunn and Henry Kissinger in hopes of discovering what levels of future defense spending would be sufficient to induce the two to express support for SALT II. Finally, on December 12, Carter announced plans for average real growth in military appropriations of 4.5% over the next five years; a rate of increase only slightly lower than the 5% level which Nunn had publicly advocated (Burt, 701979; Burt, 1979i; Burt, 1979j; Smith, T., 1979a).

Even this, however, left many critics unconverted. Henry Jackson and other Senators expressed skepticism about the sincerity of the Administration's commitment to higher defense spending. Paul Nitze (Quoted in Smith, T., 1979b) called Carter's proposal "inadequate in quantity" and "misdirected in quality". Carter's concession neither brought an immediate treaty endorsement from Nunn nor did it stop the Senate Armed Forces Committee from issuing a report critical of SALT II one week after the announcement (Burt, 1979k). In the wake of the Soviet invasion of Afghanistan, Carter requested that the SALT II treaty be withdrawn from consideration by the Senate. This reflected his recognition that Soviet actions had spoiled whatever chances the treaty had for passage. Yet its prospects were quite doubtful in any case. Prior to the invasion, the Foreign Relations Committee recommended ratification of the treaty by a lukewarm 9-6 vote. The Committee report included, however, a call for increased defense spending to make up for the treaty's inadequacies. Led by Henry Jackson, the Armed Services Committee voted out a report (Quoted in Burt, 1979k) recommending against ratification which concluded that the SALT II treaty "is not in the national security interests of the United States." Howard Baker, with Presidential aspirations, was expected to lead the fight against ratification. None of this boded well for the treaty. Senate head counts by Americans for SALT, the Conservative Caucus and Senator Alan Cranston each indicated that SALT II was headed for defeat even prior to the invasion of Afghanistan (Caldwell 1990, 2). It is probable that the Soviet action, by forcing Carter to withdraw the treaty, spared him a humiliating personal defeat.

The battle over ratification of the SALT II treaty revealed the stunning degree to which conservatives managed to parlay their organizational and ideological strengths into control over the terms of debate on national security issues. Throughout 1979, the Carter Administration was placed on the defensive by conservative attacks on the treaty and its overall foreign and defense policies. As public polls and readings of Congressional opinion revealed the growing momentum behind conservative perspectives, the Administration spent most of the year backpedaling in an attempt to regain domestic legitimacy. Instead of defending Detente and arms control in positive terms, Carter adopted a defensive posture: stressing that things would be worse without SALT II, promising to speed up strategic modernization and increase defense spending, and attempting to cultivate an image of toughness toward the Soviet Union. Many liberal appointees left the Administration during 1979 and 1980, culminating in the resignation of Cyrus Vance. During the same period, domestic considerations led the Administration to dramatize, or oversell, external threats, as, for instance, during the Soviet brigade in Cuba incident and the Soviet invasion of Afghanistan.[13] Though it won him little political credit, Carter's responses to an asymmetrical interest group environment considerably narrowed the distance between he and his critics.

EXPLAINING ASYMMETRIES IN INTEREST GROUP MOBILIZATION

Some have argued (Platt, 1982), convincingly, that Carter or his aides mishandled various aspects of the Administration's campaign to sell the

---

13. On Carter's response to Afganistan, see Skidmore (forthcoming).

SALT II treaty. How critical these mistakes may have been to the ultimate outcome is difficult to ascertain. We argue, however, that attention to Carter's tactical political errors should not blind us to broader structural characteristics of the domestic political landscape in which debates over arms control and national security took place during the late seventies.

We have focused in particular on the ways in which broad and enduring interest group coalitions dominated the environment in which Carter was forced to maneuver. A potent alliance of conservative interest groups stiffened Congressional resistance to SALT II, contributed to an erosion of public support for the treaty and created a climate in which Carter felt compelled to steer his national security policies to the right in an attempt to appease conservative critics. A weaker liberal coalition proved unable to effectively counterbalance these pressures on the Administration.

These conclusions are consistent with our argument that national security issues can indeed serve to evoke group mobilization and conflict. They also demonstrate, at least in this instance, that institutional arrangements in the national security realm do not serve as insuperable obstacles to interest group influence. The decentralized, open and democratic nature of the American political system and its shared authority between the legislative and executive branches—in short, the "weakness" of the American state—provides interest groups with routes of access and means for influencing policy which might not be available in a more hierarchical system. While a weak state structure is a necessary condition for interest group influence, it is not a sufficient one. Under what conditions are interest groups most likely to be effective in influencing national security policy? This question is impossible to answer satisfactorily based upon a single case. The SALT II experience nevertheless suggests a number of hypotheses which may serve as starting points for future research.

The evidence in this case suggests that interest groups are most likely to be influential when:

1. There exists no broad consensus on national security issues. A breakdown in consensus is most likely during periods of rapid international change. Under such conditions, the external environment offers no fixed reference for establishing the national interest. The seventies constituted such a period. The U.S. failure in Vietnam, declining relative American power, the softening of East-West ideological rivalry, international economic instability, the broadening of the foreign policy agenda and the growing complexity of the international system all contributed to a heightened sense of ambiguity about the U.S. role in the world and allowed for divergent interpretations of events and U.S. interests. In the wake of these disturbances, opinion gravitated toward two poles: a conservative camp which believed that these changes provided no serious challenge to the basic structure of world politics and therefore continued to embrace Cold War policies; and a liberal camp which argued for policies of adjustment to a changing international climate. This division led to competitive elite mobilization during the seventies as each side sought to advance its own agenda while blocking the initiatives of the other. A proliferation of foreign policy interest groups accompanied this process. The SALT II debate represented one of the climactic battles between these two interest blocs during the seventies.

2. **Interest groups form broad, enduring coalitions.** Interest groups are far more likely to be influential when they work in cooperation with other groups. Conservatives succeeded, during the late seventies, in cementing a broad yet coherent coalition which persisted across issues (e.g., Panama Canal treaties, Warnke nomination, B-1 bomber, SALT II) and over time. Although no permanent apparatus formalized this arrangement, successive ad hoc organizational umbrellas brought together many of the same groups as new issues and debates arose. This informal coalitional structure allowed the pooling of resources, the coordination of themes and activities, and a division of labor and responsibility. The whole thus became more than the sum of its parts.

3. **The strategies and objectives of groups rooted in material interests coincide with those of more ideologically-oriented groups.** The conservative coalition managed to generate harmony between its two major wings: the cold war establishment and the New Right. The former groups felt threatened by the liberal direction of Carter's early foreign policy orientation. They found themselves shut out of accustomed positions of power and Carter's policies promised to lock in undesired shifts in institutional status. The New Right was motivated more by opportunity than threat. Their campaign against Carter's foreign policies constituted only one dimension of a broader attack on the hegemony of liberalism in American politics. The demise of Cold War liberalism in the aftermath of Vietnam drove these disparate political forces together and cemented a marriage of necessity.

4. **Opposition groups are weak and divided.** When opposing interest group coalitions are matched in strength and organization, their efforts might be expected to cancel out. Thus, group influence is most likely when there exists a political asymmetry between or among competitors. In the SALT II case, liberals simply found themselves out-gunned by conservatives. This was true in terms of money, numbers of groups, media access, grass roots presence, and organizational sophistication. Moreover, the liberal camp was ideologically divided. Carter's policies appealed first to the most internationally committed sectors of American business. Sensitive to international trends, many such firms appreciated the rationales for policy adjustment put forward by the Administration. The problem with relying heavily upon this set of allies was that such interests were concentrated in elite circles and possessed little grassroots organization or appeal. They were also vulnerable to populist attacks, and therefore weak pre-

cisely where conservatives were strong. For different reasons, Carter's early policies appealed to ideological liberals. Carter, however, avoided close ties with those to his left as well. Not only did liberals lack the resources to serve as potent allies, but they often favored more far reaching reforms than Carter was willing to contemplate (Sanders 1983, 267). Carter also feared, probably correctly, that explicit association with groups considerably to the left of the general public might hurt more than it would help politically.

5. **The issue has high salience and public debate is protracted.** In the modern era, well endowed interest groups can hope to counter through paid media and direct mail campaigns, the President's natural advantage in reaching the public. Moreover, the more significant and protracted the issue, the more likely that the news media will feel compelled to air dissident voices. A drawn out debate also allows groups the time needed to raise money, engineer working coalitions and generate grass roots campaigns.

6. **Congressional involvement or approval is necessary.** As various episodes discussed in this paper suggest (e.g., Team B, PRM 10, etc.), the Executive branch is not entirely closed to direct interest group influence. Nevertheless, Congress is a far more open and decentralized institution. It is easier to gain access to and bring pressure to bear upon the legislative branch. The treaty ratification process provides the most promising opportunity for interest groups to intervene in national security issues. Even if an anti-treaty campaign ultimately fails, vigorous opposition may force Presidential concessions on the treaty's terms or on related security issues. If the treaty is unpopular with the public at large, then opposition groups are likely to expand their base of support in the course of the battle and may even find it possible to exact electoral retribution against supporters at a later date. Treaty ratification debates, however, present by no means the only or most common opportunities for interest group influence through the Congress. Congressional battles over national security issues may also take place, for instance, when Presidential appointments or security related fiscal appropriations are considered.

7. **Presidential popularity is low.** Conservatives took advantage of Carter's low popularity and overall image of political incompetence. By driving home common themes and criticisms, conservatives largely succeeded in wresting control over the national security agenda from the Carter Administration. The President, by contrast, found it difficult to articulate a consistent, positive and coherent message. Although each of these conditions was present in the SALT II case, it seems unlikely that all are required before interest group influence becomes consequential. Some are undoubtedly more crucial than others and the particular combination of conditions in various cases is likely to produce different results. A more precise weighting of these or other factors can be obtained only through

carefully designed comparative case study research in which initial conditions as well as outcomes are allowed to vary.

Conclusion

Scholars have generally assigned interest groups little weight in the study of U.S. national security policy. This neglect stems from the common assumption that the political environment surrounding national security policy differs dramatically from that associated with domestic policy. The former fails to evoke group activity due to the existence of a shared national interest with regard to such issues. Moreover, the institutional structure of national security policy-making denies access to even mobilized interest groups. This paper has suggested that these pervasive assumptions bear reexamination. Only under circumstances of extreme threat does the international environment impose a singular version of the national interest upon a society. Instead, conceptions of the national interest are socially constructed and vary with the interests and values of the society's participants. The degree to which a specific version of the national interest is widely shared will also vary over time. A peculiar set of international and domestic conditions made possible the cultivation of a relative consensus around a particular conception of U.S. national interest during the Cold War period. Yet as historical circumstances changed, consensus gave way to division during the seventies. In the post-Vietnam era, national security issues once again became available for interest group mobilization and contestation, much in the same way that domestic issues had been all along.

The institutional structure of the American state never posed quite the obstacle to interest group influence on national security issues that many analysts claimed. It is more accurate to say that the U.S. has had a "weak" state all along, making it potentially accessible to interest group influence. State strength and autonomy were not seriously put to the test, however, for much of the Cold War period due to the near consensus surrounding national security issues. Once exposed to social divisions and interest group pressure during the seventies, however, it quickly became apparent that national security policy-makers were not as insulated from society as observers had commonly believed. Moreover, institutional structure does not remain static, as evidenced by the growing role of Congress in foreign policy and national security issues during this period.

The principal purpose of this paper has been to illustrate, using the SALT II case, that the study of interest group politics offers a potentially rich and largely unexplored vein of evidence for students of national security policy-making. Gaining access to the new perspectives this evidence might inspire requires that we test traditional assumptions which have long discouraged attention to such factors.

PART THREE

Transnational Approaches

9

Expanding the Foreign Policy Discourse

TRANSNATIONAL SOCIAL MOVEMENTS AND THE GLOBALIZATION OF CITIZENSHIP

Ellen Dorsey

A fundamentally new form of political participation has begun to challenge our thinking about the nature and practice of global politics. Over the last twenty years there has been a growing number of people acting upon an emerging global consciousness. These individuals are linked by their belief in the universality of human dignity and the inherent responsibility of man for its fundamental realization, regardless of state affiliation. Acting in concert to promulgate various ideological and policy agendas, communities of these individuals have forged a set of transnational social movements. A primary impetus to the evolution of this consciousness and a central theme in the policy programs pursued by these transnational social movements has been the concern that the Cold War national security imperative, the unjust distributive effects of the international capitalist economic order, and modern foreign policy practices threaten the dignity and security of people globally. These movements have spawned creative attempts to alter the pattern of interstate relations. Frustrated with the traditional forms of recourse to the foreign policy practices of the state, citizen diplomats have invented new ways to realize their objectives by transcending the system of *inter*state relations and by simultaneously expanding the parameters of debate in which states forge their foreign policy objectives. Through a framework of participatory democracy, transnational social movements are attempting to broaden the realm of political participation and concurrently expand public discourse on foreign policy issues.

These activities have sparked growing interest in the renewed exploration of the contributions that social movement theory can provide for an understanding of citizen participation in political life. Although much attention has been devoted to the philosophical origins of these new movements, very little systematic analysis has been granted either to the impact of social movement activity upon global relations in general or on the substantive ways in which citizen diplomacy can influence the foreign policy processes of states. Traditionally foreign policy analysis has embodied pluralist assumptions about societal group influences on foreign policy. Pluralist interpretations typically relegate societal factors to one of several variables acting as inputs into the state-based process of policy construction. These influences are primarily measured through the role that specific and formal interest group organizations can wield in the governmental arena or in terms of the influence that public opinion writ large has upon those constructing the actual foreign policies. But such interpretations obscure the larger impact these forces have upon the range of phenomenon relevant to global relations.

Although social movement forces are often channelled into formal organizational structures that engage in standard competitive politics suited to the pluralist model, much of their political participation falls outside of that pattern. Promulgating the efficacy of practices of participatory democracy, social movement activists are attempting to create an alternative point of political pressure within the traditional domain of state-society relations. Social movement behavior cannot be represented in the standard framework of interest group activity, even when social movements in their organizational form assume the practices associated with interest groups. Such an interpretation misrepresents not only the depth of potential influence upon world politics, but the philosophical character of social movements as well. There needs to be an expansion of the existing framework of foreign policy analysis, where the interaction of social movement behavior with the standard methods of foreign policy formulation is explored in an attempt to construct a more comprehensive picture of transnational relations.

To this end, this paper will be concerned with four major themes. First, it will evaluate transnational social movements as political actors of international significance. Second, it will explore the origins of these movements, and the philosophical character of and commonalities between them. Third, this paper will look at how, through their novel forms of political participation, social movements are specifically influencing world politics. This will be done by constructing a model in which social movement interaction with state foreign policy practices can be viewed. Then specific examples of such practices and influences will be elaborated. Finally, the implications of the analysis of transnational social movements for the study of foreign policy and its relationship to the larger field of international relations now and in the future, will be addressed. Suggestions for future research and an analysis of some methodological problems to be tackled will be sketched.

SOCIAL MOVEMENTS AS POLITICAL ACTORS

The social movement literature is rich, both descriptively and conceptually. Typically, however, it deals with movements that operate within one political context or societal framework. Very little has been written on the phenomenon of transnational social movements. Most of the literature that is relevant to the transnationalization of social movement activity deals with the philosophical character of the emerging global consciousness that underlies particular movements and organizations, but does not wrestle with characterizations of the phenomenon, transnational social movement activities, or forms of influence.

Social movements, whether domestic or transnational, have three defining features: an ideology upon which a movement is founded and integrated, the particular structure of the movement as a unique form of political entity, and the nature of actions taken to realize objectives. Thus social movements unite individual participants along a commonality in beliefs or set of preferences, with a primary objective to alter certain societal practices or change institutional structures deemed grievous to the realization of the unifying agenda. The result is action taken outside of the standard methods of political participation. (Heberle, 1951; Tarrow, 1990; Tilly, 1978)

Gerlach and Hine (1970) provide a framework for evaluating the structure of social movements. They argue that three characteristics distinguish social movements from other types of political actors: decentralization, segmentation, and reticulation. A decentralized structure is one where no central authority exists which is charged with decision making for the entirety of the movement. There are no specific requirements for membership or obligatory restrictions upon activities taken in the name of the movement. Segmentation is the process by which the movement evolves over time. New members come into participation, participation expands and contracts, and a shifting pattern of organizations affiliated with the movement occurs. Reticulation speaks to the binding nature of social movement collectivities. Although the structure is decentralized and constantly changing, the totality of social movements comprise more than simply a commonality of interests. It implies linkage in activities through processes of cross fertilization, where individuals participating within one organizational context interact with or participate in the activities of other organizations embedded in the larger movement. (Gerlach and Hine, 1970, Gerlach, 1983.)

It is useful to distinguish between social movements and social movement organizations. Seldom does a social movement become embodied in one organizational form, as that would lead to the institutionalization of its political practices and render social movements indiscernible from interest groups or non-state organizations. McCarthy and Zald (1973, 1977) capture the relationship of social movement organizations to the broader social movements. Social movement organizations are seen as "a complex, or formal, organization which identifies its goals with the preferences of a social movement or a counter movement and attempts to implement those goals." (McCarthy and Zald, 1977)

A readily identifiable example of the relationship between social movements and social movement organizations is seen in the ecological movement, where the larger movement has come to be embodied in the organizational form of Greenpeace, Friends of the Earth, Earth First, etc. Clearly their specific agendas and organizational structures may differ significantly, but the set of preferences upon which these groups are founded are consistent with the broader ideology of the ecological movement. (Taggart, 1990) Correspondingly, Amnesty International, the Human Rights Watch Committees, and the International Commission of Jurists are all organizations associated with the transnational human rights movement evolved out of the framework laid down with the Universal Declaration of Human Rights forged at the United Nations.

Social movement organizations, through their embodiment of the ideological foundation that links a broader movement, are distinguishable as unique societal actors with political significance through their commitment to restructuring agendas. Unlike interest groups that may simply operate upon a calculation of advancing particularistic interests through institutionalized political practices, social movements seek to transform the environment in which political decisions are made to effect structural change in either societal conduct or political practices.[1]

Social movements in their organizational forms can operate outside of established political institutions to condition societal values and frame policy debate. Simultaneously, interest group methods of agenda advancement in the institutionalized sphere can be employed when deemed appropriate. Thus social movements may target the behavior of individuals within societies, as many of the ecological organizations attempt to do in their promotion of conservation and recycling. Or they can seek to change policy decisions made within the institutionalized political framework by shaping the environment in which decisions are evaluated, a process of

---

1. Two primary exceptions to this is the work of Chadwick Alger and Richard Falk. While focusing on different aspects of citizen participation in global politics, both attempt to define the methods of influence that are employed by citizen diplomats.

parameter setting which is accomplished extra-institutionally. Or they can attempt to engage in the 'pushing and hauling' acts of direct engagement in the political processes of the state. Interest groups only operate in the latter form, while social movements can simultaneously utilize all three methods in both movement and organizational forms.

With this overview of the basic characteristics of social movements in general, a framework can be sketched for the definition of *transnational* social movements. There are four characteristics that can be said to define a transnational social movement:

1. A transnational social movement is a community of individuals linked by a solidarity of concerns and commonality in agendas. Their shared consciousness is global in nature and transcends the particularistic interest of one societal or political context. That which defines them as transnational is a sense of *identity* with a broad community of individuals transcending the state structure. Existing transnational social movements have been typically concerned about issues of human dignity and security and have incorporated notions of participatory democracy as central to their philosophical orientation.

The earliest international peace and justice movements typically constituted a small minority of people from middle class backgrounds living in the countries of the advanced industrialized world who have had an international education or experience that provided them with a global consciousness (Alger, 1990). But these movements are much more diversified today. The vast majority of participants in the various movements still hail from advanced industrialized societies, yet the need for international experience to develop a global awareness has receded with advances in telecommunications and with the inculcation of global concerns into popular culture. While this access to information does not necessarily translate into a global consciousness, it does demonstrate that in the modern era a global consciousness can be created without the benefit of direct experience.

2. These transnational social movements operate as loosely constructed webs of activism with smaller organizations linked through different organizational forms, overlapping memberships, and direct contact between the participants. Modern technology has again been central for bringing the individual actors and organizations associated with the larger movement together.

3. Transnational social movement activity is characteristically a non-institutional means of participation; a politics of non-violence, of challenging state accountability, of resistance and delegitimation, and of creating alternative sources of information. (Walker, 1988) What distinguishes transnational social movements as a method of political participation is precisely the autonomy provided by their extra-institutional character. This autonomy grants the option of engaging in institutional processes when deemed strategically advantageous, but in simultaneously allowing for

resistance practices.[2] Resistance can take the form of counteracting the effects of state foreign policies that are perceived as damaging to human dignity and security of the individual or it can take the form of policies designed to create positive alternatives to state practices. The latter can be accomplished through direct participation in global affairs unmediated by the foreign policy structures of the state in which the individual resides.

4. The self conscious recognition of the global movement by the participants themselves. The perception of linkage creates a solidarity that is essential for the strength of the movement, both in shaping the nature of its activities and in its capacity to attract new participants.

ORIGINS OF TRANSNATIONAL SOCIAL MOVEMENTS

Political participation that does not operate solely within the established foreign policy institutions of the state has proliferated in the last twenty years. Often labeled as new politics, these movements have begun increasingly to take on a transnational character around issues of social justice and the promotion of human dignity in an era of increasing insecurity. To assess how this global consciousness has developed, we must look at the origins and history of the evolution of social movements in the 20th century and expansion into the pattern of the transnationalization of identity. Only then can an attempt be made to analyze the influence that these movements have upon the foreign policy process and the conduct of world politics.

The quest for protection is the primary motivating force for the conscious or unconscious individual participation in economic, social, or political phenomenon. The individual is concerned fundamentally with the protection of certain levels of economic and social well being. This can only be achieved within an environment of basic security from forces which threaten to disrupt the acquisition of these primary needs. It is within this quest for the minimal provision of security that the logic of institutionalized governance and the evolution of the social contract can be found. The state was seen to have the capacity to reduce uncertainty by regulating the capricious and arbitrary exercise of power by individuals within social contexts and across social collectivities.

---

2. Institutional here refers to the established foreign policy decision making processes where decision makers are petitioned directly or through the electoral process. Institutional participation constrains individuals to the rules of the game as defined by the state and implies the legitimacy of the decision making process- an implication many of the social movement participants reject.

Citizenship was only rendered meaningful in a state-based relationship. But increasingly the state's capacity to guarantee the security of the individual has been questioned, a pattern of increasing frustration about the states' ability to uphold expectations concerning different domains of security has been produced. The terms of the social contract have been called into question. Therefore the expansion of the realm in which responsibilities and benefits of citizenship can be derived and the generation of a new public political space for activity taken for the insurance of individual and communal security becomes a necessity.

A variety of different conditions have produced the erosion of the state's capacity to realize its contractual obligations: the relative failure of the two major modern conceptions of the preferred relationship of state-citizen relations (Marxism and Liberalism) to fulfill the expectations of individuals across the various security domains, the development of global economic patterns, actors and social problems in which the state has a diminished capacity to control events, and the unleashing of the post World War II national security apparatus, distinguished by the threat of nuclear destruction, that has inherently undermined the very essence of security across the global system.

The interaction of these different factors created the conditions in which individuals were driven to reformulate the nature of their relationship to the state and their methods of recourse to entrenched power structures. The new social movements are founded upon the logic of expanding public space for the realization of fundamental interests excised out of the social contract. Social movement participation is an attempt by the individual to redress the deficiencies in the state's capacity to provide security and to reclaim the polity. True to the Aristotelian conception of the polity as the totality of space in which each person realizes his potential as an individual through the fulfillment of communal obligations, the social movement participant seeks to re-establish the domain in which the individual can participate in public discourse, where security is derived, and the obligations and accoutrements of citizenship will simultaneously be acquired.

With the erosion of faith in the traditional governmental capacity to provide security, there now appears a growing awareness of the interrelated nature of societal struggles. This perception of the commonality in struggle is the force precipitating a global consciousness as individuals confront problems of international economic decline, environmental degradation, and global militarization. As such, the resolution of these problems cannot be found within the parameters of one particular polity. They call for creative alternatives to the existing institutions held responsible for unleashing these global phenomena. This new consciousness links concerns for human dignity and individual security to democratic renewal, realizable in participatory frameworks unconstrained by the mandates of institutional and bureaucratic governance.

An individual's identity is a complex amalgam of associations with discrete communities-national, religious, ethnic. The different levels of commitment that individuals will give to those communities are reflected in the sacrifices that they are willing to make to support the community. For one community they might be willing to sacrifice their life, for another they will sacrifice their time and energy, and for another they will sacrifice their money (Cottam, 1977). Increasingly larger communities of individuals have begun to incorporate a global community into their identity profile and are willing to apportion various sacrifices to its protection. Individuals sacrifice money for Greenpeace, time and energy to write letters for Amnesty International, or work construction in a war zone in Nicaragua for Peace Brigades. Each is a sacrifice demonstrating differing levels of commitment to an identity profile with a global component. Such sacrifices illustrate that growing numbers of the world population that have begun to internalize their sense of global responsibility.

It is this confluence of transnationally derived patterns of social and economic change with the emergence of a global consciousness encompassing a range of differing and often compatible issue areas that precipitated the transnational social movement formation. The desire to generate a new public space represents an attempt to integrate the peculiar particularistic and universalistic natures of political concern and activity characteristic of modern social relations. The expansion of the terrain of community is a functional necessity for the effective realization of political, economic, and social agendas within the post-industrial context. And it is a by product of the compression of the world, where, paradoxically individual identity correspondingly expands. Precisely because of the dictates of an inclusive, participatory orientation, political activism can necessarily only be realized in a particular locale. Yet there is a universalistic pattern in method of action and symbolic orientation that demarcates the new social movements as having a fundamentally transnational character to them (Falk, 1977).

Transnational social movements are emerging out of a locale based political strategy that is both tangibly linked across issues and methods and is simultaneously ground in reaction to global level stimuli. Spontaneous and de facto linkages begin to emerge between discrete local and regional movements cutting across national boundaries. And from there the foundations for transnational organization have been laid, representing a complex web of affiliations, collaboration, and reciprocal exchange. An exploration of these linkages reveals not a similarity in activity within a new public space existing within the confines of the state, but the realization of a transnational public space for the promotion of individual interests and rights. Previously these fell under the domain of the state's provision of security. This realization that an increased range of options are available for the promotion of the global agenda for social change has ultimately come about through the conscious and strategic manipulation of the institutions of the state and in confrontation with the non-state actors shaping global trends.

The realization of the potential for an expanding public space is grounded in the recognition that insecurity is manifested both locally and globally as a product of linked social, economic, and political phenomenon. This reconceptualization of security provides the fundamental basis for empowerment. (Walker, 1988) The challenge of the new social movements has been the translation of this empowerment into a programmatic attempt to employ effective leverage for the realization of concrete objectives.

The Peace Movement is an interesting case study with its transnational character, its coherence of symbolic nature and confrontational form, its explicit manipulation of political processes for the generation of a new political space, and for the organizational linkages that have been laid cross-nationally. The anti-nuclear peace demonstrations originating in Holland in 1981 set in motion the social and political expressions that have come to be called the Peace Movement. The Peace Movement, with its historical and organizational roots in the dramatic movements of the late 1960's, drew participants from across religious, ethnic, and gender cleavages and integrated single issue social movements into a larger conglomerate with a unifying commitment to freeing citizens globally from the dictates of the Cold War-defined international system. The fundamental theme of the promotion of security in the modern world gave the various initiating actors with discrete origins their global coherence. They were united in their confrontation with the modern national security apparatus. In turn, they challenged the non-democratic processes of the state that prioritized secrecy over disclosure to shield its foreign policies from public scrutiny.

The basic appeal of democratic renewal and insurance of security provided the foundation for the confluence of disparate concerns and interests intra-nationally. It also served to produce a transnational issue that could link organizational efforts around a common theme that extracted out particularistic concerns with the forms and manifestations of conflict. Thus security became a collective interest globally defined and brought into public discourse. And the emphasis upon democratic renewal provided the framework for a coherent articulation of strategic actions to be employed along distinct and potentially disparate locales.

An autonomous political space has been increasingly generated that could empower a community of individuals previously cast outside of the public domain. The fundamental issues of security and democratic renewal that the Peace Movement articulates served as a unifying force for disparate issues. And with it a new mechanism for the exertion of political power had emerged. By focusing upon the issues of security and democratic denial transnationally, the peace movement has created a standard of accountability that decision makers in the advanced industrialized states must be held responsible to for electoral purposes. If decision makers are not held accountable, they must at the minimum cast their policies in the context of the critiques employed by the peace activists- indicating a triumph of shaping the agenda through the expansion of public discourse. Although the capacity of the Peace Movement to do this varied across different governments and time periods contingent upon the perception of societal opposition they were able to project, the effects of their actions were clearly felt and the nature of public discourse was altered.

TRANSFORMING GLOBAL POLITICS:
THE RELATIONSHIP OF TRANSNATIONAL SOCIAL MOVEMENT ACTIVITY
TO THE FOREIGN POLICY PROCESS

Transnational social movements through their unique forms of political participation are altering foreign policy processes of states and transforming global interaction. There are two broad ways in which these movements attempt to realize their globally relevant concerns and objectives. As argued previously, what distinguishes social movements from interest groups is the dualistic nature of their capacity to influence political dynamics both institutionally and extra-institutionally, both operating as standard participants within the foreign policy institutions of the state and by operating outside of those established processes. Social movements in their organizational form can enter into the traditional political process as deemed appropriate; but even in their institutional practices they act within an altered environment conditioned by the consciousness raising dynamics of the larger social movement activities. Organizations and activists may seek to extend beyond state practices either by subverting and resisting state policies or by reaching out into the global system directly to realize their own objectives. The capacity to do this is a purely modern phenomenon only possible in an age of advanced telecommunications, complex economic interdependence, and internationalized standards of ethical state behavior that can be drawn upon for legitimation.

To categorize the many ways in which transnational social movements are shaping world politics, it is useful to think in terms of two levels. Transnational social movements can participate as actors within the national context in which they exist, or they can act directly in global relations as a separate actor. They can tactically target different sites of authority that may wield leverage over globally relevant political practices world-wide. The method of action is contingent upon the specific objectives.

TARGETING THE STATE

The most basic form of participation in the national context is environment setting; *to establish the parameters in which issues are evaluated and debated.* This can be accomplished by information dissemination and consciousness raising about policy issues and by holding state decision makers accountable to universally accepted principles of state behavior. Whether as a conscious design or as a product of the perceptions of the decision makers themselves, central to the realization of social movement objectives is the *shaping of societal values.* Changing societal values in a general sense will ultimately shape the decision making process by constraining the *decisional latitude of the foreign policy elite.*

One of the primary goals of social movement activists has been to disseminate information about a range of issues associated with the foreign policy discourse. Such consciousness raising serves the function of challenging the state's authority to interpret events, represent problems, and provide meaning to policy debates. Consistent with the participatory framework in which the social movement activists commonly operate, information is central to the reassertion of a functioning democratic process. It also serves to create a more informed populace in an attempt to expand the parameters of debate around specific foreign policy issues.

Within the context of a pluralist or non-democratic policy process, policy formulation is often a conflictual process, where different interests compete to have their agendas incorporated into the decision being made. Cobb and Elder (1972) have argued that the very rendering of a problem as relevant to the public interest is a product of the nature of group conflict that surrounded the policy. The larger the public to which an issue or problem is exposed, the larger the degree to which the conflict is expanded, and the greater potential for the issue to be introduced for policy consideration. Thus consciousness raising in churches, unions, and in schools by human rights groups and by Central American peace organizations about the magnitude of human rights abuses perpetrated by the military in El Salvador is designed to expand public concern about the United States' involvement in that civil war. By challenging the way in which the administration defines national security objectives, an informed public in opposition to the policy line will directly alter the perceptual environment in which foreign assistance decisions are made. The nature of environment alteration is contingent upon the perception that decision makers have of the level of societal resonance to the values and agenda that the social movement advocates. Consciousness raising activities are designed to explicitly broaden the totality of the polity from below, to bring into policy making discourse larger segments of the society.

A second tactic of consciousness raising for the alteration of the policy environment is the consistent evocation of standards of international accountability to which the state must be held responsive. Thus consciousness raising is designed to assert control both over the definition of a problem and to challenge the validity of the state's representation in light of obligatory standards of state behavior that have previously been subscribed to and universally codified legally or customarily.

The Universal Declaration of Human Rights has been a profoundly important instrument for human rights activists to evoke as a gauge of state foreign policy practices. In the case of the Transnational Anti-Apartheid Movement, South Africa's violation of virtually every right embodied in the Universal Declaration was a central mobilizing device for activists and served as the justification for the enactment of state trade sanctions against South Africa. When social movement organizations lobbied to have their national governments impose sanctions upon the Apartheid regime of South Africa, the Universal Declaration of Human Rights was consistently cited both as the standard by which South Africa must be judged and as a measure of accountability for the other states in the international system. Given the permeability of international standards of state behavior, such consciousness raising does not necessarily preclude states continuing to conduct inconsistent or illegitimate policies. It transforms the environment in which the continuation or construction of a new policy will be evaluated by state decision makers. And it provides the opportunity for such challenges to be mounted.

The influence of social movements over the foreign policy process of the state is typically realized through organizations associated with the broader goals of the social movement. These organizations can be national or international in character in terms of the target of their activities, but they are founded upon an ideological association with the global movement. Much like traditional interest groups, social movement organizations can participate as one actor in the policy communities that forge specific policy lines.[3] It is important to recognize that what distinguishes even these more traditional institutionalized attempts to influence the policy process is that they are being realized in the context of a policy environment already conditioned by the activities of the larger movement. *The transnational social movement organizations come together in the policy community to bring the changed parameters of the policy environment into the debate on specific policy*

---

3. Policy communities is a useful organizing construct to define the forces relevant to the construction of certain policy lines. It is useful for tracing the interplay of vested interests in policy formulation. As it looks at the intellectual underpinnings of certain policy processes, it allows for the incorporation of the role of interest groups, agencies and various governmental administrative bodies, elite representatives of social forces, and even interested academicians, journalists, and local government officials. Kingdon, Cobb and Elder, 1972.

alternatives. And the success of movement organizations to promote their objectives in this capacity are typically contingent upon their ability to open or capitalize upon policy windows or new opportunities for policy change.

TRANSCENDING THE STATE

The second level at which social movements influence global relations is by transcending the state-based foreign policy process. This is done both by bypassing the state and directly targeting other global actors or by manipulating the state decision making process through subversion of its policy lines. The subversion of state policies can be accomplished by resisting local implementation of federal policies, by creating alternative sources of authority to make foreign policy decisions that will achieve a different set of objectives (using local structures of government to promote foreign policy agendas), or by seeking to transform societal practices which will erode the conditions and assumptions upon which the foreign policy objectives are based. The lines between these methods are often overlapping and social movements use several of these tactics simultaneously.

Citizen diplomacy is not a new phenomenon, by any means. Examples of individuals trekking across borders in an unofficial capacity to attempt to regulate state interaction, promote the interests of one community of people, or to erode state hostility through interpersonal communication have coexisted with the state system itself. Nevertheless, incidences of what have been labeled Track Two diplomacy have been steadily increasing in the last several decades. The Dartmouth conference of 1960, the brain child of Norman Cousins, has become a model for current day problem solving frameworks. The Chautauqua Conferences have brought Soviet and American intellectuals, local officials, journalists, and concerned individuals into direct discourse about a range of environmental, health and security concerns.[4]

One important factor that distinguishes the contemporary period from previous periods is the ease by which such direct diplomacy can occur through modern technological advances. A major emphasis of Peace Movement activists has been the provision of alternative sources of information both to facilitate communication between societies and as a way to liberate individuals from their dependence upon their governments and media as their sole sources of information. The effects of such provision of 'counter-intelligence' can be quite significant, as it can counteract the government's capacity to effectively detach the human dimension of conflict by demon-

---

4. "Citizen Diplomacy: Coming of Age", US Institute of Peace, In Brief, #15 December 1989

izing enemies and stereotyping opponents. The dissemination of information represents an attempt at counter-socialization, an attempt to provide a complexity of interpretation and analysis beyond that which is constructed by the foreign policy apparatus and mediated by the press. The erosion of stereotypical portrayals of Soviet citizens has consistently been a primary tactic of the Peace Movement; massive weapons deployment are not likely to be sustainable if the populace does not perceive a high level of threat from the Soviet Union. Correspondingly, the alteration of public perceptions not only denies the state a powerful weapon by which it can define the national interest, but the erosion of consensus around this world view will serve to redefine the definition of the situation employed by official decision makers.[5]

Consistent with the participatory democratic framework, information exchange challenges the state's claim that secrecy is mandated by national security concerns. Such direct initiatives go beyond consciousness raising and changing the parameters of policy debates. They actually subvert the capacity of the national government to legitimate policies perceived as potentially lacking public approval and to construct policies outside of public scrutiny. This can have profound effects for the implementation of foreign policy objectives, if the very assumptions upon which these policies are predicated are eroded from below.

The innovative use of technology has transformed citizen initiatives in consciousness raising and direct diplomacy. (Shuman and Warner, 1986/87) For example, over the last decade much effort has been placed upon citizen-to-citizen exchanges based upon technology transfer, where U.S. scientists have been interacting with Soviet scientists to provide them with computer training. In some cases, individuals have organized local initiatives to import personal computers into the Soviet Union to facilitate greater access to outside information. Another example of the transformative potential of modern technology for social movement mobilization is the computer based Peacenet program. Peacenet was designed to link peace and justice organizations internationally through a computerized system that details upcoming political activities and also provides a forum to disseminate alternative documentation and analysis of events by activists and academicians that is not provided in the mainstream press. Similarly constructed programs exist for human rights and environmental issues, providing up to the minute information about concerns over violations and expanding outreach into the larger, global movement to maximize support for particular initiatives undertaken by local organizations.

---

5. See Richard Cottam's Foreign Policy Motivations for an elaboration of the relationship between the world view, the definition of the situation, and the motivations of policy makers that serve to shape policy decisions.

Another example of non-institutional participation by citizens in global affairs is the case of direct economic assistance across state boundaries. Charity has historically been central to the work of most religious denominations as a primary mechanism to unite ecumenical communities outside of the state framework. Such direct economic assistance has provided an alternative private system of supplementing the inadequacies of public provision for basic human needs. But along with challenging the hierarchical and non-democratic practices of state foreign policies, the practices of churches were increasingly called into question. The association of missionary zeal with the imperialist practices of the state caused many to question whether the institutions of the Church were the most beneficial for just economic development. Individuals began to seek new methods for extending economic assistance to other communities, incorporating the interfaith commitment to global social provision but seeking to speak to the needs of the target population and not the interests of the hierarchy of the churches.

Sister city programs are a modern reflection of this shift in venue for direct assistance. Although each city-to-city relationship has its unique mix of cultural, economic, and political objectives, the movement has typically been born out of a desire to bond individuals across boundaries independent of the nature of the relationship perpetuated by their state governments and devoid of the particularistic interests of the specific religious denominations. Currently over 800 communities in 87 nations have over 1,200 sister city relationships.[6] There are two primary types of sister city relationships. In the case of animosities existing between the states, sister city relationships attempt to forge links to create understanding and to compensate for the material costs accrued in the playing out of hostilities between their governments. The clearest example is that of US-Nicaraguan relations. Currently there are 90-100 US cities that have adopted towns in Nicaragua providing badly needed assistance to offset the economic costs of the war.[7]

The second type of relationship is one of promoting sustainable development and resource redistribution from the Northern countries to those of the South. Where they share a desire to provide assistance to impoverished populations independent of their state affiliation, city twinning is designed to make a break with the types of assistance practices that are associated with creating dependent development relationships. The philosophy of development underlying these associations is not simply charity. Community initiatives typically seek to avoid the dependency relationships that are often a consequence of top-down approaches to development assistance. Frustrated with the lack of programs supported by their national govern-

6. St. Paul's Pioneer Dispatch, July 9, 1988
7. In These Times, Sept 6-12, 1989, . 6

ments, individuals in the advanced industrialized countries have come to recognize the material and human wealth that their local governments can provide for health care, infrastructure development and education.

The innovation and commitment of activists promoting direct assistance to alleviate poverty and the hardships of war through sister city projects or by other types of citizen-based social movement organizations, has provided unique alternatives to both governmental and non-governmental organizations concerned with promoting development in Third World countries through a hierarchical model. An interesting twist to the evolution of community assistance projects is the involvement of the larger institutions of the churches. In the late 1960's the mainstream churches began to move in the direction of supporting the national liberation struggles of all individuals to self determination free from colonial interference (Shepherd 1977). What were once considered radical ideas were now being embraced by churches. Indeed secular movements spawned by the sense of inadequacy of the churches capacity to affect real change, ultimately turned back to convert the church into its framework uniting the ecumenical and secular social change communities. The heritage of charity provided by the church enabled individuals to support programs that are often antithetical to the stated objectives of the state foreign policy bodies. Furthermore, the rather innocuous character of programs like the sister city relationships have mobilized individuals across the ideological spectrum by operating upon a solidarity of concern for the provisions of basic human needs and a consensus that the present state-based structures are either inadequate or inappropriate to the task.

The final example of *direct* citizen participation in global relations is that of the human rights movement. Embodied in the work of the largest international organization representing the transnational human rights movement, Amnesty International's approach is predicated on the power of the individual voice in transforming state practices. Members of local community groups launch letter writing campaigns to target human rights violations by other states in the international system. By adopting specific prisoners of conscience, the individual human rights activist is linked directly in solidarity with the person whose rights have been violated. What Amnesty brings to bear is the weight of moral condemnation. They do not seek to target governments that have relations of leverage over the perpetrator of the abuses. Instead they rely upon a grass roots demonstration of moral outrage to precipitate changes in the target practices of social coercion. The individual activist's participation legitimated by international standards embodied in the Universal Declaration of Human Rights and the individual's expanding perception of communal responsibility is derivative of the value associated with these standards.

Direct economic assistance, sister city projects, Amnesty International's human rights work, and Track Two diplomacy are only one aspect of direct citizen participation in global affairs. They typically constitute direct campaigns for the provision of human needs and the maintenance of security that are independent of the initiatives of the state.

Another method of participation is resistance. Resistance can take several forms; it can be designed to physically subvert the implementation of state policies or to mobilize mass sentiments against specific policies. The "purpose is symbolic communication beyond the framework of lawful activity. Resistance implies negation and it expresses both the urgency of the challenge and the impotence of mainstream responses." (Falk, 1980 180) Two significant examples are the Central American sanctuary movement in the U.S. and the international campaign for a nuclear freeze. From its origins in 1982, the sanctuary movement has attempted to undermine the counter-insurgency strategy that the United States government has pursued in its involvement in the civil wars in El Salvador and Guatemala. The massive influx of refugees into the U.S. fleeing the wars in their own countries presented a serious challenge to the validity of U.S. policy. Should the U.S. accept the claim of the refugees that they were escaping political violence and not seeking economic improvements, the U.S. would be forced to accept the human rights violations of the regimes that it was upholding. By turning back from its borders massive numbers of refugees, the U.S. attempted to avert a challenge to the morality of its policies. The sanctuary movement maintained that the refugees had a legitimate right to seek refuge in the U.S. under international law and appealed to those laws as a higher authority to justify their provision of safe haven to the Central Americans in the U.S. Risking imprisonment for their activities, the Sanctuary movement not only resisted the principles behind U.S. policy towards Central America, but simultaneously resisted the implementation of Immigration and Naturalization Services policies to force these refugees to return to their home countries. (McConnell, 1989)

Similarly, the international movement for a Nuclear Freeze was founded on the principle of resistance. Rejecting the foundations of deterrence as antithetical to individual security, the anti-nuclear movement activists held their national governments accountable for the nuclear arms race. Unable to reign in the excesses of the national security apparatus, the Freeze sought to undermine the very viability of the security imperative of the state at the local sites of deployment and manufacturing.

Resistance can also take the form of constructing alternative policy lines that not only *subvert* states policies but *transform* events in the target environment independent of the actions being pursued by national governments. In effect, transnational social movements can create their own alternative method of seeking change. A classic example of this is the transnational Anti-Apartheid Movement. Meeting resistance in their attempts to lobby Western governments to impose sanctions against the South African government, the AAM sought, through its international campaign for corporate disinvestment, to directly erode the solvency of the South African economy. The intention was to precipitate internal change in the practices of Apartheid. The local organizations associated with the AAM have resisted their government's attempts to control the pace of change in South Africa and to retain South Africa's de facto participation in the Western alliance system through the years of the Cold War. Instead the transnational movement sought to erode the linkages that existed between state governments and Pretoria to force that government deeper into a pariah status.

The practices of the AAM have served as the model for recent efforts to conduct an international boycott of Salvadoran coffee. Within days after the November 1989 brutal murder of eight people, including six Jesuit priests, a campaign was launched to boycott coffee manufacturers that purchased Salvadoran coffee. Rejecting the validity of US assistance to that government on human rights grounds, the sponsors of the boycott sought their own method of sanctioning the regime for its abuses. In the United States, the Neighbor to Neighbor organization began a boycott of Folger's coffee with the support of the Lieutenant Governor of California, the mayors of Minnesota, San Francisco, and Berkeley, the Los Angeles and Chicago City Councils, the Attorney General of Massachusetts and 40 US Senators and Congressman.

Central to the transcendence and subversion of the state's policies has been the creation of new sites of authority to serve as alternative mechanisms for the empowerment of social movement initiatives, as the targeting of local authorities in the coffee boycott indicates. Thinking globally and acting locally is more than just the practice of participatory democracy on foreign policy issues; it is the recognition of a capacity to exert leverage upon global affairs. Locale-based strategies make global issues manageable and capitalize upon the often vast resources of local government. The locality is a perfect site to join global concerns with the desire for meaningful participation in issues deemed central to individual's communal responsibility while simultaneously diminishing the sense of increasing alienation from the actions of the national government. Institutional resources free of the bureaucratic dynamics and ideological baggage typically associated with the self-perpetuating national security apparatus are utilized to implement strategies of subversion, resistance, and transformation. The activation of often significant local resources has great transformative potential for social movement initiatives and the novelty of approach allows for much creativity in advancing globally relevant agendas. Local activities also serve an important consciousness-raising function, as they present opportunities to bring home to local communities the tangible costs of national foreign policy lines. As such, "Municipal Foreign Policies" have become a central organizing device. (Shuman; 1987, Alger; 1990) Some examples are illustrative of the expanding domain and novel nature of local foreign policy strategies:

> Between 1,000 and 2,000 counties and 32,000 local government bodies have passed municipal foreign policy initiatives in the United States alone.

> 176 local communities have passed nonbinding resolutions to support comprehensive test ban treaties.

> The Netherlands has 14.5 million people living in 700 towns and over 380 of them are involved in development cooperation to assist Third World countries.

> Los Angeles, Pittsburgh, and Baltimore have passed ordinances requiring their staffs to prepare and publish annual reports on the impact of military spending for the local economies.

> After the Soviet downing of KAL 007, local governments denied Soviet UN representatives access to local airports and passed resolutions banning the sale of Soviet Vodka.

> The Center for Innovative Diplomacy is a non-profit organization formed to promote citizen participation in global politics. It has steadily expanded its membership of local elected officials and interested citizens. It also publishes the Bulletin of Municipal Foreign Policies to disseminate information about different locally based initiatives.

> Local Elected Officials for Social Responsibility was founded in 1982 as a coalition of 600 mayors, city council members and county supervisors committed to using their offices to reverse the arms race.

> The Cambridge, Massachusetts Peace Commission spends 20,000 a year of local taxes for such activities as educating citizens on arms control matters, promoting a sister city relationship with Soviet Armenia, sanctuary for Central American refugees and encouraging local military contractors to convert their production for no-military usages.

Relying upon a combination of localistic tactics and the construction of long term strategies, different social movements have also sought to eradicate the conditions that might precipitate unwanted foreign policies. Referred to as transformative politics, some social movement activity seeks to produce programs for the fundamental restructuring of certain societal values and practices that become embedded in foreign policy objectives. One particular emphasis has been the patterns of energy consumption which have been directly linked to the advanced industrialized societies' increasing dependence on foreign oil. Given these relationships, energy conservation can be a microlevel program with dramatic macrolevel implications.

There are a multitude of different ways in which an individual can seek to directly alter the state of security for individuals and the preceding examples illustrate the creative approaches that have been employed. But the study of the strategy and tactics of social movements and social movement organizations is inadequate for an understanding of the impact that such a unique form of political participation has for transnational politics. This can only be determined in an examination of the context in which social movement behavior occurs.

IMPLICATIONS FOR FOREIGN POLICY ANALYSIS,
GLOBAL POLITICS, AND STATE-SOCIETY RELATIONS

One of the most critical issues to be addressed in the study of the relationship of transnational social movements (TSMs) to the practice of global relations is the relative influence that is wielded in comparison to other social, political, and institutional influences. An evaluation of this influence requires a conception of the power of social movements. Distinguishing the power of any political actor becomes the central currency of political theory. As the power of the actor is derivative of the political context in which it operates, the new political space created by transnational social movements demands novel conceptions of power.

Any attempt to define the power of TSMs to influence global relations must transcend classic notions of the levels of analysis problem in international relations theory. *Global conditions have precipitated the formation of TSMs, whose targeted effects are global in scope. They engage, however, in political acts at a subnational level. Thus they operate upon state interaction from above and below the structures of the state and are ultimately embedded within a national level of analysis, yet clearly the conditions that give rise and present opportunities for their activities are derivative of system level processes.* The TSM construct is problematic to the formulation of a neat causal model that can be circumscribed into a levels of analysis framework with discrete spaces cordoned off as unique variables. No longer can we attribute each level of analysis independent causality.

For example, one cannot clearly delineate the effects of the international system level changes upon the state foreign policy decision making from those of TSMs. The dictates of the Cold War cannot simply be viewed as a system level input into the foreign policy process unique from the influence that social movements wield. The Cold War and the evolution of TSMs are intimately interrelated. Neither represent mutually exclusive independent variables. Instead there is a paradoxical relationship between the dictates of the Cold War and the conditions under which TSM's have been able to advance their own foreign policy objectives. It took the high threat conditions of the Cold War to create the international conditions of insecurity produced by the hostage-holding nature of the deterrence strategy, the

containment-induced US and USSR interventions into Third World conflicts, and the domestic costs of economic redistribution to finance the
national security apparatus. The insecurity produced by the national security imperative became the foundation of the human dignity orientation of
the transnational peace and human rights movements.[8] But it also took the
diminishing sense of threat in the Cold War period of the 1970's to produce
the conditions in which the challenges of the social movement organizations could be launched. The diminishing sense of threat was central to the
mobilization of popular support at the grass roots level for the types of
initiatives being posed by the social movement organizations. These practices in turn fueled the demise of the Cold War by eroding societal consensus
around the perceived necessity of these national security policies, altering
the parameters of the national debate within the Western alliance system,
and giving impetus to oppositionary activities in the Eastern Bloc.

Therefore, to understand the power of TSMs and to attempt to gauge the
relative success of their initiatives, we must look at three factors:

1. The conditions under which TSMs originate and under which they are
able to advance their ideologically based agendas.

2. The effectiveness of the movements to alter the parameters of debate on
foreign policy issues and to shape societal values.

3. How specific social movement organizations are able to advance their
particular agendas by promoting change in state based practices or in
creating alternative paths outside of the state system for the realization of
their objectives.

The difficulties presented in attempting to conceptualize power for
social movements is that there is not one discrete organization or even one
clearly linked set of organizations upon which to focus. A social movement
is a construct aggregating the activities of different communities of individuals acting in concert upon shared values, as such they are not likely to
have a clearly defined strategy (Falk, 1987). Strategy must be inferred and
attributed in an ex post facto fashion. Nonetheless we are capable of tracing
the process by which social movements become empowered. There are two
diverse bodies of literature that provide compatible frameworks: the political opportunity structures literature primarily emanating out of sociology
and the literature analyzing initiating capacity in state-society relations.
Combined, they represent a framework that deals with the environmental
conditions in which actors have the greatest range of options for the

---

8. See E. Dorsey, "Towards A Post Cold War Strategy For The Promotion of Human Rights"
paper presented at the Northeast Political Science Association Conference, Providence, RI;
Nov. 1990 for an analysis of the relationship of the dynamics of the Cold War with the
international movement for the protection of human rights.

promotion of their objectives and gives the basis for determining the appropriate sites of authority or places where authority can be captured. Ultimately social movement formation is based upon individual sense of inefficacy and powerlessness in the face of the lethargy or stagnanation of institutional politics. But social movement activity, in turn, represents a reconstitution of state-society relations by seizing opportunity and opening a political space from which a new form of power and authority is created.

There has emerged within the social movement literature two bodies of analysis that can contribute to a characterization of the processes by which social movements become empowered in the political process. Attempting to characterize how the collective action that social movement activity represents is related to fundamental political processes, the notions of political opportunity structures and social movement sectors have been advanced (Tarrow 1988, 428). Political opportunity structure characterizes the openings within the political environment for the advancement of the social movement agenda contingent upon the unique construction of the polity, relative positions of political influence held by different social groups, and the structure of mass-elite relations within a society (Kitschel, 1986; Jenkins, 1983). Similarly, the social movement sector analysis attempts to delineate the relationship between social movements and social movement organizations. And it defines the environment or culture in which different social movement organizations recruit members and the pattern in which these organizations interact with each other to produce a particular outcome for the realization of the common objectives of the larger movement. (McCarthy and Zald, 1977)

The concept of political opportunity structure is specific to one societal and state context; social movements are empowered given the nature of a given political context shaped by the type of polity, regime, and political configuration of key actors. This context will determine the social movement's capacity to advance an agenda. But the notion of political opportunity structure does not immediately translate into a power paradigm for the study of transnational social movements. When dealing with social movements that are transnational in scope but targeting the foreign policy process, much as an interest group might, then political opportunity structure is a useful concept. But when attempting to classify transnational activities which transcend one societal context and one discrete polity, the concept of political opportunity structure must be expanded to incorporate the international system level context. Thus political opportunities will be determined by the nature of the international system.

International system dynamics present only the broadest of environmental parameters in which TSM activity can occur. We still have not characterized how transnational social movements become empowered and the specific conditions under which they advance their agendas. "Power is not a thing or easily measurable substance but rather an abstract capacity to act produced by organizing people." (Malloy 1991, 9) The ability of any political actor to influence policy is derivative of shifting 'points of initiating capacity'. (Malloy, 1991; Hegedus, 1987) The capacity to define, launch, and sustain policies, is a form of socially produced power and 'reflects the particular patterns of relationships current in a socio-political formation at any point in time'. (Malloy 1991, 9) Such a construct, devised to describe authority relations in the state-civil society context, can facilitate an explanation of how social movements can open political space within and external to the institutional framework of the state. The different issues and different time periods that are contingent upon the unique dynamics of civilian relations with officials of the state will determine the relative power of social movement actors to frame policy debates, advance their agendas and wield influence over policy making processes. And these patterns are equally applicable when social movements are seeking to target national foreign policy processes or to directly transform the behavior of other international actors. A tracing over time of the shifts in the sites of authority where power can be captured will lead to discernible patterns of social movement activity in relation to state authority. Such a tracing will ultimately contribute to a characterization of the patterns by which social movement actors wield influence.

This construct has great analytical utility for a number of reasons. It can accommodate the expansion of the conception of the polis to be a transnational public space in a way that traditional conceptions of authority relations bound within the state-civil society context cannot. While the 'shifting points of initiating capacity' construct provides only a broad framework in which social movement activity is defined in a state-society context, taken with the notion of political opportunity structures, the foundations of a model have been laid.

Social movements define the context in which social movement organizations can advance specific policy agendas and create options for realization of these objectives. Political opportunities present the conditions for mobilization of movements and the analysis of points of initiating capacity will lend itself to the creation of a strategy in which specific activities of social movement organizations can be forged. Social movements will define the environment in which the actions of social movements organizations will be taken, both in terms of constructing new societal values which will frame policy debates and in terms of the perceptions of the targeted actors responsible for charting new policy courses and interpreting their viability.

The integration of the notions of political opportunity structures with that of shifting points of initiating capacity into a framework will manage the first factor for understanding social movement activity and influence. The second and third factors deal explicitly with the characterization of the levels of influence of different social movement activity over discrete policies and political phenomenon. For these we must develop unique methodological approaches to attempt to weight this influence.

There are some very serious obstacles to a clear depiction of the causal relationship of social movement activity with changes in practices. The first problem lies in the dichotomous nature of the relationship of social movements to social movement organizations. While it may be possible to assert the relationship of one policy change with the activities of one particular organization associated with a larger movement, it is quite a bit more problematic to demonstrate the influence of a movement at large. Operating upon the assumption that one of the strongest levers that social movement activists have is of altering the parameters of policy debates through consciousness raising techniques, the measurement of altered consciousness is a difficult task. There may be two methods for measuring this altered consciousness. The first would be to examine the opinions of the public on certain policy issues across time to determine if changes have occurred and then correlate such changes to growth in social movement activity. Aside from the problems associated with the polling of political attitudes, even an altered consciousness of the public at large does not demonstrate that it was influential in the decision making processes. Another approach is to evaluate the perceptions of the targeted decision makers themselves. If they perceive a changed environment, then that would imply a direct relationship between the activities of the social movement activists and a changed policy environment.

But this approach also has its problems. First, it assumes that the decision makers consciously recognize the changed environment and attribute it to the activities of the social movement itself. Secondly even if there was a conscious recognition of the altered societal parameters, it may be questionable that the decision makers would find it in their interests to explicitly attribute their behavior to the influence exerted by the TSM or even public opinion at large. Nonetheless, there are a variety of different ways in which the influence of TSMs can be evaluated. First, case study analysis can be utilized to suggest examples of the impact that social movement activity has had upon the foreign policy process and directly upon the nature of world politics. Such illustrations would only be suggestive without the benefit of a framework which would attempt to disaggregate the multilevel influences that operate upon decision making processes. A second approach would be to evaluate the rhetorical statements of policy makers to determine if they explicitly assert a relationship of policy choices to social movement pressure or, more likely, to assess whether the rhetoric that they employ evokes the language or concerns of the social movement as a legitimation of policy choices. A third approach would attempt to trace the ways in which states operate in a transnational arena as a product of the pressures of social movement activities.

Case study analysis may be the most straight forward approach to the measurement of social movement influence. One can look at examples of how the targets of social movements have changed their policy decisions and then chart patterns of such changes to suggest correlations. The following list of examples of changes associated with the activities of the various peace and justice movements operating globally should be instructive.

The case of the transnational Anti-Apartheid Movement may be the most dramatic. In January of 1991, the newly appointed South African Ambassador to the United States directly attributed President F. W. DeKlerk's dismantling of Apartheid laws to the international sanctions imposed against that government and further maintained that it was the efforts of the American people in particular that were responsible. Within the context of the larger sanctions strategy, divestment is one of the most innovative tactics employed by citizen diplomats. Directly targeting institutions with investments in corporations doing business in South Africa, community groups were able to erode the financial solvency of the corporations by diminishing the pool of stockholders willing to support their investments. In the early 1980's over 350 US-based corporations were doing business in South Africa, in 1991 only 120 remained.[9]

The Helsinki Accords are exemplary not simply of the influence of a TSM in producing a new regime for human rights protection, but were instrumental in empowering local and regional movements for human rights throughout the international system. Vaclav Havel, the first President of the new Czechoslovakia has often attributed the success of the Charter 77 human rights organization, the precursor to the ruling Civic Forum Party, to the conditions presented by the international human rights movement. The transformation of that country and those of the Eastern Bloc region to multiparty systems in turn enhanced the sense of efficacy of human rights and social change agents throughout the international system. We have now begun to talk of a new wave of democracy.

Three thousand communities internationally passed Nuclear Freeze Zone initiatives to prevent the manufacturing, deployment, transportation of nuclear weapons in local areas. These resolutions were generally passed by local authorities that had been targeted by community groups working within the global anti-nuclear movement. Although in many respects the Freeze logic may have precluded real initiatives for arms reduction, the psychological effect on consciousness raising across societal groups and for parameter setting in the public policy realm was significant. It has been stated by peace activists, academic analysts, and government officials alike, that these efforts directly contributed to Reagan's launching the START talks at Geneva.

120 cities in the United States also refused to cooperate with the Federal Emergency Management Agencies 'crisis relocation planning' and pre-

9. Cable Network News, February 5, 1991

vented the implementation of Reagan's civil defense program.

As a result of a direct campaign by Mayor Feinstein and seven other mayors appealing to Soviet officials in Moscow, the Soviet Union agreed to allow 36 people to emigrate to the United States.

Amnesty International's human rights efforts, taken in the form of citizen letter writing to officials of their states regarding their treatment of political prisoners, is a dramatic success story for non-institutionalized methods of individual participation in global affairs. Not only has there been extensive documentation of cases in which the numbers of letters generated correlated to releases of prisoners and improvement in their treatment, but it is defensible to argue that these actions have altered the entire human rights climate.

Another general method of charting the transformative potential of social movements over policy decisions is rhetorical analysis. If policymakers increasingly use human rights as a justification for their policies then some link with the activities of the international human rights movement can be established. This is obviously not a precise measure of social movement influence, but it can be suggestive for future research considerations.

Another piece of evidence that would suggest the long term effects of social movement behavior is the extensiveness of governmental participation in transnational structures. Peter Wolf has found a strong correlation between the level of citizen participation in transnational affairs and the number of intergovernmental organizations in which their governments participate. This type of analysis can serve as a model for illustrating specific consequences of citizen initiatives in global affairs (Wolf, 1978).

The preceding examples demonstrate some of the ways in which social movement influence can be correlated with changes in policy environments, decisions, and agendas. They are certainly not all inclusive.

CONCLUSION

By creating a new political space for the realization of individual objectives a form of power and authority has been created. With it, the entire nature of state-society relations has the potential to be transformed. Citizenship extends beyond the traditional reciprocity of state-society relations, because the conception of relevant societies is transformed. As individuals begin to think in terms of the coexistence of their global identities with their traditional state-based identities, the social contract, the parameters of the operative polity, and the basic notion of citizenship are increasingly reconstituted.

Individual rights are increasingly seen as inherent rights to be recognized and validated by the international community. For the transnational social movement participant, the social contract is redefined on a transnational scale to constitute a commitment to the solidarity in activity among like minded individuals across state boundaries. While such an expansion of the notion of the social contract is surely problematic and potentially fuzzy, it may nonetheless represent an instructive analytical construct capable of highlighting the pyschological and philosophical bonds between individuals operating upon internationalized conceptions of rights. These bonds in turn have important implications for the expansion of individual identity to incorporate globality and transnational responsibility with the nationalistic, religious, and ethnic sources of identity traditionally operative.

Thus the disenfranchised individual, alienated from the community associated with the state is seeking to redefine his own individuality through localistic participation in a global movement to protect the dignity, security, and survival of individuals world wide. In response a new political space has begun to be created and a new source of power to mobilize has been added to existing mechanisms of participation in the institutionalized political process.

The future place of the citizen diplomat remains to be seen. Although the ranks of the citizen diplomatic corps may shrink in the face of diminished attention to international problems in different times frames and across different international configurations, it is reasonable to argue that the expansion of the public realm to accommodate new points of initiating capacity for the realization of globally-linked political objectives is permanent. The economic, ecological, and political interdependence of global communities of people will not likely be reversed. The numbers of people that have a shared concern of security and individual dependence on the other for the realization of basic human needs and self-actualization will likely increase. The effects of the increasing transnationalization of identity and the corresponding sense of obligation that embodies the terms of citizenship will continue to be felt.

This growing trend of citizen involvement in foreign affairs speaks to the importance of incorporating the analysis of TSMs into our study of global relations and the construction of state foreign policies. An emerging body of literature speaks to this changing face of state-society relations through a global pattern of resistance practices. Reflecting the influence of the postmodernist, deconstructivist trends of analysis currently permeating the social sciences and humanities, the works of Ashley and Walker have begun to conceptualize alternative political practices along the themes of dissidence, resistance, and evolving identity structures. This analysis is primarily a dissection of how culturally derived practices of discourse that shape meanings and create interpretive frames effect individual conceptions of self as political beings. They seek to analyze non-institutionalized sites of empowerment created by struggle and resistance to the oppressive societal structures and orthodox political practices. Cast in the metaphor of exile, the analysis of 'marginal sites of modern politics' represents a marked departure from traditional conceptions of international relations (Ashley and Walker, 1990).

Unfortunately these dissident works on 'marginal sites' often become, in their own words, exiled works. But the self-induced exploration of the dynamic that relegates such works to exile from the orthodoxy of the discipline tends to overwhelm the original task of providing analysis of exiled practices of individuals within society. As such, much of the theorizing from within this alternative paradigm is heavily influenced by critical theory that is directed towards questions of epistemology and methodology and does not represent systematic analysis of the links between these newly formed political spaces, political behavior, and the consequences such practices have for the global political environment.

Similarly pluralist conceptions of foreign policy are no longer adequate. They deflect attention away from the range of political participation that is increasingly relevant to the study of foreign policy. Foreign policy analysis that treats social movement behavior as operative only in its organizational form evaluates social movements in a constrained interest group formula. Such treatment is an indication of the liberal pluralist bias of foreign policy analysis that supplants the analysis of nascent participatory methods of political expression for a normative preference for pluralistic practices. Not only does this predisposition ultimately deny the changing reality of global relations, but it threatens to further exacerbate the philosophical and methodological disputes that currently plague the field of international relations theory. It is precisely because transnational social movement participants reject the efficacy of the institutionalized approach of interest articulation employed by traditional groups that they have sought alternative methods of influence. By seizing the initiative and forging a new political space within which to operate, a fundamentally new form of globally relevant behavior has been created. And we need to construct a theoretical discourse befitting its novelty.

A first step towards that end is to attempt to merge the critiques of international relations theory emanating from the deconstructivist works of exile with existing frameworks of foreign policy and interest group analysis. Such a merger should establish a new domain of discourse that can be applied to an understanding of international problems characteristic of the modern era and the unique initiatives being undertaken to address them. It has been the purpose of this analysis to bring the concerns of this dissident scholarship into discourse with the established domain of the study of foreign policy practices. But it is a crude first step. There are serious conceptual issues that will need to be addressed and methodological problems that will need to be tackled. I would suggest several direction for future research:

We need to begin to redefine a conception of power for social movement actors both in the foreign policy process and as global actors in their own right. Charting the sites of authority and the opportunities to utilize them is only a primitive first step in that direction. We must move towards attempting to analyze the strategies of social movements and the conditions under which they are likely to be successful in the promotion of their objectives.

Such an emphasis will lead to a reconsideration of the levels of analysis issues. Clearly our traditional notions of systemic, regional, national, and domestic levels cannot neatly incorporate movements that exist outside of the institutional parameters, operate upon international norms, and have the capacity to transform global relations in their own right. Similarly our very depiction of global interactions as *international* relations or *foreign* affairs is caught within the state-centric framework which precludes the transnational phenomenon that is either economic or social in nature. It may be more instructive to think as a discipline in terms of transnational or world politics to capture the totality of operative forces.

As such, we must also place renewed emphasis upon the study of identity and its great implications for the behavior of individuals, collectivities, and states. Within the discipline of international relations, the study of identity has been relegated to a relatively unimportant status given the tendency to assert the primacy of the state and associate the individual with that entity. As the explosions of ethnic conflict occurring globally are increasing, the constraining nature of such state-centrism is obvious. But it is the multidimensional nature of identity that is both problematic and raises essential questions for explaining world politics. Given international economic dependencies, the erosion of the state's capacity to manage global affairs and provide for the basic needs of its populace, how intense is the individuals attachment to the state likely to be in the future? Already we have found that there is a population of individuals existing internationally that have incorporated a global dimension into their identity profile and are acting politically to balance their differing loyalties—locally, religiously, ethnically, nationally, and globally. We need to understand if this trend will continue and what the implications are for individual behavior. Identity theory will be an essential first step.

We also need to develop more rigorous methods to measure the relative influence that social movements in their broad construction and in their organizational form wield over the policy formulation processes of the state. As outlined previously, there are several approaches that may be taken, but with the hydraheaded nature of the phenomenon being evaluated, they lack precision.

Finally, we might begin to evaluate how social movement activity differs given the types of foreign policy decision making apparatus that it seeks to influence. Are there certain patterns of foreign policy decision making that are more sensitive to the types of initiatives characteristic of social movements? Much work exists on the relationship of social movement activity to institutional political structures, but it has all been done in the domestic context. (Tarrows, Kitschelt) This work could serve as a foundation for the expansion of analysis into the foreign policy-making realm. It is clear that we need to expand the foreign policy discourse to incorporate transnational social movement activity, but not by only discussing resistance politics as a unique phenomenon or by engaging in ideological and methodological polemics. Instead we must attempt to merge the diverse bodies of literature that capture the different facets of social movement activity into the existing scholarship on foreign policy formulation, in an attempt to create a more holistic and thus descriptive framework of analysis of global relations.

10

Below, Beyond, Beside the State

PEACE AND HUMAN RIGHTS MOVEMENTS AND THE END OF THE COLD WAR

David S. Meyer

The cold war ended in 1989 and international politics should never be the same again. Mikhail Gorbachev continued a program of economic restructuring and political reform in the Soviet Union that radically altered the terms of the challenge from the East. These substantial changes were far outstripped by domestic reforms elsewhere in the Eastern bloc. State communist governments fell throughout Eastern Europe, scuttling the notions that the East bloc was monolithic, immune to internal forces for change, or a military threat to Western Europe. A year which opened with analysts and scholars debating the extent and permanence of reforms in the East ended with East and West Germans dancing atop the Berlin wall.

Political analysts and policymakers alike have yet to respond fully, or to account credibly for these unprecedented changes. Clearly, however, the explanations we derive for the end of the cold war, and indeed, for improving the prospects for democratic change anywhere, will shape policy in the future. The processes of analysis and reformulation of policy have begun slowly; the revolutions of 1989 were a theoretical as well as political shock. Not even the most optimistic analysts envisioned a chain of events remotely resembling what actually occurred. A plethora of competing analyses, addressing domestic political coalitions in the Soviet Union, state systems of deterrence, long wave economic cycles, and a host of other

* I presented an earlier version of this paper, "How the Cold War Was Really Won: A View From Below," at the annual meeting of the International Studies Association, March 24, 1991. I want to thank Terry Boswell, Matthew Evangelista, Paul Joseph, Sam Marullo, and David Skidmore for helpful comments on earlier versions of the paper.

potential explanations is at the floodgates. This chapter is intended to contribute to the emerging debate on the end of the cold war by suggesting an important contributing cause that to date has been neglected. I will argue that grassroots peace and human rights activists played an important role in precipitating and shaping the revolutions of 1989. I begin by briefly describing the changes in international politics that characterize the "end of the cold war," then examine the importance of establishing coherent causal narratives in assessing political changes and developing policy responses. After reviewing the dominant explanations of the end of the cold war, I suggest ways in which independent political movements could have contributed to a change in the international order, identifying three potential routes of influence. I then examine the evidence for the influence of the peace movements in the United States and Western Europe and the human rights movements in Eastern Europe on international politics and on each other. I conclude with a preliminary evaluation of the evidence, several suggestions for further research, and a comment on the significance of this kind of analysis.

THE END OF THE COLD WAR

The cold war was a political and military competition between the United States and the Soviet Union (and their respective allies); it dominated international politics over the past four decades, often intruding upon domestic politics in both blocs (Kaldor, 1991). At the core of the competition was an arms race between the superpowers, each trying to deter the other from aggression and extend its own influence. The Soviet Union and the United States each served as the military anchor of a relatively stable military alliance based in Europe, and competed for advantage in the third world. The cold war ended when it became clear that the Soviet Union would no longer keep up its end of the competition. Its "sphere of influence" declined dramatically, as the Soviets lost sway in the third world in the 1970s, then even in the buffer states surrounding them in the late 1980s.

Picking a starting point for the end of the cold war suggests the sort of conclusions one wants to reach. Since we are interested in the relations between the superpowers and the role of non-official actors, we might properly begin with November 1984, when Ronald Reagan was reelected president of the United States in an overwhelming landslide. At first glance, this seems a point of continuity. In fact, while Reagan's first term had created a great deal of controversy, especially regarding his stance toward the Soviet Union, the reelected Reagan promised a radically different stance. In his first campaign and upon assuming office, Reagan intensified the period of superpower hostility than had begun in the last years of Jimmy Carter's administration. Challenger Ronald Reagan promised a more aggressive approach toward the Soviet Union, and substantial increases in both military spending and capacity. His administration also unleashed a stream of exceptionally bellicose rhetoric, provoking an unprecedented oppositional movement.[1] Once reelected, however, Reagan claimed a mandate for a return to arms control and reviving a sort of detente with the Soviet Union.

The Soviet Communist Party appointed a potential negotiating partner, Mikhail Gorbachev, to succeed Konstantin Chernenko as its General Secretary in March of 1985. Following a long period of first stagnant, then transitional leadership, Gorbachev confronted an economic crisis in the Soviet Union. After working to consolidate power, he sought to pursue arms control with the United States in order to redirect his efforts toward restructuring the Soviet economy (*perestroika*) (Holloway, 1989/90; Hough, 1990; Scanlan, 1988). For Gorbachev, arms control and detente with the West were necessary both to limit the threat to his position from the Soviet military, and to free economic and political resources for domestic purposes (Meyer, 1988). By moderating the threat from the United States, he hoped to reduce the domestic political strength of the Soviet military, and create political space for his own initiatives.

Gorbachev initiated a withdrawal of Soviet troops from Afghanistan, and embraced virtually every potential opportunity for detente and arms control the West offered, including U.S. proposals for domestic political effect with little expectation Soviet response. He generally countered each Western proposal with a broader and more comprehensive one. Shortly after taking office, he announced a unilateral moratorium on deploying SS-20 missiles in the Western portion of the Soviet Union and on nuclear warhead testing, calling for reciprocation from the United States. At a summit with Reagan at Reykjavik in October of 1986, Gorbachev's proposal to eliminate all nuclear weapons dominated discussion, only to be stymied by his insistence on linking arms control to limits on Reagan's "Star Wars" Strategic Defense Initiative. Shortly afterward, however, his acceptance of the Reagan administration's "zero-zero" proposal served as the basis for an agreement on Intermediate Range Nuclear Forces (INF), signed at the Washington summit in December 1987 (Hough, 1985–86; Risse-Kappen, 1988, 1991a, b). After the ratification of the INF agreement, Gorbachev unleashed a new set of arms control proposals intended to restructure the Soviet military to a less offensive posture, explicitly adopting a "common security" approach, as articulated by an independent

---

1. On rhetoric, see Scheer (1982); on the strategy and details of the new strategic posture, see Posen and Van Evera (1983); on arms control, see Talbott (1984); on opposition to Reagan's strategic policy, see Meyer (1990).

international commission headed by Swedish prime minister Olof Palme. The Palme Commission (1982) had called for increased international cooperation and massive cuts in offensive weaponry (Snyder, 1988).

Gorbachev intended the foreign policy detente and restructuring to allow a breathing space for reforming the Soviet economy and polity, and he encouraged similar reforms throughout the Eastern bloc. He also made it clear that the Soviet Union would no longer prop up other repressive and unpopular regimes. A wave of popular movements swept across Eastern Europe, the character and content of each varying from country to country (Bunce, 1990; Gwertzman and Kaufman, 1990; Kramer, 1989/90).

The diversity of approaches to economics, politics, and especially security and foreign policy, has dramatically undercut any potential Soviet threat. Rather than "containment," the West now struggles with a process of inclusion and incorporation, as Eastern nations struggle to reform. The road to economic restructuring and the struggle for political democratization will not be easy. It is clear, however, that the dominant foreign policy goal of the West must be altered radically. The Warsaw Treaty Organization has disappeared, and the decades long struggle between East and West has evaporated. Clearly, the significance of the dramatic changes of the past several years will be felt in years to come, and they demand careful analysis and examination in order to devise policy for the future.

COMPLEXITY AND OPERABLE CAUSES: EXPLAINING EVENTS

The revolutionary events of 1989 demand a reevaluation and restructuring of United States policy, as well as a reexamination of the dominant paradigms in international relations. Clearly, the virtual collapse of the Eastern bloc provides a wealth of information useful to both projects. Despite the best efforts of political scientists, however, complex events do not easily surrender to monocausal explanations. Numerous prescriptions for change, for inducing reform in the Soviet Union, and for ensuring world peace competed throughout the cold war period, offering contradictory strategies and approaches (Evangelista, 1990a). Unfortunately for social scientists, the United States did not clearly choose one approach over another to provide a test case; indeed, it vacillated between policies of conciliation and moderation and those of confrontation and conflict. Indeed, policy throughout the cold war, even while oddly consistent over the long run, reflected conflict rather than consensus (Freedman, 1983; Meyer, 1991a). Advocates of similarly incompatible strategies now battle for primacy in shaping policy in the post-cold war period, seeking evidence for the power of their approaches in the unfolding story of the end of the cold war.

Although the events of 1989 mark a turning point in history, it is not the revolutions themselves, but the accepted explanations of those events which will shape subsequent policy. Analysts and political actors interpret events of the past in light of contemporary policy options, seeking historical precedent to inform or justify contemporary decisions (Neustadt and May, 1986). Causal narratives compete for acceptance and adherents, their support determined partly by the strength of their explanatory power, and partly by their resonance with dominant cultural values and intellectual paradigms. Each narrative suggests a differing set of significant factors which shape historical events, notes distinct occurrences as "problems," and identifies some situations as amenable to political intervention and others as effectively immutable, or at least beyond the scope of purposive action (Stone, 1989). Historical and political analysis is thus inseparable from contemporary policy debate. In studying history we are concerned not only with explaining past events, but also with learning from them. We look to the past for help in making better decisions in the future.

Within any series of events, there are numerous possible historical narratives and innumerable contributing causes. In reviewing the emerging explanations for the end of the cold war, we need to evaluate critically their explanatory power, their generalizability, and the operability of the causes they suggest (Zinn, 1970).

EXPLAINING THE END OF THE COLD WAR: THE CURRENT DEBATES

Sadly, the dominant explanations of the historic thaw in the cold war leave little guidance for the future. Within the political mainstream, political actors seek vindication of the positions they had previously espoused rather than insight into current policy problems. Thus, Republican supporters of the Reagan-era military build-up claim that their efforts forced the Soviet Union into submission. Most Democrats are hardly more insightful, arguing that it was the long bipartisan application of containment which made the expansion of the Soviet empire impossible, eventually spurring the reforms of the past few years. Left critics of the cold war mainstream have suggested that the reforms were solely the result of internal processes within the Soviet Union, particularly Mikhail Gorbachev's ascent to power (Marullo, 1990).

The evidence supporting any of these analyses is extremely limited, and more immediately relevant, all these approaches lead us to make misjudgments about policy in the future. Left critics underestimate the influence external events may have on the processes of reform. By denigrating the role of US policy in stalling reform in both the East and West, they suggest that military policy is essentially irrelevant, and that reevaluation and remaking of policy is important only for domestic reasons. The international context can in fact have a dramatic influence on domestic politics within a state (Gourevitch 1978, 1986). The Democratic and Republican perspectives overestimate the importance of US military strength by contending that the United States can force other nations to initiate internal reforms by applying external pressure, at least if continued over a period of decades. The best future policy for the United States, in this view, is essentially more of the same.

The first order of more analytic—and less explicitly political—explanations is little better, attributing the end of the cold war to the fortitude, commitment, flexibility, and/or resilience of the leaders of the superpowers, Ronald Reagan and Mikhail Gorbachev. Gorbachev's champions applaud his willingness to experiment with substantial reforms in the Soviet Union and respond to a terrible economic crisis. Reagan's supporters laud the buildup he presided over during his first term, and the hard line he took toward the Soviet Union. Reagan's approach, they contend, exacerbated and underscored the economic problems in the Soviet Union, and foreclosed the possibility of continuing without reforms.[2]

"Great man" explanations such as these neglect the importance of larger political forces and the constraints under which even the most visionary political leaders operate. Further, in their simplest articulation they offer little guidance for future political decisions besides choosing wise, committed, or daring leaders. In Gorbachev's case, there is considerable evidence that a substantial reevaluation of Soviet foreign and economic policy was underway well before Gorbachev (or Reagan, for that matter) came to power. Soviet intellectuals began publicly (and very tentatively) exploring notions of fundamental reform in the late 1970s. Indeed, Gorbachev's fast track to leadership was evident in the 1970s, and though he was certainly no wild reformer, he had shown sympathy for economic restructuring. Evidence of a new Soviet willingness to reform surfaced clearly in Leonid Brezhnev's speech to the 26th Party Congress in May 1980. The Soviet leader announced a priority for detente with the United States, a continuation of the SALT process, and even an openness to "different roads to socialism" in Eastern Europe (Brown, 1989; Meissner, 1981). Brezhnev's successor, Yuri Andropov, had established alternate sources of information and legitimation on military strategy, in an attempt to build an institutional alternative to the Soviet General Staff likely to be more sympathetic to arms control. Even the Soviet military, however, had expressed an interest in new defensive strategies such as non-provocative defense and

---

2. The award of the 1990 Nobel Peace Prize to Gorbachev reflects the esteem in which he is held outside the Soviet Union. Reagan's champions included Krauthammer (1989) and Weinberger (1990). Former U.S. Ambassador to the United Nations, Jeanne J. Kirkpatrick (1989/90) manages to give credit to and find exceptional qualities in both men.

concepts of "mutual security" (Meyer, 1988). As Secretary for Ideology under Chrenenko, Gorbachev gave voice to diverse claims for restructuring, including both certain elite demands for reform, and dissatisfaction and demands for social change at the grassroots (Hough, 1990). Although Gorbachev's political skills were surely important in shaping the course of Soviet reforms, it is critical to recognize his place in a larger current of "new thinking." The Soviet president's survival of the attempted August 1991 military coup demonstrates, more than anything else, how dependent Gorbachev was on the broader social networks he unleashed.

The case for ascribing the end of the cold war to Gorbachev is limited, but the one for attributing it to Ronald Reagan is much weaker. Like Gorbachev, Reagan accelerated trends set into motion by his predecessor. The harder line approach to the Soviet Union that Reagan championed was commenced under Jimmy Carter, partly in response to the Soviet invasion of Afghanistan, and partly (and paradoxically) to win support in the Senate for SALT II ratification. Virtually all of the weapons associated with Reagan's strategic buildup—MX, Pershing II, Trident II, and cruise missiles—were already on line under Carter (Komer, 1985). Reagan continued Carter's policies, adding a few weapons (notably the B-1 bomber and two additional nuclear powered aircraft carriers), a more hostile attitude toward arms control, more bellicose rhetoric, and a tremendous amount of money (Kaufmann, 1984; Stockman, 1986). It is far from clear that what James Fallows (1986) called Reagan's "spend-up" substantially improved the United States' strategic posture, or translated into many new weapons, increased capabilities, or enhanced the threat to the Soviet Union (Arkin, 1989). Indeed, it is quite likely that the administration's hostility to (and internal division on) arms control cost both superpowers the possibilities of attaining significant agreements on both nuclear and conventional weapons more easily and earlier, including a still-unnegotiated test ban treaty (Doty, 1987; Johansen, 1983, 1984; Mandelbaum and Talbot,t 1986/ 7; Sharp 1984; Talbott, 1984). Of course, Reagan's willingness to negotiate arms control with the Soviet Union was critical to the success of Gorbachev's reform efforts, but it is unwise to attribute this to the President's style or character. Rather, as I will argue below, Reagan was constrained by Western allies and popular pressure in the United States; essentially, he was forced to make at least an symbolic attempt at arms control.

Clearly, although the styles and concerns of Reagan and Gorbachev influenced the shape of events in 1989, those influences were likely marginal, and themselves shaped by larger historical forces. The focus on political leadership is unsatisfying, and ultimately of little utility, leaving far too much to historical contingency. In contrast, alternative macropolitical explanations of the end of the cold war can point to larger forces and their influence, but bear the weight of undue determinism, again providing little guidance to policymakers for the future. I will briefly discuss explanations which emphasize ideology, economics, and security.

Perhaps the weakest of the macropolitical explanations focuses on ideology. In an exceptionally controversial essay, Frank Fukuyama (1989) adopts an odd neo-Hegelian approach, arguing that the triumph of liberal democracy over communism was inevitable and, now that the major struggle of the modern era has been resolved, history as we know it has ended. Although few critics have been willing to stake out as polemic a position, the notion that Eastern Europe and the Soviet Union suddenly recognized the superiority of liberal capitalism to their own systems resonates deeply in popular discourse. In the popular version of this myth, Soviets and East Europeans will now rush headlong to open their markets and imitate the United States. This explanation offers little on the mechanisms of change, or why the governments of the East collapsed when they did and in sequence. More to the point, many of the dissidents have expressed substantial doubts about liberal capitalism and/or democracy. Hungary, for example, seems determined to carve out a social welfare state similar to Sweden, and Poland, though currently committed to radical free market reforms in its economy, seems likely to give the Catholic church a political role which is distinctly illiberal. In Romania and Bulgaria, neither capitalism nor liberalism appear likely to flourish soon. Further, the collapse of repressive governments throughout the East has unleashed a rash of nationalist and anti-Semitic movements, which are antithetical to liberalism and democracy.

The economic explanations offer a more convincing first cut at the collapse of state communism. The Soviet Union, along with all the East European governments, faced continuing economic crises, burdened with debt, unable to deliver consumer goods, and beset by continually declining productivity. Although the rate of economic growth worldwide declined significantly in the 1980s, it was a substantially steeper decline in state socialist economies (Boswell and Peters, 1990; Vanuous, 1982). Scholars differ on the causes of this relative decline. Liberals and conservatives argue that the economic crises reflected inherent weaknesses of state socialism, for example, in setting prices (e.g. Heilbronner 1990). Marxist and neo-Marxist analysts emphasize the changing nature of the world economy, and the failure of state socialist societies to adapt to new patterns of technological innovation and economic organization. Further, as all analysts note, a technological revolution in global communications made the failings of the East bloc all the more evident to both leaders and citizens, as did increased communication between East and West.

Clearly, the economic troubles of the Eastern bloc provided substantial pressure for economic and political reform, and set the context within which reform movements operated. Athough economic explanations demonstrate the pressure of crisis, however, they do not explain the differing political responses states make to these crises. The government crackdown on both economic and political reform in China provides a critical counterpoint for the generally more liberal responses in Eastern Europe (Boswell and Peters, 1990). It is important to recognize the economic crises as the backdrop for political reform, but it is crucial to develop an analysis which explains the varieties of response.

REALISM AND CHANGE

The explanation most likely to influence subsequent policy decisions derives from *realism*, the dominant approach to security analysis in the post-war period. This is odd and troubling, as realist thought offered little indication of how or why events like the revolutions of 1989 took place. Realism is predicated on the assumption that the causes of war are rooted in state competition for pursuit of interests within a system of "international anarchy" (Morgenthau, 1978; Waltz, 1979). Realists contend that the nature of domestic political systems within the "black box" of a state is essentially irrelevant to the pursuit of state interests. Democratic states are no less likely to use violence or coercion to pursue their interests than totalitarian ones. Absent a world government with the power to implement substantial sanctions, international norms and agreements are of minimal importance.

The best protection against international aggression and conflict, according to the realists, is military deterrence. A state can reliably be expected to refrain from aggressive behavior only when the clear costs of doing so outweigh the potential benefits. Individual states must then protect themselves by seeking either independent deterrent capability or alliance with a state that has such capabilities. History has shown, say the realists, that the most stable system is one of bipolar deterrence in which two states or state systems provide an essential international stalemate, each deterring the other's aggressive behavior. The post-war order, at least in the Northern world, has roughly approximated such a system and has coincided with an unprecedented period of relative stability, what Gaddis (1987) has termed "the long peace." The moderation of Soviet foreign policy in the middle 1980s, in the realist paradigm, is considered separately from the concommitant domestic reforms, and is by definition seen as a reaction to the international climate. Since the state is seen as a unitary actor responding rationally to a world system, there is little alternative.

This systemic view also bears the burden of overdetermination and inevitability. Essentially, not only Gorbachev, but any Soviet leader responding to the same external circumstances would respond as Gorbachev did.[3] The narrow view of a realist perspective disallows the influence of political choice or domestic politics, and thus we look to the world system for an explanation of moderation. The bipolar cold war system, however, was supposed to be stable; nation-states can win or lose in internaional conflicts, but they are not supposed to "give up" in the international competition. Any realist explanation is therefore an odd synthetic addendum to the theory: the Soviet Union retreated from the bipolar system because it was unable to continue keeping up its end of the competition. Gaddis (1989) attributes this to thirty years of Western resolve in keeping up the other end of the competition. Specifically, he praises Reagan for rebuilding American self-confidence, "spook[ing] the Soviets" and defusing the peace movement, negotiating from strength, and responding to Gorbachev.

If this explanation is something less than satisfying, the realist agenda for the future is even more troubling. Since realists believe the bipolar stalemate to be the most stable international system, they confess a nostalgia for the costly—but surely stable—cold war. Indeed, realist analysts have been much less interested in explaining the end of the cold war than in devising a stable multipolar system to replace it. Recent analysts have, with varying degrees of trepidation, prescribed a course of managed nuclear proliferation to ensure stability (Mearsheimer, 1990a, b; Weber, 1990/91).[4]

Since it was first propounded, realism has faced waves of criticism which take the approach to task for failing to recognize the complexity of states' decision-making processes. By looking inside the "black box," analysts have found considerably greater diversity of opinion, less rational thinking, and more contingency and uncertainty than realist thinking recognizes.[5] In the case of the end of the cold war, the realist narrative gives little indication about why the Soviet bloc collapsed when it did, why Eastern European states have shown a considerable diversity in their approaches to both foreign policy and democracy, and perhaps most important, why the peculiar mix of bellicosity (Reagan I, 1980-84) and conciliation (Reagan II, 1984-88) somehow proved to be the magical combination needed to bring down the Eastern system. Given the troubling realist vision of the future, we would do well to examine alternative explanations and agendas before accepting this narrative.

---

3. For discussion and criticism of this explanation, see Evangelista (1990c).
4. Mearsheimer's work, predictably, has generated a great deal of controversy. For the first wave of critical responses, see the correspondence between Mearsheimer et. al. (1990).
5. For a recent summary indictment of realism, see Kober (1990).

PEACE MOVEMENTS:
ROUTES FOR DOMESTIC AND TRANSNATIONAL INFLUENCE

Toward that end, in this section I will suggest the importance of domestic politics, specifically grassroots-based peace movements, as a contributing cause of the end of the cold war. Peace movements emerged strongly in the United States and Western Europe in the early 1980s, shortly preceding the waves of reform in the East. Human rights and democracy movements in Eastern Europe, often affiliated with the Western peace movements, preceded the revolutions of 1989 in Poland, Hungary, Czechoslavakia, and East Germany. In many cases, the human rights activists and political dissidents of the 1970s and 1980s are now part of the reformed governments they had recently challenged. Before beginning, it is useful to identify the potential ways subnational and transnational movements could influence international politics. There are three distinct routes through which a peace movement could exercise influence on international politics: domestic influence on the state through direct or indirect means, direct influence on foreign governments, and indirect influence on foreign governments by alliance with movements in other countries.

First, a protest movement may influence the policy of the state in which it operates by a) changing political discourse or the larger political environment within that country, thereby altering perspectives on politically viable solutions (see Gusfield, 1980); b) bringing elite attention to certain political problems; c) suggesting and supporting policy alternatives; d) increasing the difficulty and costs of policy implementation to the extent that the government alters its conduct; and/or e) changing coalition conditions and thus altering a government's policy options.

Second, peace movements may influence the policies of their own governments by changing the behavior of foreign governments in much the same ways outlined above. They may also serve as conduits for ideas, as foreign governments can use activists as non-official channels to explore ideas for political negotiations. John Kennedy, for example, knowing that editor and antinuclear activist Norman Cousins was going to the Soviet Union to interview Soviet General Secretary Khrushchev, asked Cousins to explain the US position on a nuclear test ban. Cousins' shuttle diplomacy early in 1963 proved critical in bringing the two leaders together later in the year to negotiate a treaty (Seaborg 1981, 207–8). Reciprocally, critics of peace movements in the West have often charged that American and West European activists were actually manipulated by and serving the interests of the Soviet government (e.g. Barron, 1982; Bukovsky, 1982; Herf, 1986; Vermaat, 1982; US Department of State, 1982).

Finally, proposals may arise from below and be passed transnationally through conferences and informal contacts. As example, Evangelista (1990b), by tracing the movement of ideas, makes a convincing case that international conferences between Soviet and American scientists, specifically the Pugwash meetings, influenced the Soviet scientists' view of antiballistic missiles (ABM) systems, and that the scientists then influenced the Soviet Union's posture in subsequent arms control negotiations. Peace movements may then influence international policy by strengthening citizen movements inside other states or by altering the conditions of coalition formation in other countries. Activists may draw public attention to peace and antinuclear movements in other countries, thus strengthening them, and weakening governments' capacities to claim consensus.

The peace and human rights movements of the 1980s, I will argue, exercised influence through all of these channels. In summary, I contend that although reform in the Soviet bloc was domestically based and motivated, a posture of conciliation from the West gave Eastern reformers room to operate. American and Western European peace activists applied pressure on their own governments to allow the possibility of a new detente and Soviet reform, and constrained the Carter-Reagan military build-up. They built a domestic constituency of support for arms control, forcing their governments to revive the process. Through a policy of international citizen-level contacts, they drew attention to Eastern reformers and dissidents, and provided them with support. They created a political climate in the United States which forced government officials to respond to the Soviet Union's steps toward detente and reform.

WESTERN PEACE MOVEMENTS AND POLICY: A BRIEF HISTORY

Peace movements undoubtedly have as long a history as war. As DeBenedetti (1980, p.xii) notes, movements have had two distinct goals: to oppose war and the preparations for war, and to devise alternative means of international dispute resolution. Given these goals, it is understandable that peace movements have always had a strong transnational component. International contacts can be traced back at least as far as 1843, when activists held the first international citizen's peace conference in London (ibid, p.46). In the United States, movements have waxed and waned in response to the perceived urgency of the threat of war. Thus antiwar movements emerged strongly prior to United States entry into the first and second world wars, during the Vietnam war, and most recently in opposition to the war in the Persian Gulf. After the second world war, however, when the United States firmly established itself as an international actor and developed a large and permanent military establishment and the shadow of nuclear weapons hung over both potential wars and the peace, citizen movements were faced with both a substantially different world and a new urgency.

The relative consistency of post-war United States military policy masks the political conflicts underlying it. Indeed, for the past forty years peace movements have reined in the very worst aspects of the arms race, preventing an even more aggressive US posture (Meyer, 1991b; Wittner, 1988). Since the dawn of the nuclear age, small groups of people have consistently opposed both the strategy and the conduct of the arms race. A broad peace movement has united groups with dramatically differing views of the problem only when there has been a general atmosphere of crisis about the arms race. During these times, they have been able to build new organizations, put forward strong demands, command mainstream attention, and, on occasion, even influence policy. Immediately after World War II, a movement led by scientists involved in developing the atomic bomb called for the international control of nuclear weapons. Although quashed by the red scare and McCarthyism of the 1950s, they left in place the organizations which would serve as a base of support for subsequent movements. By the late 1950s, a broader peace movement was resurrected, focusing on the dangers of ongoing atmospheric testing. Mobilizing around public fear of radioactive fallout, the movement called for a ban on nuclear testing. Responding to this public concern, and to the real issues the movement raised, President Kennedy created the Arms Control and Disarmament Agency (ACDA), and negotiated the Limited Test Ban Treaty. The movement fragmented shortly afterward, partly in response to its partial victory, partly as a result of increased concern about more immediately pressing issues, particularly the struggle for civil rights and the war in Vietnam (Boyer, 1986; DeBenedetti, 1980; Katz, 1986; Wittner, 1984).

The movement to stop the war in Vietnam was certainly the most volatile and broadly based of the post-war peace movements. Although the war dragged on even as the movement grew, popular opposition stymied Lyndon Johnson's conduct of the war and convinced Johnson not to seek reelection in 1968. After the election, citizen activism constrained President Nixon's early plans to escalate militarily in Vietnam, and helped end the draft (DeBenedetti and Chatfield, 1989; Zaroulis and Sullivan, 1984).

At the end of the 1960s, a smaller peace movement coalition re-emerged. Comprised of scientists, dissident strategists, and local activists, the movement focused on stopping new technological innovations that threatened to accelerate the arms race, particularly multiple-warhead nuclear missiles (MIRVs) and antiballistic missiles (ABM). Working primarily through Congress, the movement succeeded in pressuring President Nixon to redefine the mission and citing of ABM systems. Instead of deploying large systems near major cities for population defense, Nixon limited development of ABM to a much smaller system devoted to defense of American missile fields. This meant that ABM systems were deployed in rural North Dakota rather than suburban Chicago, and then only for a few months in 1974. This success was the product of an alliance between strategists who doubted the utility of ABM, scientists who questioned its viability, and local activists who opposed it in any case (Primack and von Hippel, 1974).

WESTERN PEACE MOVEMENTS IN THE 1980s

There has been a consistent pattern in the relationship between peace movements and policy. Activists have used opposition to a particularly dangerous aspect of nuclear weapons policy to mount broad-based campaigns challenging the basic tenets of government policy. They have generally won a moderation in policy, but certainly not an end to the arms race. The partial concessions have, however, made it far more difficult for opposition campaigns to mobilize support and activity (Meyer, 1991b). The nuclear freeze movement, and its counterparts throughout Western Europe, followed much the same pattern. Like its predecessors, the freeze emerged when the arms race became more expensive and threatened to become much more dangerous (Marullo and Lofland, 1990; McRae and Markle, 1989; Meyer, 1990; Solo, 1988; Waller, 1987). More than any of its historical antecedents, however, the freeze developed in concert with sympathetic movements in Eastern and Western Europe.

The first large wave of international peace activism in the recent period surrounded NATO's 1979 "dual track" decision to respond to Soviet SS-20 intermediate range nuclear missiles. The United States would deploy Pershing II and ground launched cruise missiles carrying nuclear warheads in Western Europe, while simultaneously conducting arms control negotiations on this category of weaponry. President Jimmy Carter's December 1979 announcement of this policy spurred an immediate response in the countries scheduled to host the weapons. The movements took distinct forms in different countries. In the Netherlands, much of the opposition was coordinated by the Dutch Interchurch Peace Council (IKV), with strong opposition across the political spectrum. In Britain, antinuclear activism revived the moribund Committee for Nuclear Disarmament (CND), a membership organization, and carried substantial influence within the British Labour Party. Much of the Italian dissent was carried by the Communist Party, while the antinuclear movement spurred the formation of a new political party, the Greens, in West Germany. Parallel French and Flemish speaking organizations developed in Belgium to coordinate the antinuclear forces (Johnston, 1984; Kaldor and Smith, 1982; Myrdal et al., 1982; Risse-Kappen, 1988, 1991a,c; Rochon, 1988). The movements also spurred the creation of European Nuclear Disarmament (END), a specifically international organization based in Britain, dedicated to coordinating the movements, and to linking peace activism with campaigns for human rights in the East (Thompson, 1982; Thompson and Smith, eds., 1981). The

European activists saw the United States as the power behind the NATO decision, and set out to stop INF deployment by joining with a peace movement in the United States. Early efforts were unsuccessful.

At the same time, a broad range of activists in the United States were searching for a new approach to link their own efforts. The idea of a bilateral freeze had circulated periodically throughout the 1960s and 1970s; a freeze represented a simple, verifiable, confidence building first step toward arms control and disarmament. The proposal contained in Randall Forsberg's "Call to Halt the Arms Race" was different from the earlier versions in one central respect: Forsberg (1984) envisioned the freeze not only as an arms control position, but also as the centerpiece of a popular campaign. In December 1979, at the annual meeting of Mobilization for Survival, she proposed the freeze as a strategy for organizing opposition to President Carter's military build-up. The freeze won early support from several pacifist and left disarmament groups, but had a difficult time making inroads among supporters of arms control. Resurrecting SALT II then appeared possible, and without a mass base, activists were unable to command political attention.

Organizers took the freeze proposal to the Democratic national convention in New York during the summer of 1980, but both the Kennedy and Carter campaigns worked to keep it off the convention floor. When Carter won the party's nomination and promised more aggressive and expensive foreign and military policies, things appeared desperate to activists. Carter had already withdrawn SALT II from Senate consideration, endorsed PD-59, which codified plans for an extended nuclear war, begun plans for deploying the MX, Trident II, Pershing II, and cruise missiles, and commenced a large increase in military spending.

In November, however, things appeared much worse. Ronald Reagan, running far to Carter's right, won the presidency in a landslide. For the only time in his career, Reagan had coattails, and he brought enough Republicans into office to win his party control of the Senate for the first time in nearly 30 years. The ousted Senators included some of the strongest arms control advocates in Congress, and they were replaced by conservative Republicans either hostile or indifferent to arms control. On the eve of the 1980 election, more than one third of the electorate reported that they feared that as President Reagan would lead the United States into war. The November returns were both dispiriting and terrifying to both peace activists and more moderate advocates of detente, as Reagan promised to "rebuild" what he saw as America's neglected military forces.

Dispirited with the prospects of exercising influence within government, advocates of detente and arms control turned their efforts toward other routes to influence. Importantly, the polemic position struck by the Reagan administration allowed activists to build alliances with dissident elites. Activists saw one bright spot in the electoral returns. In Western

Massachusetts, a nuclear freeze proposal won 59 percent support in three state senate districts, all of which had supported Reagan for president. In one stroke, the election demonstrated a soft spot in Reagan's popular support, the domestic appeal of the freeze proposal, and a tactic for exploiting both. The freeze quickly won broad support in public opinion polls, town meetings, and state and local referenda. Without other visible alternatives or initiatives from government, arms control groups and Congressional supporters now flocked to it. It demonstrated clear political support useful for political campaigns and fundraising, and won large margins in public opinion polls and referenda while there were no alternatives on the political horizon. At its height, the movement included an exceptionally broad range of political activity, including civil disobedience and direct action, lobbying and campaign contributions in Congress, large demonstrations, and broad educational programs. The freeze was the only viable antinuclear game in town, and it made substantial inroads in both the Democratic and Republican parties.

Mass media coverage of European antinuclear activism in the fall of 1981 and the following spring helped the freeze campaign grow. Large demonstrations in Bonn, London, Amsterdam, Rome, and Paris gained prominent coverage in American newspapers and magazines. Seeking to exploit the publicity, peace groups in the United States organized solidarity tours of Western European activists, which served to generate publicity for both movements, and aided in political mobilization and organization building (Meyer 1990, 119–35).

POLITICAL RESPONSES

Throughout the Western alliance, government coalitions were threatened by the new movements. Although both the United States and the five nations scheduled to host the INF weapons held to the original dual track decision, their decisions were not without political cost. Most dramatically, a split within the West German Social Democratic Party led to the fall of Helmut Schmidt's coalition government and to new elections in early 1983 (Markovits, 1983). Although a conservative coalition prevailed, as was the case in much of Western Europe, the left was enlivened and the governments' foreign policies were tempered. Political responses in the case of the United States are instructive.

In 1983 the House of Representatives overwhelmingly passed a nonbinding nuclear freeze resolution, and the following year the Democratic Party nominated as its presidential candidate someone who ostensibly embraced the freeze proposal. Even more significant, the Reagan administration was compelled to respond to the broad concern about nuclear weapons the freeze demonstrated (Cortright, 1991). Reagan refused to allow the movement to demonize him and his policies. He and his administration backed away from the cavalier rhetoric about nuclear warning shots, recallable missiles, improvised fallout shelters, and limited nuclear wars that had characterized the early years of the administration and animated the movement. Instead, they learned the utility of guarded language about "options" and "flexibility."

The administration engaged in a propaganda war to rob the freeze of the political space it commanded. One front involved playing on fears of the Soviet Union by accusing the Soviets of chemical warfare and treaty violations. At the same time, the administration reopened arms control talks with the Soviet Union, proposing treaties such as the "zero-zero" proposal for intermediate nuclear forces in Europe and START. The proposals called for deep (and what the administration thought would be unacceptable) cuts in the Soviet arsenal, in exchange for modest reductions in US plans (Talbott, 1984). The final piece of the Reagan political strategy was the Strategic Defense Initiative. On March 23, 1983, Reagan abandoned talk of prevailing in nuclear war and instead asked Americans if it wouldn't be "better to save lives than to avenge them." Taken together, the administration's approach prevented the 1984 election from serving as a referendum on Reagan's nuclear policy. Importantly, however, the price of electoral protection was a stifling of the "rollback" posture. Reagan proclaimed his mammoth reelection landslide a mandate for arms control, and ironically, he was right.

The Reagan who campaigned in 1984 was substantially different from the one who took office in 1981. In January of 1984 Reagan had announced his intention to resume arms control negotiations with the Soviet Union, and he was defensive about his failure to meet with any Soviet leaders, promising to do better in his next term. He no longer spoke of "winnable" nuclear wars. Indeed, he memorized and frequently repeated the phrase "nuclear war cannot be won and must never be fought (Bundy, 1989)." Between the freeze campaign and his own Star Wars plan, Reagan had become convinced that the system of mutually assured destruction was morally intolerable. Importantly, this all took place well before Mikhail Gorbachev ascended to power in March of 1985.

DOMESTIC CONTAINMENT

The peace movement's popular clout limited NATO's policy options and those of the Reagan administration. Although NATO succeeded in deploying the unpopular INF missiles, it was, as Dutch analyst Martin Huygen (1986) notes, a "pyrrhic victory." The NATO governments expended so much political capital in placing the weapons that there was insufficient political will or resources to sustain further nuclear modernization (also see Mueller and Risse-Kappen, 1987). Essentially, the movements made subsequent escalation politically untenable. The dual track decision fragmented what domestic consensus on security had previously existed throughout Europe. The United States had to relinquish its appearance as a leading force in NATO, and the NATO governments, even when ruled by conservative coalitions, were far more sensitive to the concerns of their own peace movements. They were also much more reluctant to follow United States leadership on matters of national security.

Although the movement became far less visible, it was now entrenched in domestic political institutions. Even as the freeze faded in the United States, the organizations which had supported it continued their own activities, working to build a knowledgable and effective opposition. Freeze-supported political action committees made some $6 million in contributions to the campaigns of arms control supporters in 1984, and somewhat more in 1986, when they helped bring Democrats back into control of the Senate. The arms control caucus in Congress was stronger, better educated, and more aggressive than ever before. The House of Representatives pushed for restraint in military spending, anti-satellite weapons development, research on star wars projects, and deployment of first strike weapons such as the MX missile. They also consistently pressed for more active pursuit of arms control (Fascell, 1987; Magraw, 1989).

Members of Congress had good reason to be more concerned about nuclear weapons and arms control. The freeze groups remained active locally, and held representatives accountable to the wishes of their districts. Activists around the country developed peace studies programs at universities and high schools, staged community eduction forums, and generally raised the national level of nuclear awareness. Political leaders could no longer count on ignorance or apathy about nuclear issues among their constituents. They had to be more aware and more responsive.

As a result of raised awareness and activism in both Congress and mass public opinion, Reagan's initial approach to nuclear weapons and foreign policy was no longer possible. The president could not effect further increases in military spending or nuclear capabilities; he could not abandon arms control or ignore signs of willingness to negotiate or moderation from the East. He was forced to make at least a show of openness toward arms control and detente. When Gorbachev accepted the zero-zero proposal for nuclear weapons in Europe, a proposal the Reagan administration originally designed to counter the peace movement, Reagan had no alternative but to negotiate (Griffith, 1989; Lapidus and Dallin, 1989).

Within the Western alliance, peace movements in the United States and Western Europe were responsible for restoring some semblance of detente to US and NATO policy. The West European governments, virtually without exception, were always less enthusastic about military escalation and the end of detente than the Reagan administration, and they used the peace movements as an excuse to resist the hardest line US policies. By mobilizing public opinion and gaining influence within center and left parties, they shifted the balance of visible consensus, essentially forcing their leaders to adopt a more conciliatory policy to the East, and to respond to initiatives for detente and arms control from the Soviet Union.

THE SPREAD OF IDEAS

The movements also set out to influence Soviet behavior more directly, first by explicitly criticizing Soviet weapons and human rights violations, second, by proffering alternative visions of international security. Criticism of the Soviet Union, and indeed of bloc politics, was an essential component of many peace groups' strategies. This approach was controversial within movement coalitions, as groups debated how, for example, to deal with the official Eastern peace councils. Tactically, however, it was largely successful in dispelling the notion that the Western peace movements were intentionally serving Soviet interests (although charges of naievete remained) (e.g., Vermaat, 1982). The nuclear freeze movement in the United States emphasized first bilateralism, then gradual step-wise reciprocal moratoriums and reductions in certain categories of weaponry. Similarly, and even more aggressively, a significant component of the West European peace movements criticized Soviet conduct generally, SS-20 weapons specifically, and the repression of democratic movements in Eastern Europe, particularly martial law in Poland.

Although NATO governments continued to use the repression of human rights in the East to discredit their own oppositional movements, most peace groups refused to allow their governments to define the dissident position. By criticizing the Soviets and state communism on the same grounds, activists challenged the East to do better, and publicly questioned the efficacy of the policy of containment in doing anything to improve the prospects for human rights and democracy. Peace movement criticism of both superpowers aided in establishing and preserving the credibility of campaigns specifically designed to influence the policies of the West. Even more important over the long run, however, were efforts explicitly designed to undermine balance of power politics and support ways to establish an alternative world order. A long term goal of undermining the bloc system established in Yalta, articulated most clearly and frequently by END founder E.P. Thompson (1982), animated many of the West European movements. Alternative paradigms differed significantly in the details, but activists were aggressive in seeking to demonstrate how their proposals would provide a more hopeful route to political democratization than containment.[6]

The Western movements also promoted new ideas of national defense which would allow this to happen. Peace activism served as impetus for research on alternative defense postures and common security paradigms. Peace groups provided forums for discussion of these issues, and published and disseminated the ideas.[7] Although security planners in the West were reluctant to acknowledge, much less accept these approaches, Soviet leaders adopted Western peace movement proposals one after another, beginning with the adoption of a "no first use" declaration on nuclear weapons, then calling for a test ban, a nuclear freeze, nuclear weapons free zones, common security, and non-offensive defense (Wettig, 1988).

CHANGE FROM BELOW, TRANSNATIONALISM, AND NEW POLITICS

These efforts supported and publicized the work of dissidents in the East. END and other peace groups provided forums for exiled dissidents such as East Germans Rudolf Bahro and Wolf Biermann, explicitly making common cause with the insurgent forces, rather than the governments, of the East. Publicity strengthened the reformers and human rights activists, helping to establish a powerful and legitimate alternative outside of government. Most importantly, peace activists in the West and the East looked beyond their governments to develop a new peace process.

In order to understand the role that transnational contacts played in strengthening dissidents in both blocs, it is useful to begin by reviewing the strategies emerging for democratic change within the East bloc. The structure of political institutions and alignments in a state, what scholars (e.g. Kitschelt, 1986; Rochon, 1988; Tarrow, 1989; Tilly, 1978) have called the "structure of political opportunity," constrains dissident activists' choices about issues, strategies, and tactics. Within Eastern Europe, the available political space for dissent was severely circumscribed by Soviet military power. For activists, the invasions of Hungary in 1956 and Czechoslovakia in 1968 underscored the impossibility of conventional national independence movements, and the difficulty of establishing even a reform oriented Communist government. The dominance of the party over not only gov-

---

6. cf., Forsberg (1984) who argues that liberalization in Eastern Europe and the unification of Germany would follow the establishment of a non-intervention regime; and Ammon and Brandt (1982) who contend that the unification of Germany would be a first step toward untangling the blocs.
7. See Herf (1986) who, in seeeking to discredit the importance of peace research institutes, overstates their importance. On alternative defense, see e.g., Galtung (1984), Kaldor (1983), Saperstein (1987), and Sharp (1985).

ernment, but virtually every facet of social life, stifled the development of reform movements or advocacy groups. The first step in initiating meaningful social change was working to develop autonomous social institutions and social life, what activists and analysts have called a "civil society."

According to Sarah Terry (1989), this analysis was first articulated by exiled Polish philosopher, Leszek Kolakowski in 1970, and served as a basis for building the workers' defense committees, a large number of unofficial political groups, and eventually Solidarity. The notion of inciting revolutionary changes not by seeking power, but by building an autonomous social sector, became the central tenet of the Eastern dissidents' theory of social change.

As improbable a notion for revolution as this might be, it was clearly far more hopeful than the model promised by Western containment, which Hungarian dissident George Konrad (1984) argued, reinforced the Yalta agreement and the system of blocs, virtually forcing the Soviet Union to respond in kind, and preventing internal reform. Even if one accepts the notion that Eastern reforms would come in response to Western pressure from above, this vision of change leaves little purpose to activity below, effectively isolating activists for democratic change. In contrast, the dissident model of change emphasized a congruity between means and ends, through positive social development as both a means and an end in itself. The clearest articulation of this approach is in Vaclav Havel's remarkable essay, "The Power of the Powerless," written shortly after the establishment of Charter 77, but before the Solidarity uprising in Poland. According to Havel (1985, 65), dissident movements "emerge, like the proverbial one-tenth of the iceberg visible above the water, from...the independent life of society...just as the independent life of society develops out of living within the truth..." The revolution begins when people live in truth, rather than *as if* the demands of the state had some validity (see also Michnik, 1982). For the dissidents, the key is instead to behave *as if* one's activity had the potential of effecting change. The first signs of openness from above unleashed insurgent movements that had been building for some time.

When Gorbachev demonstrated a new tolerance to innovation, independence, and diversity in the East bloc, Hungary and Poland responded quickly; indeed, in many ways the Hungarian economy served as a model for Soviet restructuring (Ash, 1989b; Gati, 1989; Schopflin, Tokes, and Volgyes, 1988; Shipler, 1989). In both cases, a strong and public opposition existed before the opportunity for reform was presented; in Hungary much of it within the Communist Party; in Poland, a broad range of government opponents and reformers grouped under the banner of the Solidarity trade union. As the summary below shows, most of the activity which comprised the revolutions of 1989 is not fully explained by Gorbachev's posture, nor can it be captured by an analytic approach which focuses on top-down reforms.

The roots of reform ran deeply in Hungary, and President Janos Kadar, who had taken power with the aid of the Soviet Union after the invasion of 1956, guided a continual and very gradual process of economic reform during his 31 years in office. These reforms preempted and coopted much of the potential pressure for change, as many dissidents saw the Kadar regime going about as far as possible without provoking Soviet intervention (e.g. Konrad, 1984). As a result, dissidents were not so estranged from either the state or the party as elsewhere in the East. Indeed, Kadar welcomed the opposition into government, including his initial successor, Karoly Grosz, a reformer promoted by Gorbachev and the Soviet Union. Grosz replaced Kadar in May 1988, at the Hungarian Socialist Worker's Party Conference (its first since 1957), when the party also endorsed a quicker pace of reform. The following summer, the party officially rehabilitated Imre Nagy, who had led the Hungarian government during the revolt of 1956, and Grosz was superceded by leaders more committed to reform. By October the party was split, when it officially announced both a name change. (to the Hungarian Socialist Party) and its intent to adopt a West European-style democratic socialist approach. This ushered in a series of multiparty elections.

The opposition in Poland had a more dramatic history (Ash, 1989b; Connor, 1980; Crighton, 1985; Karpinski, 1987; Terry, 1989; Wescheler, 1989; Weydenthal, 1980). Workers' revolts and dissent among intellectuals frequently erupted throughout the post-war period, but had been discontinuous, divided, and largely ineffectual. A wave of strikes during the summer of 1976 created a coalition between students, intellectuals and workers, symbolized by the formation of a committee for worker's self defense, KOR, then KSS-KOR. These intellectuals provided support and guidance for the Solidarity trade union movement when it emerged in the summer of 1980. Their presence helped make the trade union the leading edge of a much broader social movement. The movement grew and made substantial gains in negotiating with the government until General Jaruzelski declared martial law on December 13, 1981, outlawing Solidarity in the process. The movement continued, however, generating a *samizdat* literature, organizing house and church meetings, and continuing to develop a network of dissent and social action groups. The banned union staged a series of strikes in the summer of 1988, demonstrating sufficient strength to win new negotiations with Jaruzelski in February of 1989. These negotiations produced an agreement to hold free elections and ensure a gradual transition to democracy. When Solidarity demonstrated overwhelming support in the June elections, the timetable for transition was speeded, and a Solidarity-led government took control in August, 1989.

The governments of Czechoslavakia and East Germany had been far more resistant to reform efforts, producing the potential for faster and more violent conflicts in transition. In Czechoslavakia, dissent and civil society developed through Charter 77, an explicitly non-political defense of human rights (Skilling, 1985). The signatories, or Chartists, committed to monitor human rights. The existence of the Charter undermined what Miroslav Kusy (1985) called the ideology of "as if," by calling for a move to a socialist utopia, exposing what Czechoslavakia and existing socialism were not. The Chartists were consistent in refusing to establish an alternative political organization, or to address the state on its own terms. Rather, they worked to build a civil society through engaging in what they saw as normal life, writing, speaking, meeting, to the degree that the state allowed them to do so. In this context, the production of *samizdat* literature was a critical political activity. Czechoslavakia's persecution of the Chartists also demonstrated the nature of the state in which they lived. The invisibility of any opposition beyond the actual Chartists until the demonstrations of hundreds of thousands of people in the fall of 1989, seems to vindicate Havel's iceberg metaphor.

In Prague, a student led-march on November 17, 1989—one of many emerging across the country—provoked a violent response from riot police (Ash, 1990; Elon, 1990). Determinedly non-violent, the marchers lit candles, chanted, and sang, as they endured beatings from the police. In what came to be known as "the massacre," the police wounded more than 100 people, sparking a wave of similar marches across the country. Citizen-initiated marches, posters, and leaflets spurred the formation of a coordinating effort, "Civic Forum," a new human rights group which had grown out of Charter 77. The Soviet embassy in Prague received a Forum delegation with courtesy, making it clear to the Czechoslavakian government that it would not support military suppression of the rebellions, and the Soviets encouraged the government to undertake reforms. Lacking the capacity or will to put down the revolt, the government opened negotiations with the Forum; the President and his entire cabinet resigned on November 24. The Czechoslavakian parliament then appointed a coalition caretaker government, led by party reformers, which was also unable to reform quickly enough to stall the dissident movement. By the end of the year, the parliament elected playwright and Charter 77 dissident Vaclav Havel to administer the state until free elections could be held.

East Germany's communist leader, Erich Honecker remained resistant to calls for reform from either the Soviet Union or dissidents within the country (Ash, 1989a; Pond, 1990; Tismaneanu, 1989). The international environment provided increased pressure, however, as Czechoslavakia and Hungary allowed East Germans to pass through their borders en route to West Germany. Waves of immigrants from the East entered West Germany throughout the fall, and by October 7, when Gorbachev visited to commemorate East Germany's fortieth anniversary, the pressures on Honecker were immense. Demonstrators, coordinated by "New Forum," which had grown out of church-based peace and human rights movements, chanted "Gorby, Gorby," and, "No violence," as they faced beatings by police.

Gorbachev himself publicly warned Honecker on the necessity of reform. Within two weeks, the Communist Party forced Honecker to resign, recognizing the domestic and foreign policy costs of holding off the reforms sweeping neighboring countries. The Party replaced him with former state security chief, Egon Krenz. Rallies and protests continued, however, as did the exodus to the West. Seeking to stem the tide of emigration, Krenz ordered the Berlin wall opened on November 9, 1989. Krenz' past limited his credibility and his capacity to preside over reform, and the Communist Party ousted him less than a month later, establishing a caretaker government and calling for new elections. With widespread disenchantment with the government and the presence of an apparently viable alternative in unification with the West, the prospects for the continuation of two Germanies quickly evaporated.

Where religious institutions, another transnational and subnational actor, were accorded some room to operate in Eastern Europe, they provided political space and moral legitimacy to the emerging dissident movements. In Poland, the Catholic church provided a voice for human rights throughout the 1970s, and gained enhanced visibility and authority with the election of Pope John Paul II in 1977. The first Polish pope was consistent in his advocacy of human rights in the East, and his visit to Warsaw in June 1979 gave impetus to the emerging human rights struggle. Although the church's initiative was superceded by Solidarity one year later, during the 1980s, it served as a mediator between the state and the insurgents, and provided a space for meeting and support when the trade union was banned. Even Adam Michnik, an avowed atheist, consistently emphasized the importance of the Catholic church in protecting human rights (Hall, 1986; Nowak, 1982).

The church was also a critical asset to the human rights struggle in East Germany. Initially, its primary role was to provide support and guidance to young men opposed to compulsory military service; it had begun pressing for recognition of equivalent alternative service for conscientious objectors in the middle 1970s. By the 1980s, however, the Evangelical church provided a base of operations for an independent peace movement (Hall, 1986; Ramet, 1984; Sanford, 1983; Tismaneanu, 1989). In November 1980, the East German churches began an annual fall ritual of "peace weeks," ten days of prayer and remembrance against war. Out of the first peace week, young activists designed a patch of a Soviet statue showing a figure beating swords into ploughshares. (The choice to use a rendering of a Soviet statue as the symbol of a dissident independence movement reflected the sense of irony that characterized many of the democratic movements.)

The patch quickly became fashionable, and was banned by the government. Dissident youth then conspicuously displayed blank patches. In May 1981, a Christian group proposed that the parliament debate the introduction of alternative "Community Peace Service," a notion quickly rejected by the government. In January 1982, dissident Robert Havemann and Evangelical pastor Rainier Epplemann circulated the "Berlin Appeal," which called for nuclear disarmament in both the East and West, and the end to Soviet and American intervention in either Germany. The Church itself never officially supported the appeal, which eventually gained more than 2,000 signatures and invited state repression. Without Church support, Epplemann continued to play a leading role in the dissident movement, sending a letter to Honecker in 1985 which endorsed the earlier appeal, and called for the demilitarization of public life. In the next years, the independent peace movement began holding regular meetings with the West German Greens, who were critical players in the Western peace movements. In January 1989, the independent peace movement in Leipzig distributed a leaflet calling for "the democratic renewal of our society." It is important not to underestimate the power of such words, especially when the very production and distribution of documents constitutes a political act. Leipzig was the site of the first in a wave of marches that eventually toppled the East German government, and Epplemann was East Germany's last defense and disarmament minister.

The human rights movements in the East, including the independent peace movements, were publicized, supported, and encouraged by the Western peace movements. By the middle of the 1980s, the West German Greens held regular meetings with the independent peace movements in East Germany, even adopting the "swords into ploughshares" emblem in much of their own literature. Such meetings strengthened the resolve of Eastern activists, legitimating their efforts, and building their confidence (Tismaneanu 1989). When the Germanies were united, the Greens negotiated an electoral alliance with the independent "Civic Forum," including many of the activists who actually started the October revolution (although both wings of the alliance did badly at the polls) (Ash 1991). Both the Greens and the democratic activists of the East were upstaged by Chancellor Kohl and his promises of rapid unification and economic growth.

END played an even larger role in uniting activists in the West and East. The END appeal (Thompson and Smith 1981, 163–65), launched on April 28, 1980, called for a united and nuclear-free Europe, from "Poland to Portugal." In July of 1982, END held its first annual conference in Brussels, inviting human rights activists from the East to attend. The conference was an important political event, linking activists across the European continent in common effort, providing a forum for exchanging information and passing documents. Perhaps even more importantly, organizing the conference "as if" Eastern and Western Europe were not divided, and "as if" borders could be easily crossed, brought movement activists into conflict with their own governments through such seemingly mundane activity as obtaining visas (Chilton, 1990). END actively sought out and supported independent peace activists elsewhere in the East, snubbing the official communist party dominated peace committees. Instead, it published the work of Eastern dissidents, bringing their *samizdat* writings above ground— at least in the West (e.g., "Perugia Papers" 1984/5).

Since the Western peace movements shared with the Eastern activists the concern of making their nations more receptive to democratic reforms, the bases for alliance were obvious. While government officials in the West often accused their domestic peace movements of serving Soviet interests and ignoring the suppression of human rights, many of the notable Eastern dissidents expressed their support not for the Reagan approach to the East, but for the peace activists in the West, sensing a reciprocity in their efforts. Said Havel (Kavan and Tomin, eds. 1983, 42, as cited in Havel 1985, 22), "I consider these young, long-haired people who keep demonstrating for peace in various western cities and whom I saw almost daily when I was in jail, where we were forced to watch the TV news, to be my brothers and sisters: they aren't indifferent to the fate of the world and they voluntarily take upon themselves a responsibility outside the sphere of their own personal well-being, and that—though in more difficult circumstances—is exactly what we are doing."'

Despite the difficulties of transition, establishing essentially new governments staffed with committed and competent admistrators, rebuilding economies crippled by debt, and coping with a global recession, the longterm prospects for democracy in Poland, Hungary, Czechoslavakia, and Germany are good. They are much less so in Bulgaria and Romania, where revolutionary transitions have yet to bring about comparable restructuring. At Gorbachev's urging, the Bulgarian Communist Party ousted longtime leader Todor Zhivkov, and established new elections, which it won. A visible, much less coherent, opposition has yet to emerge. In Romania, Nicolae Ceacusescu refused all entreaties for reform from both the Soviet Union and the stifled opposition within his own country. The government violently suppressed protests in Timisoara, leading to thousands of deaths. As the protests continued, however, Romanian soldiers finally refused to fire on the citizens. By the end of the year, Ceausescu was overthrown, summarily tried, and executed. For a brief period, the transitional government filled state stores with food and other goods bound for foreign markets. New elections brought old allies of the dictator into power, however, and the potential for significant change is unclear. Thus we see that international pressure may induce a change at the top of a government without bringing about restructuring in society below.

Similarly, the prospects for successful reform in the Soviet Union are also unclear; Gorbachev's extensive restructuring has engendered substantial criticism from both conservatives and more radical reformers. He has also been considerably less tolerant to independence movements and reformers within the Soviet Union than those in Eastern Europe. Throughout much of 1990, Gorbachev installed old-line Communist Party loyalists in high positions in government to stave off the challenge from his right. When Gorbachev began shifting his policies to favor the reformers in 1991, these new appointees attempted a coup against him. The coup's failure, primarily due to the challenging junta's inability to control the apparatus of repression and the strong resistance from the grassroots, suggests that the reformers will be stronger in the near future, and that a true civil society is taking root. This history, however, is just beginning to unfold.

CONCLUSION

In this chapter, I have shown the connections between the East European movements for human rights and the peace movements in the United States and Western Europe, and the ways in which these movements influenced the revolutions of 1989, and could continue to influence the developing post-cold war order. The case here has been suggested, not proven unequivocally, and several issues merit more discussion, research, and debate.

I contend that domestic unrest in the United States and Western Europe influenced Western policy, circumscribing further military build-ups after 1984, and forcing leaders to adopt a more conciliatory posture toward the Soviet Union, resurrecting the arms control regime in the process. Even peace activists are not unanimous on this point, some emphasizing the limits, rather than the extent of the movements' achievements. Clearly, Pershing II and cruise missiles were deployed in Western Europe, an unambiguous defeat for the European movements. However, the latest arms control proposals by Bush nad Garbychev in the fall of 1991 offer some hope. Such unevenness suggests a more complicated process of exercising influence. We need more historical studies of the relationship between protest and policy, and the ways in which dissident movements have influenced policy (Meyer, 1991a,b).

I argue that the peace movements provided a conduit for new ideas about security to both Eastern Europe and the Soviet Union, ideas ultimately expressed by the Soviet leadership. There is a great deal of circumstantial evidence on this point, but this issue is important enough to merit extensive studies tracing the movement and development of specific ideas. As more documents from the Soviet Union become available to scholars, it is important to undertake such process-tracing research. It is especially important to examine the internal debates within the Soviet Union's leadership about reform. In this way, we can discover how the decisionmakers themselves responded to various Western initiatives.

Finally, I also contend that the development of autonomous political institutions in Eastern Europe, or "civil society," provided a basis and direction for major reforms. Here too, there is strong circumstantial evidence, but the history of the 1989 revolutions needs to be written, and the distinct processes of change in each country need to be described and analyzed. The relative nonviolence of the transitions in Hungary, Poland, East Germany, and Czechoslavakia, especially in comparison with Romania, underscores the importance of autonomous institutions and political opportunity structures. In Romania, where Ceaucescu prevented the emergence of any independent institutions, dissent has been spontaneous and violent, and democratic values or institutions seem to be totally undeveloped. In contrast, in Hungary where the Communist party itself accomodated change, distinctions between conservatives and reformers are more difficult to draw, but stability seems ensured. In Czechoslavakia, where the government offered no access or tolerance to dissidents, the government has been completely replaced by a wide variety of leaders with autonomous bases of support, unidentified by a common program or approach. Large long-established institutions have played a large role in Poland and East Germany. The Catholic Church has had an important influence in shaping post-cold war Poland, as the only non-Communist institution with established authority. Independent East German institutions were stalled in their development because of the ever present alternative of grafting the state to West Germany. The West German parties, for example, quickly expanded to include the new territory, replacing the outmoded state communist institutions exogenously. These events suggest that there are critical research questions on the influence of state structures and independent political institutions in shaping dissent. The details of these transitions, and of course the ultimate implications of different paths of political development, provide the promise of answering these questions, and an ample agenda for a generation of scholars.

Arguments that subnational and transnational forces have an important impact on international security, as I have articulated here, often find little support within mainstream literature on international relations. This is a significant deficit in the dominant theories, and it merits analytic remedy. Clearly, as this analysis shows, a focus on the state can be myopic if it excludes the environment within which states operate. I suggest a broader and more inclusive approach to our studies of history and security. There is much more systematic thinking, theory building, and research to be done. More immediately important, a narrative which finds a place for grassroots activism in critical historic events calls for a reevaluation of policy. If grassroots activism, citizen diplomacy, and military restraint were effective strategies for supporting internal democratic reform in Eastern Europe and the Soviet Union, we should consider what this means for subsequent democratic movements and security problems. Above all else, we should consider not only optimum state policies, but how we as citizens can implement them.

References

Adams, G. 1984. *The Iron Triangle. The Politics of Defense Contracting.* New York: Council on Economic Priorities.

Adkin, M. 1989. *Urgent Fury: The Battle for Grenada.* Lexington: Lexington Books.

Aggarwal, V. K. et al. 1987. The Dynamics of Negotiated Protectionism. *American Political Science Review* 81(2):345–366.

Aggawal, V. 1985. *Liberal Protectionism: The International Politics of Organized Textile Trade* Berkeley: University of California Press.

Alber, J. 1989. Modernization, Cleavage Structures, and the Rise of Green Parties and Lists in Europe. In *New Politics in Western Europe,* edited by F. Muller-Rommel, 175–194. Boulder, CO: Westview Press.

Aldrich, J. L. et al. 1989. Foreign Affairs and Issue Voting: Do Presidential Candidates Waltz Before a Blind Audience? *American Political Science Review* 83(1):123–141.

Alger, C. 1984-5. Bridging the Micro and the Macro in International Relations Research. *Alternatives.* (Winter):319-344.

Alger, C. 1990. The World Relations of Cities: Closing the Gap Between Social Science Paradigms and Everyday Human Experience, in *International Studies Quarterly,* Volume 34, Number 4, Dec. 1990.

Allison, G. 1969. Conceptual Models and the Cuban Missile Crisis. *American Political Science Review* 63: 698-718.

Allison, G. 1971. *The Essence of Decision: Explaining the Cuban Missile Crisis.* Boston: Little, Brown.

Almond. G. 1950. *The American People and Foreign Policy.* New York: Harcourt Brace.

American Heritage. 1969. *The American Heritage Dictionary of the English Language* Boston: Houghton Mifflin.

Ammon, H. and P. Brandt. 1982. The German Question. *Telos.* (Spring):32-44.

Appleton, S. 1975. The Role of the Opposition in Foreign Policymaking. In *Foreign Policy Analysis,* edited by R. Merritt, 55–60 Lexington, Mass.: Lexington Books.

Arian, A., I. Talmud, and T. Hermann. 1988. *National Security and Public Opinion in Israel.* Boulder, Co.: Westview Press.

Arian, A. 1989 A People Apart: Coping with National Security Problems in Israel. *Journal of Conflict Resolution,* (33): 605–631.

Arkin, W. M. 1989. The Buildup that Wasn't. *Bulletin of the Atomic Scientists.* (January-February):6-10.

Art, R. 1973. Bureaucratic Politics and American Foreign Policy: A Critique. *Policy Sciences.* 4 (4): 467-490.

Ash, T. G. 1991. Germany at the Frontier. *The New York Review of Books.* (January 17):21-22.

Ash, T. G. 1989a. The German Revolution. *The New York Review of Books*. (December 21):14-19.

Ash, T. G. 1989b. Revolution in Hungary and Poland. *The New York Review of Books*. (August 17):9-15.

Ash, T. G. 1990. The Revolution of the Magic Lantern. *The New York Review of Books*. (January 18):42-51.

Ashley, R. K. and R.B.J. Walker. 1990. Speaking the Language of Exile: Dissident Thought in International Studies in *International Studies Quarterly*, vol. 34, No. 3.

Avarbanel, M. and B. Hughes 1975. Public Attitudes and Foreign Policy Behavior in Western Democracies. In *The Analysis of Foreign Policy Outputs*, edited by W. Chittick, 46–72. Columbus, Ohio: Charles Merrill.

Azar, E.E., C.A. McClelland, and R.A. Brody, eds. 1972. *International Events Interaction Analysis*. Beverly Hills, CA: Sage Publications.

Bar On, M. 1985. *Peace Now: A Portrait of a Movement*. Tel Aviv: Hakibutz Hameuhad. [In Hebrew.]

Barber, J. and M. Spicer. 1979. Sanctions Against South Africa—Options for the West. *International Affairs* 55:385-401.

Barnett, M. 1990. High Politics is Low Politics: The Domestic and Systemic Sources of Israeli Security Policy, 1967-77. *World Politics*. 42 (4): 529-562.

Barnett, M. and Levy, J. 1991. Domestic Sources of Alliances and Alignments: The Case of Egypt, 1962-73. *International Organization*, 45 (3): 369-395. 67

Barron, John. 1982. The KGB's Magical War for Peace. *Reader's Digest*. (October):206-59.

Barzilai, G. 1987. Democracy in War—Attitudes, Reactions and Political Participation of the Israeli Public in Processes of Decision Making. The Hebrew University, Jerusalem. Ph.D diss. [In Hebrew.]

Bauer, R., I. Poole, and L. Dexter. 1963. *American Business and Public Policy*. New York: Atherton.

Ben Gurion. D. 1950. On War and Immigration Absorption (excerpts from a speech in Ein Harod). Cited in *"Ihud" Bulletin Ner* (28.4.50). [In Hebrew.]

Bennett, W. L. 1988. *News: The Politics of Illusion*. New York: Longman Inc.

Berry, J. 1989. *The Interest Group Society*. Glenville, Il.: Scott, Foresman.

Bialer, U. 1980. *East and West: Israel's Foreign Policy Orientation*. 1948–1956. Cambridge: Cambridge University Press.

Birand, M. A. 1988. A Turkish View of Greek-Turkish Relations. *Journal of Political and Military Sociology* 16 (Fall):173-83.

Bissell, R. 1982. *South Africa and the United States: The Erosion of an Influence Relationship*. New York: Praeger.

Blank, S. 1978. Britain: The Politics of Foreign Economic Policy, the Domestic Economy, and the Problems of Pluralistic Stagnation. In Katzenstein (1978) 89–138.

Blau, P. M. 1967. *Exchange and Power in Social Life*. New York: John Wiley and Sons.

Blechman, B. M. and Kaplan, S. S. 1978. *Force Without War: U.S. Armed Forces as a Political Instrument*. Washington D.C.: Brookings.

Bloom, J. 1986. *Black South Africa and the Disinvestment Dilemma*. Johannesburg: Jonathan Ball Publishers.

Bobrow, D. 1989. Japan in the World: Opinion from Defeat to Success. *Journal of Conflict Resolution* 33 (4):571–603.

Boggs, C. 1986. *Social Movements and Political Power*, Philadelphia: Temple University Press.

Boswell, T. and R. Peters. 1990. State Socialism and the Industrial Divide in the World Economy: A Comparative Essay on the Rebellions in Poland and China. *Critical Sociology*. (Fall):3-34.

Boyer, P. 1986. *By the Bomb's Early Light: American Thought and Culture at the Dawn of the Nuclear Age*. New York: Pantheon.

Brecher, E. 1972. *The Consumers Union Report: Licit and Illicit Drugs* Boston: Little, Brown.

Brecher, E. 1975. *Decisions in Israel's Foreign Policy*. New Haven: Yale University Press.

Brecher, M. 1972. *The Foreign Policy System of Israel: Setting, Images, Process*. New Haven: Yale University Press.

Brock, P. 1972. *Pacifism in Europe to 1914*. Princeton: Princeton University Press.

Brown, A. 1989. Political Change in the Soviet Union. *World Policy Journal*. (Summer)471-.

Bruun, K., L. Pan, and I. Rexed. 1974. *The Gentleman's Club: International Control of Drugs and Alcohol* Chicago: University of Chicago Press.

Bueno de Mesquita, B. 1981. *The War Trap*. New Haven: Yale University Press.

Bukovsky, V. 1982. The Peace Movement and the Soviet Union. *Commentary*. (May):19-26.

Bunce, V. 1990. The Struggle for Liberal Democracy in Eastern Europe. *World Policy Journal*. (Summer):397-430.

Bundy, M. 1989. The Emperor's Clothes. *The New York Review of Books*. (July 20):5-8.

Burrows, R. A. 1988. *Revolution and Rescue in Grenada: An Account of the U.S.-Caribbean Invasion*. New York: Greenwood Press.

Burt, R. 1979a. Money Is Already Starting to Flow From Both Sides in Treaty Debate. *New York Times*, January 23: A-12.

Burt, R. 1979b. A New Approach to Selling the Arms Pact. *New York Times*, April 6: A-11.

Burt, R. 1979c. Ex-Aides Assail Soviet Arms Treaty. *New York Times*, April 12: A-13.

Burt, R. 1979d. Senator Nunn Sees U.S. Arms-Lag Peril. *New York Times*, May 1: A-5.

Burt, R. 1979e. At Arms Length: The Chances for SALT II May Improve with Time. *New York Times*, May 13: section 4, 1.

Burt, R. 1979f. Vance Warns that Senate Changes Could Doom Arms-Limitation Pact. *New York Times*, May 14: A-13.

Burt, R. 1979g. In a Diplomatic Corner. *New York Times*, Sept. 14: A-1.

Burt, R. 1979h. Some U.S. Aides Fear a Directive by Carter Will Slow Arms Curbs. *New York Times*, September 21: A-12.

Burt, R. 1979i. Are the Russians Outspending the U.S. on Weapons? *New York Times*, September 23: Section IV, 3.

Burt, R. 1979j. Carter Accepting Substantial Rise in Arms Budget. *New York Times*, November 29: A-1.

Burt, R. 1979k. Senate Panel l Votes Anti-Treaty Report New York Times, December 21: A-10.

Burton, J. 1972. *World Society*. Cambridge: Cambridge University Press.

Bühl, W. 1978. *Transnationale Politik. Internationale Beziehungen zwischen Hegemonie und Interdependenz*. Stuttgart: Klett-Cotta.

Calder, K. 1988. *Crisis and Compensation: Public Policy and Political Stability in Japan, 1949–1986* Princeton NJ: Princeton University Press.

Caldwell, D. 1990. The SALT II Treaty Ratification Debate. Unpublished manuscript presented at the Annual Meeting of the International Studies Association held April 10–14 in Washington, D.C.

Callahan, P., L. P. Brady, and M. G. Hermann, eds. 1982. *Describing Foreign Policy Behavior.* Beverly Hills, CA: Sage Publications.

Cardoso, F. H. 1973. *Sociologie du developpement en Amériquelatine.* Paris.

Carter, J. 1982. *Keeping Faith: Memoirs of a President.* New York: Bantam Books.

Caspary, W. R. 1970) The Mood Theory: A Study of Public Opinion and Foreign Policy. *American Political Science Review,* (64): 536–47.

Chan, S. 1984. Mirror, Mirror on the Wall. Are the Freer Countries more Pacific? *Journal of Conflict Resolution* 28(3):617–648.

Charlton, L. 1977. Groups Favoring Strong Defense Making Gains in Public Acceptance. *New York Times,* April 4: 50.

Chilton, P. 1990. Transnational Relations and the End of the Cold War. Unpublished talk delivered at Harvard University Center for International Affairs, November 28.

Chomsky, N. and Herman, E. 1988. *Manufacturing Consent.* New York: Pantheon.

Clogg, R. 1987. *Parties and Elections in Greece.* London: C. Hurst.

Clymer, A. 1979. G.O.P. Leaders Support Dissent in Foreign Policy. *New York Times,* February 4: A-1.

Cohen, B. 1983. The Influence of Special Interest Groups and Mass Media on Security Policy in the United States. In *Perspectives on American Foreign Policy,* edited by Charles Kegley and Eugene Wittkopf, 222–41. New York: St. Martins Press.

Cohen, B. and M. El-Khawas. 1975. *The Kissinger Study of Southern Africa.* Nottingham: Spokesman Books.

Cohen, B. J. 1990. The political economy of international trade. *International Organization* 44(2):261–281.

Coker, C. 1987. *British Defence Policy in the 1990s. A Guide to the Defence Debate.* London: Brassey's Defence Publisher.

Coker, C. 1986. *The United States and South Africa, 1968–1985.* Durham, NC Duke University Press.

Collier, R. B. 1982. *Regimes in Tropical Africa.* Los Angeles: University of California Press.

Comisso, E. 1986. Introduction: State Structures, Political Processes, and Collective Choice in CMEA States. *International Organization* 40:195-238.

Connor, W. D. 1980. Dissent in Eastern Europe: A New Coalition. *Problems of Communism.* (January-February):1-17.

Cortright, D. 1991. Assessing Peace Movement Effectiveness in the 1980s. *Peace and Change.* 16:46-63.

Cottam, R. W. 1977. *Foreign Policy Motivations.* Pittsburgh: University of Pittsburgh Press.

Coufoudakis, V. 1988. Greek Foreign Policy Since 1974: Quest for Independence. *Journal of Modern Greek Studies* 6 (May):55-79.

Couloumbis, T. A. 1983. The Structures of Greek Foreign Policy. In *Greece in the 1980s,* edited by Richard Clogg, 95-122. London: Macmillan.

Cox, A. M. 1980. The CIA's Tragic Error. *The New York Review of Books,* 27: 21–24.

Crabb, C. and P. Holt. 1980. *Invitation to Struggle: Congress, the Presidency and Foreign Policy*. Washington, D.C.: CQ Press.

Crawford, A. 1980. *Thunder on the Right: The New Right and the Politics of Resentment*. New York: Pantheon.

Crighton, E. 1985. Resource Mobilization and Solidarity: Comparing Social Movements Across Regimes. in Bronislaw Misztal, ed., *Poland After Solidarity*. New Brunswick, NJ: Transaction, 113-132.

Cowell, A. 1986. Mixed Signals To Pretoria. *New York Times* 21 October, p. D30.

Czempiel, E.-O. 1963. Der Primat der auswärtigen Politik. *Politische Vierteljahresschrift* 4:266-287.

Czempiel, E.-O. 1979. *Amerikanische Außenpolitik*. Stuttgart: Kohlhammer.

Czempiel, E.-O. 1981. *Internationale Politik*. Paderborn: Schöningh.

Czempiel, E.-O. 1986. *Friedensstrategien*. Paderborn: Schöningh.

Czempiel, E.-O. 1989a. *Machtprobe. Die USA und die Sowjetunionin den achtziger Jahren*. München: Beck.

Czempiel, E.-O. 1989b. Internationalizing Politics: Some Answers to the Question of Who Does What to Whom. In E.O. Czempiel and J. N. Rosenau (1989)

Czempiel, E.-O. and Rosenau, J. N. eds. 1989. *Global Changes and Theoretical Challenges* Lexington MA: Lexington Books.

Czerwick, E. and Muller, H. 1976. Rüstungskonzerne, ökonomisches Interesse und das Konzept des 'militärisch-industriellen Komplexes.' *Friedensanalysen* (6):153-177. Frankfurt/M.: Suhrkamp.

Dahl, Robert A., ed. 1973. *Regimes and Oppositions*. New Haven, CT: Yale University Press.

Dalton, R. J. 1988. *Citizen Politics in WesternDemocracies*. Chatham, N.J.: Chatham House.

Danaher, K. 1984. *In Whose Interest? A Guide to U.S.-South Africa Relations*. Washington D.C.: Institute for Policy Studies.

Danaher, K. 1985. *The Political Economy of U.S. Policy Toward South Africa*. Boulder, CO: Westview Press.

Daoudi, M. and M. Dajani. 1983. *Economic Sanctions* Boston: Routledge and Kegan Paul.

Davenport, J. 1982. The Impact of Economic Sanctions Against South Africa on the Strategic Mineral Position of the United States. Ph.D. Dissertation. New York: Columbia University.

Davies, J. 1962. Toward a Theory of Revolution. *American Sociological Review* 6(February):5-19.

Davies, J. 1986. Roots of Political Behavior. In *Political Psychology*, edited by Margaret G. Hermann, 39-61. San Francisco: Jossey-Bass.

De Rivera, J. 1968. *The Psychological Dimensions of Foreign Policy*. Columbus, Oh.: Merrill.

DeBenedetti, C. 1980. *The Peace Reform in American History*. Bloomington: Indiana University Press, 1980.

Dehio, L. 1961. Ranke und der deutsche Imperialismus. In *Deutschland und die Weltpolitik im 20. Jahrhundert*, ed. L. Dehio, 33-62. Munich.

Destler, I. 1974. *Presidents, Bureaucrats and Foreign Policy: The Politics of Organizational Reform*. Princeton: Princeton University Press.

Destler, I. M. 1978/79. Treaty Troubles: Versailles in Reverse. *Foreign Policy*, 33: 45-65.

Deutsch, K. W. 1966. External Influences on the Internal Behavior of States. In *Approaches to Comparative and International Politics*, ed. R.B. Farrell, 5–26. Evanston IL: Northwestern University Press.

Dimitras, P. E. 1985. Greece: A New Danger. *Foreign Policy* 58 (Spring): 134-50.

Dixon, J. 1984. The Congressional Black Caucus and U.S. Policy in Southern Africa. *Africa Report* 29:12–15 (May-June).

Dollard, J., L. W. Doob, N. E. Miller, O.H. Mowrer, and R. R. Sears. 1967. *Frustration and Aggression*. New Haven, CT: Yale University Press.

Doran, C. and Parsons, W. 1980. War and the Cycle of Relative Power. *American Political Science Review* 74: 947-965.

Doty, P. 1987. A Nuclear Test Ban. *Foreign Affairs*. (Spring):750-769.

Downs, A. 1957. *An Economic Theory of Democracy* New York: Random House.

Doxey, M. 1987. *International Sanctions in Contemporary Perspective*. New York: St. Martins Press.

Doyle, M. 1983. Kant, Liberal Legacies, and Foreign Affairs. *Philosophy and Public Affairs* 12(4):323–353.

Doyle, M. 1986. Liberalism and World Politics. *American Political Science Review* 80(4):1151–1169.

Duvall, R. and M. Stohl. 1983. "Governance by Terror." In *The Politics of Terrorism*, edited by Michael Stohl. New York: Marcel Dekker, Inc.

East, M. A., S. A. Salmore, and C. F. Hermann, eds. 1978. *Why Nations Act*. Beverly Hills, CA: Sage Publications.

Easton, D. 1953. *The Political System: An Inquiry into the State of Political Science*. New York: Knopf.

Easton D. 1965. *A Systems Analysis of Political Life*. New York: John Wiley.

Eberwein, W.-D. and Siegmann, H. 1985. *Bedrohung oder Selbstgefährdung? Die Einstellungen sicherheitspolitischer Führungs-schichten aus fünf Ländern zur Sicherheitspolitik*. West Berlin: International Institute for Comparative Social Research, Science Center Berlin.

Eckstein, H. 1975. "Case Study and Theory in Political Science." In Fred I. Greenstein and Nelson W. Polsby, eds. *Handbook of Political Science*. vol. 7. Reading, MA: Addison-Wesley, 79-138.

Edelman, M. 1977. *Political Language: Words That Succeed and Policies That Fail*. New York: Academic Press inc.

Eichenberg, R. 1989. *Public Opinion and National Security in Western Europe*. Ithaca NY: Cornell University Press.

Elon, A. 1990. Letter from Jerusalem. *The New Yorker*, April 23, 1990, 92–101.

Elon, A. 1990. Prague Autumn. *The New Yorker*. (January 2):125-132.

Evangelista, M. 1988. *Innovation and the Arms Race. How the United States and the Soviet Union Develop New Military Technologies*. Ithaca NY: Cornell University Press.

Evangelista, M. 1989. Issue-area and foreign policy revisited. *International Organization* 43(1):147–171.

Evangelista, M. 1990a. Sources of Moderation in Soviet Security Policy, in Robert Jervis, Philip Tetlock et al., eds., *Behavior, Society, and Nuclear War*. Vol. 2. New York: Oxford University Press, 255-354.

Evangelista, M. 1990b. Soviet Scientists as Arms Control Advisers: The Case of ABM. University of Michigan, unpublished paper, June.

Evangelista, Matthew. 1990c. Transnational Alliances and Soviet Demilitarization, University of Michigan, unpublished paper.

Evans, P.B. et al. eds. 1985. *Bringing the State Back In*. Cambridge: Cambridge University Press.

Evans, P. 1989. Declining Hegemony and Assertive Industrialization: U.S.-Brazil Conflicts in the Computer Industry. *International Organization* 43:207-38.

Evans, P. 1979. *Dependent Development: The Alliance of Multinational, State and Local Capital in Brazil*. Princeton: Princeton University Press.

Evans, R. and R. Novak 1977. A Complaint from the Democratic Cente. *Washington Post*, January 31: A-19.

Everts, P. 1983. *Public Opinion, the Churches, and Foreign Policy in the Netherlands*. Leiden: Institute for International Studies.

Everts, P. 1985. *Controversies at Home: Domestic Factors in the Foreign Policy of the Netherlands*. Dordrecht: M. Nijhoff.

Everts, P. 1990. The Peace Movement and Public Opinion. Paper presented at the 13th General Conference of the International Peace Research Association, The Netherlands, Groningen, July 1990.

Everts, P. and Faber, A. 1990. Public Opinion, Foreign Policy, and Democracy. Paper presented at the Workshop on "ForeignPolicy, Public Opinion, and the Democratic Process," European Consortium of Political Research, Bochum. 2–7 April.

Everts, P. 1991. Continuity and Change in Public Attitudes on Questions of Security in the Netherlands: The Role of the Peace Movement. In *Debating National Security*. ed. H. Rattinger and D.Munton: 203–238. Frankfurt/M.: Peter Lang.

Falk, R. 1987. The Global Promise of Social Movements: Explorations at the Edge of Time, *Alternatives*, XII.

Fallows, J. 1986. The Spend-Up. *The Atlantic Monthly*. (July):27.

Fascell, D. 1987. Congress and Arms Control. *Foreign Affairs*. (Spring):730-749.

Featherstone, K. and D. K. Katsoudas. 1987. *Political Change in Greece Before and After the Colonels*. New York: St. Martin's Press.

Felder, B. 1986. I.B.M. To Pull Out From South Africa As Problems Grow. *New York Times* 22 October, 1, D22.

Ferguson, T. and J. Rogers 1980. The Empire Strikes Back. *The Nation*, 231: 436–40.

Ferguson, T. 1984. From Normalcy to New Deal: Industrial Structure, Party Competition and American Public Policy in the Great Depression. *International Organization*. 34 (1): 95-129.

Finn, J. 1985. The Peace Movement in the United States. In *The Peace Movements in Europe and the United States*, edited by W. Kaltfleiter and R. Pfaltzgraff 162–72. New York: St. Martins Press.

Fitzsimmons, B. et al. 1969. *World Event Interaction Survey Handbook and Codebook*. World Event Interaction Survey Technical Report 1, University of Southern California, January.

Flynn, G. and Rattinger, H. eds. 1985. *The Public and Atlantic Defense*. London: Croom Helm.

Foltz, W. 1978. U.S. Policy Toward Southern Africa: Economic and Strategic Constraints. In American Policy in Southern Africa: The Stakes and the Stance, edited by R. LeMarchand, 279–307. Washington: University Press of America.

Forde, S. 1986. Thucydides and the Causes of Athenian Imperialism. *American Political Science Review* 80(2):433–448.

Forsberg, R. 1984. The Freeze and Beyond: Confining the Military to Defense as a Route to Disarmament. *World Policy Journal.* (Winter):287-318.

Franck, T. and E. Weisband 1979. *Foreign Policy by Congress.* New York: Oxford University Press.

Frank, A. G. 1969. *Capitalism and Underdevelopment in Latin America.* New York: Monthly Review Press.

Freedman, L. 1983. *The Evolution of Nuclear Strategy* . New York: St. Martin's.

Frieden, J. 1988. Sectoral Conflict and Foreign Economic Policy, 1914-1940. In *The State and American Foreign Economic Policy,* edited by G. John Ikenberry G. J., David Lake and Michael Mastanduno, eds. *The State and American Economic Policy* Ithaca: Cornell University Press.

Friman, H. 1990. *Patchwork Protectionism: Textile Trade Policy in the United States, Japan, and West Germany* Ithaca: Cornell University Press.

Fukuyama, F. 1989. The End of History? *The National Interest.* Vol. 16 (Summer):3-18.

Gaddis, J. L. 1989. Hanging Tough Paid Off. *Bulletin of the Atomic Scientists.* (January-February):11-14.

Gaddis, J. L. 1987. *The Long Peace.* New York: Oxford University Press.

Gallhofer, I. N. and Saris, W.E. 1979. Strategy Choices of Foreign Policy Decision Makers. *Journal of Conflict Resolution* 23: 425-445.

Gallup G. 1981-1991., *The Gallup Report.* Princeton: Gallup Poll.

Gallup, G. 1979. *The Gallup Poll: Public Opinion, 1978.* Wilmington, Del.: Scholarly Resources.

Galtung, J. 1975-80. *Essays in Peace Research. vol. 1-5.* Copenhagen: Ejlers.

Galtung, J. 1984. Foreign Policy Opinion as a Function of Social Position. *Journal of Peace Research,* I (1964):206-31.

Galtung, J. 1984. *There are Alternatives.* Nottingham: Spokesman.

Gantzel, K.-J. 1987. Tolstoi statt Clausewitz!? Überlegungen zum Verhältnis von Staat und Krieg seit 1816 mittels statistischer Beobachtungen. *Kriegsursachen. Friedensanalysen* (21):25-97.Frankfurt/M.: Suhrkamp.

Garthoff, R. 1984. *Detente and Confrontation: American-Soviet Relations from Nixon to Reagan.* Washington D.C.: Brookings.

Gati, C. 1989. Reforming Communist Systems: Lessons from the Hungarian Experience. in Griffith, ed., (1989):218-240.

Gaubatz, K. 1991. Election Cycles and War. *Journal of Conflict Resolution* 35: 212-244.

Gelb, L. and R. Halloren 1983. CIA Analysis Now Said to Find U.S. Overstated Soviet Arms Rise. *New York Times,* March 3: A-1.

Geller, J. 1988. *Domestic Factors in Foreign Policy. A Cross-National Statistical Analysis.* Cambridge MA.

George, A. L. 1979. "Case Studies and Theory Development: The Method of Structured, Focused Comparison." In Paul G. Lauren, ed. *Diplomacy: New Approaches in History, Theory and Policy.* New York: Free Press, 43-68.

George, A.L.1980. Domestic Constraints on Regime Change in U.S. Foreign Policy: The Need for Policy Legitimacy. In *Change in the International System,* edited by O. Holsti, R.M. Siverson, and A.L. George, 233-63. Boulder, Co.: Westview Press.

Gerlach, L. P. 1983. Movements of Revolutionary Change: Some Structural Characteristics, in *Social Movements of the Sixties and Seventies,* edited by Jo Freeman. New York: Longman.

Gerlach, L. P and V. Hine. 1970. *People, Power, Change: Movements of Social Transformation*, Indianapolis: Bobbs Merrill.

Gerschenkron, A. 1962. *Economic Backwardness in Historical Perspective*. Cambridge MA: Belknap Press of Harvard University Press.

Gill, S. 1990. *American Hegemony and the Trilateral Commission*. Cambridge: Cambridge University Press.

Gilpin, R. 1981. *War and Change in World Politics*. New York:Cambridge University Press.

Gilpin, R. 1987. *The Political Economy of International Relations*. Princeton NJ: Princeton University Press.

Ginsberg, B. 1986. *The Captive Public: How Mass Opinion Promotes State Power*. New York: Basic Books.

Gleditsch, N.P. and Njøstad, O. eds. 1989. *Arms Races: Technological and Political Dynamics*. London: Sage.

Goldstein, J. 1988. Ideas, Institutions, and American Trade Policy. *International Organization* 42:179-218.

Gordon, M. 1974. Domestic Conflict and the Origins of the First World War: The British and the German Cases. *Journal of Modern History* 46:191–226.

Gourevitch, P. 1984. Breaking with Orthodoxy: The Politics of Economic Policy Responses to the Depression of the 1930s. *International Organization* 38:95-129.

Gourevitch, P. 1978. The Second Image Reversed: The International Sources of Domestic Politics. *International Organization* 32: 881–911.

Gourevitch, P. 1986. *Politics in Hard Times. Comparative Responses to International Economic Crises*. Ithaca NY: CornellUniversity Press.

Graham, T. 1988. The Pattern and Importance of Public Knowledge in the Nuclear Age. *Journal of Conflict Resolution* 32(2):319–334.

Graham, T. 1989. *American Public Opinion on NATO, Extended Deterrence, and Use of Nuclear Weapons*. Cambridge MA: Center for Science and International Affairs, Harvard University.

Grieco, J. 1990. *Cooperation Among Nations: Europe, America, and Non-Tariff Barriers to Trade* Ithaca: Cornell University Press.

Griffith, W. E. 1989. Central and Eastern Europe: The Global Context. 1-11. in Griffith, ed., *Central and Eastern Europe: The Opening Curtain?* Boulder, CO: Westview.

Guetzkow, H. 1963. *Simulation in International Relations: Developments for Research and Teaching*. Englewood Cliffs: Prentice Hall.

Gusfield, J. 1980. Social Movements and Social Change: Perspectives of Linearity and Fluidity. in Louis Kriesberg, ed., *Research in Social Movements, Conflict, and Change*. 317-339.

Gwertzman, B. and M. T. Kaufman, eds. 1990. *The Collapse of Communism*. NY: Random House/Times Books.

Habermas, J. 1981. New Social Movements, *Teleos*, No. 49, (Fall), pp. 33-37.

Habermas J. 1973. *Legitimation Crises*. Boston: Beacon Press.

Haftendorn, H. 1985. *Security and Détente. West German Foreign Policy 1955–1982*. New York: Praeger.

Hagan, J. D. 1987. Regimes, Political Oppositions, and the Comparative Analysis of Foreign Policy. In C.F. Hermann et al.(1987), 339–365.

Hagan, J. D. 1980. Regimes, Oppositions and foreign Policy: A Cross-National Analysis of the Impact of Domestic Politics on foreign Policy Behavior. Dissertation, University of Kentucky.

Hagan, J. 1987. Regimes, Political Oppositions, and the Comparative Analysis of Foreign Policy. In *New Directions in the Study of Foreign Policy*, edited by Charles F. Hermann et al, 339-65. Boston: Allen and Unwin.

Hagan, J. 1989. Conceptualizing Political Opposition for Comparative Foreign Policy Analysis. Paper presented at the 30th annual International Studies Association convention, London, United Kingdom, March 28-April 1.

Hagan, J. (Forthcoming) *Political Opposition and Foreign Policy in Comparative Perspective*. Boulder, CO: Lynne Rienner Publishers.

Haggard, S. 1988. The Institutional Foundations of Hegemony: Explaining the Reciprocal Trade Aggreements Act of 1934. In *The State and American Foreign Economic Policy*, edited by G. John Ikenberry, David Lake and Michael Mastanduno, 91-120. Ithaca: Cornell University Press.

Haggard, S. and B. Simmons 1987. Theories of International Regimes. *International Organization* 41:491-517.

Hall, B. Welling. 1986. The Church and the Independent Peace Movement in Eastern Europe. *Journal of Peace Research*. (June):193-208.

Hall, D. S. 1986. The Emergence and Structure of the Israeli Peace Movement. Master's thesis, Oxford University.

Hallenberg, J. 1990. The Image of the Soviet Union in American Politics: The Role of Public Interest Groups, 1977–1980. Unpublished manuscript presented at the Annual Meeting of the International Studies Association held April 10–14 in Washington, D.C.

Halperin, M. 1974. *Bureaucratic Politics and Foreign Policy*. Washington, D.C.: Brookings.

Hamilton, M., ed. 1986. *American Character and Foreign Policy*. Grand Rapids: Eerdmans.

Hanrieder, W. 1967. Compatibility and Consensus. A Proposal for the Conceptual Linkage of External and Internal Dimensions of Foreign Policy. *American Political Science Review* 61:971–982.

Hanrieder, W. F., ed. 1971. *Comparative Foreign Policy: Theoretical Essays*. New York: David McKay.

Harkavi. Y. 1986. *Fatal Decisions*. Tel Aviv: Am Oved. [In Hebrew.]

Hartz, L. 1955. *The Liberal Tradition in America*. New York: Harcourt, Brace.

Hattis, S.L.1970. *The Bi-National Idea in Palestine During Mandatory Times*. Haifa: Shikmona.

Hauck, D. 1986. *Can Pretoria Be Moved? The Emergence of Business Activism in South Africa*. Washington: Investor Responsibility Research Center.

Hauck, D., M. Voorhes, and G. Goldberg. 1983. *Two Decades of Debate: The Controversy Over U.S. Companies in South Africa*. Washington D.C.: Investor Responsibility Research Center.

Havel, V. 1985. The Power of the Powerless. 23-86 in Havel et al, *The Power of the Powerless*. Armonk, NY: M.E. Sharpe.

Hayes, J. 1987. *Economic Effects of Sanction on Southern Africa*. Brookfield, VT: Gower.

Heberle, R. 1951. *Social Movements: An Introduction to Political Sociology*, New York: Appleton-Century-Crofts.

Hegedus, Z. 1987. The Challenge of the Peace Movement: Civilian Security and Civilian Emancipation, *Alternatives*, XII

Heilbroner, R. 1990. Reflections: After Communism. *The New Yorker*. (September 10):91-100.

Herf, J. 1986. War, Peace, and the Intellectuals: The West German Peace Movement. *International Security*. (Spring):172-200.

Hermann, C.F. et al. eds. 1987. *New Directions in the Study of foreign Policy*. Boston: Allen&Unwin.

Hermann, M.G. and C.F. 1989. Who Makes Foreign Policy Decisions and How: An Empirical Inquiry. *International Studies Quarterly*, 33(4): 361-387.

Hermann, C. F. 1987. Political Opposition as Potential Agents of Foreign Policy Change: Developing a Theory. Paper presented at the 28th annual International Studies Association convention, Washington, DC, April 14-18.

Hermann, C. 1972. Policy Classification: A key to the Comparative Study of Foreign Policy. In *The Analysis of International Politics*, edited by J. Rosenau and V. Davis and M. East,58-79. New York: The Free Press.

Hermann, M. G., C. F. Hermann, and J. D. Hagan. 1987. "How Decision Units Shape Foreign Policy Behavior." In *New Directions in the Study of Foreign Policy*, edited by Charles F. Hermann, Charles W. Kegley, and James N. Rosenau, 309-36. Boston: Allen and Unwin.

Hermann, T. 1989. From Peace Covenant to Peace Now: The Pragmatic Pacifism of the Israeli Peace Camp in Comparative Perspective. Ph.D. diss., Tel Aviv University. [In Hebrew.]

Hermann, T. 1991. The Contemporary Peace Movements—Between the Hammer of Pacifism and the Anvil of Realism. Paper recently submitted for publication to the *Western Political Quarterly*.

Hilferding, R. 1910/1968. *Das Finanzkapital. Eine Studie über die jüngste Entwicklung des Kapitalismus*. Frankfurt/M.

Hilton, A. 1986. Impact of the Report of the Panel of Eminent Persons. *The CTC Reporter* 22:23-25.

Hintze, O. 1906. *Staatsverfassung und Heeresverfassung. In Staatund Verfassung. Gesammelte Abhandlungen zur allgemeinen Verfassungsgeschichte*, O. Hintze: 52-83. Göttingen.

Hogan, M. 1986. *The Panama Canal in American Politics: Domestic Advocacy and the Evolution of Policy*. Carbondale: Southern Illinois University Press.

Holloway, D. 1989-90. State, Society, and the Military Under Gorbachev. *International Security*. (Winter):5-42.

Holsti O. and J. Rosenau. 1984. *American Leadership in World Affairs*. Boston: Unwin and Allen.

Holsti, O. R. and Rosenau, J. N. 1986. Consensus Lost. Consensus Regained? Foreign Policy Beliefs of American Leaders 1976–1980. *International Studies Quarterly* 30(4):375-409.

Holsti, O.R. and Rosenau, J. N. 1988. The Domestic and Foreign Policy Beliefs of American Leaders. *Journal of Conflict Resolution* (322):248-294.

Holusha, J. 1986. G.M. Plans to Sell South Africa Unit To A Local Group. *New York Times* 20 October, 1, D30.

Holzman, F. 1980. Are the Soviets Really Outspending the U.S. on Defense? *International Security*, 4: 86-104.

Horowitz, D. 1985. *The Israeli Doctrine of National Security*. Jerusalem: The Hebrew University, Eshkol Institute. [In Hebrew.]

Hough, J. F. 1985-86. Beyond the Summit: Managing the US-Soviet Relationship. *World Policy Journal*. (Winter):1-28.

Hough, J. F. 1990. Gorbachev's Endgame: Positioning for Radical Reform. *World Policy Journal.* (Fall):639-672.

Howorth, J. and Chilton, P. eds. 1984. *Defence and Dissent in Contemporary France.* New York: St. Martin's Press.

Höll, O. ed. 1983. *Small States in Europe and Dependence.* Wien: Braunmüller.

Hrebenar, R. and R. Scott 1990. *Interest Group Politics in America.* Englewood Cliffs, N.J.: Prentice Hall, 2nd ed.

Hudson, V. M. 1984. "Domestic Opposition and Regime Foreign Policy Behavior: A Conceptual Investigation." Paper presented at the Annual Meeting of International Society of Political Psychologists. Toronto, June 23-24.

———. 1988. "Building an Explanatory Framework Linking Domestic Opposition and Regime Foreign Policy Behavior: Greek Politics and the Aegean Sea Incident." Paper presented at the 29th annual International Studies Association convention, St. Louis, MO, March 29-April 3.

Hudson, Valerie M. and Susan M. Sims. 1989. "Expected Foreign Policy Effects of Regime Response Tactics." Unpublished mimeo. Brigham Young University.

Hudson, V. and E. Singer 1992. *Political Psychology and Foreign Policy,* Boulder, CO: Westview Press.

Hufbauer, G. and J. Schott. 1985. *Economic Sanctions Reconsidered: History and Current Policy* Washington D.C.: Institute for International Economics.

Hughes, B. 1978. *The Domestic Context of American Foreign Policy.* San Francisco: W.H. Freeman.

Huntington, S. 1984. *Renewed Hostility. In The Making of America's Soviet Policy,* edited by Joseph Nye, 265–89. New Haven: Yale University Press.

Hurwiz, J. 1989. Presidential Leadership and Public Followship. In *Manipulating Public Opinion,* edited by M. Margolis and G.E. Mauser, 222–49. Pacific Grove, Ca.: Brooks/Cole.

Huth, P and Russet, B. 1984. What Makes Deterrence Work? Cases From, 1900 to, 1980. *World Politics* 36: 496-526.

Huygen, Maarten. 1986. Dateline Holland: NATO's Pyrrhic Victory. *Foreign Policy.* (Spring):193-227.

Ikenberry, G. J. 1986a. The irony of state strength: comparative responses to the oil shocks in the 1970s. *International Organization* 40(1):105–137.

Ikenberry, G. J. 1986b. The State and Strategies of International Adjustment. *World Politics* 39(1):53–77.

Ikenberry, G. J. 1988. Conclusion: an institutional approach to American foreign economic policy. in *International Organization* (1988).

Ikenberry, G., D. Lake, and M. Mastaduno. 1988. Introduction: Approaches to Explaining American Foreign Economic Policy. *International Organization* 42:1-14.

Ilchman, W. and Bain, J. S. eds. 1973. *The Political Economy of the Military-Industrial Complex.* Berkeley CA: University of California Press.

Inglehart, R. 1990. *Cultural Shifts in Advanced Industrial Society.* Princeton: Princeton University Press.

International Organization 1988. Explaining American Foreign Economic Policy. Special Issue, 42(1).

Isaac, R. J. 1976. *Israel Divided—Ideological Politics in the Jewish State.* Baltimore: The Johns Hopkins University Press.

Ishida, T. 1983. *Japanese Political Culture.* New Brunswick.

Iyengar, S. and Kinder, D. 1987. *News That Matters: Television and American Opinion.* Chicago: University of Chicago Press.

Jackson, J. 1984. The United States and Africa Under a Jackson Administration *Africa Report* 29:4-8 (May–June).

James, P. and Oneal, J. 1991. The Influence of Domestic and International Politics on the President's Use of Force. *Journal of Conflict Resolution* 35: 307-332.

Janda, K. 1980. *Political Parties: A Cross-National Survey.* New York: Free Press.

Janis, I. 1982. *Groupthink.* 2nd ed. Boston: Little, Brown.

Jenkins, J. Craig. 1983. Resource Mobilization Theory and the Study of Social Movements, *Annual Review of Sociology,* Vol. 9: 527-53.

Jensen, L. 1982. *Explaining Foreign Policy.* Englewood Cliffs, N.J.: Prentice Hall.

Jervis, R. 1977. *Perception and Misperception in International Politics.* Princeton, N.J.: Princeton University Press.

Jervis, R. et al. 1985. *Psychology and Deterrence* Baltimore MD: Johns Hopkins University Press.

Johansen, R. C. 1983. How to Start Ending the Arms Race. *World Policy Journal.* (Fall):71-100.

Johansen, R. C. 1985. The Future of Arms Control. *World Policy Journal.* (Spring):193-227

Johnson, C. 1982. *MITI and the Japanese Miracle: The Growth of Industrial Policy.* Stanford: Stanford University Press.

Johnson, C. 1982. *Revolutionary Change.* Stanford, CA: Stanford University Press.

Johnson, B. 1975. Righteousness Before Revenue: The Forgotten Moral Crusade Against the Indo-Chinese Opium Trade. *Journal of Drug Issues* 5:304-26.

Johnstone, D. 1984. *The Politics of the Euromissiles.* New York: Schocken.

Joseph, P. (forthcoming). Realizing the Peace Dividend: The End of the Cold War and the Emergence of Progressive Politics. manuscript. *Journal of Conflict Resolution* (1991) Democracy and Foreign Policy: Community and Constraint, Special Issue. 35(2).

Kaldor, M. 1983. Beyond the Blocs: Defending Europe the Political Way. *World Policy Journal.* (Fall):1-21.

Kaldor, M. 1991. *The Imaginary War.* London: St. Martin's.

Kaempfer, W., J. Lehman, and A. Lowenberg. 1987. Divestment, Investment Sanctions and Disinvestment: An Evaluation of Anti-Apartheid Policy Instruments. *International Organization* 41:457–473.

Kaiser, D. 1990. *Politics and War. European Conflict from Philip II to Hitler.* Cambridge MA: Harvard University Press.

Kaiser, K. 1969. Transnationale Politik. In *Die anachronistische Souveränität,* ed. E.-O. Czempiel, 80–109. Köln-Opladen: Westdeutscher Verlag.

Kaldor, M. and D. Smith, eds. 1982. *Disarming Europe.* London: Merlin Press.

Kampelman, M. 1984. Introduction. In *Alerting America: The Papers of the Committee on the Present Danger,* edited by Charles Tyroler, II, xv–xxi. Washington, D.C.: Pergamon-Brassey's.

Kaplan, M. 1957. The Balance of Power, Bipolarity, and Other Models of the International System. *American Political Science Review* 51:684-695.

Kaplan, S. 1981. *Diplomacy of Power: Soviet Armed Forces as a Political Instrument.* Washington D.C.: Brookings.

Karpinski, J. 1987. Polish Intellectuals in Opposition. *Problems of Communism*. (July-August):44-57.

Katz, M. S. 1986. *Ban the Bomb: A History of SANE*. New York: Greenwood.

Katzenstein, P. 1976. International Relations and Domestic Structures: Foreign Economic Policies of Advanced Industrialized States. *International Organization* 30(1):1–45.

Katzenstein, P. ed. 1978a. *Between Power and Plenty*. Madison WI: University of Wisconsin Press.

Katzenstein, P. 1978b. International Relations and Domestic Structures: Foreign Economic Policies of Advanced Industrialized States. In *Between Power and Plenty: Foreign Economic Policies of Advanced Industrialized States*, edited by Peter Katzenstein, Madison: University of Wisconsin Press.

Katzenstein, P. 1978c. Introduction and Conclusion. In P. Katzenstein (1978a)

Katzenstein, P. 1984. *Corporatism and Change*. Ithaca NY: Cornell University Press.

Katzenstein, P. 1985. *Small States in World Markets*. Ithaca NY: Cornell University Press.

Katzenstein, P. 1989. *Policy and Politics in West Germany*. Philadelphia: Temple University Press.

Kaufmann, W. W. 1984. *The 1985 Defense Budget*. Washington, DC: Brookings.

Kavan, J. and Z. Tomin, eds. 1983. *Voices from Prague, Czechoslovakia, Human Rights and the Peace Movement*. London: END and Palach Press.

Kegley, C. 1987. *The Domestic Sources of American Foreign Policy: Insights and Evidence*. New York: St. Martins Press.

Kehr, E. 1928/1977. Anglophobia and Weltpolitik. In *Economic Interest, Militarism, and Foreign Policy. Essays on German History*, E. Kehr. Berkeley CA: University of California Press.

Kelleher, C. 1987. Nation-State and National Security in Postwar Western Europe. In *Evolving European Defense Policies* ed. C.M. Kelleher and G.A. Mattox: 3–14. Lexington MA: Lexington Books.

Keohane, R. 1984. *After Hegemony: Cooperation and Discord in the World Economy* Princeton: Princeton University Press.

Keohane, R. 1989. *International Institutions and State Power: Essays in International Relations Theory* Boulder: Westview Press.

Keohane, R. and Nye, J. S. 1977. *Power and Interdependence*. Boston: Little, Brown.

Keohane, R. 1986. Theory of World Politics: Structural Realism and Beyond. In *Neorealism and Its Critics*, edited by Robert Keohane, 158-203. New York: Columbia University Press.

Kessler, F. 1985. Goodyear Toughs It Out. *Fortune* 30 September, 24–26.

Key, V. O. 1961. *Public Opinion and American Democracy*. New York: Knopf.

Kies, S. 1975. The Influence of Public Policy on Public Opinion. *State. Government and International Relations*, 8:36-53. [In Hebrew.]

Kilgour, M. 1991. Domestic Political Structure and War Behavior. *Journal of Conflict Resolution* 35: 266-284.

Kirkpatrick, J. J. 1989-90. Beyond the Cold War. *Foreign Affairs*. (Winter):1-16.

Kitschelt, H. P. 1986. Political Opportunity Structures and Political Protest: Anti-Nuclear Movements in Four Democracies. *British Journal of Political Science* 16:57–85.

Kober, S. 1990. Idealpolitik. *Foreign Policy*. (Summer):3-24.

Kohler-Koch, B. ed. 1989. *Regime in den internationalen Beziehungen*. Baden-Baden: Nomos.

Kolko, G. 1968. *The Politics of War: The World and United States Foreign Policy, 1943–1945.* New York: Random House.

Kolko, G. and J. Kolko 1969. *The Roots of American Foreign Policy.* Boston: Beacon Press.

Komer, R. 1985. What Decade of Neglect? *International Security.* (Fall):73-.

Konrad, G. 1984. *Antipolitics: An Essay.* (Translated by Richard E. Allen) San Diego: Harcourt Brace, Jovanovich.

Konrad, G. 1985. (interviewed by Richard Falk and Mary Kaldor) The Post-Yalta Debate. *World Policy Journal.* (Summer):451-466.

Knorr, K. 1977. Economic Interdependence and National Security. In *Economic Issues and National Security*, eds. K. Knorr and F. N. Trager, 1–13. Lawrence KS.

Kramer, M. 1989-90. Beyond the Brezhnev Doctrine: A New Era in Soviet-East European Relations? *International Security.* (Winter):25-67.

Krasner, S. 1972. Are Bureaucracies Important? *Foreign Policy.* 7: 159-179.

Krasner, S. 1978. *Defending the National Interest: Raw Materials Investments and U.S. Foreign Policy.* Princeton, N.J.: Princeton University Press.

Krasner, S. ed. 1983. *International Regimes.* Ithaca NY: Cornell University Press.

Krasner, S. 1976. State Power and the Structure of International Trade, *World Politics* 28:317-47.

Krauthammer, C. 1989. Universal Dominion: Toward a Unipolar World. *The National Interest.* (Winter):46-49.

Kreile, M. 1978. *Ostpolitik und Osthandel.* Baden-Baden: Nomos.

Krell, G. 1976. *Rüstungsdynamik und Rüstungskontrolle. Die gesell-schaftlichen Auseinandersetzungen um SALT in den USA 1969–1975.* Frankfurt/M.: Haag&Herchen.

Krell, G. 1981. Capitalism, Business Cycles, and Defense Spending. *Journal of Peace Research* 18:221–240.

Kubbig, B. W. 1988. *Amerikanische Rüstungskontrollpolitik. Dieinnergesellschaftlichen Kräfteverhältnisse in der ersten Amtszeit Ronald Reagans.* Frankfurt/M.: Campus.

Kurkowski, D. 1982. The Role of Interest Groups in the Domestic Debate on SALT II. Ph.D. dissertation. Temple University.

Lakatos, I. and A. Musgrave, eds. 1974. *Criticism and the Growth of Knowledge.* Proceedings of the International Colloquium in the Philosophy of Science, Bedford College, 1965, vol. 4. London: Cambridge University Press.

Lake, A. 1976. *The "Tar Baby" Option: American Policy Toward Southern Rhodesia.* New York: Columbia University Press.

Lake, D. 1988. *Power, Protection and Free Trade: International Sources of U.S. Commercial Strategy, 1887-1939.* Ithaca: Cornell University Press.

Lake, D. 1988b. The State and American Trade Strategy in the Pre- Hegemonic Era. *International Organization* 42:33-58.

Lamborn, A. C. and S. P. Mumme. 1989. *Statecraft, Domestic Politics and Foreign Policy-Making: The El Chamizal Dispute.* Boulder, CO: Westview Press.

Lanouette, W. 1977. The Battle to Shape and Sell the New Arms Control Treaty. *National Journal.* 9: 1984–93.

Lanouette, W. 1979. The Senate's SALT II Debate Hinges on 'Extraneous' Issues. *National Journal*, 11: 1564–1567.

Lapidus, G. W. and A. Dallin. 1989. The Pacification of Ronald Reagan. *Bulletin of the Atomic Scientists.* (January-February):14-17.

Lasswell, H. D. and A. Kaplan. 1976. *Power and Society: A Framework for Political Inquiry.* New Haven, CT: Yale University Press.

Lebow, R. N. 1981. *Between Peace and War. The Nature of International Crisis.* Baltimore MD: Johns Hopkins University Press.

Lebow, R. and Stein, J. 1987. Beyond Deterrence. *Journal of Social Issues* 43:5-71

Lebow, R. and Stein, J. 1989. Rational Deterrence Theory: I think, Therefore I Deter. *World Politics* 41: 208-24.

Lehman-Wilzig, S. 1990. *Stiff Necked People, Bottle-Necked System: The Evolution and Roots of Israeli Public Protest. 1949-1986.* Bloomington: Indiana University Press.

Lenin, V. 1975. Imperialism: The Highest Stage of Capitalism In *The Lenin Anthology,* edited by Robert Tucker, New York: W. W. Norton.

Levy, J. 1989. The Diversionary Theory of War: A Critique. In *Handbook of War Studies.* ed. M. I. Midlarsky, 259-288. Boston: Unwin, Hyman.

Levy, J. 1988. Domestic Politics and War. *Journal of Interdisciplinary History.* 43 (4): 653-673.

Levy, Jack S. and Lily Vakili. 1989. External Scapegoating by Authoritarian Regimes: Argentina in the Falklands/Malvinas Case, paper presented at the annual meeting of the American Political Science Association, Atlanta, 31 Aug-3 Sept.

Light, P. 1982. *The President's Agenda: Domestic Policy Choice from Kennedy to Carter.* Baltimore: The Johns Hopkins University Press.

Lijphart, A. 1975. The Comparable-Case Study in Comparative Research. *Comparative Political Studies* 8 (July):158-77.

Lijphart, A., T. C. Bruneau, N. P. Diamandourous, and Richard Gunther. 1988. A Mediterranean Model of Democracy? The Southern European Democracies in Comparative Perspective. *West European Politics* 11 (January): 7-25.

Limberes, N. M. 1986. The Greek Election of 1985: A Socialist Entrenchment. *West European Politics* 9 (January): 142-47.

Lindblom, C. 1977. *Politics and Markets.* New York: Basic Books.

Lindsay, J. 1986. Trade Sanctions as Policy Instruments. *International Studies Quarterly* 30: 153-73.

Link, W. 1978. *Deutsche und amerikanische Gewerkschaften und Geschäftsleute 1945-75: Eine Studie über transnationale Beziehungen.* Düsseldorf: Droste.

Lipson, L. 1954. *The Great Issues of Politics: An Introduction to Political Science.* New York: Prentice-Hall.

Lissner, J. 1977. *The Politics of Altruism: A Study of thePolitical Behavior of Voluntary Development Agencies.* Geneva: Lutheran World Foundation.

Longmyer, K. 1985. Black American Demands. *Foreign Policy* 60:3-17.

Loomis, B. 1986. Coalitions of Interests: Building Bridges in the Balkanized State. In *Interest Group Politics,* edited by Burdett Loomis and Alan Cigler, 258-78. Washington, D.C.: CQ Press.

Loomis, B. and A. Cigler, Introduction: The Changing Nature of Interest Group Politics. In *Interest Group Politics,* edited by Burdett Loomis and Alan Cigler, 1-26. Washington, D.C.: CQ Press.

Losman, D. 1979. *International Economic Sanctions.* Albuquerque NM: University of New Mexico Press.

Loulis, J. C. 1984. Papandreou's Foreign Policy. *Foreign Affairs* 63 (Winter): 375-91.

Lowes, P. 1966. *The Genesis of International Narcotics Control* Geneva: Librairie Droz.

Lowi, T. 1964. American Public Policy, Case-Studies, and Political Theory *World Politics* 16:677–715.

Lowi, T. 1979. *The End of Liberalism: The Second Republic of the United States.* New York: Norton, 2nd ed.

Lowi, T. 1985. *The Personal Presidency: Power Invested, Promise Unfulfilled.* Ithaca: Cornell University Press.

Machiavelli, N. *The Prince.* translated by R. Adams 1977. New York: Norton.

Macridis, R. C. 1984. *Greek Politics at a Crossroads: What Kind of Socialism?* Stanford, CA: Hoover Institution Press.

Magraw, K. 1989. The Nuclear Weapons Policy Debate in the 1980s: A Reevaluation of the Role of Congress. Unpublished paper delivered at the American Political Science Association Annual Meeting, September.

Mahood, H.R. 1990. *Interest Group Politics in America: A New Intensity.* Englewood Cliffs, N.J.: Prentice Hall.

Malloy, J. M. 1991. Statecraft, Social Policy, and Governance in Latin America, in *The State and Public Policy;* ed. James F. Hollifield and B. Guy Peters, forthcoming.

Mandelbaum, M. and S. Talbott. Reykjavik and Beyond. *Foreign Affairs.* (Winter):215–235.

Mansbach, R. W., Ferguson, Y. H. and Lampert, D. E. 1976. *The Web of World Politics. Nonstate Actors in the Global System.* Englewood Cliffs NJ: Prentice Hall.

Mann, M. 1987. The Autonomous Power of the State: Its Origins, Mechanisms, and Results. In *States in History,* edited by J. Hall, pp. 109-36. London: Basil Blackwell.

Maoz, Z. 1990. *National Choices and International Processes.* Cambridge: Cambridge University Press.

Maoz, Z. and Abdolali, N. 1989. Regime Types and International Conflict, 1816–1976. *Journal of Conflict Resolution* 33(1):3–35.

Maoz, Z. and Russett, B. 1991. Alliances, Contiguity, Wealth, and Political Stability: Is the Lack of Conflict Among Democracies a Statistical Artifact? *International Interactions* 17.

Marder, M. 1977. The Arms Muddle: Some Aides Feel U.S. Miscalculated. *The Washington Post,* April 2: A-1.

Marra, R. and Ostrom, C. and Simon, D. 1990. Foreign Policy and Presidential Popularity. *Journal of Conflict Resolution* 34: 588-623.

Marullo, S. 1991. Lessons of the Peace Movement. Unpublished paper. Georgetown University.

Marullo, S. and J. Lofland, eds. 1990. *Peace Action in the Eighties: Social Science Perspectives.* New Brunswick, NJ: Rutgers University Press.

Marx, K. 1978. On the Jewish Question. In Robert C. Tucker, ed. *The Marx-Engels Reader.* New York: Norton. 26-54.

Maslow, A. H. 1943. A Theory of Motivation. *Psychological Review* 50:370-96.

Mastanduno M., J. Ikenberry and D. Lake 1989. Toward a Realist Theory of State Action. *International Studies Quarterly.* 33 (4): 457-474.

Mathias Jr., C. 1981. Ethnic Groups and Foreign Policy *Foreign Affairs* 59 :975-998.

McCarthy, J. D. and Mayer N. Zald. 1977. Resource Mobilization and Social Movements: A Partial Theory, *American Journal of Sociology,* Vol. 82, No. 6: 1212-1241.

McCaskill, C. W. 1988. US-Greek Relations and the Problems of the Aegean and Cyprus. *Journal of Political and Military Sociology* 16 (Fall): 215-33.

McClelland, C. 1961. The Social Sciences, History, and International Relations. In *International Politics and Foreign Policy*. Edited by J. Rosenau, 24-35. The Free Press of Glencoe.

McConnell, M. 1989. A View From The Sanctuary Movement, in *The Moral Nation*, eds. Bruce Nichols and Gil Loescher. Notre Dame, IN: Univ. of Notre Dame Press.

McPherson, C.B. 1977. *The Life and Times of Liberal Democracy*. New York: Oxford University Press.Mandelbaum, M. and Schneider, W. 1979. The New Internationalism: Public Opinion and American Foreign Policy. In *Eagle Entangled: U.S. Foreign Policy in a Complex World*. ed. K. Oye et al.: 34–90. New York: Longman.

McRae, F. B. and Gerald E. Markle. 1989. *Minutes to Midnight: Nuclear Weapons Protest in America*. Newbury Park, CA: Sage.

Mearsheimer, J. 1990a. Back to the Future: Instability in Europe after the Cold War. *International Security*. (Summer):5-56.

Mearsheimer, J. 1990. Why We Will Soon Miss the Cold War. *The Atlantic*. (August):35-50.

Mearsheimer, J., S. Hoffmann, and R. Keohane. 1990. Exchange. *International Security*. (Fall):191-199.

Medick, M. 1976. *Waffenexporte und auswärtige Politik der Vereinigten Staaten*. Meisenheim a. Glan: Verlag A. Hain.

Meissner, B. 1981. The 26th Party Congress and Soviet Domestic Politics. *Problems of Communism*. (May-June):1-23.

Melman, S. 1970. *Pentagon Capitalism. The Political Economy of War*. New York: McGraw Hill.

Melzer, J. 1985. Peace Now Agony. In *The Limits of Obedience*, edited by Y. Menuchin and D. Menuchin. 151–59. Tel Aviv: The 'Yesh Gvul' Movement & Siman Kri'a Books.

Menzel, U. 1985. *In der Nachfolge Europas. Autozentrierte Entwicklung in den ostasiatischen Schwellenländern Südkorea und Taiwan*. München.

Menzel, U. 1986. *Auswege aus der Abhängigkeit. Die entwicklungspolitische Aktualität Europas*. Frankfurt/M.: Suhrkamp.

Menzel, U. and Senghaas, D. 1986. *Europas Entwicklung und die Dritte Welt*. Frankfurt/M.: Suhrkamp.

Merritt, R. 1973. Public Opinion and Foreign Policy in West Germany. In *Sage International Yearbook of Foreign Policy Studies*, edited by P. McGowan, vol. 1, 255-74. Beverly Hills, Calif.: Sage.

Merritt, R. 1975. Public Perspective in Closed Societies. In *Foreign Policy Analysis*. 101–17. Lexington Mass.: Lexington Books.

Metz, S. 1985. The Anti-Apartheid Movement And the Formulation of American Policy Toward South Africa, 1969-1981. Ph.D. Dissertation. Baltimore, MD: Johns Hopkins University.

Mever, D. 1990. *A Winter of Discontent: The Nuclear Freeze and American Politics*. New York: Preager.

Meyer, D. S. 1991a. Peace Movements and National Security Policy: A Research Agenda. *Peace and Change*. (April):131-161.

Meyer, D. S. 1991b. Peace Protest and Policy: Explaining the Rise and Decline (and Rise and Decline) of Antinuclear Movements in Postwar America. Paper presented at the annual meeting of the American Political Science Association. Washington, DC. August.

Meyer, S. M. 1988. The Sources and Prospects of Gorbachev's New Thinking on Security. *International Security*. (Fall):124-163.

Michnik, A. 1982. We are All Hostages. *Telos*. (Spring):173-181.

Milbrath, L. 1967. Interest Groups and Foreign Policy. In *Domestic Sources of Foreign Policy*, edited by James Rosenau, 231–252. New York: Free Press.

Milburn, T and Billings, R. 1976. Decision-Making Perspectives and Psychology. *American Behavioral Scientist* 20: 111-126.

Miller, J. 1978. *The Black Presence in American Foreign Affairs*. Washington: University Press of America.

Miller, J. 1979. Black Legislators and African-American Relations, 1970-1975. *Journal of Black Studies* 10 :245-261.

Miller, W. and D. Stokes. 1963. Constituency Influence in Congress. *American Political Science Review*. 57 (1963): 45–56.

Mills, C. W. 1956. *The Power Elite*. New York: Oxford University Press.

Milner, H. 1988. *Resisting Protectionism. Global Industries and the Politics of International Trade*. Princeton NJ: Princeton University Press.

Milner, H. and D. Yoffie. 1989. Between Free Trade and Protectionism. *International Organization* 43:239-72.

Modelski, G. 1983. *Long Cycles of World Leadership*. in *Contending Approaches to World System Analysis* edited by W. Thompson, 115-140.

Moffett, G. 1985. *The Limits of Victory: The Ratification of the Panama Canal Treaties*. Ithica, N.Y.: Cornell University Press.

Mohr, C. 1979. Senator Garn Guides Foes of Arms Treaty. *New York Times*, May 29: A-2.

Moore, B. 1966. *Social Origins of Dictatorship and Democracy: Lord and Peasant in the Making of the Modern World*. Boston: Beacon Press.

Moorsom, R. 1986. *The Scope for Sanctions: Economic Measures Against South Africa*. London: Catholic Institute for International Relations.

Moravscik, A. 1990. Integrating International and Domestic Explanations of World Politics: A Theoretical Introduction. manuscript. Cambridge MA, Harvard University.

Morgan, T. and Cambell, S. 1991. Domestic Structure, Decisional Constraints, and War: So Why Can't Democracies Fight? *Journal of Conflict Resolution* 35: 187-211.

Morgenthau, H. 1973. *Politics Among Nations: The Struggle for Power and Peace* New York: Alfred A. Knopf.

Morse, E. 1970. The Transformation of Foreign Policies: Modernization, Interdependence and Externalization. *World Politics*. 22 (3): 371-392.

Most, B. and H. Starr. 1989. *Inquiry, Logic, and International Politics*. Columbia, SC: University of South Carolina Press.

Most, B. and Siverson, R. M. 1987. Substituting Arms and Alliances, 1870–1914: An Exploration in Comparative Foreign Policy. In C.F. Hermann et al. (1987), 131–157.

Mueller, Harald and Thomas Risse-Kappen. 1987. Origins of Estrangement: The Peace Movement and the Changed Image of America in West Germany. *International Security*.(Summer):52-88.

Mueller, J. 1973. *War, Presidency, and Public Opinion*. New York: Columbia University Press.

Muller, J. 1973. *War, Presidents and Public Opinion*. New York: Wiley.

Musto, D. 1973. *The American Disease: Origins of Narcotics Control* New Haven: Yale University Press.

Myrdal, A. et al. 1982. *The Dynamics of European Nuclear Disarmament*. Chester Springs, PA: Dufour Editions.

Müller, E. 1985. *Rüstungspolitik und Rüstungsdynamik: Fall USA*. Baden-Baden: Nomos.

Müler, H. 1989a. *Vom Ölembargo zum National Energy Act. Amerikanische Energiepolitik zwischen gesellschaftlichen Interessen und Weltmachtanspruch. 1973–1978*. Frankfurt/M.: Campus.

Müller, H. 1989b. Regime analyse und Sicherheitspolitik. Das Beispiel Nonproliferation. In *Kohler-Koch* (1989), 277–313.

Müller, H. 1991. The Internalization of Principles, Norms, and Rules by Governments: The Case of Security Regimes. Paper prepared for the Conference "The Study of Regimes in International Relations," Tübingen, July 14–18.

Müller, H. and Risse-Kappen, T. 1990. Internationale Umwelt, gesellschaftliches Umfeld und außenpolitischer Prozeß in liberal-demokratischen Industrienationen. In *Theorien der Internationalen Beziehungen* ed. V. Rittberger, 375–400. Opladen: WestdeutscherVerlag.

Nadelmann, E. 1990. Global Prohibition Regimes: The Evolution of Norms in International Society. *International Organization* 44:479- 526.

Nau, H. 1989. Domestic Trade Politics and the Uruguay Round: An Overview. In *Domestic Trade Politics and the Uruguay Round*, ed. idem, 1–28. New York.

Neal, F. 1979. Inertia on SALT. *New York Times*, January 22: A-21.

Neustadt, R. 1990. *Presidential Power and the Modern Presidents: The Politics of Leadership from Roosevelt to Reagan*. New York: The Free Press.

Neustadt, R. E. and E. R. May. 1986. *Thinking in Time: The Uses of History for Decision-Makers*. New York: Free Press.

Nincic, M. 1990. U.S. Soviet Policy and the Electoral Connection. *World Politics*. 62: 370–96.

Noel-Seumann, E. 1981. *The Germans*. Westport, CT.: Greenwood Press.

Noer, T. 1978. *Briton, Boer, and Yankee: The United States and South Africa 1870-1914*. Kent, OH: Kent State University Press.

Nolt, J. 1992. Business Power and National Strategy in the American Century: Objectives in Disarmament, Appeasement and War. Ph.D. dissertation, University of Chicago.

Nordlinger, E. 1981. *On the Autonomy of the Democratic State* Cambridge: Harvard University Press.

Nordlinger, E. 1988. The Return to the State: Critiques. *American Political Science Review* 82:875-85.

Novicki, M. 1984. Interview: Tom Bradley, Mayor of Los Angeles. *Africa Report* 29 :17-18 (May–June).

Nowak, Jan. 1982. The Church in Poland. *Problems of Communism*. (January-February):1-16.

Nyangoni, W. 1981. *United States Foreign Policy and South Africa*. New York: SCI Press

Nye, J. 1986. The Domestic Environment of U.S. Policy-Making. In *U.S.-Soviet Relations: The Next Phase*, edited by Arnold Horelick, 111–126. Ithica: Cornell University Press.

Nye, J.S. and S. Lynn-Jones, 1988. International Security Studies: A Report of a Conference on the State of the Field. *International Security* 12 (4):5–27.

Nye, J. and R. Keohane 1971. *Transnational Relations and World Politics.* Cambridge: Harvard University Press.

Offe, C. 1984. *Contradictions of the Welfare State.* Cambridge: MIT Press.

Offe, C. 1985. New Social Movements: Challenging the Boundaries of Institutional Politics, *Social Research*, Vol. 52, No. 4, (Winter), pp. 817-866.

Office of National Drug Control Policy. 1989. *National Drug Control Strategy* Washington, D.C.: Government Printing Office.

Olsen, M. 1982. *The Rise and Decline of Nations—Economic Growth, Stagflation, and Social Rigidities.* New Haven: Yale University Press.

Opp, K. D. 1989. *The Rationality of Political Protest.* Boulder, CO.: Westview Press.

Organski, A.F.K. and Kugler, J. 1980. *The War Ledger.* Chicago: University of Chicago Press.

Orman, J. 1980. *Presidential Secrecy and Deception: Beyond the Power to Persuade* Westport: Greenwood Press.

Ostrom, C.W. and Job, B. 1986. The President and the Political Use of Force. *American Political Science Review.* 80: 554–566.

Owen, D. 1934. *British Opium Policy in China and India* New Haven: Yale University Press.

Oye, K. ed. 1986. *Cooperation Under Anarchy* Princeton: Princeton University Press.

Packenham, R. 1973. *Liberal America and the Third World.* Princeton: Princeton University Press.

Page, B. and Shapiro, R. 1983. Effects of Public Opinion on Policy. *American Political Science Review* (1):175–190.

Palme, Olof et al. (Independent Commission on Disarmament and Security Issues). 1982. *Common Security: A Blueprint for Survival.* New York: Simon and Schuster.

Paul, L. T. 1990. Social Movements and the Interface of Domestic and International Politics: A Study of Peace Activism paper presented at the 1990 Annual Meeting of the American Political Science Association, San Francisco.

Payne, R. and E. Ganaway. 1980. The Influence of Black Americans on U.S. Policy Towards Southern Africa African Affairs 79 :585–598.

Peele, G. 1984. *Revival and Reaction: The Right in Contemporary America.* Oxford: Clarendon Press.

Pempel, T.-J. 1982. *Politics and Policy in Japan: Creative Conservatism.* Philadelphia: Temple University Press.

Perugia Papers. 1984-85. *ENDpapers.* 9 (Winter).

Petras, J. 1987. The Contradictions of Greek Socialism. *New Left Review* 163(May):3-26.

Philippas, S. C. 1986. *The Panhellenic Socialist Party (PASOK): Ideology and Politics.* Dissertation, George Washington University.

Pipes, R. 1976. Team B: The Reality Behind the Myth. *Commentary.* 82: 25–40.

Platt, A. 1982. The Politics of Arms Control and the Strategic Balance. In *Rethinking the U.S. Strategic Posture,* edited by Barry Blechman, 155–78. Cambridge, MA.: Ballinger Publishing Co.

Pond, E. 1990. A Wall Destroyed: The Dynamics of German Unification in the GDR. *International Security.* (Fall):35-66.

Posen, B. and S. Van Evera. 1983. Defense Policy and the Reagan Administration: Departure from Containment. *International Security.* (Summer):3-45.

Primack, J. and F. von Hippel. 1974. *Advice and Dissent: Scientists in the Political Arena.* New York: Basic.

Prinsloo, D. 1978. *United States Foreign Policy and the Republic of South Africa*. Pretoria: Foreign Affairs Association.

Purkitt, H. E. 1991. Intuitive Foreign Policy Makers. *Artificial Intelligence and International Politics*. ed. by Valerie Hudson, Boulder, CO: Westview.

Purkitt, H. E. 1992. Political Decision Making in the Context of Small Groups: The Cuban Missile Crisis Revisited—One More Time. In *Political Psychology and Foreign Policy*, edited by E. Singer and V. Hudson. Boulder: Westview Press.

Putnam, R. 1988. Diplomacy and Domestic Politics: The Logic of Two Level Games. *International Organization*. 42 (3): 427-460.

Putnam, R. D. and Bayne, N. 1984. *Hanging Together. The Seven Power Summits*. Cambridge MA.

Ramet, P. 1984. Church and Peace in the GDR. *Problems of Communism*. (July-August):44-57.

von Ranke, L. 1836/1973. A Dialogue on Politics. In *The Theory and Practice of History*, ed. Ranke, Leopold von. Indianapolis: Bobbs-Merrill.

Razis, V. 1986. *The American Connection: The Influence of United States Business on South Africa*. New York: St. Martin's Press.Reilly, J. 1988. America's State of Mind: Trends in Public Attitudes Towered Foreign Policy. In *The Domestic Sources of American Foreign Policy*, edited by C. Kegley, Jr. and E. Wittkopf, 45–56. New York: St. Martins Press.

Rielly, J. 1975. *American Public Opinion and U.S. Foreign Policy, 1975*. 97 Chicago: Chicago Council on Foreign Relations.

Rielly, J. 1979. *American Public Opinion and U.S. Foreign Policy, 1979*. Chicago: Chicago Council on Foreign Relations.

Risse-Kappen, T. 1988a. *Die Krise der Sicherheitspolitik. Neuorientierungen und Entscheidungsprozesse im politischen Systemder Bundesrepublik Deutschland, 1977–1984*. Mainz-München: Grünewald-Kaiser.

Risse-Kappen, T. 1988b. *The Zero Option: INF, West Germany, and Arms Control*. Boulder CO: Westview.

Risse-Kappen, T. 1991b. Anti-Nuclear and Pro-Détente? The Transformation of the West German Security Debate. In *Debating National Security*, eds. D. Munton and H. Rattinger, 269–299. Frankfurt/M.:Peter Lang.

Risse-Kappen, T. 1991a. Did 'Peace Through Strength' End the Cold War?: Lessons From INF. *International Security*. 16 (Summer) 1:162-188.

Risse-Kappen, T. 1991b. Public Opinion, Domestic Structure, and Foreign Policy in Liberal Democracies. *World Politics* 43(4):479–512.

Risse-Kappen, T. 1991c. Transnational Relations, States, and Security Policy: Lessons From Three Case Studies. Paper presented at the International Studies Association Annual Meeting. Vancouver, British Columbia.

Rittberger, V. 1987. Zur Friedensfähigkeit von Demokratien. Betrachtungen politischen Theorie des Friedens. *Aus Politik und Zeitgeschichte* (44):3–12.

Roberts, S. 1979. Arms Pact Friends and Foes Rally for Senate Battle. *New York Times*, April 13: A-2.

Robinson, J., J. Rusk, and K. Head. 1968. *Measures of Political Attitudes*. Ann Arbor: University of Michigan, Survey Research Center.

Rochon, T.R. 1988. *Mobilizing for Peace: The Anti-Nuclear Movement in Western Europe*. Princeton: Princeton University Press.

Rode, R. 1988. *Die Zeche zahlen wir. Der Niedergang der amerikanischen Wirtschaft.* München: Beck.

Rode, R. and Jacobsen, H.-D. eds. 1985. *Economic Warfare or Détente.* Boulder CO: Westview.

Rogowski, R. 1989. *Commerce and Coalitions. How Trade Affects Domestic Political Alignments.* Princeton NJ: Princeton University Press.

Rosati, J. 1981. Developing a Systematic Decision Making Framework: Bureaucratic Politics in Perspective. *World Politics* 33:234-251.

Rose, J D. 1982. *Outbreaks: The Sociology of Collective Behavior.* New York: Free Press.

Rosecrance, R. 1986. *The Rise of the Trading State.* New York: Basic Books.

Rosen, S. ed. 1973. *Testing the Theory of the Military Industrial Complex.* New York.

Rosenau, J. and O. Holsti 1984. *American Leadership in World Affairs: Vietnam and the Breakdown of Consensus.* Boston: Allen and Unwin.

Rosenau, J. N. 1961. *Public Opinion and Foreign Policy.* New York: Random House.

Rosenau, J. N. 1966. Pre-theories and Theories of Foreign Policy. In *Approaches to Comparative and International Politics,* ed. Farrell, R. Barry, 27–92. Evanston IL: Northwestern University Press.

Rosenau, J. N. 1980. *The Scientific Study of Foreign Policy.* Rev. ed. London: Frances Pinter.

Rosenau, J. N. 1981. *The Study of Political Adaptation.* London: Frances Pinter.

Rossiter, Caleb. 1984. The Financial Hit List A publication of *The Center For International Policy.*

Rothchild, D. and J. Ravenhill. 1987. Subordinating African Issues to Global Logic: Reagan Confronts Political Complexity. In *Eagle Resurgent,* edited by K. Oye, R. Lieber, and D. Rothchild, 393–429. Boston: Little, Brown.

Rummel, R. J. 1963. "Dimensions of Conflict Behavior Within and Between Nations." In *General Systems: Yearbook of the Society for General Systems Research.* Society for General Systems Research.

Rummel, R. J. 1983. Libertarianism and International Violence. *Journal of Conflict Resolution* 27(1):27–71.

Russett, B. 1963. The Calculus of Deterrence. *Journal of Conflict Resolution* June, 1963: 97-109.

Russett, B. 1974. The Revolt of the Masses: Public Opinion on Military Expenditures. In *New Military-Civil Relations,* edited by J. Lovell and P. Kronenberg, New Brunswick: Transaction Books.

Russett, B. 1983. International Interactions and Processes: TheInternal vs. External Debate Revisited. In *Political Science. The State of the Discipline,* 541–568. Washington DC: American Political Science Association.

Russett, B. 1989. *Economic Decline, Electoral Pressure, and the Initiation of Interstate Conflict. In Prisoners of War? Nation-States in the Modern Era.* ed. C. Gochman and A.N. Sabrosky. Lexington MA: Heath.

Russett, B. 1990. *Controlling the Sword. The Democratic Governance of Nuclear Weapons.* Cambridge MA: Harvard University Press.

Russett, B. and Hanson, E.C. 1975. *Interest and Ideology: The Foreign Policy Beliefs of American Businessmen.* New York: W.H. Freeman.

Russett, B. and Starr, H. 1989. *World Politics: The Menu For Choice.* New York: Freeman.

Sabin, P. 1986. *The Third World War Scare in Britain.* London: Macmillan.

Salmore, B. G. and Stephen A. Salmore. 1978. "Political Regimes and Foreign Policy." In *Why Nations Act*, edited by Maurice East et al. Beverly Hills: Sage Publications.

Sanders, J.W. 1983. *Peddlers of Crisis. The Committee on the Present Danger*. Boston: South End Press.

Sanford, J. 1983. *The Sword and the Ploughshare: Autonomous Peace Initiatives in East Germany*. London: Merlin Press/END.

Saperstein, A. M. 1987. An Enhanced Non-Provocative Defense: Attrition of Aggressive Armed Forces by Local Militia. *Journal of Peace Research*. (March):47-60.

Scanlan, J. 1988. Reforms and Civil Society in the USSR. *Problems of Communism*, (March-April):41-46.

Schattschneider, E. E. 1960. *The Semisovereign People*. New York: Holt, Rinehart, and Winston.

Scheer, R. 1983. *With Enough Shovels: Reagan, Bush and Nuclear War*. rev. ed. New York: Vintage Books.

Schlozman, K. and J. Tierney 1986. *Organized Interests and American Democracy*. New York: Harper and Row.

Schneider, W. 1983. Conservatism, Not Interventionism: Trends in Foreign Policy Opinion, 1974–82. In *Eagle Defiant: United States Foreign Policy in the 1980's*, edited by Kenneth Oye, Robert Lieber, and Robert Rothchild, Boston: Little, Brown.

Schneider, W. 1987. "Rambo" and Reality: Having It Both Ways. In *Eagle Resurgent*, edited by K. Oye, R. Lieber, and D. Rothchild, 41–72. Boston: Little, Brown.

Scholarly Resources. 1974. *The Opium Trade, 1910-1941* Wilmington, Delaware: Scholarly Resources.

Schopflin, G., R. Tokes, and I. Volgyes. 1988. Leadership Change and Crisis in Hungary. *Problems of Communism*. (September-October):23-46.

Schlotter, P. 1975. *Rüstungspolitik in der Bundesrepublik Deutschland. Die Beispiele Starfighter und Phantom*. Frankfurt/M.:Campus.

Schmitter, P. 1984. Still the Century of Corporatism? *The Review of Politics*. 36: 85–131.

Schössler, D. and Weede, E. 1978. *West German Elite Views on National Security and Foreign Policy Issues*. Königstein: Athenäum.

Schweigler, G. 1985. *Grundlagen der außenpolitischen Orientierung der Bundesrepublik Deutschland*. Baden-Baden: Nomos.

Scolnick, J. M., Jr. 1988. How Governments Utilize Foreign Threats. *Conflict* 8: 12-22.

Scott, J. 1990. *Domination and the Arts of Resistance* New Haven: Yale University Press.

Seaborg, G. T. 1981. *Kennedy, Khrushchev, and the Test Ban*. (With Benjamin S. Loeb) Berkeley: University of California.

Senghaas, D. 1968. *Abschreckung und Frieden. Studien zur Kritik organisierter Friedlosigkeit*. Frankfurt/M.: Europäische Verlagsanstalt.

Senghaas, D. 1972. *Rüstung und Militarismus*. Frankfurt/M.:Suhrkamp.

Senghaas, D. 1982. *Von Europa lernen. Entwicklungsgeschichtliche Betrachtungen*. Frankfurt/M.: Suhrkamp.

Sethi, S., ed. 1987. *The South African Quagmire: In Search of a Peaceful Path to Democratic Pluralism*. Cambridge MA: Ballinger.

Shahabuddeen, M. 1986. *The Conquest of Grenada: Sovereignty in the Periphery*. Guyana: University of Guyana.

Shannon, T. 1989. *An Introduction to the World-System Perspective* Boulder: Westview Press.

Shapira, A. 1988. *Visions in Conflict*. Tel Sviv: Am Oved. [In Hebrew.]

Shapiro, R. Y. and Page, B. 1988. Foreign Policy and the Rational Public. *Journal of Conflict Resolution* 32(2):211–247.

Sharet, M. 1971. *Political Diary*. Tel Aviv: Am Oved, vol. II. [In Hebrew.]

Sharlet, R. 1989. Human Rights and Civil society in Eastern Europe. in Griffith, ed. (1989):156-177.

Sharp, G. 1985. *Making Europe Unconquerable*. London: Taylor and Francis.

Sharp, J. M. O. 1984. Are the Soviets Still Interested in Arms Control. *World Policy Journal*. (Summer):813-849.

Shepherd, G. 1977. *Anti-Apartheid: Transnational Conflict and Western Policy in the Liberation of South Africa*, Westpoint, Conn: Greenwood Press.

Shipler, D. K. 1989. Letter from Budapest. *The New Yorker*. (November 20):74-101.

Shuman, M. 1986-1987. Dateline Mainstreet: Local Foreign Policies. *Foreign Policy*, 65(Winter).

Shulman, M. 1979. An Overview of U.S.-Soviet Relations. Statement before the Subcommittee on Europe and the Middle East of the Committee on International Relations, House of Representatives, September 26, 1978. In *American Foreign Relations, 1977: A Documentary Record*, edited by Elaine Adam, New York: New York University Press.

Simmons, L. and A. Said. 1974. *Drugs, Politics and Diplomacy* Beverley Hills: Sage.

Simon, D. and Ostrom, C. 1988. The Politics of Prestige: Popular Support and the Modern Presidency. *Presidential Studies Quarterly* 18: 741-759.

Simon, H. A. 1976. *Administrative Behavior* Third edition. New York: Collier Macmillan Publishers.

Sims, S. M. 1989. "Tactic Strength Prerequisites." Unpublished mimeo.

Skidmore, D. 1992. The Politics of National Security Policy: Interest Groups, Coalitions, and the SALT II Debate. In *The Limits of State Autonomy: Societal Groups and Foreign Policy Formulation*, edited by D. Skidmore and V. Hudson, Boulder, CO: Westview Press.

Skidmore, D. (forthcoming). The Politics of Decline: International Adjustment Versus Domestic Legitimacy During the Carter Presidency. *Political Science Quarterly*.

Skilling, H. G. 1985. Independent Currents in Czechoslovakia. *Problems of Communism*. (January-February):32-49.

Sklar, H., ed. 1980. *Trilateralism: The Trilateral Commission and Elite Planning for World Management*. Boston: South End Press.

Skocpol, T. 1979. *States and Revolutions: A Comparative Analysis of France, Russia, and China* Cambridge: Cambridge University Press.

Skocpol, T. 1985. Bringing the State Back In: Strategies of Analysis in Current Research. In *Bringing the State Back In*, edited by Peter Evans et. al., 3-37. Cambridge: Cambridge University Press.

Small, M. 1988. *Johnson, Nixon, and the Doves*. New Brunswick NJ: Rutgers University Press.

Smith, G. 1986. *Morality, Reason, and Power: American Diplomacy in the Carter Years*. New York: Hill and Wang.

Smith, H. 1977. Carter Study Takes More Hopeful View of Strategy of U.S. *New York Times*, July 8: A-4.

Smith, H. 1979a. Three Cornered Arms Talks. *New York Times*, April 14: A-2.

Smith, H. 1979b. Poll Shows Belief Soviet Leads in Arms. *New York Times*, June 13: A-15.

Smith, H. 1983. CIA Report Says Soviet Arms Spending Slowed. *New York Times*, November 19: A-6.

Smith, T. 1979a. President Calls for 4.5% Increases in Military Budgets for Five Years. *New York Times*, December 13: A-1.

Smith, T. 1979b. Carter's Plans for Arms Rise. *New York Times*, December 14: A-7.

Snyder, J. 1988. Limiting Offensive Conventional Forces : Soviet Proposals and Western Options. *International Security*. (Spring):48–77.

Snyder, J. 1989. International Leverage on Soviet Domestic Change.*World Politics* 42(1):1–30.

Snyder, J. 1991. *Myths of Empire. Domestic Politics and Strategic Ideology*. Ithaca NY: Cornell University Press.

Sobel, R. 1989. Public Opinion about United States Intervention in El Salvador and Nicaragua. *Public Opinion Quarterly*. (53): 114–28.

Solo, P. 1988. *From Protest to Policy: Beyond the Freeze to Common Security*. Cambridge: Ballinger.

South Africa: Time Running Out. 1981. Report of the Study Commission on U.S. Policy Toward Southern Africa. Berkeley: University of California Press.

Spanier, J. and E. Uslaner. 1982. *Foreign Policy and the Democratic Dilemmas* New York: Holt, Rinehart, and Winston.

Spanier, J. 1985. *American Foreign Policy-Making and the Democratic Dilemmas*. 4th ed. New York: Holt, Rinehart and Winston.

Spanier, J. and J. Nogee 1981. *Congress, the Presidency and American Foreign Policy*. New York Pergamon Press.

Spencer, D. 1988. *The Carter Implosion: Jimmy Carter and the Amateur Style of Diplomacy*. New York: Praeger.

Spourdalakis, M. 1988. *The Rise of the Greek Socialist Party*. London: Routledge.

Spring, M. 1977. *Confrontation: The Approaching Crisis Between the United States and South Africa*. Sandton, South Africa: Valiant Publishers.

Stanley, H. and R. Niemi. 1990. *Vital Statistics on American Politics*, second edition. Washington: Congressional Quarterly Press.

Starr, S. F. 1988. Soviet Union: A Civil Society. *Foreign Policy*. (Spring):26–41.

Steele, C. 1941. *Americans and the Chinese Opium Trade in the 19th Century* Chicago: The University of Chicago Libraries.

Stein, S. 1985. *International Diplomacy, State Administration, and Narcotics Control: The Origins of a Social Problem* Aldershot, Hampshire, England: Gower Publishing.

Steinbrunner, J. 1974. *The Cybernetic Theory of Decision*. Princeton: Princeton University Press.

Stockman, D. 1986. *The Triumph of Politics: Why The Reagan Revolution Failed*. New York: Harper and Row.

Stoll, R. J. 1984. The guns of November: presidential re-elections and the use of force. *Journal of Conflict Resolution* 28(1).

Stone, D. A. 1989. Causal Stories and the Formation of Policy Agendas. *Political Science Quarterly*. 104 (Summer) 2:281–300.

Stuart, P. 1979. Anti-SALT Lobbyists Outspend Pros 15-1. *Christian Science Monitor*, March 23: 1, 7.

Swank, D. 1988. The Political Economy of Government Domestic Expenditure in the Affluent Democracies. *American Journal of Political Science* 32:1120-50.

Szabo, S. 1988. West German Public Attitudes and Arms Control. In *The Silent Partner. West Germany and Arms Control*, ed. B. Blechmanet al., 195–230. Cambridge MA: Ballinger.

Taggart, P. 1990. Green Parties and the Politics of Ecologism: Green Parties as New Social Movement Organizations. Paper presented at the Northeastern Political Science Association Annual Conference, Providence, Rhode Island. Nov 15-17, 1990.

Talbott, S. 1979. *Endgame: The Inside Story of SALT II*. New York: Harper and Row.

Talbott, S. 1984. *Deadly Gambits: The Reagan Administration and the Stalemate in Arms Control*. New York: Alfred A. Knopf.

Tanter, R. 1966. Dimensions of Conflict Behavior Within and Between Nations, 1958-60. *Journal of Conflict Resolution* 10(March):41-64.

Tarrow, S. 1988. National Politics and Collective Action, *Annual Review of Sociology*, 14

Tarrow, S. 1989. *Struggle, Politics, and Reform: Collective Action, Social Movements, and Cycles of Protest*. Ithaca, NY: Cornell University Center for International Studies.

Taylor, A. 1969. *American Diplomacy and the Narcotics Traffic, 1900-1939: A Study in International Humanitarian Reform* Durham: Duke University Press.

Terry, S. M. 1989. The Future of Poland: Perestroika or Perpetual Crisis. In Griffith, ed. (1989):178-217.

Tetlock, P. 1985. Integrative complexity of American and Soviet foreign policy rhetoric. *Journal of Personality and Social Psychology* 49(6):1565–1585.

Thompson, E.P. and Dan Smith, eds. 1981. *Protest and Survive*. New York and London: Monthly Review Press.

Thompson, E.P. 1982. *Beyond the Cold War*. New York: Pantheon.

Thompson, W. 1983. Uneven Economic Growth, Systemic Challenges, and Global Wars. *International Studies Quarterly* 27: 341-355.

Tilly, C. 1978. *From Mobilization to Revolution*. Reading, MA: Addison-Wesley.

Tismaneanu, V. 1989. Nascent Civil Society in the German Democratic Republic. *Problems of Communism*. (March-June):91-111.

Touraine, A. 1981. *The Voice and The Eye: An Analysis of Social Movements,* Cambridge: Cambridge University Press.

Tryman, M. and Z. Mwamba, eds. 1987. *Apartheid South Africa and American Foreign Policy*. Dubuque, IA: Kendall/Hunt.

Tyroler, C. ed. 1984. *Alerting America: The Papers of the Committee on the Present Danger*. Washington, D.C.: Pergamon-Brassey's.

Tyson, L. 1986. The Debt Crisis and Adjustment Responses in Eastern Europe: A Comparative Perspective. *International Organization* 40:239-86.

United Nations Centre on Transnational Corporations. 1984. Policies and Practices of Transnational Corporations Regarding Their Activities in South Africa and Namibia. New York.

United Nations Panel of Eminent Persons and the Secretary-General. 1986. *Transnational Corporations in South Africa and Namibia: UN Public Hearings* vol. 1, New York.United States Department of State. 1982. World Peace Council: Instrument of Foreign Policy. *Foreign Affairs Note*. (April).

Vanderbilt Television News Archives, Jan, 1972-, Television News Index and Abstracts. Nashville: Vanderbilt Television News Archives.

Vanuous), J. 1982. East European Slowdown. *Problems of Communism*. (July-August):1-19.

Vermaat, J. A. Emerson. 1982. Moscow Fronts and European Peace Movements. *Problems of Communism*. (November-December):43-56.

Waller, D. 1987. *Congress and the Nuclear Freeze: An Inside Look and the Politics of a Mass Movement*. Amherst: University of Massachusetts Press.

Walker, R.B.J. 1988. *One World, Many Worlds: Struggles for a Just World Peace*, Boulder: Lynne Rienner Publishers.

Walker, S, ed. 1987. *Role Theory and Foreign Policy Analysis*. Durham, NC: Duke University Press.

Walker, W. 1981. *Drug Control in the Americas* Albuquerque: University of New Mexico Press.

Waltz, K. 1964. The Stability of a Bipolar World. *Daedelus, 1964.*

Warnke, P. 1975. Apes on a Treadmill. *Foreign Policy*, 18: 12–25.

Warnke, P. 1976/77. We Don't Need a Devil (To Make or Keep Our Friends). *Foreign Policy*, 25: 78–87.

Watson, C. 1990. *U.S. National Security Policy Groups: Institutional Profiles*. New York: Greenwood Press.

Weber, S. 1990-91. Cooperation and Interdependence. *Daedalus.* 120 (Winter)1:183-201.

Wehler, H.-U. 1969. *Bismarck und der Imperialismus*. Köln: Kiepenheuer & Witsch.

Weil, M. 1974. Can Blacks Do For Africa What Jews Did For Israel? *Foreign Policy* 15:109–130.

Weinberger, C. W. 1990. *Fighting for Peace: Seven Critical Years in the Pentagon*. New York: Warner.

Weinraub, B. 1979. U.S. Military Strength Dwindling, Republicans Say. *New York Times*, March 2: A-11.

Weintraub, S., ed. 1982. *Economic Coercion and U.S. Foreign Policy*. Boulder CO: Westview Press.

Weiss, F. D. 1989. Domestic Dimensions of the Uruguay Round: The Case of West Germany in the European Communities. In *Domestic Trade Politics and the Uruguay Round*, ed. H. Nau, 69–90. New York.

Wells, S. 1979. Sounding the Tocsin: NSC 68 and the Soviet Threat. *International Security.* 4: 116–58.

Weschler, L. 1989. A Grand Experiment. *The New Yorker.* (November 13):59-104.

Wettig, G. 1988. 'New Thinking' on Security in East-West Relations. *Problems of Communism.* (March-April):1-14.

Weydenthal, J. B. Workers and Party in Poland. *Problems of Communism.* (November-December):1-22.

White, P. 1969. The Black American Constituency for Southern Africa, 1940–1980. In *The American People and South Africa*, edited by A. Hero and J. Barratt, 83–101. Lexington, MA: D.C. Heath.

Whyte, J.D. and A. MacDonald. 1989. The Dissent and National Security and Dissent Some More. In *Dissent and the State*, edited by C.E.B. Franks, 21–39. Toronto: Oxford University Press.

Wildavsky, A. 1966. *The Two Presidencies*. Transaction. 7–14.

Williams, W. 1969. *Roots of the Modern American Empire.* New York: Random House.

Williams, W.A. 1962. *The Tragedy of American Diplomacy.* New York: Dell.

Wilkins, R. 1985. Demonstrating Our Opposition. *Africa Report* 30: 29-32 (May-June).

Wilson, J.Q. 1973. *Political Organizations*. New York: Basic Books

Wittkopf, E. 1987. Elites and Masses: Another Look at Attitudes Toward America's World Role. *International Studies Quarterly* 31(2):131–159.

Wittkopf, E. 1990. *Faces of Internationalism: Public Opinion and American Foreign Policy*. Durham, NC: Duke University Press.

Wittkopf, E.R. and J.M. McCormick. 1990. The Domestic Politics of Contra Aid: Public Opinion, Congress and the President. Paper presented at the conference on Public Opinion and U.S. Foreign Policy: The Case of Contra Funding. May, 1990. Woodrow Wilson School, Princeton University.

Wittner, L. S. 1984. *Rebels Against War: The American Peace Movement, 1982-1983*. Philadelphia: Temple University Press.

Wittner, L. S. 1988. The Transnational Movement Against Nuclear Weapons, 1945-86: A Preliminary Survey. In Charles Chatfield and Peter Van den Dungen, eds. *Peace Movements and Political Cultures*. Knoxville, University of Tennessee Press. pp. 265-294.

Wolf, C. 1987. *The Fourth Dimension: Interviews with Christa Wolf*. (Translated by Hilary Pilkington) London: Verso.

Wolf, P. 1978. International Social Structure and the Resolution of International Conflicts, 1920–1965 in *Research in Social Movements, Conflicts, and Changes, Vol 1*; ed. Louis Kriesberg, Greenwich, Connecticut: SAI Press.

Wolsfeld, G. 1990. *The Politics of Provocation: Participation and Protest in Israel*. Albany, New York: State University of New York Press.

Woodward, B. 1987. *Veil: The Secret Wars of the CIA 1981-1987*. New York: Pocket Books.Waltz, K. 1979. *Theory of International Politics*. Reading, Ma.: Addison Wesley.

Wright, P. 1987. *Spy Catcher*. New York: Dell Publishing.

Wright, S. 1985. Constructive Disengagement: U.S. Sanctions Against South Africa. *The Black Scholar* 16 :2–11 (November/December).

Wörmann, C. 1982. *Der Osthandel der Bundesrepublik Deutschland*. Frankfurt/M.: Campus.

Young, O. 1989. *International Cooperation*. Ithaca NY: Cornell University Press.

Yoffie, D. 1983. *Power and Protectionism: Strategies of the Newly Industrializing Countries* New York: Columbia University Press.

Zaroulis, N. and G. Sullivan. 1984. *Who Spoke Up? American Protest Against the War in Vietnam, 1963-1975*. New York: Holt, Rinehart, and Winston.

Zeidenstein, H. 1978. The Reassertion of Congressional Power. *Political Science Quarterly*. 93: 293–410.

Ziegler, A. 1987. The Structure of Western European Attitudes towards Atlantic Cooperation: Implications for the Western Alliance. *British Journal of Political Science* 14(4):457–477.

Zimmerman, W. 1973. Issue Area and Foreign-Policy Process: A Research Note in Search of a General Theory. *American Political Science Review* 67(December).

Zinn, H. 1970. *The Politics of History*. Boston: Beacon.

Zinnes, D. A. and J. Wilkenfeld. 1972. "Analysis of Foreign Conflict Behavior." In *Peace, War, and Numbers*, edited by Bruce Russett. Beverly Hills: Sage Publications.

Other

Athens News Agency. *Daily News Bulletin*.

Atlanta Journal.

Embassy of Greece. Press and Information Office. *Greece: The Week in Review*.

Economist.

Los Angeles Times.

New York Times.

Reuters Library Service.

Common Sense and the Common Danger: Policy Statement of the Committee on the
102 Present Danger. 1984. In *Alerting America: The Papers of the Committee on the
Present Danger*, edited by Charles Tyroler, II, 3–9. Washington, D.C.: Pergamon-
Brassey's.

Countering the Soviet Threat. 1984. In *Alerting America: The Papers of the Committee on
the Present Danger*, edited by Charles Tyroler, II, 178–83. Washington, D.C.: Pergamon-
Brassey's.

The 1980 Crisis and What We Should Do About It. 1984. In *Alerting America: The Papers
of the Committee on the Present Danger*, edited by Charles Tyroler, II, 170–77.
Washington, D.C.: Pergamon-Brassey's.

What Is the Soviet Union Up To? 1984. In *Alerting America: The Papers of the Committee
on the Present Danger*, edited by Charles Tyroler, II, 10–15. Washington, D.C.:
Pergamon-Brassey's.

Opinion Roundup: Americans and the World. 1979. *Public Opinion*. 2: 22–31.

Opinion Roundup: SALT Support Shaky. 1979. *Public Opinion*. Oct./Nov.: 40.

Excerpts From Criticism of Arms Pact. 1979. *New York Times*, April 12: A-13.

Jackson Calls Approval of Pact 'Appeasement'. 1979. *New York Times*, June 13: A-14.
Congressional Digest, (1979). 58: 202–24.

About the Editors and Contributors

Ellen Dorsey is a doctoral candidate in the Department of Political Science at the University of Pittsburgh in Pittsburgh, Pennsylvania. She is currently serving as research fellow at the University of Witwatersrand in Johannesburg, South Africa.

H. Richard Friman is an Assistant Professor in the Department of Political Science at Marquette University in Milwaukee, Wisconsin. He is also Associate Director of the UWM/Marquette Center for International Studies.

Tamar Hermann is a Lecturer at the Open University and the Hebrew University, both in Tel Aviv, Israel.

Valerie M. Hudson is an Associate Professor with the David M. Kennedy Center for International and Area Studies at Brigham Young University in Provo, Utah.

David S. Meyer is an Assistant Professor in the Department of Urban and Environmental Policy at Tufts University in Medford, Massachusetts.

Harald Müller is a Senior Research Associate and the Director of International Programs at the Peace Research Institute in Frankfurt, Germany.

Thomas Risse-Kappen is an Associate Professor in the Department of Political Science at the University of Wyoming in Laramie, Wyoming.

Elizabeth S. Rogers is a Visiting Assistant Professor in the Department of Political Science at Case Western Reserve University in Cleveland, Ohio.

Susan M. Sims is Associate Managing Editor of publications with the David M. Kennedy Center for International and Area Studies at Brigham Young University in Provo, Utah. She is also a recent graduate of the Master of Arts program at the Kennedy Center.

David Skidmore is an Assistant Professor in the Department of Political Science at Drake University in Des Moines, Iowa.

John C. Thomas is a doctoral candidate at Indiana University in Bloomington, Indiana.

Douglas Van Belle is a doctoral candidate in the Department of Political Science at Arizona State University in Tempe, Arizona.